A SHORT HISTORY OF GLOBAL EVANGELICALISM

This book offers an authoritative overview of the history of evangelicalism as a global movement, from its origins in Europe and North America in the first half of the eighteenth century to its present-day dynamic growth in Africa, Asia, Latin America and Oceania. Starting with a definition of the movement within the context of the history of Protestantism, it follows the history of evangelicalism from its early North Atlantic revivals to the great expansion in the Victorian era, through to its fracturing and reorientation in response to the stresses of modernity and total war in the late nineteenth and early twentieth centuries. It describes the movement's indigenisation and expansion towards becoming a multi-centered and diverse movement at home in the non-Western world that nevertheless retains continuity with its historic roots. The book concludes with an analysis of contemporary worldwide evangelicalism's current trajectory and the movement's adaptability to changing historical and geographical circumstances.

Mark Hutchinson is University Historian at the University of Western Sydney. He has also served as founding Director of the Centre for the Study of Australian Christianity (1991–1999), and as Reader in History and Society at Alphacrucis College. His research has been published in the *Journal of Religious History, Church History, The History of Education Review* and the *Australian Journal of Politics and History.*

John Wolffe is Professor of Religious History at The Open University where he previously served as Head of the Religious Studies Department and as Associate Dean (Research) in the Faculty of Arts. He is the author of several books and numerous articles and book chapters on evangelicalism and British national identities, most recently *The Expansion of Evangelicalism* (2006).

A Short History of Global Evangelicalism

MARK HUTCHINSON
University of Western Sydney

JOHN WOLFFE
The Open University

CAMBRIDGE UNIVERSITY PRESS
Cambridge, New York, Melbourne, Madrid, Cape Town,
Singapore, São Paulo, Delhi, Mexico City

Cambridge University Press
32 Avenue of the Americas, New York, NY 10013-2473, USA

www.cambridge.org
Information on this title: www.cambridge.org/9780521746052

First published 2012

Printed in the United States of America

A catalog record for this publication is available from the British Library.

Library of Congress Cataloging in Publication data

Hutchinson, Mark, 1958–
A short history of global evangelicalism / Mark Hutchinson, John Wolffe.
p. cm.
Includes bibliographical references and index.
ISBN 978-0-521-76945-7 (hardback) – ISBN 978-0-521-74605-2 (paperback)
1. Evangelicalism – History. I. Wolffe, John. II. Title.
BR1640.H88 2012
270.8′2–dc23 2012006873

ISBN 978-0-521-76945-7 Hardback
ISBN 978-0-521-74605-2 Paperback

Contents

Preface

This book is the fruit of twenty years of friendship and collaboration in the study of global evangelicalism. As young scholars in the early 1990s, we came together in an informal network with others from all five continents who shared a common awareness of the need to see the contemporary upsurge of evangelicalism both in a worldwide comparative perspective and in a long-term historical one. The resulting conversations, especially at conferences hosted by the Institute for the Study of American Evangelicals at Wheaton College in Illinois and the Centre for the Study of Australian Christianity (CSAC) in Sydney, proved to be exhilarating and formative ones. They bore immediate fruit in the publication by CSAC in 1998 of *A Global Faith: Essays on Evangelicalism and Globalization.*

Since then, with the manifold distractions of busy professional and personal lives, we have had ample cause to ponder the wisdom of Matthew Arnold's lines:

> And long the way appears, which seem'd so short
> To the less practised eye of sanguine youth . . . .[1]

Nevertheless, the field has advanced substantially in the intervening years, through much distinguished individual work and two major collaborations funded by the Pew Charitable Trusts: Currents in World Christianity (which incorporated the Evangelicalism and Globalization project) and Evangelical Christianity and Democracy in the Global South. It therefore seemed timely in 2008 when Donald Lewis of Regent College in Vancouver and Andy Beck of Cambridge University Press suggested that we jointly undertake the synthesis offered in the present book.

The endeavour to write a 'short' history of such a historically and geographically wide-ranging movement is obviously in tension with any prospect of achieving comprehensive coverage. We bring to the task our particular perspectives and expertise as historians of nineteenth-century Anglo-American evangelicalism (Wolffe) and evangelical and pentecostal networks in the twentieth-century global south (Hutchinson). Our selection of material should be judged in the context of our central aim of tracing the remarkable development of a religious movement with diverse origins in eighteenth-century central Europe, Britain and New England through numerous subsequent mutations to become a major force

[1] 'Thyrsis', lines 141–2.

in the global south in the early twenty-first century. It is inevitable that along the way we have had to bypass or only pause briefly to discuss many issues and topics that have received much more extensive attention from scholars who have studied particular national, denominational and local manifestations of evangelicalism. We hope, however, that our footnotes will suggest useful initial lines of enquiry for those who want to pursue such cases in more depth. We are also aware that Edith Blumhofer is currently writing a companion *Short History of Pentecostalism* and, although our narrative naturally overlaps with hers at various points, we have avoided detailed discussion of movements, notably in Latin America, that more properly belong in her volume.

The same information and communication technologies that have had a profound impact on evangelicalism over the last quarter of a century have greatly facilitated our long-distance collaboration between Britain and Australia. We met once in 2008 to plan the book, but have otherwise communicated by e-mail and Skype. We apportioned the initial drafting of the text between us, but have worked closely together on subsequent revision, and take joint responsibility for the result.

Among the numerous debts we have incurred we would first pay tribute to three inspirational scholars of evangelicalism who were fellow-travellers in the earlier stages of this journey but are now sadly deceased: Ogbu Kalu, George Rawlyk and W.R. (Reg) Ward, pioneers, respectively, of the study of African, Canadian and European evangelicalism. We also acknowledge with gratitude the encouragement, friendship and advice of David Bebbington, Edith Blumhofer, Stewart J. Brown, John Coffey, Larry Eskridge, Paul Freston, David Hempton, Bruce Hindmarsh, J.W. (Hoffie) Hofmeyr, Timothy Larsen, Donald Lewis, Mark Noll, R.V. (Dick) Pierard, Stuart Piggin, Mark Smith, Brian Stanley, Geoffrey R. Treloar, Andrew Walls and John Walsh. Our sometimes challenging bibliographical demands have been ably met by the Open University Library, the British Library, the Library of Congress, the archives of the Billy Graham Center, and the J.R. Flower and Alphacrucis Pentecostal Heritage Centres. Last, but by no means least, we enormously appreciate the readiness of Helen and David, Alfonsa, James, Sonia and Andrew to support and divert respective husbands and fathers amidst the pressures of book authorship.

Milton Keynes, England, and Sydney, Australia
August 2011

Abbreviations

ADEB	B. Dickey (ed.), *Australian Dictionary of Evangelical Biography*, Adelaide: Flinders University/ EHA, 1999, online at http://webjournals.alphacrucis.edu.au/journals/adeb/
AICC	African Institute of Corporate Citizenship
AKP	Justice and Development Party
AMP	Australian Mutual Provident Society
BAAC	Business Action Against Corruption
BGEA	Billy Graham Evangelistic Association
BL	British Library
C&MA	Christian and Missionary Alliance
CCM	Christian Contemporary Music
CESA	Church of England in South Africa
CICCU	Cambridge Intercollegiate Christian Union
CIM	China Inland Mission
CMF	Christian Medical Fellowship
CMS	Church Missionary Society
CWLF	Christian World Liberation Front
DEB	Donald M. Lewis, ed., *The Blackwell Dictionary of Evangelical Biography*, 2 vols, Oxford: Blackwell, 1995
GAFCON	Global Anglican Futures Conference
HCJB Radio	*Hoy Cristo Jesus Benedice* Radio
ICFG	International Church of the Foursquare Gospel
ICMDA	International Christian Medical and Dental Association
IVCF	InterVarsity Christian Fellowship
IVF	Intervarsity Fellowship, when without country ascription, refers to IVF (UK)
IVP	InterVarsity Press
JHU	Jathika Hela Urumaya Party
KICC	Kingsway International Christian Centre
LAM	Latin American Mission
LES	League of Evangelical Students
MMD	Movement for Multiparty Democracy
mss	manuscript
NGO	non-governmental organisation
OAPEC	Organization of Arab Petroleum Exporting Countries
ODNB	*Oxford Dictionary of National Biography*, Oxford University Press, 2004; online at http://www.oxforddnb.com.

OICCU	Oxford Intercollegiate Christian Union
PF	Prison Fellowship
PNG	Papua New Guinea
ROC	Russian Orthodox Church
SIM	Sudan Interior Mission
SSEC	South Seas Evangelical Church
SVM	Student Volunteer Movement
TEAR Fund	The Evangelical Alliance Relief Fund
tss	typescript in the possession of the authors
USA	United States of America
WATC	World Action Team for Christ
WBU	Wesley Bible Union
WCD	*World Christian Database*
WCE	*World Christian Encyclopedia*
WEC	World Evangelization Crusade
YFC	Youth for Christ
YMCA	Young Men's Christian Association

Understanding Evangelicalism

In October 1757, Thomas Haweis, a young Cornishman, was ordained to the curacy of St Mary Magdalen church in Oxford. His ministry rapidly stirred strong reactions. According to Charles Wesley, a co-founder of Methodism, Haweis preached 'Christ crucified, with amazing success' and drew large crowds both from the university and the city. On the other hand, students jeered Haweis in the street, shouting 'There goes the saver of souls!' Stones were thrown through the church windows while he was preaching, and 'This is the back way to Hell' was chalked on the church doors. More orderly, but ultimately more effective, critics eventually forced Haweis to leave Oxford in 1762.[1] Not to be repressed, Haweis subsequently published a selection of the sermons he had delivered in Oxford under the overall title of *Evangelical Principles and Practice.* It was one of the earliest attempts systematically to set out the theological outlook of the developing evangelical movement and its implications for Christian devotion and practice. Haweis's starting point was 'The Divinity of the SON and SPIRIT, co-eternal and co-equal with the FATHER'. He affirmed 'the inability of man in his fallen state to do any thing but evil' and the impossibility of human compliance with God's Law. Hence, 'the one great glorious and all-sufficient oblation of the SON of GOD for the sins of the world, as a true and real sacrifice, atonement and propitiation is pleaded for; its necessity and influence proved; and the various blessings obtained for sinners thereby, set forth.'

Justification and acceptance with God came, Haweis believed, through faith alone, but 'works of piety and virtue' were a necessary outcome of faith.[2] True holiness lay in becoming a new creation through faith in Jesus Christ, leading a life empowered by the indwelling of the Holy Spirit.[3] The believer should seek to grow in holiness through study and meditation on the Scriptures, through self-examination and prayer and through converse with other believers and devout attendance at Holy Communion.[4]

The historical background to Haweis's preaching will be more fully explored later, but for the present let us fast-forward to August 1846. More than nine

[1] J.S. Reynolds, *The Evangelicals at Oxford 1735–1871*, Oxford: Blackwell, 1953, pp. 25–33.
[2] Thomas Haweis, *Evangelical Principles and Practice*, London: Oliver, 1762, pp. iv–v.
[3] Ibid., pp. 215–60.
[4] Ibid., pp. 283–300.

hundred delegates from the British Isles, continental Europe and North America were gathered at Freemasons Hall in London for the founding conference of the Evangelical Alliance. The participants were conscious of being part of an even wider network, as numerous messages of support came from as far away as India, South Africa and Tasmania. The meeting opened amidst a sense of euphoria, that evangelicalism was not merely gaining worldwide presence and influence, but that its striking advance foreshadowed the dawn of the millennium and the eventual second advent of Christ.[5]

Almost immediately, however, the conference was brought down to earth by the more prosaic, but essential, task of setting up the new organisation and defining what it stood for. It was thus a seminal moment in the articulation of evangelical identity. The meeting quickly endorsed the name 'Evangelical Alliance', but in so doing it was rejecting weighty advice from Thomas Chalmers, leader of the Free Church of Scotland, who feared the word 'Evangelical' would prove divisive and difficult to define. 'It is a truly possible, nay frequent thing,' Chalmers wrote, 'for men to think alike and to feel alike yet when brought to verbal explanations not to explain alike.' He would have preferred the title 'Protestant Alliance' on the grounds that this would have obviated the need for 'any other test than a declaration that the Bible and the Bible alone is the religion of Protestants'.[6] A rousing speech by a German delegate drew an analogy between the military triumph of the allies over Napoleon at 'La Belle Alliance' (Waterloo) and the Evangelical Alliance as a spiritual standard under which Christians would rally against their enemies.[7] However, as French- and German-speaking participants struggled to communicate effectively with the overwhelming majority of English-speakers, it was apparent that the very word 'Evangelical' had different resonances in different linguistic and national contexts.

The basis of faith subsequently discussed by the conference covered similar ground to Haweis's sermons nearly a century before, but with interesting differences of emphasis. For example, the Evangelical Alliance began by affirming 'The Divine Inspiration, Authority, and Sufficiency of the Holy Scriptures', with 'The Unity of the Godhead, and the Trinity of Persons therein' following as the second article. Subsequent clauses upheld utter human depravity, Christ's incarnation and atonement (but not 'sacrifice' and 'propitiation'), justification by faith, the work of the Holy Spirit and the 'right and duty of private judgement in the interpretation of the Holy Scriptures'. These matters were in general uncontentious, but

[5] John Wolffe, *The Expansion of Evangelicalism: The Age of Wilberforce, More, Chalmers and Finney*, Nottingham: Inter-Varsity, 2006, pp. 231–2.

[6] Evangelical Alliance, *Report of the Proceedings of the Conference, held at Freemasons' Hall, London from August 19th to September 2nd 1846*; London: Partridge and Oakey, 1847, pp. 67–8; Thomas Chalmers, *On the Evangelical Alliance*, Edinburgh: Oliver and Boyd, 1846, pp. 23–8.

[7] Evangelical Alliance, *Report of Proceedings*, p. 72.

there was some debate over forms of words, and it was reported that a meeting of continental delegates 'regretted the admission of certain Articles, and perhaps also the omission of others'.[8] Then the conference found itself more sharply divided over the last two clauses. One of these affirmed the 'Divine institution of the Christian Ministry, and the authority and perpetuity of the ordinances of Baptism and the Lord's Supper'. Despite concerns that it tended to a Roman Catholic view of priesthood and would exclude Quakers, the clause gained general support when 'authority' was changed to 'obligation'.[9] The final clause was a late addition to the draft and proved particularly problematic, not in general because delegates did not believe it themselves, but because they feared it would prove too exclusive: 'The Immortality of the Soul, the Resurrection of the Body, the Judgement of the World by our Lord Jesus Christ, with the Eternal Blessedness of the Righteous, and the Eternal Punishment of the Wicked'. It was eventually agreed to, but only when a rider was added to the whole statement to make it clear that it was not 'a Creed or Confession' but merely 'an indication of the class of persons whom it is desirable to embrace within the Alliance'.[10] The endeavour to embrace a wide range of beliefs and practices within the Alliance almost required that it *not* have a creed or confession. Defining the theological boundaries of evangelicalism was thus no easy matter. Nor were practical implications any more straightforward. In the end, the most serious and lasting split in the Alliance proved to be not over theology at all, but over the question of whether American slaveholders should be excluded from membership.

Eighty years later, events across the Atlantic in the small town of Dayton, Tennessee, reflected more rigid and combative understandings of the boundaries of acceptable evangelical belief, boundaries which became part of popular religious culture. In Dayton, according to the journalist H.L. Mencken, 'people . . . not only accept the Bible as an infallible handbook of history, geology, biology and celestial physics, but . . . also practice its moral precepts – at all events, up the limit of human capacity.'[11] When in 1925 the Tennessee state legislature passed a law prohibiting teaching of the theory of evolution in schools, this was accordingly a natural location in which to launch a test prosecution against a young biology teacher, John Scopes. The trial opened in Dayton on 10 July 1925 amidst enormous publicity and a high-profile clash between a former presidential candidate, the prosecutor William Jennings Bryan, and the celebrated defence lawyer, Clarence Darrow. The event was a symbolic moment in the development of fundamentalism as a variant of evangelicalism. This movement can be traced back to the publication between 1910 and 1915 of a series of booklets, collectively entitled *The Fundamentals*, which had crystallized a theological reaction not only against modernism but against

[8] Ibid., pp. 122–9, 148.
[9] Ibid., pp. 129–52.
[10] Ibid., pp. 160–93.
[11] H.L. Mencken, *A Religious Orgy in Tennessee*, Hoboken: Melville, 2006, pp. 46–7.

liberalizing tendencies within evangelicalism. Amidst the sense of religious and moral crisis which accompanied and followed the First World War, fundamentalism acquired sharper focus and a broad popular base.[12] In a speech drafted for the trial, but never in fact delivered, Bryan employed characteristic fundamentalist high-stakes rhetoric, in which the specific controversy over human origins was widened into a confrontation over the status of the Bible and the truth of Christianity itself:

> [T]he question, "What shall I do with Jesus?" must be answered. A bloody, brutal doctrine – evolution – demands, as the rabble did nineteen hundred years ago, that He be crucified. That cannot be the answer of this jury representing a Christian state and sworn to uphold the laws of Tennessee. Your answer will be heard throughout the world; it is eagerly awaited by a praying multitude. If the law is nullified, there will be rejoicing wherever God is repudiated, the Saviour scoffed at and the Bible ridiculed. Every unbeliever of every kind and degree will be happy. If, on the other hand, the law is upheld and the religion of the school children protected, millions of Christians will call you blessed . . .[13]

Scopes was convicted and fined. Militant fundamentalism was seeking to reshape evangelicalism, dogmatically highlighting supernaturalist convictions as a means to offer determined counter-cultural resistance to contemporary secularism.

In 1986, in the dying years of the Soviet Union, a Nigerian student, Sunday Adelaja, won a scholarship to study journalism at the Belarus State University in Minsk. Shortly before leaving Nigeria, he had been converted by a televangelist, William F. Kumuyi. As a student he led an African Christian students' fellowship, and in 1989, after graduating, he remained in the country and founded the Word of Faith Church. He subsequently moved to Kiev, the capital of Ukraine, where in 1994 he founded a church that subsequently became known as the Embassy of the Blessed Kingdom of God for All Nations. Within a decade it had grown from a house fellowship with seven members to a mega-church with more than 20,000 members in Kiev alone, and was developing an extensive network of associated churches in Eastern Europe and beyond. Pastor Sunday, as he is known, has also pursued an extensive itinerant, print and media ministry, with an explicit agenda for world evangelization. The church demonstrates strong social engagement and claims to have helped in the reclamation of more than 5,000 drug addicts and alcoholics. Belief and preaching are centred on the proclamation of Jesus Christ as 'the only way to God', with an emphasis on the contemporary reality of the Holy Spirit in worship and the lives of believers. The authority of the 'Word of God' is paramount, and so a core activity is biblical education for Christians in order to equip them for mission. Multimedia and Internet strategies have developed as

[12] Mark A. Noll, *A History of Christianity in the United States and Canada*, Grand Rapids: Eerdmans, 1992, pp. 282–3.

[13] Leslie H. Allen, ed., *Bryan and Darrow at Dayton*, New York: Russell, 1925, pp. 196–7.

an extension of its face-to-face ministry, reaching a potential worldwide audience. Pastor Sunday's apparently remarkable success in cross-cultural mission from Africa to Eastern Europe, employing American methodologies, epitomises the continuing dynamism and expanding global linkages of evangelicalism at the turn of the twenty-first century.[14]

This rapid journey from mid-eighteenth-century Oxford to early-twenty-first-century Kiev serves at the outset of this book both to illustrate some of the consistent characteristics of evangelicalism over the course of the last three centuries and to indicate the changing dynamics of the movement. There is something paradoxical about a religious category which is very extensively used both by scholars and practitioners, but which is much less easily defined and described. Indeed, one recent analyst has argued that the very concept distorts historical reality. According to D.G. Hart, 'evangelicalism, as the term is used, is a construct developed over the last half of the twentieth century. Prior to 1950 the word had not been used in the way religious leaders and academics now use it, and even then it was not a coherent set of convictions or practices.'[15]

Another leading historian, Nathan Hatch, has stated even more baldly that '[i]n truth, there is no such thing as evangelicalism'.[16] In addition, there are the issues arising from the use of the cognate terms in non-English-speaking settings where evangelical Christianity took root. For instance, in Germany, where many of the theological distinguishing features of evangelicalism were born, 'evangelisch' emerged out of the Reformation to indicate the recovery of the 'gospel', and hence came to mean 'gospel-like', 'Protestant', or even merely 'non-Catholic' – a far broader sense than the standard post-eighteenth-century usage of 'evangelical' in English. Hence since the 1960s, Germans have increasingly used the word 'evangelikal/e' specifically to distinguish movements comparable to Anglo-American evangelicalism.[17] The word 'evangelicalism' does indeed have a significantly shorter history than the movements to which it is has been applied by historians (although the word 'evangelical' has a much longer history, as both a noun and an adjective). The earliest usage of 'evangelicalism' recorded by the *Oxford English Dictionary* was in 1831, in an article in the *Edinburgh Review* by William Empson, but this was predated by a reference in 1820 by a writer in the *Christian Remembrancer* to 'what may be called Evangelicalism'.[18] Whatever the precise date at which people began to write and talk about 'evangelical*ism*' as a concept or movement, rather than about

[14] www.godembassy.com, accessed 8 August 2011; J. Kwabena Asamoah-Gyadu, 'Spirit, Migration and Mission in an African-led Mega-Size Church in Eastern Europe', *Evangelical Review of Theology*, 34 (2010), 71–8.

[15] D.G. Hart, *Deconstructing Evangelicalism*, Grand Rapids: Baker, 2004, p. 19.

[16] Nathan O. Hatch, Response to Carl F.H. Henry, in Kenneth S. Kantzer and Carl F.H. Henry, eds, *Evangelical Affirmations*, Grand Rapids: Zondervan, 1990, p. 97.

[17] Eric Geldbach, "'Evangelisch', 'Evangelikal' & Pietism", in M. Hutchinson and O. Kalu, eds, *A Global Faith*, Sydney: CSAC, 1998, pp. 155–6.

[18] *Christian Remembrancer*, 2 (1820), 577.

'evangelicals' as individuals or 'evangelical' as a descriptor of theology or religious style, it is likely to have been the better part of a century after the start date of David Bebbington's influential survey, *Evangelicalism in Modern Britain: A History from the 1730s to the 1980s*. Nevertheless, although the lack of contemporary use of the word is certainly suggestive, there is an analogy to be drawn with the emergence in the late eighteenth and early nineteenth centuries of other now familiar '-isms' such as nationalism (whose first usage recorded in the *Oxford English Dictionary* was in 1798), liberalism (1819), socialism (1833) and imperialism (1858). In all these cases, there are good historical grounds for arguing that the word was invented to designate a reality that already existed. These analogies have further value in typifying the nature of evangelicalism as a similarly broad and multifaceted movement. It must therefore be distinguished from '-isms' focused on adherence to a specific theology or ideology originating with a particular individual – such as Calvinism or Marxism – or one defining adherence to a particular organisational structure – such as Methodism or Presbyterianism. The task of understanding evangelicalism needs to start from the recognition that it is a phenomenon that defies precise definition, partly because it was 'held' by its practitioners in ways different from those used by its categorizers.

It is helpful to frame an initial understanding of evangelicalism by reference to nineteenth-century usage of the word, from the period when it first came into current usage. Early use of the word tended to be disparaging or polemical. Thus the 1820 *Christian Remembrancer* article portrayed evangelicalism as a rudimentary form of Calvinism, unwittingly promoted by those who disavowed fully developed Calvinist convictions.[19] In his 1831 *Edinburgh Review* article, Empson thought that 'the worst things about Evangelicalism were its exclusiveness – which led to narrow views of God and the divine government – and its misrepresentation of, and consequent want of sympathy with, human nature.'[20] An 1851 pamphlet characterised 'Evangelicalism (so called)' as 'a disparagement of Grace' and saw it as defined by opposition to belief in the sacramental character of baptism.[21]

In the 1850s, more nuanced and objective analyses of evangelicalism began to appear, notably from W.J. Conybeare in an article in the *Edinburgh Review* in 1853, and from George Eliot (the pen name of Marian Evans) in her novella 'Janet's Repentance', published as part of *Scenes of Clerical Life* in 1858. Writing specifically about evangelicals in the Church of England in the late eighteenth century, Conybeare offered a concise summary of their distinctive theological emphases:

> Of the tenets that then became, and have since continued, the watchwords of the Evangelical camp, the most conspicuous were the two following; first, '*the universal*

[19] *Christian Remembrancer*, 2 (1820), 578.
[20] *Edinburgh Review*, 53 (1831), 305.
[21] 'A Liverpool Layman', *A Letter to... H. MacNeile containing strictures on his recent letter to the... Bishop of Exeter*, Liverpool: Deighton and Laughton, 1851.

> *necessity of conversion,*' and secondly '*justification by faith.*' A third was added, to which subsequent controversy gave more than its original prominence, namely, '*the sole authority of Scripture as the rule of faith.*'[22]

Conybeare thus corroborated the impression that arises from comparing Haweis's sermons with the Evangelical Alliance basis of faith. Between the mid-eighteenth century and the mid-nineteenth century, the authority of the Bible became more prominent as an evangelical tenet. His article was also helpful in making a distinction between those who treated these doctrines as 'a living principle of action' and those who used them rather as 'the cornerstone of a technical system'. The latter, he suggested, were apt to produce rigid and exaggerated forms of evangelicalism.[23]

George Eliot had a complex love-hate relationship with evangelicalism. In her youth she held evangelical beliefs, but as a young woman in the 1840s, she moved to a freethinking position and rejected orthodox Christianity. In 1855, she published a savage attack on 'Evangelical Preaching' as personified by Dr John Cumming, a prominent London Presbyterian.[24] Thereafter her attitude to her erstwhile adolescent faith became more mellow and balanced. 'Janet's Repentance' recounts the impact of evangelicalism, mediated through the ministry of the Anglican curate Mr Tryan, in transforming the lives of both Janet, the abused wife of Robert Dempster, and the town of Milby (modelled on Eliot's native Nuneaton) in which she lives. As Tryan counsels the despairing Janet, Eliot puts into his mouth her understanding of the spiritual dynamics of evangelical conversion:

> You are weary and heavy laden; well, it is you Christ invites to come to Him and find rest. He asks you to cling to Him; to lean on Him;... He neither condemns nor reproaches you for the past, He only bids you come to Him that you may have life:... That is what is meant by faith. Your evil habits, you feel, are too strong for you; you are unable to wrestle with them... But when once we feel our helplessness... and go to Christ, desiring to be freed from the power as well as the punishment of sin, we are no longer left to our own strength.[25]

Tryan's version of evangelical theology has softer edges than more formal statements such as Haweis's sermons and the Evangelical Alliance's basis of faith, reflecting the mature Eliot's distaste for doctrines such as absolute human depravity and subsitutionary atonement. However, it is also a plausible representation of what evangelicalism could sound like in face-to-face pastoral practice. Like Conybeare, Eliot was well aware that a common source of spiritual inspiration was being refracted, for better or worse, through the prism of the behaviour and experience of diverse and fallible human beings. Thus she wrote of the effect of evangelicalism

22 W.J. Conybeare (ed. Arthur Burns), 'Church Parties', in Stephen Taylor, ed., *From Cranmer to Davidson*, Woodbridge: Boydell/Church of England Record Society, 1999, p. 262. Emphases are in the original.

23 Ibid., p. 262.

24 Reprinted in T. Pinney, ed., *Essays of George Eliot*, London: Routledge, 1963, pp. 158–89.

25 George Eliot (ed. Thomas A. Noble), *Scenes of Clerical Life*, Oxford University Press, 2000, p. 260.

on 'Milby' as a whole: 'Religious ideas have the fate of melodies, which, once set afloat in the world, are taken up by all sorts of instruments, some of them woefully coarse, feeble or out of tune, until people are in danger of crying out that the melody itself is detestable.'[26] Nevertheless, for Eliot, the movement had had positive social and moral consequences by bringing 'into palpable existence and operation in Milby society [the] idea of duty, that recognition of something to be lived for beyond the mere satisfaction of self.'

As the movement became more diversified in the late nineteenth century, growing ambiguity about evangelical identity led to significant restatements. In 1867, the leading evangelical Anglican and future bishop, J.C. Ryle, published his summary of 'Evangelical Religion: What it is, and what it is not'. He identified five 'leading features' of evangelicalism, as follows:

> (a) . . . the absolute supremacy it assigns to Holy Scripture, as the alone rule of faith and practice, the alone test of truth, the alone judge of controversy.
> (b) . . . the depth and prominence it assigns to the doctrine of human sinfulness and corruption.
> (c) . . . the paramount importance it attaches to the work and office of our Lord Jesus Christ, and to the nature of the salvation which He has wrought out for man.
> (d) . . . the high place which it assigns to the inward work of the Holy Spirit in the heart of man.
> (e) . . . the importance which it attaches to the outward and visible work of the Holy Ghost in the life of man.

Ryle did not see these beliefs as unique to evangelicalism, but he argued that non-evangelicals 'do not give them the prominence, position, rank, degree, priority, dignity and precedence which we do'.[27] His formulation, however, drew a riposte from a critic who found it insufficiently rigorous, especially in its implicit discounting of explicitly Calvinist doctrines as essential to evangelicalism.[28]

In significant contrast to their British counterparts, nineteenth-century American evangelicals seemed to feel little need to offer theological definition of evangelicalism. Robert Baird's *Religion in the United States of America* (1844),[29] which was subtitled *An Account of the Origin of the State, and Present Condition of the Evangelical Churches in the United States, with Notices of the Unevangelical Denominations*, identified evangelicals primarily on a denominational basis. In his view, the evangelical denominations comprised much the greater part of American organised religion, with only Roman Catholics, Universalists, 'Christians', Jews, Mormons, and other small radical groups excluded, although he acknowledged that there

[26] Ibid., p. 227.
[27] In *Truths for the Times*, London: William Hunt, n.d. (BL acquisition 1867), pp. 138–44.
[28] T.H. Gregg, *Evangelical-ism! Or "Evangelical Religion: What it is"*, London: Marlborough, n.d. (BL acquisition 1869).
[29] Glasgow: Blackie.

were 'unevangelical' minorities in the Protestant Episcopal Church and the Society of Friends.[30] Baird's theological understanding of evangelicalism initially emerges somewhat in passing, particularly in explaining why he classified certain groups as 'unevangelical'. Thus he explained that what Roman Catholics and Unitarians have in common was that they were not churches 'whose religion is the Bible, the whole Bible, and nothing but the Bible'.[31] He offered the following sketch of the preaching of 'unevangelical' Episcopalians: 'Their sermons are of too negative a character; neither are the sinner's sin and danger as fully and earnestly set forth as they should be, neither is the glorious sufficiency of Christ unfolded, and salvation by faith alone fully and clearly presented.'[32] In his view, evangelicals were united in opposing 'the errors of Rome, and . . . the heresy that denies the proper divinity and atonement of Christ', and 'on no point are all these churches more completely united, or more firmly established, than on the doctrine of the supremacy of Christ in his church, and the unlawfulness of any interference with its doctrine, discipline, and government, on the part of the civil magistrate.'[33]

Baird thus affirmed those who had recently seceded from the Church of Scotland in the Disruption of 1843, and his perspective suggested a significant point of divergence from evangelicals in the British state churches. Only towards the end of his book did Baird attempt any systematic analysis of 'the extent of doctrinal agreement and diversity in and among the communions classed together as evangelical'.[34] Similarly, W.F.P. Noble, in his 1876 survey of the growth of 'evangelical religion' in the United States in the century since independence, adopted an institutional approach, equating his subject with the history of that majority of denominations he classified as 'evangelical'.[35]

In 1889, the prominent English Congregationalist R.W. Dale offered his assessment of *The Old Evangelicalism and the New*.[36] Dale saw the evangelicalism of the eighteenth-century revivals as characterised by interdenominationalism and disregard for ecclesiastical structures. It was marked by a tendency to individualism, urging personal commitment to 'a devout and godly life' but having 'very little to say about the relations of the individual Christian to the general order of human society'. Above all, Dale conceived of the early evangelicals as motivated by zeal for the salvation of the lost, who, they wholeheartedly believed, would be condemned to eternal fire if they did not repent and turn to Christ in this life. He summed up 'the characteristic doctrines of the Revival' as 'the Death of Christ for the sins of men which they maintained was the ground of the Divine forgiveness, and the only hope of a sinful race; Justification by Faith; the reality and necessity of the

[30] Baird, *Religion in America*, pp. 506, 598, 612–64.
[31] Ibid., p. 613.
[32] Ibid., p. 506.
[33] Ibid., p. 499.
[34] Ibid., p. 658.
[35] W.F.P. Noble, *1776–1876: A Century of Gospel-Work*, Philadelphia: Watts, 1876.
[36] R.W. Dale, *The Old Evangelicalism and the New*, London: Hodder and Stoughton, 1889.

supernatural work of the Holy Spirit in Regeneration; and the Eternal Suffering to which they believed that those are destined who have heard the Christian Gospel in this life and rejected it.'[37]

Dale judged that among his own evangelical contemporaries, a zeal for the salvation of souls had given way to a rather self-indulgent preoccupation with 'truth', that there was no longer any consensus about the eternal fate of the unregenerate, that belief in human corruption had become attenuated, that there was less emphasis on the necessity of a definite conversion experience, and that a growing emphasis on the incarnation of Christ was obscuring more specific emphasis on atonement and justification.[38] The broader understanding of evangelicalism developing in the late nineteenth and early twentieth centuries was further reflected in 1912 in a short book by R.C. Gillie. This summed up evangelicalism as a recognition of 'Man's desperate need' and 'the all-sufficiency of Christ's sacrifice' leading to emphasis on conversion and real repentance. Gillie attacked any tendency to impose rigorous doctrinal tests of evangelical identity: 'Our bond is a common experience, not a unanimous interpretation of that experience; a common devotion to our Lord, not an exact statement concerning His mysterious yet all-sufficient work.' In his view, it was possible for people, for example, not to believe in eternal punishment or in the verbal infallibility of the Bible and still be friends of 'Evangelical Truth'.[39] Fundamentalism, as evident at Dayton in 1925, was a reaction to this kind of thinking.

Some stocktaking will be helpful before turning to consider some more recent and contemporary approaches to the definition and understanding of evangelicalism. We have seen that there was considerable variation within significant theological common ground. In addition to doctrines common to all orthodox Christians, particularly the Trinity and the divinity and incarnation of Christ, evangelicals particularly emphasised

- the inherent sinfulness of unredeemed human beings (but disagreed about the eternal punishment of the unregenerate);
- justification by faith alone (but disagreed over whether this entailed a distinctively Calvinist belief in predestination and election);
- the work of Christ as the means for the salvation of humankind (but disagreed over the degree of emphasis to be placed on substitutionary atonement and over the language used to describe it);
- the active work of the Holy Spirit in the life of the believer (but disagreed as to whether specific datable experiences of conversion and 'baptism in the spirit' were essential);

[37] Dale, *Old Evangelicalism*, pp. 16–22, 37–8.
[38] Ibid., pp. 23–8, 38–58.
[39] R.C. Gillie, *Evangelicalism: Has it a Future?*, London: Cassell, 1912, pp. 11–24.

- the importance of the Bible as the authoritative guide to faith and devotion (but disagreed as to the extent to which it was verbally infallible).

When the theology of evangelicals is stated in these broad terms, it is not immediately obvious what distinguishes them from other orthodox Protestants. As the leading late-twentieth-century British evangelical, John Stott, put it, 'not all evangelical *essentials* are evangelical *distinctives*.'[40] Hence it was plausible in the mid-nineteenth-century United States for Baird to equate evangelicalism with Protestant orthodoxy, as identified by reference to a list of specified denominations. The patterns of migration which had established religious cultures as demographic realities made his account very credible in the American setting. In the United Kingdom – and hence around the British Empire – the theologically hybrid nature of the Church of England and the way in which many of its clergy distanced themselves from evangelicalism meant that matters were never so straightforward. However, the very difficulty of drawing precise theological boundaries is an important indication of an underlying complex historical reality in which individuals – especially, but not only, Anglicans – adopted aspects of an evangelical outlook with varying degrees of commitment and enthusiasm.

The theological emphases previously described are therefore better interpreted not as a definition of evangelicalism, but as preconditions for it. In pinpointing what distinguished evangelicals from other Protestants, particular attention needs to be given to the manner in which such ideas were 'wired' together in evangelical minds, in generating zeal and energy for the salvation of others. Evangelicals believed that they had a commission from God to spread the good news that inherently sinful human beings could be saved by personal faith in Jesus Christ. The Arminian John Wesley famously wrote in defiance of the constraints of the Church of England's parochial system: 'I look upon all the world as my parish; thus far I mean, that, in whatever part of it I am, I judge it meet, right, and my bounden duty to declare unto all that are willing to hear, the glad tidings of salvation.'[41]

Popular hymns effectively articulated and fostered this imperative to save the lost wherever they might be found, as in these lines written in 1869 by the American Methodist Fanny Crosby:

> Rescue the perishing, care for the dying;
> Snatch them in pity from sin and the grave;
> Weep o'er the erring ones, lift up the fallen;
> Tell them of Jesus, the mighty to save.[42]

[40] John Stott, *Evangelical Truth: A Personal Plea for Unity, Integrity and Faithfulness*, Leicester: Inter-Varsity, 1999, p. 11, emphasis added.

[41] Nehemiah Curnock, ed., *The Journal of the Rev John Wesley*, 8 vols, London: Epworth, 1938, ii.218.

[42] *The Church Hymnary*, Edinburgh: Frowde, 1898, no. 434.

Whereas the primary focus of such zeal was on the proclamation of the gospel, its impetus readily extended to a wider social and political engagement in challenging perceived sins and obstacles to effective repentance, such as slavery and oppression, illiteracy, intemperance and sexual immorality.

This characteristic evangelical sense of personal responsibility for the salvation of others explains the movement's ambivalent relationship to Calvinism, with its characteristic emphasis on the sovereignty and initiative of God in the salvation of humankind. It is true that many prominent evangelicals have also been Calvinists, above all two seminal eighteenth-century figures, Jonathan Edwards and George Whitefield. Thus Edwards, in his auspiciously entitled Faithful Narrative of the Surprising Work of God, describing the revival in Northampton, Massachusetts in the mid-1730s, had no doubt that 'God has so ordered the manner of the work in many respects, as very signally and remarkably to shew it to be his own peculiar and immediate work, and to secure the glory of it wholly to his own almighty power, and sovereign grace'.[43]

Whitefield's underlying Calvinist conviction that salvation was a work of God alone, did not prevent him literally working himself to death in preaching the gospel.[44] For evangelicals who believed themselves to be agents of divine providence, Calvinism was no grounds for fatalistic inertia, but rather a spur to redoubled efforts. The leading nineteenth-century British Calvinist, Charles Spurgeon, remarked:

> Our Saviour has bidden us to preach the gospel to every creature; he has not said, "Preach it only to the elect;" and though that might seem to be the most logical thing for us to do, yet, since he has not been pleased to stamp the elect in their foreheads, or to put any distinctive mark upon them, it would be an impossible task for us to perform; whereas, when we preach the gospel to every creature, the gospel makes its own division.[45]

On the other hand, from the earliest days of the movement, other evangelicals found their own expansive zeal for the salvation of others to be at odds with the underlying Calvinist conviction that the saving grace of God was limited and circumscribed only to those he had predestined. Hence there were significant tensions in the 1740s between Wesley and Whitefield, which sowed the seeds of subsequent distinct institutional legacies. In the later eighteenth and nineteenth centuries, there were substantial explicit and implicit controversies and divergences between Calvinist and Arminian[46] evangelicals. The latter followed Wesley in believing that

[43] Jonathan Edwards, *A faithful narrative of the surprising work of God in the conversion of many hundred souls in Northampton*, London: Oswald, 1737, p. 129.

[44] Harry S. Stout, *The Divine Dramatist: George Whitefield and the Rise of Modern Evangelicalism*, Grand Rapids: Eerdmans, 1991, pp. 278–80.

[45] *Metropolitan Tabernacle Pulpit*, 19, Sermon 1124 (1873), 427–8.

[46] Jacobus Arminius (1560–1609) argued against Calvin that Jesus died for all, not only the elect.

it was theoretically possible that zealous preaching of the gospel could eventually bring all human beings to repentance and saving faith. In practice, too, many evangelicals from historically Calvinist traditions such as Presbyterianism softened their practical application of Calvinism. Evangelicalism has thus been incompatible with hyper-Calvinist fatalism at one extreme or universalistic complacency at the other, but its commitment to seek the salvation of those lost in sin came to cover a range of specific theological rationalisations of the task. It follows that both specifically Calvinist and anti-Calvinist definitions of evangelicalism can appear narrow and tendentious.

Eschatology has also been a significant source of tension within evangelicalism. In general, early evangelicals implicitly espoused an optimistic postmillennial eschatology, perceiving the gradual advance of the gospel as ushering in a golden age of peace and Christian triumph without any radical discontinuity in human history. However, in the aftermath of the French Revolution, darker premillennial visions of the future began to gain ground, teaching that only the second advent of Christ to establish his reign on earth would overcome the turmoil and sinfulness of fallen humanity. According to their particular sense of calling, premillennialists could be fatalistic or relentlessly activist, but they shared an underlying pessimism about the potentialities of human society. Their impact has been interpreted as a key factor in the later emergence of fundamentalism, which in the eyes of one influential historian 'ought to be understood partly if not largely as one aspect of the history of millenarianism [i.e., premillennialism].'[47] That specific judgement is open to debate, but there can be no doubt that differing perceptions of the eventual course of future history carried with them significant implications for modes of social engagement.

The resurgence of evangelicalism in the second half of the twentieth century has led – from the 1980s onwards – to increased scholarly attention to the problem of definition. Recent evangelical growth has been a global phenomenon, however, which has tended to produce treatments in which the American experience is implicitly regarded as normative. A further distorting factor has been the understandable but regrettable tendency of evangelical writers themselves to produce definitions – for example, the 1978 Chicago Statement on Biblical Inerrancy – that reflected their own theological convictions and current preoccupations rather than objective observation of the range of beliefs and attitudes plausibly associated with historic and contemporary evangelicalism. Thus definitions can become polemical tools oriented towards seeking stable places in a rapidly changing world, rather than genuine aids to understanding.[48]

[47] Ernest R. Sandeen, *The Roots of Fundamentalism: British and American Millenarianism 1800–1930*, Chicago: University of Chicago Press, 1970, p. xix.

[48] For further details, see Rob Warner, *Reinventing English Evangelicalism 1966–2001: A Theological and Sociological Study*, Milton Keynes: Paternoster, 2007, pp. 4–15, 192–200. Cf. David Neff et al., 'A Call to Evangelical Unity', *Christianity Today*, 14 June 1999, pp. 49–56.

A full account of recent definitional debates would therefore rapidly become somewhat sterile and add little to the reader's essential understanding of evangelicalism. Rather, we shall here limit ourselves to discussing three approaches to defining and understanding evangelicalism that are historically rather than theologically grounded, and hence the most appropriate basis for the historical survey undertaken in this book. They are also representative of three continents, coming from the American George Marsden, the Briton David Bebbington and the Australian Stuart Piggin. It should nevertheless be borne in mind that Marsden, Bebbington and Piggin are all white male academics – a potentially limiting factor in their perspectives.

Marsden's approach is especially helpful in distinguishing between different senses of the word 'evangelicalism':

> We can avoid many of the pitfalls in speaking about . . . 'evangelicalism' if we simply distinguish among three distinct, though overlapping, senses in which evangelicalism may be thought of as a unity. The first two are broad and inclusive, the latter more narrow and specific. First, evangelicalism is a conceptual unity that designates a group of Christians who fit a certain definition. Second, evangelicalism can designate a more organic movement. Religious groups with some common traditions and experiences, despite wide diversities and only meager institutional interconnections, may constitute a movement in the sense of moving or tending in some common directions. Third, within evangelicalism in these broader senses is a more narrow, consciously 'evangelical' transdenominational community with complicated infrastructures of institutions and persons who identify with 'evangelicalism'.[49]

Marsden goes on to expand his delineation of these three categories, beginning with the 'conceptual unity':

> Evangelicals in this sense are Christians who typically emphasize
>
> 1) the Reformation doctrine of the final authority of Scripture;
> 2) the real, historical character of God's saving work recorded in Scripture;
> 3) eternal salvation only through personal trust in Christ;
> 4) the importance of evangelism and missions; and
> 5) the importance of a spiritually transformed life.[50]

Even though the specific language of Marsden's summary of evangelical belief differs from that we have offered earlier, there is substantive similarity *except* that inherent human sinfulness is merely implicit in his definition. The weakening of this historic evangelical emphasis may well reflect his primary focus on the later-twentieth-century United States, where in a 1996 survey, only 34 percent of

[49] George Marsden, ed., *Evangelicalism and Modern America*, Grand Rapids: Eerdmans, 1984, p. ix.

[50] Ibid., pp. ix–x.

self-identified evangelicals said they believed human nature to be wholly sinful.[51] As R.W. Dale observed a century earlier, in Britain, evangelical belief in absolute human corruption was already becoming attenuated.[52]

It is no criticism of Marsden to note that his conceptualization of evangelicalism, in the introduction to a book entitled *Evangelicalism in Modern America*, is primarily applicable to the United States. It remains useful for understanding evangelicalism in other national contexts. Marsden's second category refers to a wide range of denominations and religious groups that would be at least loosely classified as evangelical. It is important, however, to consider what is meant by 'some common traditions and experiences'. Marsden goes on to highlight democracy and materialism as two background 'experiences' shared by all American evangelicals.[53] Evangelicals in other societies and continents did not necessarily share these particular experiences, at least not in the same way and with the same chronological incidence. For evangelicals in Africa, for example, poverty and political oppression would seem more widespread shared experiences, whereas for evangelicals in other parts of the globe, the experience of living as religious minorities – in historically Roman Catholic cultures in southern Europe and Latin America and in Buddhist, Hindu or Muslim ones in Asia – has been more formative. Evangelicalism in Britain and in parts of continental Europe has been shaped by the persistence of links between church and state, which are so anomalous, even offensive, to Americans. In Ireland, its history has been closely interwoven with the sectarian and political conflicts of that divided island. In many non-European societies, the initial advent of evangelicalism was closely bound up with British or – more recently – American imperialism. Indeed, the very centrality of American influence for globalisation meant that the emergence of the evangelicalism described by Marsden was also critical to the emergence of other forms which diverge from his categories. The challenge, therefore, for a book such as the present one, concerned with evangelicalism as a worldwide phenomenon, is to consider the extent to which Marsden's concept of an 'organic movement' applies on a global canvas, or whether it is in reality only meaningful on a national or regional scale.

In exploring this question, Marsden's third category of specific institutional and personal trans-denominational associations may well offer the most accessible starting point. Once again, however, it is important to note how his model has been shaped by the specificities of the context in the United States, particularly the very extensive infrastructure of parachurch agencies, colleges, businesses, publications and media networks that sustained the late-twentieth-century evangelical subculture. At the present time, no other country has such a well-developed

[51] Christian Smith, *American Evangelicalism: Embattled and Thriving*, Chicago: University of Chicago Press, 1998, p. 23.

[52] Dale, *Old Evangelicalism*, p. 42.

[53] Marsden, *Evangelicalism and Modern America*, p. xi.

evangelical 'machinery', although, as Marsden points out,[54] its origins lie in the early-nineteenth-century transatlantic impulse to found evangelical voluntary societies. In the Victorian era in Britain, there was indeed a comparable network of evangelical organisations, focused on Exeter Hall in the centre of London, which provided many of them with an office base, and also hosted a season of annual meetings every May, which gave visible social coherence to their diverse activities and memberships.[55] Although many individual associations survived, this sense of a coherent wider movement in Britain declined in the early twentieth century, before reviving somewhat in recent decades, notably with the resurgence of the Evangelical Alliance under the leadership of Clive Calver, and the advent of the Spring Harvest gatherings, which attracted many thousands in the 1980s, 1990s and 2000s.[56] Nevertheless, British interdenominational evangelical infrastructure has remained small scale relative to that in the United States. Elsewhere, despite the emergence of some pan-evangelical groups to promote particular moral, political and social agendas, organisational development is even more limited. In such places, personal networks are strong at both national and global levels, where they have been centred on such high-profile figures as the American Billy Graham, the Argentinian Luis Palau, the Nigerian Sunday Adelaja (as described earlier) and the Korean David Yonggi Cho. More informal networks arising from the migration of people have also been very important in shaping evangelical identity, for example, in the movement of a diversity of European evangelicals to North America, Australia and New Zealand, and more recently the 'reverse' migration and mission of Africans and Latin Americans to Europe and the United States.

The strength of Marsden's definition lies in its highlighting of the complex meanings and organisational dynamics of evangelicalism in a manner that, if applied flexibly, offers a useful tool for understanding the movement in other national contexts. By contrast, David Bebbington's definition is useful for its incisive clarity and brevity: 'There are . . . four qualities that have been the special marks of Evangelical religion: *conversionism*, the belief that lives need to be changed; *activism*, the expression of the gospel in effort; *biblicism*, a particular regard to the Bible; and what may be called *crucicentrism*, a stress on the sacrifice of Christ on the cross.'[57]

Although Bebbington formulated this definition with particular reference to Britain, it has during the last twenty years gained widespread currency as a tool for understanding evangelicalism in all parts of the world. There are aspects of the movement's beliefs that it arguably does not sufficiently highlight, for example, human sinfulness (although this can be seen as implicit in conversionism) and the importance of revivalism (although this may be implicit in activism). It also

[54] Ibid., p. xii.
[55] Leonard W. Cowie, 'Exeter Hall', *History Today*, 18 (1968), 390–7.
[56] Warner, *Reinventing English Evangelicalism*, pp. 41–86.
[57] D. W. Bebbington, *Evangelicalism in Modern Britain: A history from the 1730s to the 1980s*, London: Unwin Hyman, 1989, pp. 2–3. All emphases are in the original.

takes quite a lot as read – for example, the sovereignty and omnipotence of God, and the uniqueness of Christ – although such convictions are shared with other orthodox Christians rather than being distinctive to evangelicals. Such objections have, however, hitherto not been translated into convincing refinements, and even scholars apparently less than fully comfortable with Bebbington's definition have nevertheless tended to defer to it.[58]

A particular strength of the Bebbington definition is its short-circuiting of controversy on theological specifics. Thus it accommodates the variety of evangelical views on the precise process of conversion, the exegesis of Scripture, priorities for engagement with the wider world, and the significance of Christ's sacrificial death in the divine plan of salvation. It also reflects the theological imprecision common in lay and popular evangelicalism. Its very ascendancy in the literature, however, carries the risk of leading to an overly homogeneous impression of evangelicalism, obscuring those committed to sharper theological definition, as well as significant distinctive local emphases and features of belief and practice not explicit in Bebbington's short summary of four evangelical qualities.

Finally, Stuart Piggin, in the 'Preface' to his historical survey of evangelicalism in Australia, offers a three-stranded interpretative model:

> Evangelicalism is concerned to foster an intimate, even intense, personal relationship with Jesus Christ. The creation and development of this relationship is understood as the work of the Holy Spirit. It is the Spirit who converts and regenerates believers and gives them the desire for personal holiness. Consistent with the Reformation, evangelicalism holds salvation by faith alone (*sola fide*) as its central doctrine and the Bible understood as the Word of God, as its sole authority (*sola scriptura*). The evangelical faith is crystallised in the Gospel which the early generations of evangelicals understood not only as the divinely given instrument for the rebirth of the individual soul, but as for the renovation of society and culture. Evangelicalism, then, is experiential, Biblicist and activist. It is concerned with the Spirit, the Word and the world.[59]

For those anxious for theological precision, Piggin's definition is even less satisfying than Bebbington's. However, as a summary of an historical phenomenon, it has much to recommend it. Piggin notes the continuities with the Reformation in respect of the authority of the Bible and justification by faith, but also highlights the movement's experiential and activist dimensions that, taken together, lie at the heart of its identity as a distinctive form of Protestantism. Exploration of the interplay of 'Spirit, Word, and world' also offers a convenient tool for interpreting change and diversity within evangelicalism, in terms of the ascendancy or relative

[58] For example Nathan A. Finn in *Themelios*, 33:3 (2008). For a survey of its reception, see Timothy Larsen, 'The Reception given *Evangelicalism in Modern Britain* since its publication in 1989', in Michael A.G. Haykin and Kenneth J. Stewart, eds, *The Emergence of Evangelicalism: Exploring Historical Continuities*, Nottingham: Inter-Varsity, 2008, pp. 21–36.

[59] Stuart Piggin, *Evangelical Christianity in Australia: Spirit, World and World*, Melbourne: Oxford University Press, 1996, p. vii.

recession of one or other strand. Thus pentecostalism and charismatic evangelicalism have tended to emphasise the Spirit, whereas central to fundamentalism has been a particularly rigorous interpretation of the Word. A particular emphasis on the world and its transformation through 'the renovation of society and culture', as Piggin puts it, produced evangelical movements for social and moral reform in the nineteenth century, whereas in the later twentieth century both the 'New Christian Right' in the United States and the radical evangelicalism of the developing world reflected a heightened concern for social change.[60]

Intelligent analysis of evangelicalism needs to start from the recognition that it is a fluid and diverse phenomenon, with boundaries that cannot be rigidly defined. It is this fluidity that has given it much of its power, even as it contributes to confusion about evangelicalism on the part of opinion makers in public culture. Hence in this book, rather than articulate and defend a single definitional model, we shall develop an interpretation that draws on all the three approaches just discussed, as well as on the longer-term historical self-understanding of evangelicals, as explored earlier in the chapter. Although emphasising that evangelicalism cannot be intellectually or organisationally pigeonholed and circumscribed, we would still emphatically affirm its existence as a meaningful concept, representing a recognisable, self-aware distinct style of Protestantism undergirded by shared convictions and assumptions. Indeed, when we place Nathan Hatch's provocative assertion that 'there is no such thing as evangelicalism' in its context, it is apparent that he is making a very similar point. He immediately follows this generalisation with the statement that 'the vitality of conservative Protestantism in America, since the very early 19th century, has been directly related to its entrepreneurial quality, its populist and decentralized structure, and its penchant for splitting, forming and reforming.'[61]

While in this sentence Hatch carefully avoids using the word 'evangelical', it comes back into his analysis in the following paragraph as he discusses developments in the United States since the Second World War. Here he makes it clear that his essential point is not that evangelicalism does not exist, but that its 'dynamic . . . decentralized, competitive'[62] character means that it is not – and probably never can be – a coherently structured whole.

It should also be noted that Hatch's and Hart's reservations about the term 'evangelicalism' relate to its use in relation to the later-twentieth-century United States. Hart – who prefers to identify himself as a 'reformed christian' – is correct to recognize that in this period and national context, evangelicalism has taken distinctive and specific forms,[63] but incorrect in inferring that evangelicalism,

[60] Steve Bruce, 'Zealot Politics and Democracy: The Case of the New Christian Right', *Political Studies*, 48 (2000), 263–82; Al Tizon, *Transformation after Lausanne: Radical Evangelical Mission in Global-Local Perspective*, Oxford: Regnum, 2008.

[61] Hatch, Response to Henry, p. 97.

[62] Ibid., p. 98.

[63] Hart, *Deconstructing Evangelicalism*, pp. 19–28.

therefore, did not exist before the mid-twentieth century. Indeed, a significant challenge for anyone taking a historically and geographically wide-ranging view of evangelicalism is to move beyond the preconceptions that arise from the visibility of the contemporary and near-contemporary American experience in order to gain a more rounded appreciation of its nature and significance. Such difficulties point to the importance of avoiding pre-definition in the study of evangelicalism as an historical subject.

Three further important dimensions of evangelicalism merit attention. First, as R.W. Dale observed in 1889, individualism is an abiding characteristic of evangelicalism.[64] This follows naturally from emphasis on salvation by faith alone, on the importance of personal conversion, and on the legitimacy and indeed spiritual duty of private reading and interpretation of the Bible. Moreover, the widespread, if not universal, evangelical experience of assurance of salvation that followed conversion could produce religious self-confidence, even arrogance. Evangelical individualism undergirded the movement's dynamism and energy and was entirely compatible with the creation of intense, mutually supportive communities, but it also does much to explain its diversity and tendency to fragmentation. Authentic aspirations for evangelical coherence have always been for 'unity in diversity' rather than uniformity. Such was the vision of the early promoters of the Evangelical Alliance, as reaffirmed by John Stott in the late twentieth century: 'While holding with a good conscience whatever our particular understanding of the evangelical faith may be, is it not possible for us to acknowledge that what unites us as evangelical people is much greater than what divides us?'[65]

Second, it follows that evangelicalism has been enormously empowering for those hitherto lacking a sense of individuality and self-worth, in the face of material deprivation or oppressive class and gender structures. Attempts to intellectualise and define evangelicalism ultimately risk obscuring its essential character as a popular movement. The point was eloquently made by George Eliot in her novel *Adam Bede*, through Dinah Morris, the female Methodist preacher modelled on the author's own aunt, Betsy Tomlinson. As Dinah gathers a group of listeners on the village green, she recalls her childhood memory of hearing the aged John Wesley and continues:

> Jesus Christ did really come down from heaven, as I, like a silly child, thought Mr Wesley did: and what he came down for, was to tell good news about God to the poor. Why, you and me, dear friends, are poor. We have been brought up in poor cottages, and have been reared on oat-cake and lived coarse; and we haven't been to

[64] Dale, *Old Evangelicalism*, pp. 18–19.

[65] John Wolffe, 'Unity in Diversity? North Atlantic Evangelical Thought in the Mid-Nineteenth Century', in R.N. Swanson, ed., *Unity and Diversity in the Church: Studies in Church History* 32, Oxford: Blackwell, 1996, pp. 363–75; Stott, *Evangelical Truth*, p. 12.

school much, nor read books, and we don't know much about anything but what happens just round us. We are just the sort of people that want to hear good news.[66]

The 'good news' preached by real-life evangelicals indeed had a powerful appeal to the poor, amidst the social stresses of the British industrial revolution, the remoteness and instability of the American frontier, the grinding oppression of the slave plantations, the squalor of twentieth-century Latin American and African shanty towns, the hardship of women raising families with absent or abusive partners, and the disorientated and fractured lives of migrants across three centuries and five continents. As the leading sociologist David Martin has convincingly argued, there are significant parallels between the social dynamics of early Methodist revivals in England and the twentieth-century upsurge of popular pentecostalism in the global south.[67] Such movements have been rooted not only in individual responses to evangelical preaching, but in the need of whole communities to find a basis for coherence, meaning and mutual support where none had previously existed.

Third, in creative tension with their individualism and groundedness in particular communities and cultural contexts, evangelicals have a sense of being part of a much wider global whole. The perception of an interconnected worldwide movement – empowered by a sense of being the spiritual church – dates back at least to the early years of the eighteenth-century revival, with significant flows of both people and news across the Atlantic and beyond. For example, the rapid publication of Jonathan Edwards's narrative in Britain as well as America ensured that the 'surprising work of God' was, within a year or two, inspiring emulation many thousands of miles away from western Massachusetts. The vision of the founders of the Evangelical Alliance extended to the remotest corners of the Christian world as they knew it. Thus Leonard Bacon, a prominent American advocate of a 'general conference' of 'evangelical bodies', believed that Christ was calling them to 'make it manifest to ourselves and to the world that we recognize as brethren, not Christians of one country and lineage alone, but all in every land who love his Gospel, and find access through him in one spirit to the Father'.[68]

Although the original global vision of the Evangelical Alliance faltered in the first half of the twentieth century, it gained fresh institutional impetus with the founding of the World Evangelical Fellowship in 1951.[69] Meanwhile, missionary magazines and deputations gave dispersed and remote congregations a sense of belonging to a much larger whole. Links that were strong even in days when communication was limited to the speed of horses and sail were reinforced by the subsequent advent of steam and the electric telegraph, and eventually radio

[66] George Eliot, *Adam Bede*, Harmondsworth: Penguin, 1985 (first published 1859), p. 69.

[67] David Martin, *Tongues of Fire: The Explosion of Protestantism in Latin America*, Oxford: Blackwell, 1990, pp. 27–46.

[68] Leonard Bacon, *Christian Unity*, New Haven: Foreign Evangelical Society, 1845, pp. 36, 42.

[69] David M. Howard, *The birth and growth of the World Evangelical Fellowship 1846–1986*, Exeter: Paternoster, 1986, pp. 27–34.

and television, air travel and the Internet. Global evangelicalism may lack the structure of global Roman Catholicism, or the explicit ideological concept of the Muslim *ummah*, but it has still been a potent vision founded on strong networks of actual connection. In 2006, the International Fellowship of Evangelical Students listed affiliated movements in 136 countries across every continent.[70] Members of migrant churches in Europe and North America link together many parts of the world.[71] As David Martin has observed, 'The expansion of evangelical Christianity, and more especially of its potent Pentecostal mutation, is closely related to the emergence of a global society.'[72]

How should we understand the relationship to evangelicalism of pentecostalism and that other major twentieth-century development of the evangelical tradition, fundamentalism?[73] Martin's description of pentecostalism as a 'mutation' of evangelicalism can also helpfully be applied to fundamentalism, in that both movements share underlying evangelical characteristics and conservative theology, but have given emphasis to particular features of Piggin's 'Spirit' and the 'Word' elements. The obvious differences (and indeed antagonisms) between fundamentalism and pentecostalism should not obscure notable similarities between them. Both emerged at the same period in the early twentieth century, in an apparent reaction to the perceived complacency of existing forms of evangelicalism. Secondly, both have a sense of eschatological expectation that is greater than in traditional evangelicalism, in the pentecostal experience of the pouring out of the Holy Spirit as a sign of the end of days and in dispensationalist beliefs closely associated with fundamentalism. Thirdly, both have been popular movements 'from below', engaging large numbers of poor, or at least less privileged, people and adopting a critical, if not hostile, attitude to established intellectual, political and social elites. Finally, both have stood in intriguingly ambivalent relationship to twentieth-century secular culture, rejecting many of its ideas and values but enthusiastically embracing its media and modes of organisation.

On the other hand, differences between fundamentalism and pentecostalism are not merely matters of theological emphasis, but also flow from religious style and geography. George Marsden once quipped that 'a fundamentalist is an evangelical

[70] Lindsay Brown, *Shining Like Stars: The Power of the Gospel in the World's Universities*, Nottingham: Inter-Varsity, 2006, pp. 205–12.

[71] For vivid personal narratives illustrating the widespread global connections of church members in one region of Germany, see Claudia Währisch-Oblau, *The Missionary Self-Perception of Pentecostal/Charismatic Church Leaders from the Global South in Europe*, Leiden: Brill, 2009, pp. 337–407.

[72] David Martin, *On Secularization: Towards a Revised General Theory*, Aldershot: Ashgate, 2005, p. 26.

[73] It should be noted that fundamentalism is here conceptualized specifically as a variant of evangelicalism rather than in the much broader comparative religious framework adopted by the Fundamentalisms Project of 1990s (Martin E. Marty and R. Scott Appleby, *Fundamentalisms Observed*, Chicago: University of Chicago Press, 1991, pp. vii–x.

who is angry about something'[74] – too superficial a judgement to be definition in itself, but one that highlights the belligerency and confrontationalism that has been a consistent feature of fundamentalism. Those who believed – like William Jennings Bryan in the Scopes trial – that essential truths were at stake saw no room for compromise. A parallel quip for a pentecostal might be 'an evangelical who is happy about something', the happiness being rooted in an experience of empowering by the Holy Spirit and leading to optimism (sometimes exaggerated) about the potentiality for further spiritual transformations. The 'anger' of fundamentalists stems from the need to define themselves against a hostile world; pentecostals also believe the world to be hostile, but have much greater confidence in God's ability to change it. Geographies also differ: while both movements have important connections to the United States, the greatest strength of fundamentalism has continued to be in America, whereas pentecostalism had multiple origins and is now growing strongly in Africa, Asia and Latin America.

This book is thus predicated on the assumption that it makes much more sense to understand fundamentalism and pentecostalism as variants of evangelicalism than as wholly discrete movements. Valid distinctions can be made, for example in highlighting the relative openness of non-fundamentalist evangelicals to biblical criticism and the particular ability of pentecostals to interact with non-evangelical movements such as African Independent Churches and Catholic charismatics. However, family resemblances are strong. Recognition that there are strong interrelationships also means that it should occasion no surprise when features reminiscent of both fundamentalism and pentecostalism are found in 'mainstream' evangelicalism. Thus it was possible for Ernest Sandeen to trace 'the roots of fundamentalism' back to early-nineteenth-century British evangelicalism. Historians of pentecostalism have been undertaking the same function for that movement,[75] with reference, for example, to the ecstatic experiences of early Methodists[76] and manifestations of spiritual gifts in Edward Irving's London congregation in the 1820s and early 1830s.[77] By the later twentieth century, characteristic pentecostal beliefs in the baptism of the Holy Spirit were not limited to the formal pentecostal denominations, but were also present in the so-called charismatic movement in the traditional churches which strongly influenced many evangelicals. Observers need to take seriously the conceit of these movements that they were rediscovering

74 George Marsden, *Fundamentalism and American Culture*, 2nd edn, New York: Oxford University Press, 2006, p. 235.

75 See, for instance, Edith Blumhofer and Randall Balmer, eds, *Modern Christian Revivals*, Chicago: University of Illinois Press, 1993, pp. 100ff; Barry Chant, *The Spirit of Pentecost: The Origins and Development of the Pentecostal Movement in Australia*, Louisville: Emeth Press, 2011.

76 See Chant, *Spirit of Pentecost*; but also Mark Hutchinson, 'The Text Repeats Itself: Of Earthquakes and Waifs and Strays in 1920s Australian Pentecostalism', http://phc.alphacrucis.edu.au/, accessed 11 August 2011.

77 Tim Grass, *The Lord's Watchman- Edward Irving*, Carlisle: Paternoster/Authentic Media, 2011.

elements of their own traditions rather than grafting *de novo* from an American stock. Indeed, just as expressions of evangelicalism vary according to location, they also change over time, with particular emphases becoming ascendant. The point has been well made by Joel Carpenter, with particular reference to the United States, but can be more broadly applied:

> The role of fundamentalism and its moderating heirs during our [i.e. the twentieth] century has been similar, then, to the influence of Methodism during the first half of the nineteenth century and the pervasive reach of the holiness movement throughout the second half of that century. Understanding that fundamentalists and their moderate heirs had a period of ascendancy also helps us perceive, by implication, that we are now entering a new chapter of evangelical history, in which the pentecostal-charismatic movement is quickly supplanting the fundamentalist-conservative one as the most influential evangelical impulse at work today. . . . A better understanding of this pattern – the rise and fall of the relative influence of one popular movement after another – adds another kind of thematic unity to the history of modern evangelicalism.[78]

In this sense too, evangelicalism's unity paradoxically lies in its diversity.

The remaining chapters of this book will fill out this inevitably schematic initial picture, exploring the shifting dynamics of evangelicalism across nearly three centuries and five continents. In Chapter 2, we turn to examine the complex question of the origins of evangelicalism, exploring continuities and discontinuities with antecedent movements stemming from the sixteenth-century Protestant Reformation, especially Pietism and Puritanism. Chapter 3 explores the growing institutionalism of evangelicalism in the late eighteenth and early nineteenth centuries, including the emergence of new evangelical denominations, the evangelicalisation of existing ones, and the initial flowering of the voluntary societies and missionary endeavour that became prominent features of the movement. In Chapter 4, we analyse the further expansion of evangelicalism in the middle decades of the nineteenth century while considering the increasing external and internal tensions that arose in the face of new scientific theories and the slide into civil war in the United States. Chapter 5 examines the new currents in late-nineteenth-century evangelicalism associated particularly with the evangelistic ministry of Dwight Moody, the impact of Keswick spiritual teaching and innovations in global mission. Chapter 6 considers the early twentieth century, especially the impact of modernity and the two world wars, which presented numerous challenges to the traditional fabric of evangelical belief and practice, resulting in the rise of fundamentalism. Chapter 7 surveys the era following the Second World War, which saw the global ministry of Billy Graham, the mushrooming of evangelicalism in the global south, and the growth of international networks, which gave some institutional identity to the

[78] Joel A. Carpenter, *Revive Us Again: The Reawakening of American Fundamentalism*, New York: Oxford University Press, 1997, pp. 237–8.

worldwide movement. Chapter 8 assesses the extent of the evangelical presence in the early-twenty-first-century world, and Chapter 9 considers developments since the 1970s, especially the resurgence of evangelical political engagement and the rise of mega-churches. This book is explicitly a 'short' history which cannot aspire to begin to fill in all the rich detail of the tapestry of the evangelical past, but it does seek to offer an overall framework in which such specific manifestations of evangelicalism can be better understood.

2

'The Surprising Work of God': Origins to 1790s

The origins of evangelicalism, like those of any great historical movement, are much debated. A widely accepted narrative dates its emergence, in the English-speaking North Atlantic world at least, quite precisely to a few years in the mid- to late 1730s. Others, however, would trace its history much further back, at least to the later seventeenth century, or even see it in essential continuity with the Protestantism of the Reformation era.[1]

Two contemporary texts provide a useful, even normative, starting point for this discussion. Jonathan Edwards's *Faithful Narrative*, first published in 1737 and recounting events in and around Northampton in western Massachusetts in 1734 and 1735, was rapidly accepted as a definitive account of evangelical revival. Edwards (1703–58) had succeeded his grandfather Solomon Stoddard as Congregational minister of the town in 1729, and a few years later experienced a remarkable response to his preaching, which, for a period at least, transformed the whole community. A 'great and earnest concern about the great things of religion' spread throughout the town, influencing all classes and age groups. Secular business became a secondary concern, and house meetings for religious purposes proliferated.[2] This was not the first time the people of Northampton had experienced a spiritual awakening: Edwards himself acknowledged that such 'harvests' had occurred five times during Stoddard's long ministry over the preceding sixty years. Nor were these occurrences by any means unique to Northampton. Nevertheless, it was clear that both he and his readers felt that there was something qualitatively new about the scale and depth of the revival of 1734–5. For them it was quite literally, as stated in the full title of Edwards's *Narrative*, 'a surprising work of God', the direct intervention of the Holy Spirit in human affairs.

The year after Edwards's *Faithful Narrative* was published, on 24 May 1738, his exact contemporary, John Wesley (1703–91), attended a religious meeting in the City of London. The child of former Dissenters, who had become High Church Anglicans, Wesley had previously sought assurance of salvation in the very different

[1] This debate in well represented in Michael A.G. Haykin and Kenneth J. Stewart, eds, *The Emergence of Evangelicalism: Exploring Historical Continuities*, Nottingham: Inter-Varsity Press, 2008.

[2] Jonathan Edwards, *A Faithful Narrative of the surprising work of God in the conversion of many hundred souls in Northampton*, London: Oswald, 1737, pp. 12–13.

environments of Lincoln College Oxford and the wilds of colonial Georgia. Now, at a gathering inspired by the spirituality of Moravian exiles from central Europe but held almost in the shadow of St Paul's Cathedral, he at last felt that God had met his need:

> In the Evening I went very unwillingly to a Society in Aldersgate Street, where one was reading Luther's Preface to the Epistle to the Romans. About a Quarter before nine, while he was describing the Change which GOD works in the Heart thro' Faith in Christ, I felt my Heart strangely warm'd. I felt I did trust in Christ, Christ alone for Salvation: And an Assurance was given me, That He had taken away my Sins, even mine, and saved me from the Law of Sin and Death.[3]

Wesley's 'strange warming' was no dramatic Damascus Road style of conversion, but rather the pivotal moment in a prolonged period of spiritual striving during which he remained sufficiently self-possessed to notice and record the time. Nevertheless, it was subsequently presented as a seminal moment in both Methodist and wider evangelical history, giving him the inspiration for the remarkable career as evangelist, writer and organiser that he was to sustain for more than half a century.

To later generations, the Northampton revival and Wesley's Aldersgate Street experience seemed important new beginnings, but even from the brief summaries in the two previous paragraphs it is clear that they were also closely tied to the past. They were weaving together the strands of English Puritanism and Scottish Presbyterianism as mediated by English Dissent and colonial Congregationalism, continental Pietism as mediated by the Moravians, and the High Anglican devotion of Wesley's youth. Completing the fabric of influences that came together in the 1730s were an already well-established sequence of outbreaks of revival and a widespread sense of political, social and religious crisis that served as a stimulus to bring other threads together. In the following section we shall consider these various factors in turn.

THE PREHISTORY OF THE EVANGELICAL MOVEMENT

The title of this subsection anticipates its overall line of argument, which is to chart a middle course between those accounts of evangelicalism (notably by David Bebbington) that present it as an essentially new phenomenon and those that view it as at most a mutation in a continuous Protestant tradition. Our contention here will be that evangelicalism as it developed from the 1730s onwards showed strong continuities with the past, but nevertheless also manifested a distinctive and innovative combination of characteristics.[4] These complex origins help to explain

[3] *An Extract of the Rev. Mr. John Wesley's Journal from February 1 1737–8 to His Return from Germany*, London: Strahan, 1740, p. 34; Henry D. Rack, *Reasonable Enthusiast: John Wesley and the Rise of Methodism*, London: Epworth, 1989, pp. 137–57.

[4] The analysis that follows draws particularly on the following works: J.D. Walsh, 'The Origins of the Evangelical Revival' in G.V. Bennett and J.D. Walsh, eds, *Essays in Modern Church*

the subsequent shifting alliances within evangelicalism. Perhaps the best metaphor for visualising that process is to think of a major river, made up of tributaries with diverse origins and courses, but eventually combining their differently coloured waters in a common stream, subsequently again divided into channels by islands.

The first and longest tributary was English Puritanism, itself a problematic concept. As a broad category, the Puritans were the more radical Protestants who were dissatisfied with the compromise religious settlement in England made at the beginning of the reign of Elizabeth I (c. 1558–63). Such dissatisfaction covered a wide spectrum of attitudes and actions, ranging from working within the Church of England in order to strengthen its Protestant ethos, to principled separation from the Anglican establishment. The latter tendency was perceived as seditious by the Elizabethan and early Stuart regimes, and its adherents were prominent among early English emigrants to the American colonies who sought to escape religious persecution. During the English Civil War and interregnum (1642–60), extreme Puritanism also appeared to triumph at home, with more Catholic and liturgical forms of Anglicanism suppressed and a proliferation of radical Protestant groups. However, the restoration of the monarchy in 1660 was followed by the re-imposition of the Anglican settlement and, in 1662, by the expulsion of erstwhile Puritan clergy who were conscientiously unable to accept it. From these expulsions originated the three major original English Dissenting denominations: the Baptists, Independents (later known as Congregationalists) and the English Presbyterians (many of whom moved towards a Unitarian theology during the eighteenth century).

There has been a tendency for later generations to perceive Puritanism in unduly monolithic terms, whether in America by seeing the separatist Pilgrim Fathers who founded Massachusetts as normative, or in England by highlighting those who held to systematic orthodox Calvinism at the expense of both Arminians and more radical sectarians. The reality was one of a highly diverse movement that included Anglican bishops such as Lewis Bayly (c. 1575–1631) and Joseph Hall (1574–1656), but also nourished fringe and eventually unorthodox groups such as the Diggers and Muggletonians. Recognition of this diversity is an essential preliminary to appreciating the variety of ways in which the Puritan legacy contributed to the emergence of evangelicalism. In New England, it is easy to establish direct personal links between a late Puritan such as Solomon Stoddard and an early evangelical such as Jonathan Edwards. In England, however, such connections were less clear-cut, particularly in the light of the suppression of Puritanism in the Church of England in 1662, and the fact that the leaders of the evangelical awakening in the 1730s were predominantly Anglicans rather than the Dissenters who were the more

History, London: Adam and Charles Black, 1966, pp. 132–62; W.R. Ward, *The Protestant Evangelical Awakening*, Cambridge: Cambridge University Press, 1992; Thomas S. Kidd, *The Great Awakening: The Roots of Evangelical Christianity in Colonial America*, New Haven: Yale University Press, 1977; John Coffey, 'Puritanism, Evangelicalism and the Evangelical Protestant Tradition' in Haykin and Stewart, eds, *Emergence of Evangelicalism*, pp. 252–77.

obvious heirs of the Puritans. However, the sixteenth- and seventeenth-century Puritans left an extensive literary legacy, notably in the works of Richard Baxter (1615–91) and John Bunyan (1628–88). This was readily accessible to eighteenth-century evangelicals, and there is evidence that the latter 'were steeped in classic Puritan texts'.[5] Moreover, Puritan devotional works were extensively translated into German, thus stimulating the growth of Pietism, which, as we shall see shortly, was another substantial tributary of evangelicalism. The sheer diversity and richness of the Puritan inheritance provided rich soil for nourishing the faith of early evangelicals. The significance of this legacy lay not so much in specific doctrinal or ideological ideas as in a rejection of Protestant nominalism and compromise, and in a quest for deeper experience of God in both individual and corporate devotion, which was also to characterise evangelicalism.

However, evangelical emphases were sometimes different from Puritan ones. The dominant strand of seventeenth-century Puritanism, for instance, espoused the Calvinist ideal of a godly commonwealth in which church and state would be closely integrated in an ideal Christian society. This was the vision the Puritans sought to implement in England when they gained temporary political ascendancy with the defeat of Charles I in the civil war, and on a smaller scale in the development of early colonial Massachusetts. Evangelicals, on the other hand, were initially focused on personal salvation rather than social and political transformation, and although their ambitions broadened as the movement matured, their strategy for changing the world differed from that of the Puritans in being founded on voluntary action rather than state ordinance. The experience of 1662 left English Dissenters with a lasting suspicion of state connection, and even Anglicans such as the Wesleys had little cause to pin much hope on the conventional Christianity of the Whig political leaders and Church of England establishment of their day. In America, whereas Puritans had played a leading role in creating church establishments in the colonial period, after independence evangelicals were enthusiastically to endorse the emphatic separation of church and state. The most significant evangelical revival of the ideal of the godly commonwealth was led by Thomas Chalmers in early-nineteenth-century Scotland, but after the British state proved unresponsive to his vision, Chalmers's campaign ended paradoxically with the creation of the Free Church of Scotland, which dramatically severed its connection with the state in the Disruption of 1843.[6]

Scottish Presbyterianism was a second significant tributary, which flowed from similar Calvinist headwaters to English Puritanism.[7] Its course differed, however, insofar as the eventual confirmation of Presbyterianism as the official

[5] Coffey, 'Puritanism, Evangelicalism', p. 273.

[6] See Chapters 3 and 4 in this volume.

[7] For a detailed account, see Marilyn J. Westerkamp, *Triumph of the Laity: Scots-Irish Piety and the Great Awakening, 1625–1760*, New York: Oxford University Press, 1988.

state-sanctioned religious establishment in Scotland, with the Westminster Confession of 1643 adopted as an explicit doctrinal standard, gave the tradition an institutional and constitutional coherence that Puritanism lacked. Moreover, from the early seventeenth century onwards, the Scottish diaspora brought Presbyterianism to a variety of regions that were later to become important centres of evangelicalism: first to Ulster, then to parts of North America, especially the middle Atlantic colonies of New York, New Jersey and Pennsylvania, the Canadian Maritimes, and eventually the frontiers of pastoral expansion in Australia and New Zealand. The Presbyterian practice of the communion season, as a concentrated period of preaching and religious devotion drawing people from a wide area to a single centre, was a significant pre-condition for later evangelical revivals. Moreover, communion seasons were later to be the starting point for some major revivals, most famously those at Cambuslang near Glasgow in 1742 and at Cane Ridge, Kentucky, in 1801.[8]

A third, and perhaps more unexpected, tributary of the revival was High Church Anglicanism, particularly in the form of voluntary religious societies that had begun to proliferate in the later seventeenth century. The most prominent and enduring products of this movement were the Society for the Promotion of Christian Knowledge (SPCK), founded in 1698, and the Society for the Propagation of the Gospel (SPG), founded in 1701. The SPCK concerned itself with promoting Christian education at home, and was especially significant in creating preconditions for revival in Wales through establishing schools and publishing Welsh-language religious literature. The SPG supported Christian ministry in the overseas colonies and missions to non-Christians. These were significant forerunners of the evangelical societies that proliferated from the late eighteenth century onwards. More immediately significant in the prehistory of early evangelicalism, however, were numerous small societies that existed primarily to strengthen the devotional life of their members, who were predominantly younger men. Adherents were expected to attend public worship, take communion monthly, and practice asceticism and frequent private prayer. They also met regularly for their own devotions as well as sharing and discussion of their spiritual problems. The famous 'Holy Club' which nurtured the spiritual lives of the Wesley brothers at Oxford should be seen in the context of this wider movement. These societies formed a pre-existing network that played an important role in the early growth of evangelical movements in England, especially in the major centres of Bristol and London. Their contribution helps to explain why Anglicans predominated among the English leaders of early evangelicalism. It also helps to explain the importance of spiritual 'method' in later evangelicalism.

[8] Arthur Fawcett, *The Cambuslang Revival*, London: Banner of Truth, 1971; John B. Boles, *The Great Revival 1787–1805*, Lexington: University Press of Kentucky, 1972.

The final major tributary was continental Pietism, a movement conventionally dated from the publication in 1675 of *Pia Desideria* by Philipp Jakob Spener (1635–1705), then a Lutheran minister in Frankfurt-am-Main. Spener had been influenced by earlier German Protestant devotional works, notably those of Johann Arndt (1555–1621). He sought to renew the Lutheran tradition particularly by stimulating the devotional life of the laity, engendering a new birth of spiritual vitality through small gatherings (*collegia pietatis*) for prayer and Bible reading with a view to making a reality of the foundational vision of a 'priesthood of all believers'. The Pietists were opposed by orthodox Lutherans who feared both the undermining of the authority of the clergy and the elevation of pious practice at the expense of explicit faith convictions. The future of the movement was secured, however, by the patronage of the Elector Frederick III of Brandenburg (who was to become King Frederick I of Prussia in 1701). Despite his own Reformed (rather than Lutheran) ecclesiastical allegiance, Frederick perceived political advantages in an association with the Pietists, an alignment reinforced by his more devout son and successor Frederick William I (reigned 1713–40). Thus, in 1691, Spener was appointed Rector of the Nikolaikirche in Berlin, where he was close to the Elector's court. More importantly for the future, in 1694, Frederick founded the University of Halle (near Leipzig) which provided Pietism with a crucial centre of activity and influence. Pietism at Halle flourished particularly under the leadership of August Hermann Francke (1663–1727), pastor of nearby Glaucha and professor of theology from 1698. Francke's particular contributions to the development of Pietism were his emphasis on the inner spiritual struggle (*busskampf*) that preceded conversion and his creation at Halle of a range of institutions, including schools, a dispensary and an orphanage accommodating 3,000 people, that set a precedent for ambitious charitable and social engagement. Pietist influence spread across many parts of Lutheran Germany and also extended north into the Baltic region and Scandinavia.

Only a portion of the Pietist stream flowed into the evangelical river. The direct antecedents of evangelical revival were to be found not so much in the institutionalised, official Pietism of Halle as in more popular movements influenced by the Pietists. Especially significant in this respect were Protestant communities suffering persecution in lands under Catholic rule: in the Austrian Habsburg dominions of Silesia, Bohemia and Moravia (corresponding to the modern Czech Republic and southern Poland) and in the prince-archbishopric of Salzburg (present-day western Austria). For many of those suffering deprivation or oppression because of their religious allegiance, or even being driven in exile from their homelands, the deepened spiritual experience and mutual human support that came with Pietism had a powerful appeal. In Silesia, the suppression of Protestant church structures forced believers back on small informal Pietist gatherings as the central means of collective worship and teaching. In 1731, the Archbishop of Salzburg expelled all Protestants over the age of twelve from his territory. Twenty thousand of them were resettled in Prussia, a smaller contingent went to the Netherlands and another group emigrated to Georgia, where they came into contact with John Wesley in his capacity as an SPG missionary in the colony between 1735 and 1737.[9] Meanwhile, refugees from Moravia formed the nucleus of the Pietist community that developed in the 1720s at Herrnhut in Saxony, on the estate of the nobleman Count Nikolaus Ludwig von Zinzendorf (1700–60). Zinzendorf had been educated at Halle and initially seemed close to the Pietist mainstream, but after Francke's death in 1727, the Halle establishment became more rigid in its spiritual and ecclesiastical prescriptions. At just the same time Zinzendorf began to develop 'irregular' rituals such as love feasts and to present conversion as an immediate experience without the prior prolonged spiritual struggle envisaged by Francke. Thus by the mid-1730s, Zinzendorf found himself in conflict with his former friends at Halle, and this erstwhile Pietist was emerging as a central figure in early evangelicalism.[10]

Clearly the particular mix of influences in early evangelicalism varied according to locality and personal connection. The High Anglican and Presbyterian streams were primarily linked to regions where their respective forms of ecclesiastical organisation prevailed, whereas the Puritan and Pietist streams were more amorphous and widespread, their diffusion dependent more on publications and the movement of people than on denominational structures. Meanwhile, the middle Atlantic colonies of New Jersey, New York and Pennsylvania saw a particular mingling of the waters, as Presbyterian Scots and Irish settled alongside Pietist emigrants from Germany, central Europe, the Netherlands and Scandinavia.[11] Zinzendorf himself was to visit Pennsylvania between 1741 and 1743.[12] The Pietist influence on the early British evangelical movement was substantial, deriving both directly from Halle and through contacts with Zinzendorf and the Moravians. It was mediated by individuals such as Anton Wilhelm Boehm, an early Halle student and minister of the German Protestant chapel in London from 1705 to 1722, and his successor from 1722 to 1776, Friedrich Michael Ziegenhagen.[13] When the young George Whitefield encountered Charles Wesley at Oxford, the first devotional book the latter lent him was Francke's *Against the Fear of Man*.[14] In late 1735, as John and Charles Wesley, Charles Delamotte and Benjamin Ingham sailed to Georgia as SPG missionaries, they found their travelling companions included a party of Moravian emigrants, whose spirituality was powerfully to influence the future leaders of Methodism. Such contacts brought a full circle to the earlier influence of English Puritan publications on the Pietists. They illustrate how early evangelicalism emerged from a

[9] Ward, *Protestant Evangelical Awakening*, pp. 103–4.
[10] Ibid., pp. 116–41.
[11] Milton J. Coalter, *Gilbert Tennent, Son of Thunder: A Case Study of Continental Pietism's Impact on the First Great Awakening in the Middle Colonies*, Westport, CT: Greenwood, 1986.
[12] Ward, *Protestant Evangelical Awakening*, pp. 141–4.
[13] Geoffrey F. Nuttall, 'Continental Pietism and the Evangelical Movement in Britain' in J. van den Berg and J.P. van Dooren, eds, *Pietismus und Reveil*, Leiden: Brill, 1978, pp. 207–36.
[14] George Whitefield, *The First Two Parts of His Life, With His Journals*, London: Strahan, 1756, p. 11.

rich confluence of tributaries in post-Reformation European and North Atlantic Protestantism, all with considerable preceding histories of their own, but creating a new and distinctive blend. It was not American religion, English religion or German religion, but a meeting of multiple post-Reformation spiritualities brought together by the geographical movement of peoples as well as by the transmission of ideas.

A GREAT AWAKENING?

In the eyes of participants, however, what happened in the 1730s and 1740s was more than a gradual confluence of streams of influence and connection. It was a point of vigorous new departure, in which the Holy Spirit was manifestly at work in the world. Although the discernment of divine agency lies outside the remit of more recent academic history, subsequent historians have in general shared a perception that this was an innovative religious movement with a substantial impact, the 'great awakening' or 'evangelical revival'. At the heart of the events of those years was an awareness of almost simultaneous movements of revival, in central Europe, the British Isles and North America, of people of a wide range of ages and circumstances coming suddenly – and seemingly miraculously – to an intense experience of God that changed the course of individual lives and, for a time at least, could transform whole communities, in the manner Edwards so eloquently described at Northampton. In a twenty-first-century world of instant communication, such simultaneous developments in widely dispersed localities occasion no surprise, but in an age where news travelled at the speed of the fastest horse or sailing ship, the coincidences appeared remarkable. As awareness of them spread, they engendered a heightened sense of significance and expectation. As Thomas Kidd puts it, 'Early American evangelicalism was distinguished from earlier forms of Protestantism by dramatically increased emphases on *seasons of revival*, or *outpourings of the Holy Spirit*, and on *converted sinners experiencing God's love personally*.'[15] Kidd pinpoints a key discontinuity that is also applicable to Europe and the British Isles.

It is true that revivals as such were hardly novel in the 1730s. Revivals linked to Presbyterian communion seasons had been widespread in southwest Scotland and Ulster as early as the 1620s and 1630s, culminating in the 'Six Mile Water' revival of 1625–33, centred on County Antrim. In 1703, it was observed, 'Communions in Scotland are for the most part very solemn, and the great Master of Assemblies is pleased so far to countenance them with his presence and power, that many hundreds, yea thousands in this Land, have dated their conversion from some of these occasions.'[16]

[15] Kidd, *Great Awakening*, p. xiv. Emphasis in the original.

[16] Quoted in Leigh Eric Schmidt, *Holy Fairs: Scottish Communions and American Revivals in the Early Modern Period*, Princeton: Princeton University Press, 1989, p. 45.

As already noted, the paradigmatic Northampton revival of 1734–5 continued a sequence of previous spiritual awakenings in the town during Solomon Stoddard's ministry. In churches across New England, the occasional practice of covenant renewal stimulated congregations to re-examine their relationship with God, and could be an occasion for bringing the unconverted but devout church members admitted by the Halfway Covenant of 1662 to a full experience of new birth. More particularly, there was a significant outbreak of revival along the Connecticut River between 1720 and 1722. Meanwhile, in Silesia in 1708, there was a remarkable revival movement led by children who gathered in camp meetings for prayer and singing. By 1720, revival had spread to neighbouring Bohemia, and in 1727, Zinzendorf's community at Herrnhut experienced a powerful revival, stimulated by the conversion of a recently bereaved eleven-year-old girl. In 1731, the outbreak of revival among the repressed Salzburg Protestants was the final straw provoking the archbishop to expel them from his territory.[17] In Britain, too, there were significant forerunners of later revival, in the ministry of John Balfour at Nigg in Easter Ross from 1730[18] and in the stirrings that accompanied the formation of the Associate Presbytery in 1733. In Wales, Griffith Jones, rector of Llandowror (Carmarthenshire), was an exceptionally powerful itinerant preacher and a significant forerunner of the later revivalists, leading a local revival at nearby Laugharne in 1713.[19]

Nevertheless, there was something both quantitatively and qualitatively different about the revivals of the 1730s and 1740s. The sheer number and geographical extent of outbreaks gave participants the sense that something new and distinctive was happening. Thus the Welsh leader, Howel Harris, wrote breathlessly in 1742 of the 'Progress of ye Gospel in Scotland, Yorkshire, Lincolnshire, Warwickshire, Wiltshire, Germany, Prussia, New England, Pennsylvania and many provinces'.[20] Much had indeed happened in the eight years since the Northampton revival. The year 1735 saw the conversion of three key leaders of the revival in Britain: the Welshmen Howel Harris and Daniel Rowland and the Englishman George Whitefield. Both Harris and Rowland soon began itinerant evangelistic ministries, drawing large crowds in many parts of south and central Wales. Whitefield did not begin to preach until he had been ordained deacon in the Church of England in June 1736, but in the ensuing months he rapidly made a considerable impact, first in his native Gloucester and then in London. The spread of revival in England stalled somewhat in 1737, when Whitefield followed the Wesley brothers to Georgia, but by the time he returned in late 1738, their conversion experiences had given fresh

[17] Ward, *Protestant Evangelical Awakening*, pp. 71–3, 79–80, 101–3, 126–8.

[18] John MacInnes, *The Evangelical Movement in the Highlands of Scotland*, Aberdeen: Aberdeen University Press, 1951, p. 156.

[19] David Ceri Jones, *'A Glorious Work in the World': Welsh Methodism and the International Evangelical Revival, 1735–1750*, Cardiff: University of Wales Press, 2004, p. 44.

[20] Quoted in Jones, *'A Glorious Work'*, p. 3.

impetus to their zeal. It was, therefore, in 1739 that the revival in England began to gather momentum, with first Whitefield and then Wesley resorting to open-air preaching after Anglican pulpits had been closed to them. A particular early focus of their efforts was the miners of Kingswood near Bristol. Then in the spring and summer months of 1739, Whitefield based himself in London, preaching to huge crowds in the open spaces around the city: Kennington Common to the south, Hyde Park to the west, and Moorfields to the east.[21] In the same year, Benjamin Ingham's preaching took the revival north to Yorkshire.[22] Across the Atlantic, the Northampton revival had stirred expectations of further such awakenings in New England, while further south, Gilbert Tennent, the Ulster-born Presbyterian minister at New Brunswick, New Jersey, was emerging as the central figure in 'a formidable revivalist contingent in the Philadelphia Synod'.[23] The catalyst that transformed revivalist aspirations into a large-scale popular movement was George Whitefield's second visit to America, from late 1739 to early 1741, during which time he travelled throughout the colonies, from Boston in the north to Savannah in the south, reportedly drawing enormous crowds and stirring intense spiritual and emotional responses.[24] Back in England, in Whitefield's absence, John Wesley was establishing himself as the central figure in the revival, beginning his continual pattern of itinerancy centred on London and Bristol but reaching as far north as Newcastle-on-Tyne by 1742.[25] After his own return to Britain, Whitefield travelled to Scotland in 1741, initially having a limited impact, but then in the summer of 1742 returning to play a central role in the large-scale revival at Cambuslang.[26]

Why did the revivals break out when they did? Although historians, whatever their personal theological convictions, can hardly be satisfied with merely attributing the revivals to divine agency, the specific human and material factors at work remain difficult to identify with confidence.[27] Some weight should be given to a sense of general religious crisis and vulnerability in the Protestant world, catalysed by awareness of the expulsion of the Salzburgers in 1731. In Britain, the challenge from persecuting Catholic authorities was less immediate, although as the 1745 rebellion was to show, there remained potential for a serious challenge to the Hanoverian regime by the Catholic Stuarts. However, in the 1730s, in the High Church Anglican circles that were to nourish the revival, there was a sense

[21] Harry S. Stout, *The Divine Dramatist: George Whitefield and the Rise of Modern Evangelicalism* (Grand Rapids: Eerdmans, 1991), pp. 66–86.

[22] C.J. Podmore, 'Ingham, Benjamin (1712–1772)', *ODNB*.

[23] Kidd, *Great Awakening*, p. 35.

[24] Stout, *Divine Dramatist*, pp. 87–132.

[25] Henry D. Rack, 'Wesley, John (1703–1791), *ODNB*.

[26] Fawcett, *The Cambuslang Revival*, pp. 113–22.

[27] J.D. Walsh, 'Elie Halévy and the Birth of Methodism', *Transactions of the Royal Historical Society*, fifth series, 25 (1975), 1–20, and for a broader analysis of explanations, see Mark A. Noll, *The Rise of Evangelicalism: The Age of Edwards, Whitefield and the Wesleys*, Leicester: Inter-Varsity Press, 2004, pp. 127–44.

of conflict both with deists on the theological front and with the corrupt anticlerical Whig government of Sir Robert Walpole on the political front. In New England, there was a consciousness of declension from the perceived higher moral and spiritual standards of the past, with fears of divine judgement awakened by a substantial earthquake in 1727. On the material front, the late 1730s were years of economic depression in Britain, arguably rendering the populace more responsive to the message of revivalists, calling them to trust in spiritual realities beyond their current hardships, than they would have been in more prosperous times. More broadly, it has been suggested that the Great Awakening coincided with substantial structural changes in Western society, with accelerating population growth and the emergence of a commercial middle class, that exposed the inability of traditional state churches to meet the spiritual needs of the people and created space for the voluntarist movements that stemmed from the revival.[28] A connection has also been made to the cultural currents of the Enlightenment, particularly its emphasis on personal experience as an essential basis for reliable knowledge, which is consistent with the evangelical preoccupation with conversion and assurance.[29]

A defining feature was the personal charisma and impact of the revivalists. Without Harris, the Wesleys and, above all, Whitefield and their networks, it is hard to envisage that the revival would have developed so rapidly into a dynamic international movement. Whitefield indeed was the most outstanding example of a distinctive feature of evangelicalism relative to the movements that preceded it, the extreme zeal and activism of the itinerant evangelist who travelled tirelessly to preach the gospel rather than basing himself in a particular settled ministry.[30] Whereas John Wesley's preaching journeys were limited to Britain and Ireland, Whitefield crossed the Atlantic numerous times, serving as a personal link between the movements in Europe and America and pioneering a style of ministry that was to be emulated by successors such as Dwight Moody in the nineteenth century and Billy Graham in the twentieth.

Once the revival was under way, the extensive dissemination of publications giving news of developments across the North Atlantic world provided it with a self-sustaining and replicating quality. Edwards's *Faithful Narrative* provided an important initial stimulus when it was published in London in 1737. Subsequently, George Whitefield proved himself an adept self-publicist, ensuring that newspapers took up the story of his activities and between 1738 and 1741 publishing seven *Journals* recounting his travels. The early 1740s saw the launching of magazines specifically designed to disseminate news of the revival: the *Christian's Amusement* (subsequently the *Weekly History*) in London, the *Glasgow Weekly History*,

[28] Noll, *Rise of Evangelicalism*, pp. 136–40.

[29] D.W. Bebbington, *Evangelicalism in Modern Britain: A History from the 1730s to the 1980s*, London: Unwin Hyman, 1989, pp. 50–55.

[30] Stout, *Divine Dramatist*.

Christian History (Boston) and *Christian Monthly History* (Edinburgh).[31] Such publications both inspired emulation of events elsewhere and fostered a sense of common evangelical identity between otherwise remote locations and individuals. For example, as David Ceri Jones has shown, participants in the early Welsh revival had a strong sense of participating in a much wider international movement.[32]

The extent to which the concept of a 'great awakening' was thus crystallised by contemporary publications has led to some scholarly questioning of its objective reality, on the grounds that it was actually made up primarily of diverse localised revivals, which often provoked considerable opposition and had a limited longer-term impact. Accordingly, it is argued that the 'great awakening' was an 'interpretative fiction' or 'invention' of excited participants which was perpetuated by subsequent historians.[33] Another variant of this argument has been to present the revivals as merely a new response to consistent primary human religious impulses 'to seek some kind of extra-human power, either for personal protection, including the cure of diseases, or for the sake of ecstatic experience, and possibly prophetic guidance.'[34] While they should not be overstated, such arguments should be taken seriously, as a corrective to other presentations of the revival that have tended to exaggerate its significance by, for example, seeing it as producing wholesale social and moral transformation in English society[35] or as a major source of the American nationalism that was to culminate in the Revolution thirty years later.[36] However, from the perspective of the evangelical movement itself, perceptions developed a life of their own, and were enormously significant in producing a sense of enduring collective identity. Even if the objective existence of the 'great awakening' and the extent of its impact on society as a whole remains a matter for legitimate debate, its importance in launching evangelicalism as a distinctive movement is undeniable.

NEW WINE AND OLD WINESKINS

> [N]o one pours new wine into old wineskins. If he does, the wine will burst the skins and both the wine and the wineskins will be ruined. No, he pours new wine into new wineskins.[37]

This New Testament metaphor provides an apt starting place for analysing the interaction of the evangelical revival with existing religious and social structures.

31 Susan O'Brien, 'Eighteenth-Century Publishing Networks in the First Years of Transatlantic Evangelicalism' in Mark A. Noll, David W. Bebbington and George A. Rawlyk, eds, *Evangelicalism*, New York: Oxford University Press, 1994, pp. 38–57.

32 Jones, *'A Glorious Work'*, pp. 102–42.

33 Jon Butler, 'The Great Awakening as Intepretative Fiction', *Journal of American History*, 69 (1982), 305–325; Frank Lambert, *Inventing the "Great Awakening"*, Princeton: Princeton University Press, 1999.

34 John Kent, *Wesley and the Wesleyans*, Cambridge: Cambridge University Press, 2002, pp. 1–2.

35 J. Wesley Bready, *England: Before and After Wesley*, London: Hodder and Stoughton, 1939.

36 Alan Heimert, *Religion and the American Mind from the Great Awakening to the Revolution*, Cambridge, MA: Harvard University Press, 1966, pp. 94, 5, 45–52.

37 Mark 2:22, *New International Version*.

Once the initial exhilaration of revival had passed, the challenge for its protagonists became one of sustaining a new movement within an inherited structure of theology and ecclesiastical organisation. The process proved divisive both for evangelicalism itself and for the existing fabric of church life on both sides of the Atlantic. Although sometimes the old wineskins proved unexpectedly flexible, sometimes they split under the pressure and at other times new wineskins were indeed created for the new wine. Only when one considers consequences does the metaphor begin to break down: The bursting of the wineskins did not 'ruin' the new wine of evangelicalism but rather enabled it to flow into a wide diversity of different channels that might otherwise have been inaccessible to it.[38]

The early evangelicals rapidly found themselves divided over two key problems. First, what theological framework should they use to interpret their common experience of new birth and personal relationship with God? Second, should they work within existing church structures, create their own new ones, or attempt to do both?

As we have seen,[39] evangelicals came from both sides of the major theological division in post-Reformation Protestantism between Calvinists and Arminians. This tension rapidly came to the surface in estrangement between Wesley and Whitefield, which began in 1739 when Wesley published a sermon directly attacking Whitefield's Calvinism. Wesley claimed that the 'horrible' doctrine of predestination made all preaching pointless, provoking Whitefield to respond in a published letter, and leading to a break between them in 1741. The damage to the larger movement was limited by a tacit acceptance of different geographical spheres of operation, with Wesley concentrating on England and Whitefield on a wider North Atlantic ministry.[40] Moreover, the issue did not make much practical difference in their approach to seeking initial converts. Despite his Calvinism, Whitefield's personal evangelistic zeal was beyond question and he wrote to Wesley in October 1741: 'Though I hold to particular election, yet I offer Jesus to every individual soul.'[41] The divergence, however, was also apparent in their views of the subsequent spiritual life of the believer. Wesley feared predestinarian teaching could become a cloak for inactivity and lack of motivation to seek holiness and Christian perfection, which he believed to be an attainable object for the truly committed disciple. On the other hand, Whitefield told him, 'You may carry sanctification to what degrees you will, only I cannot agree with you that the in-being of sin is to be destroyed in this life.'[42]

[38] The survey in this subsection draws particularly on Mark Noll's account (*Rise of Evangelicalism*, pp. 111–25, 145–79), which is the source for details not otherwise specifically referenced.

[39] See Chapter 1.

[40] John Wesley, *Free Grace: A Sermon Preach'd at Bristol*, London: Strahan, 1740, pp. 8, 15; Jones, *'A Glorious Work'*, pp. 27–8.

[41] Quoted Noll, *Expansion of Evangelicalism*, p. 257.

[42] Ibid., p. 257; Wesley, *Free Grace*, pp. 9–13.

The issue can be illuminated further from the texts of two of the most famous eighteenth-century evangelical hymns. The Wesleyan Methodist interpretation of the Arminian position is well represented by the final stanza of Charles Wesley's 'Love divine, all loves excelling', first published in 1747:

> Finish then thy new creation:
> Pure and sinless let us be;
> Let us see thy great salvation,
> Perfectly restored in thee;
> Changed from glory into glory,
> Till in heaven we take our place,
> Till we cast our crowns before thee,
> Lost in wonder, love and praise.[43]

The emendation of 'sinless' in the second line to 'spotless' in later hymnbooks reflects the embarrassment of editors at the perfectionism of the original: Wesley implies that believers can become 'pure and sinless' in this life *before*, at death ('changed from glory into glory'), they take their place in heaven. On the other hand, to the Calvinist Augustus Toplady (author of 'Rock of Ages', first published in 1776), even committed believers remained irremediably sinful and helpless, with their salvation entirely dependent on God's election and the atoning sacrifice of Christ on the cross:

> Not the labours of my hands
> Can fulfil thy law's demands;
> Could my zeal no respite know,
> Could my tears for ever flow,
> All for sin could not atone:
> Thou must save, and thou alone.
>
> Nothing in my hand I bring,
> Simply to thy Cross I cling;
> Naked, come to thee for dress;
> Helpless, look to thee for grace;
> Foul, I to the fountain fly;
> Wash me, Saviour, or I die.[44]

Although there were subsequent attempts to build bridges between Wesley and Whitefield and so avoid a lasting separation, the dynamics of organisational development made effective reconciliation impossible. By the mid-1740s, Wesley was

[43] Maurice Frost, ed., *Historical Companion to Hymns Ancient and Modern*, London: Clowes, 1962, p. 258.
[44] Ibid., p. 260.

already organising what was to become the Methodist Conference, while Whitefield, in association with Howel Harris, had set up the more loosely structured Joint Association of English and Welsh Calvinistic Methodism, which was later to benefit substantially from the patronage of Selina, Countess of Huntingdon. In the longer term, the distinctive theological emphases of Wesleyan Methodists were an important factor leading to their continuing development in both Britain and America as a separate family of denominations from the predominantly Calvinist Baptists, Congregationalists, and Presbyterians. However, even though heated controversy between Arminians and Calvinists could sometimes erupt, as in the 1770s, in other respects the practical significance of the issue should not be exaggerated. In theory, Arminians might slide into universalist perfectionism or Calvinists into fatalistic antinominianism, but in practice, moderate versions of both positions predominated. Leaders of both persuasions gave priority to the purposeful preaching of the gospel, while ordinary believers found it possible to sing both Wesley's and Toplady's hymns with equal conviction and enthusiasm.

The Moravians represented something of an anti-theological strand, going further than other evangelicals in emphasizing the importance of experience rather than precise doctrine, and remaining rooted in the reinterpretation of the Lutheran Pietist tradition by Zinzendorf and others. While they were not Calvinists, their emphasis on the possibility of quick conversion, 'stillness' and assurance of salvation seemed to Wesley to have similar consequences to Calvinist beliefs in that they risked engendering a passivity that would inhibit further striving after Christian perfection and active efforts for the conversion of others. Moravians, especially Benjamin Ingham and John Cennick (the first revivalist to itinerate in Ireland), played an important role in early evangelicalism in the United Kingdom, but suffered significant setbacks in the 1750s because of financial problems and allegations of heresy and sexual irregularity.[45] However, they also established a presence in America, notably in a settlement at Bethlehem near Philadelphia, pioneered new missionary strategies and continued to play a major role in the expansion of evangelicalism in continental Europe.

Thus within a decade or so of the initial revivals of the 1730s, theological divergences reinforced by personalities and organisational dynamics had already created two new evangelical 'wineskins' – Wesleyan Methodism and Calvinistic Methodism – alongside the longer tradition of broader, especially Moravian, Pietism. Relationships between these groups and with existing denominational structures remained, however, fluid and unpredictable. Indeed, in general, early evangelicals saw their task as regeneration of the existing churches rather than separation from them. The Moravians had already established a denominational identity in Germany, but Calvinistic Methodism did not evolve into a Dissenting

[45] Colin Podmore, *The Moravian Church in England, 1728–1760*, Oxford: Clarendon, 1998, pp. 266–89.

denomination until the 1760s and 1770s, and only when John Wesley ordained ministers for America in 1784 was his Connexion clearly set on a course to lasting separation from the Church of England.

Meanwhile, other evangelicals sought to advance their cause within the existing churches. William Grimshaw (1708–63) had a remarkable career combining his regular Anglican ministry at Haworth in Yorkshire with a wide-ranging itinerancy overseeing the growth of Methodist societies across the north of England. Although Grimshaw sailed very close to the legal wind, he gained the respect of successive archbishops of York, and accordingly escaped church discipline.[46] Other Church of England clergy, such as Henry Venn in Yorkshire, Samuel Walker in Cornwall, and William Romaine in London, were more circumspect, clearly identifying with evangelicalism but continuing to operate within the regular order of parish ministry. They were sympathetic to the Methodists and sometimes actively cooperated with them but stopped short of the irregular itinerancy and open-air preaching outside their own parishes that placed Wesley and Whitefield in obvious conflict with church authority. They played an important role in sustaining an evangelical presence in their respective localities: Venn in Huddersfield and Walker in Truro initiated evangelical traditions in significant provincial towns. In 1766, Romaine became the first evangelical beneficed clergyman in London, and in 1780, John Newton was also appointed to a London living, following his sixteen years as curate at Olney in north Buckinghamshire.[47] By the end of the century, with other notable appointments such as that of Henry Venn's son John as rector of nearby Clapham in 1792, a strategically important evangelical bridgehead in the capital and its vicinity was secured. Cambridge became another important centre of evangelical influence, with the beginning of Charles Simeon's half-century of ministry in the university city in 1782. Outside England, however, evangelical Anglicans were a rarity in the eighteenth century: only in the 1780s and 1790s did evangelicalism begin to grow in the Church of Ireland, and in America, Devereux Jarratt of Bath, Virginia was very unusual among Anglican clergy in being willing to welcome Whitefield and cooperate with the Methodists.

In general there was considerable initial opposition to evangelicals in the Anglican churches. In Wales, Howel Harris was deeply frustrated by clerical opposition to his 'irregular' activity, and – faced with the impossibility of securing ordination from a hostile episcopate – he remained technically a layman. Nevertheless, he remained, paradoxically – even perversely – loyal to Anglicanism and always hoped to see 'a reformation in this poor benighted church'.[48] It was not until the

[46] Frank Baker, *William Grimshaw 1708–1763*, London: Epworth, 1963.

[47] G.C.B. Davies, *The Early Cornish Evangelicals 1735–60*, London: SPCK, 1951; J.D. Walsh, 'The Yorkshire Evangelicals in the Eighteenth Century', PhD thesis, Cambridge University, 1956; P.N.L. Pytches, 'The Development of Anglican Evangelicalism in London 1736–1836', MPhil thesis, Open University, 2006; Bruce Hindmarsh, *John Newton and the English Evangelical Tradition*, Oxford: Clarendon, 1996.

[48] Quoted Jones, *Glorious Work*, p. 150.

early nineteenth century that the Welsh Calvinistic Methodists decisively separated from the Church of England. However, in 1763, the revivalist leader Daniel Rowland was expelled from his curacy at Llangeitho, a symbolic moment that 'inflicted untold damage on Anglicanism'[49] and confirmed the long-term course of mainstream Welsh evangelicalism away from the Church of England. In England, John Newton had considerable difficulty finding a bishop prepared to ordain him, and both Romaine and Simeon only secured appointment to their parishes after bitter disputes.[50] It was understandable that such antagonism drove some into Methodism and Dissent, but the conviction of others that evangelicalism had a legitimate place in Church of England was strong enough to enable its survival and growth.

By contrast, Presbyterianism provided more receptive soil for early evangelicalism. The revivals in 1742 at Cambuslang and Kilsyth were actively fostered by the Church of Scotland parish ministers, William McCulloch and James Robe respectively, who remained leaders and promoters of the movement in Scotland. A key figure in the next generation was John Erskine (1721–1803), minister of the strategic parish of Old Greyfriars Edinburgh from 1767 until his death. During the second half of the eighteenth century, evangelicals became an important element in the so-called Popular party in the Kirk, which opposed the Moderate advocates of lay patronage. Herein lay some of the seeds of the conflict that was eventually to tear the Church of Scotland apart in the Disruption of 1843. In the shorter term, however, the significance of that tension should not be exaggerated and the majority of evangelicals were readily assimilated.[51] Although evangelicals were involved in the two significant secessions from the Church of Scotland that occurred during the eighteenth century – the Associate Presbytery in 1733 and the Relief Church in 1761 – the precipitating factors for these splits related more to patronage and relations between church and state than to evangelical beliefs as such.

American Presbyterianism proved equally receptive, but not without initial conflict. A group of revivalist ministers in New Jersey and Pennsylvania, led by William Tennent and his sons William and Gilbert, warmly welcomed George Whitefield, but in 1741 were expelled from the Synod of Philadelphia. The evangelicals formed the rival Synod of New York, but in 1758, the two groups rejoined. At that point, there were seventy-three 'New Side' or evangelical ministers, but only twenty-three 'Old Side' or traditionalist ones, an indication of the rapid ascendancy evangelicalism had gained in the denomination.[52] In Ulster, on the other hand, mainstream

[49] Eifion Evans, *Daniel Rowland and the Great Evangelical Awakening in Wales*, Edinburgh: Banner of Truth, 1985, p. 325.

[50] Hindmarsh, *Newton*, pp. 83–118; Grayson Carter, 'Romaine, William (1714–1795)', *ODNB*; Leonard W. Cowie, 'Simeon, Charles (1759–1836)', *ODNB*.

[51] For a detailed analysis, see John R. McIntosh, *Church and Theology in Enlightenment Scotland: The Popular Party, 1740–1800*, East Linton: Tuckwell, 1998.

[52] Coalter, *Gilbert Tennent*; Noll, *Rise of Evangelicalism*, p. 171.

Presbyterianism proved more resistant to evangelicalism, with the influence of the movement initially limited to seceding groups.[53]

Initially Independent/Congregationalist and Baptist responses to the revival were patchy, but in the medium term, both denominations were to be transformed by evangelicalism. Two leading English Independent ministers, Isaac Watts and Philip Doddridge, were sympathetic to evangelicalism, but after their deaths, in 1748 and 1751 respectively, evangelical Dissent lacked obvious leadership for a while. Eventually, however, some of the chapels founded by Whitefield and the Countess of Huntingdon moved to the Independents, thus providing new momentum. Meanwhile evangelical influence inspired the formation of both the (Calvinist) Northamptonshire Baptist Association – which had a much wider geographical spread than its name implied – in 1764, and the (Arminian) New Connexion of General Baptists in 1770. In New England in the face of the established state church nature of Congregationalism, evangelicalism proved particularly divisive, both in giving rise to tensions within the denomination and also in leading some individuals and congregations to separatism. It was the Baptists, led by Isaac Backus (1724–1806), who proved to be the most dynamic force in early New England evangelicalism, with their churches growing in number from 36 in 1756 to 312 in 1804.[54] Backus himself had moved from Congregationalism to separatism to the Baptists, a progress representative of many of his co-religionists. The New England Baptists Shubal Stearns and David Marshall also played a key role in pioneering the advance of evangelicalism further south in Georgia and the Carolinas.

Developments in the English-speaking world were paralleled in continental Europe by the diffusion of Pietism within the established Lutheran churches and the spread of the radical Moravian groups outside them. Where Pietism received state patronage, as it did notably under William I and Frederick William I of Prussia and Christian VI of Denmark-Norway (reigned 1730–46), it advanced rapidly, although radical variants were discouraged.[55] Where the authorities were hostile, as in most parts of north-western Germany and in Sweden, it proved difficult to make lasting progress. The Moravians established themselves in Denmark, with a centre of activity at Christianfeld in Jutland from 1772, and moved further north into southern Sweden. Their greatest successes in the Baltic, however, were in Estonia and Livonia (modern Latvia) in a context of an existing relative religious vacuum. To the south-west, Zinzendorf and his associates took a considerable interest in Switzerland, seeking to challenge both Lutheran and Reformed establishments and stirring a notable revival in Basel in 1738. However, although small Moravian

[53] David Hempton and Myrtle Hill, *Evangelical Protestantism in Ulster Society 1740–1890*, London: Routledge, 1992, pp. 16–19.

[54] Noll, *Expansion of Evangelicalism*, pp. 169–70.

[55] Richard L. Gawthrop, *Pietism and the Making of Eighteenth-Century Prussia*, Cambridge: Cambridge University Press, 1993; Martin Schwarz Lausten (trans. Frederick H. Cryer), *A Church History of Denmark*, Aldershot: Ashgate, 2002, pp. 164–76.

congregations survived, the 'old wineskins' held together. In the Netherlands, too, existing structures proved resilient, although Dutch money was important in bankrolling Zinzendorf. When revivals did break out there in the late 1740s and early 1750s, they appear to have owed more to influence from Britain and New England than to the Moravians.[56] On the other hand, the Moravian John Cennick spearheaded the evangelical advance in Ireland between 1746 and his death in 1755, although thereafter the initiative passed to Wesley and the Methodists.[57]

This brief sketch of the impact of early evangelicalism on existing denominational structures also serves to point up the movement's expansionist zeal. Expansion manifested itself most obviously in geographical terms, in the impulse rapidly to move outward from early centres of activity such as Herrnhut, London, south-west Wales, central Scotland and New England to evangelise regions such as Cornwall, Ireland, the Scottish Highlands, Scandinavia, Nova Scotia, and the American South. Some of these were later themselves to become important centres of evangelicalism. Evangelicals, however, were also determined to cross social and cultural frontiers. It was significant that in 1739, Whitefield chose to begin his first systematic outdoor preaching campaign among the miners of Kingswood near Bristol, by no means the most immediately prepossessing group for a man looking for easy converts. In his subsequent preaching at Moorfields in east London he was placing himself in the centre of an area known for its criminality and immorality and competing with open-air showmen and street vendors of a very different kind. In 1742, he wrote that he was competing with 'drummers, trumpeters, merry andrews, masters of puppet shows, exhibiters of wild beasts, players, &c. &c. all busy entertaining their respectful auditories'.[58] Early Methodists continued to make a determined effort to communicate the gospel to poorer people, often unreached by the Church of England. At the other end of the social scale, in her patronage of Whitefield, Lady Huntingdon was seeking to challenge the religious indifference of aristocratic society, and through the conversion of influential people to bring about a wider spiritual transformation. She only enjoyed limited success, but the important role played by one of her converts, William Legge, Earl of Dartmouth, as a patron of John Newton and others demonstrated the potentialities of her strategy. Moreover, as a woman, Lady Huntingdon was merely the most prominent example of the movement's capacity to cross gender frontiers. Women played a conspicuous role in the early revivals, with their spiritual experience given equal weight to that of men. Indeed one of the charges against the revivals made by Charles Chauncy, a leading American opponent, was that 'the encouraging WOMEN, yea GIRLS to

[56] Ward, *Protestant Evangelical Awakening, passim*; Nicholas Hope, *German and Scandinavian Protestantism 1700 to 1918*, Oxford: Clarendon, 1995, pp. 154–65, 247–55.

[57] Hempton and Hill, *Evangelical Protestantism in Ulster*, pp. 5–8.

[58] Quoted D. Bruce Hindmarsh, *The Evangelical Conversion Narrative*, Oxford: Oxford University Press, 2005, p. 77.

speak in the assemblies for religious worship is a plain breach of that *commandment of the LORD*, where it is said *Let your WOMEN keep silence in the churches*.'[59]

Women could also play an important part in the organisation of early Methodism at a local level. For example, at Booth Bank in Cheshire, Alice Cross organised a local society, became a class leader and had a pulpit erected in the largest room in her house that was used as a regular place of worship.[60] They could also exercise significant spiritual leadership: during a revival at Newport, Rhode Island, in 1766, Sarah Osborn was attracting numerous people of both genders and all age groups to her house for prayer and spiritual counsel.[61] In the 1760s and 1770s, Mary Bosanquet (1739–1815) led evangelical communities at Leytonstone, Essex and Gildersome near Leeds before, in 1781, marrying John Fletcher, the evangelical vicar of Madeley, Shropshire. Thereafter, she exercised a preaching and teaching ministry, initially in partnership with her husband but continuing on her own after his death.[62] In 1771, Bosanquet had written to John Wesley to argue the case for women being allowed to preach under exceptional circumstances. He responded positively: 'It is plain to me that the work of God, termed Methodism, is an *extraordinary* dispensation of HIS providence. Therefore I do not wonder, if several things occur therein, which do not fall under the ordinary rules of discipline.'[63] Even though, apart from Lady Huntingdon, women's roles normally remained subordinate ones, evangelicalism still enabled them to challenge convention and tradition, giving them much greater scope for religious expression and influence than did the exclusively male structures of the existing churches.

In America, evangelicals also began at an early date to cross racial and ethnic frontiers in seeking converts among Native and African Americans. Revivals in Long Island in the early 1740s had a significant impact on Native Americans. Among the converts was Samson Occum (1723–92), who was subsequently to become a missionary to his own people. The paradigmatic figure, however, was David Brainerd (1718–47) important not so much because of the inevitably limited achievements of his short life, but because his journal was posthumously published by his friend and prospective father-in-law Jonathan Edwards. Between 1742 and 1746, Brainerd had worked as a missionary to Native Americans, making few converts but, through the spiritual intensity manifest in his diary, serving as an

[59] Quoted Susan Juster, *Disorderly Women: Sexual Politics and Evangelicalism in Revolutionary New England*, Ithaca: Cornell University Press, 1994, pp. 30–1.

[60] Gail Malmgreen, 'Domestic Discords: Women and the Family in East Cheshire Methodism, 1750–1830', in Jim Obelkevich, Lyndal Roper and Raphael Samuel, eds, *Disciplines of Faith: Studies in Religion, Politics and Patriarchy*, London: Routledge, 1987, pp. 57–8.

[61] Catherine A. Brekus, *Strangers and Pilgrims: Female Preaching in America 1740–1845*, Chapel Hill: University of North Carolina Press, 1998, pp. 74–5.

[62] John A. Hargreaves, 'Fletcher, Mary (1739–1815)' *ODNB*.

[63] Zechariah Taft, *Biographical Sketches of... Holy Women*, Peterborough: Methodist Publishing House, 1992 (reprint of the 1825 original), p. 24.

inspiration to others, not least his own brother John (1720–80), who sustained a mission in New Jersey from the late 1740s to the late 1770s.[64]

Evangelistic concern for African Americans in both the Caribbean and the North American mainland had predated the upsurge of revival in the late 1730s. The Moravians began a mission in St Thomas (Virgin Islands) in 1732, and during his ministry in Georgia in 1736 and 1737, John Wesley took a considerable interest in the spiritual condition of black people. The Moravians extended their work in the West Indies to Jamaica in 1754, Antigua in 1756 and Barbados in 1765, sowing the seeds for later growth.[65] Meanwhile, in mainland North America, Whitefield and other revivalists welcomed the sight of black people among their hearers and regarded them as spiritual equals. In January 1740, Whitefield addressed a published letter to the inhabitants of the southern colonies regarding their treatment of slaves. He reserved judgement on the morality of the slave trade, but condemned both the physical abuse of slaves and the spiritual abuse of keeping them ignorant of Christianity. He continued: 'Blacks are just as much, and no more, conceived and born in sin as white men are. Both, if born and bred up here . . . are naturally capable of the same improvement. And as for the grown negroes, I am apt to think, whenever the Gospel is preach'd with power amongst them, that many will be brought home to God'.[66]

At this period, evangelicals stopped short of condemning slavery as such. Indeed, both Edwards and Whitefield owned slaves, and John Newton, famously, was a slave ship captain in his youth. Even slave converts were prepared to see their situation as providential, in bringing them to a knowledge of Christianity that they would not have obtained in Africa. Nevertheless, evangelical acceptance of black people as actual and potential brothers and sisters in Christ was a recognition of common humanity and an essential point of departure for later evangelical opposition to the slave trade and eventually to slavery itself. In the shorter term, the evangelical sense of the immediacy of the supernatural gave them a ready affinity with African spirituality, as demonstrated in the success of pioneer revivalist ministries such as that of the Presbyterian Samuel Davies in Hanover County, Virginia, who in 1757 reported having baptized 150 adults during the preceding 18 months,[67] and the Baptist Elhanan Winchester in South Carolina in the 1770s. From the 1760s onwards, Methodism began to have a substantial impact on black people in both Antigua and the American south. Before the end of the century, specifically

64 Kidd, *Great Awakening*, pp. 189–212.

65 Sylvia R. Frey and Betty Wood, *Come Shouting to Zion: African American Protestantism in the American South and British Caribbean to 1830*, Chapel Hill: University of North Carolina Press, 1998, pp. 83–91.

66 *Three Letters from the Rev Mr G. Whitefield*, Philadelphia: Franklin, 1740, pp. 13–15.

67 Robert M. Calhoon, *Evangelicals and Conservatives in the Early South, 1740–1861*, Columbia: University of South Carolina Press, 1988, p. 14.

African-American churches were beginning to emerge, notably George Liele's First African Church of Savannah, founded in 1775.[68]

In some respects evangelicals appeared ahead of their time, in others they found themselves swimming with the social and cultural tides. The point is well made by the subtitles of two influential biographies of George Whitefield: Harry Stout's *The Divine Dramatist* and Frank Lambert's *Pedlar in Divinity*.[69] To Stout, Whitefield was the consummate showman who successfully employed all the acting techniques of the eighteenth-century theatre, even as he rejected its perceived immorality. To Lambert, his self-advertisement and offer of an individualistic Christianity challenging the religious monopoly of conventional Anglicanism was reminiscent of contemporary traders who challenged mercantilist commercial monopolies leading to the advent of the free market and the emergence of genuine consumer choice. Where they agree is in pointing out the importance of the evangelical co-optation of popular cultures. In these respects, Whitefield's spectacular transatlantic career was reflected at a more localised level by the activities of numerous more obscure preachers, who offered their hearers a dynamic and culturally progressive spiritual alternative to both established Christianity and traditional popular religion.[70]

A conventional narrative of evangelical history places the 'First Great Awakening' in the late 1730s and 1740s, followed by the 'Second Great Awakening' in the 1790s and early 1800s. This chronology is useful up to a point. There was, of course, discontinuity of personnel with the deaths of Edwards in 1758, Whitefield in 1770 and, eventually of both John Wesley and the Countess of Huntingdon in 1791. In the 1770s, the American Revolution and the subsequent war with Britain disrupted the structures of colonial evangelicalism and weakened the ties with Europe that had been so important in the early years of the revival. There was also, as we shall see in the next chapter, a dramatic acceleration in the expansion of evangelicalism in the years after 1790. Nevertheless, the historical construct of two 'awakenings' tends to obscure significant continuities across the later eighteenth century. Revivals certainly did not cease between the 1740s and the 1790s, and there was a particularly notable outbreak in New England and elsewhere between 1762 and 1765.[71] Rapid Methodist expansion in America began in the early 1770s and accelerated after the War of Independence concluded in 1783.[72] In Nova Scotia, New Brunswick and northern New England, Henry Alline enjoyed enormous success as an itinerant evangelist in the decade between his conversion in 1775 and his death in 1784.[73] In Ireland, similarly, Methodist progress had been slow in the middle decades of

68 Frey and Wood, *Coming Shouting to Zion*, pp. 95–116.

69 Frank Lambert, *Pedlar in Divinity: George Whitefield and the Transatlantic Revivals 1737–1770*, Princeton: Princeton University Press, 1994; Stout, *Divine Dramatist.*

70 Cf. Hindmarsh, *Evangelical Conversion Narrative*, p. 77.

71 Kidd, *Great Awakening*, pp. 267–87.

72 Noll, *Rise of Evangelicalism*, p. 205.

73 G.A. Rawlyk, *Ravished by the Spirit: Religious Revivals, Baptists and Henry Alline*, Kingston and Montreal: McGill-Queen's University Press, 1984, pp. 8–12; G.A. Rawlyk, *The Canada Fire:*

the century, but membership nearly doubled in the 1770s, from 3,124 to 6,109, and more than doubled again in the 1780s.[74] In Britain, even if the intensity of the early revivals receded, it was the 1750s, 1760s and 1770s that saw the gradual consolidation of the Methodist movement, the securing of the evangelical presence in the state churches through the work of men like Erskine, Newton and Romaine, and the emergence of a distinctively evangelical group of Protestant Dissenters. The new wine was indeed maturing in both new *and* old wineskins.

THE APPEAL OF EVANGELICALISM

It remains in this final section of the chapter to illuminate more fully the reasons why early evangelicalism had a powerful appeal to many people, sustaining itself and gathering momentum. This task is approached through three different sources: first, a small sample of sermons, to illustrate some central emphases of preachers; second, hymns, a further medium for spiritual and doctrinal instruction, readily internalised by singers as authentic articulations of their own convictions and experience; and finally, spiritual autobiographies and narratives of conversion, which provide insights into the mental and spiritual worlds of ordinary believers.

Three sermons have been selected to illustrate a little of the geographical, demominational and chonological range of early evangelicalism. The first comes from George Whitefield's first sustained London preaching campaign and was delivered at Moorfields on 20 May 1739.[75] Whitefield took his text from Luke's account of Jesus's encounter with the tax collector Zacchaeus: 'For the Son of Man is come to seek and to save that which was lost' (19:9–10). He began by attacking nominal Christians who made the 'fatal error' of believing they could secure their own salvation rather than depending on 'the free Gift of God'. Zacchaeus was unpopular, rich and corrupt, but unlike many rich people he did not think himself 'too wise to be instructed'. He came to see Jesus merely out of curiosity, like many came to see Whitefield, but did not expect to be noticed. However, Jesus is 'God over all' and he knew Zacchaeus, just as 'he knows every one that is come to hear me this morning'. Christ called him 1,700 years before, and called them now. This might be their last opportunity to respond as they could be launched into eternity that very day. The Christian life is joyful, not melancholy, and faith in Christ is a 'living principle' in the soul calling the believer to praise and good works. Whitefield concluded with a direct appeal to his listeners:

> I invite you all to come to Jesus Christ this day; make haste then, come down and receive him as your Lord and Saviour. If you apprehend you are in a lost condition,

Radical Evangelicalism in British North America 1775–1812, Kingston and Montreal: McGill-Queen's University Press, 1994, pp. 5, 16.

[74] Hempton and Hill, *Evangelical Protestantism in Ulster*, p.11.

[75] George Whitefield, *An Exhortation to Come and See Jesus*, London: Whitefield, 1739.

> he came to save such: such as labour and are heavy laden; such as feel the weight and the load of sin on their souls, a burden too heavy for them to bear, are weary of it, and lie down under the pressure of it, I, in the name of my Lord and Master, invite you to come to him that ye may find rest for your souls.[76]

Even on the dry printed page, the forcefulness and emotional power of Whitefield's sermon is apparent. When one also takes into account the effect of the powerful dramatic delivery for which he was renowned, it is easy to understand how he stirred such a strong response. He skilfully turns his hearers' mixed motives to his advantage, addressing himself directly to those who have come merely out of curiosity. He makes the uncertainty of life grounds for immediate decision and anticipates the objections of those who see Christianity as dull or themselves as either too good to need to respond or too bad to be able to do so. Prospective converts are offered peace of mind for the present and eternal salvation for the future.

The second example is a sermon delivered in 1755 by John Cennick, the pioneer Moravian itinerant in Ireland, at Ballymena, an early centre of evangelical activity in Ulster.[77] The immediate context of his text, 'Behold the Lamb of God, which taketh away the sin of the world' (John 1:29), was John the Baptist's initial recognition of Jesus at the beginning of his ministry. However, Cennick rapidly turned to wider reflection on the title 'Lamb of God' itself, building up to an extended meditation on the crucifixion. Jesus, he said, had many of the qualities of a lamb, such as a tender nature so that 'the most affrighted and fearful soul may approach him, and come into his presence without danger'. The most important reason, however, for identifying Jesus as a lamb was the use of lambs for sacrifice 'from the beginning of the world', but no earlier sacrifice 'could take away sin, make peace or atone for our Fall, or avert the just wrath of Almighty God.' Only the offering of Jesus, God's 'eternal Son, his dearest Lamb, his coessential and beloved Child', could be a sufficient substitute for 'sinful creation'. Cennick thus built up to a graphic exhortation to experience almost as a present physical reality the figure of Jesus himself suffering on the cross, offering comfort and salvation to the believer:

> Behold him! Behold the Lamb of God! These open arms are extended to embrace you, that pained breast was made bare, that you might lean there and be comforted, that cross of his was raised up to screen and shelter you like a great tree, from the burning heat of the wrath of Almighty God; these wounds are the cities of refuge [see Numbers 35: 9–15], set open that you might turn in and be safe; that reverend head was bowed down to listen to your complaint and sighs, and those dear lips stooped to kiss you, the blood which runs down from all parts, from head to foot, hastened to make a river of life, that you might drink and live for ever, that you might wash and be clean. O go to him, venture near him, spread your hands and hearts towards

[76] Ibid., pp.11–12 (spelling, capitalization and punctuation modernized).

[77] John Cennick, *The Beatific Vision; or Beholding JESUS Crucified*, London: Lewis, 1755.

> this temple; make your prayer towards this gate of heaven and apply, fearless and with truth, to him who was lifted up and slain, and you shall find help.[78]

Theologically, Cennick's sermon serves as a classic statement of full-blooded evangelical Christology and what David Bebbington calls crucicentrism,[79] the pivotal significance of Jesus's death on the cross as a propitiatory sacrifice for the sins of humankind. Moreover, it illustrates how abstract doctrine could be given a powerful devotional appeal to those troubled by guilt or burdened by the hardships and insecurities of eighteenth-century life. Moravians were particularly prone to such intense visualisation of Jesus's sufferings, but they highlighted a strain of spirituality common to the evangelical movement as a whole. The imagery may be disturbing to later post-Freudian generations, troubled by perceived sexual connotations, or confused by the paradoxical notion of washing in blood, but it appears to have struck a powerful chord with the original hearers.

Finally we come to a sermon preached under distressing personal circumstances by Isaac Backus, the leading American Baptist, at Middleborough, Massachusetts, on 5 February 1769.[80] Backus had just received news of his own mother's death, but turned this bereavement into a pastoral opportunity. His text (I Thessalonians 4:14) affirmed the resurrection hope: 'For if we believe that Jesus died, and rose again, even so them also which sleep in Jesus, will God bring with him.' It was first essential to be 'in Jesus', which Backus defined as 'by faith to take him as our refuge from all evil' and having a living union with him 'as the branch hath with the vine'. Death, Backus argued, 'is but a sleep to those who are in Jesus'. But morning will come and God will awaken those who sleep in Jesus and give them a new glorious body. Hence, provided one has confidence of being 'in Jesus', death offers the prospect of rest from labours and suffering. There is, therefore, 'much support under the loss of Christian friends. Did I say *loss*? Must I not retract the expression? For we are not wont to call our weary friends lost, when they are gone to rest in a quiet sleep; and none sleep so quietly as those who sleep in Jesus.'[81] Those left behind should lay to heart the evil of sin, the shortness of life and the importance of always being ready for death. The sermon thus uses the inevitability, and perhaps imminence, of death as a stimulus to Christian devotion and purpose in the present life. While Backus does not dwell on the terrors of Hell, he is clear that those who do not identify with Christ in life face a grim prospect after death: those who do not labour in the daytime have no right to expect rest when night comes. His hearers are comforted as to the situation of deceased loved ones, and, in a culture where even younger people had good cause to be conscious of their

78 Ibid., pp. 16–17.
79 Bebbington, *Evangelicalism in Modern Britain*, pp. 14–17.
80 Isaac Backus, *Gospel Comfort, under Heavy Tidings*, Providence: Carter, 1769.
81 Ibid., pp. 14–15.

mortality, they are given a powerful incentive to seek a closer relationship with Jesus.

Central to all three sermons is an emphasis on the believer's identification by faith with the person of Jesus as a source of support and comfort in life and the means to salvation after death. This central devotional focus of evangelicalism is also powerfully apparent in the hymns of the period, written not only for public worship, but as a means to assist believers in understanding and internalising essential teachings. While there were to be numerous American hymn-writers in later generations, in the early decades of evangelicalism, the leading authors were all British. Evangelicals utilised the hymns of significant forerunners, notably Doddridge and Watts, but through Charles Wesley's copious and sometimes powerful verse, and the significant contributions of others such as Cennick and William Williams Pantycelyn, they quickly acquired a substantial corpus of their own. Important additions were also made by the next generation, notably in the *Olney Hymns* of William Cowper and John Newton, first published in 1779.

Charles Wesley wrote 'And can it be . . . ', a testimony of his own conversion, in 1738 and it featured in the earliest Methodist hymnbooks, thus giving it a enduring normative influence in enabling less theologically literate followers to articulate and celebrate their experience:

> Long my imprisoned spirit lay,
> Fast bound in sin and nature's night;
> Thine eye diffused a quickening ray—
> I woke, the dungeon flamed with light;
> My chains fell off, my heart was free,
> I rose, went forth, and followed Thee.
>
> Still the small inward voice I hear,
> That whispers all my sins forgiven;
> Still the atoning blood is near,
> That quenched the wrath of hostile Heaven.
> I feel the life His wounds impart;
> I feel the Saviour in my heart.
>
> No condemnation now I dread;
> Jesus, and all in Him, is mine;
> Alive in Him, my living Head,
> And clothed in righteousness divine,
> Bold I approach th'eternal throne,
> And claim the crown, through Christ my own.[82]

[82] John and Charles Wesley, eds, *Hymns and Sacred Poems*, London, 1739, pp. 118–9. However, Thomas Campbell's stirring tune 'Sagina', with which this hymn is nowadays inextricably associated, was not composed until 1825.

In 1739, Charles Wesley marked the first anniversary of his conversion with 'O for a thousand tongues to sing', another hymn that subsequently became enormously popular, affirming the reality of the presence of Jesus in the believer's experience, and the consciousness of being cleansed from sin through his self-sacrifice on the cross.[83] Even if earthly life seemed burdensome, evangelical hymns offered the prospect of a better life beyond. As John Cennick put it in 1742:

Lift your eyes, ye sons of light!
Sion's city is in sight;
There our endless home shall be,
There our Lord we soon shall see.

Fear not, brethren! Joyful stand
On the borders of your land;
Jesus Christ, your Father's Son
Bids you undismayed go on.[84]

A similar sentiment was expressed in one of the greatest hymns of the Welsh revival, William Williams's 'Arglyydd, arwain trwy'r anialwch' (1745), translated into English in 1771 as 'Guide me, O thou great redeemer':

When I tread the verge of Jordan
Bid my anxious fears subside;
Death of death, and hell's destruction,
Land me safe on Canaan's side . . . [85]

A slightly later (1758) Charles Wesley hymn, 'Lo! He comes with clouds descending', inspired by similar verses by John Cennick, highlights the early evangelical preoccupation with very physical visualisation of the sufferings of Christ, as well as their anticipation of his second advent:

Every eye shall now behold Him
Robed in dreadful majesty;
Those who set at naught and sold Him,
Pierced and nailed Him to the tree,
Deeply wailing,
Shall the true Messiah see. . . .

The dear tokens of His passion
Still His dazzling body bears;
Cause of endless exultation
To His ransomed worshippers;
With what rapture,
Gaze we on those glorious scars!

[83] Charles Wesley, *Hymns and Spiritual Songs* (1758), p. 63, spellings modernised.
[84] Frost, *Hymns Ancient and Modern*, p. 302.
[85] Ibid., p. 303.

Again the immediate and enduring popularity of this hymn was indicative of the way it expressed a powerful strand in evangelical expectation. Moreover, its lasting association with the popular mid-eighteenth-century tune 'Helmsley' gives a further insight into the experience of the original worshippers.[86]

The *Olney Hymns* further broadened the resources available to evangelical worshippers. The hymns of John Newton – the more confident member of the collection's hymn-writing partnership – reflected a similar spiritual assurance to those of Charles Wesley, in for example 'Glorious things of thee are spoken', 'How sweet the name of Jesus sounds' and 'Amazing grace'.[87] However, the depressive William Cowper penned hymns that powerfully expressed the doubts and sense of spiritual weakness and striving of more fallible mortals:

> Oh! For a closer walk with God,
> A calm and heav'nly frame;
> A light to shine upon the road
> That leads me to the Lamb! . . .
>
> Return, O holy Dove, return,
> Sweet messenger of rest;
> I hate the sins that made thee mourn,
> And drove thee from my breast.[88]

It was Cowper too who wrote verses that reflected the undoubtedly widespread reality of small and struggling evangelical groups seeking to sustain themselves after the first ardour of revival had passed:

> Dear Shepherd of thy chosen few!
> Thy former mercies here renew;
> Here to our waiting hearts proclaim
> The sweetness of thy saving name. . . .
>
> Lord, we are few, but thou art near;
> Nor short thine arm, nor deaf thine ear;
> Oh rend the heav'ns, come quickly down,
> And make a thousand hearts thine own.[89]

Surviving personal testimonies from early evangelicals make it possible to explore how such published articulations of conviction and experience were mirrored in the spiritual lives of individuals. Indeed, sermons and hymns themselves could have an immediate and powerful impact. Thus, Nathaniel Hurst began

[86] John Julian, *A Dictionary of Hymnology*, 2nd edn, 2 vols, London: John Murray, 1907, i.680–1.
[87] It is worth noting, however, that 'Amazing grace' was never as popular in Britain as it subsequently became in America, and was dismissed by John Julian in his authoritative *Dictionary of Hymnology* (p. 55) as 'far from being a good example of Newton's work'.
[88] *Olney Hymns*, London: Oliver, 1779, p. 4.
[89] *Olney Hymns*, p. 235.

a narrative of his conversion by saying, 'When first the Lord sent Mr Whitfield out into the fields, I went to hear him at Moorfields.' In the course of the summer of 1739, Mary Ramsay, a schoolmistress, heard Whitefield preach thirteen times in and around London, recalling his words in considerable detail.[90] Hymns were also an important spiritual catalyst: Mary Ramsay recalled that 'Another thing that workt in me was some words of that hymn Called Christ the friend of Sinners.' John Henderson's testimony further illustrated the capacity of hymns to communicate to less-well-educated people: 'Hymns are the chief of my reading, for they may be felt without study.'[91] For Moravians above all, hymn-singing was a central part of collective and personal devotional life.[92]

The central experience of conversion was described by Elizabeth Hinsome in a letter to Charles Wesley in 1740, with an eloquence that overcame the limitations of her grammar and spelling: 'I trembled and should have fell done but the people heald me up and I was out of my sense but the lord a wakened me with peace be unto you your sins are for giving you. I went home full of joye not knowing ware to bestow my self ... I am lost in wonder when I see what god has done for my soul.'[93]

The characteristic prelude to this moment of resolution and spiritual release was a period of recognition of the inadequacy of merely formal Christian observance accompanied by an oppressive consciousness of sinfulness and the reality of divine judgement. The Moravian emphasis differed, however, in encouraging a less tortured initial struggle, and in conversion a quietist abandonment of self in contemplation of the sufferings of Christ. For some, especially women, conversion came as a recovery of human dignity in the face of very material suffering. For example, Margaret Austin had been the victim of an abusive husband who deserted her, leaving her to bring up two young children. She initially had an understandably low sense of self-worth but, encouraged and supported by other Methodist women, she eventually experienced 'such joy that I could scarce forbear speaking' in conversion.[94]

This chapter began with one classic instance of conversion, and it is therefore appropriate to end it with another. In March 1775, a few weeks before skirmishes at Lexington and Concord were to mark the outbreak of the American Revolutionary War, a few hundred miles to the north-east in Falmouth, Nova Scotia, the twenty-seven-year-old Henry Alline found release from inward spiritual and psychological turmoil in an intense experience of God's presence and love:

> O how the condescension melted me, and thought I could hardly bear, that God should stoop so low to such an unworthy wretch, crying out still, enough, enough,

[90] Hindmarsh, *Evangelical Conversion Narrative*, pp. 135–6.
[91] Ibid., p. 152.
[92] Ibid., pp. 183–6.
[93] Quoted ibid., p. 134.
[94] Ibid., pp. 147–8.

> O my God, I believe, I believe; at the same time I was ravished with his love, and saying, go on blessed God in love and mercy to me, and although I do not deserve thee, yet I cannot live without thee, and I long to drink deeper and deeper in thy love. O what secret pleasure I enjoyed![95]

The depth of Alline's experience, which, as George Rawlyk puts it, 'blended the sexual with the spiritual to produce a powerful explosive mixture',[96] was the driving force behind his subsequent enormously successful career as a revivalist, bringing in turbulent times a strong, if transient, sense of spiritual unity, with each other and with God, to the scattered communities of the colonial Maritimes.

Ontological judgements on the sources of such experience fall outside the competence of the historian. The individuals concerned believed that they had had a direct encounter with the divine, and were encouraged by their leaders to articulate and interpret what happened to them with reference to the Bible and within the particular theological frameworks of early evangelicalism. A more sceptical later generation might prefer to follow John Kent in characterising them rather as expressions of 'primary religion', fulfilling the search of the individuals concerned for an extra-human power to meet their personal fears and needs.[97] What is beyond question, however, is that the preaching, hymns and general religious excitement of early evangelicalism stirred numerous intense spiritual and emotional responses, thus giving the revivals a self-sustaining momentum. The participants believed themselves truly to be witnessing and taking forward 'the surprising work of God'.

[95] Quoted Rawlyk, *Ravished by the Spirit*, p. 14.
[96] Ibid., p. 11.
[97] Kent, *Wesley and the Wesleyans*, pp. 1–2.

3

Volunteering for the Kingdom: 1790s to 1840s

The five years between 1787 and 1792 were an important watershed in the development of evangelicalism within the wider context of world history. On 1 June 1787, eighteen months after William Wilberforce had experienced an evangelical conversion, King George III issued at his instigation a proclamation for 'the encouragement of piety and virtue'. Wilberforce formed the Proclamation Society to advance its implementation, pioneering a format that was to be adopted by a plethora of evangelical voluntary societies pursuing religious, moral and social reform. Across the Atlantic in Philadelphia on 17 September 1787, the United States Constitution was adopted. Its ratification by the former British colonies created an expanding new nation which, despite – or perhaps because of – its rigorous separation of church and state, was to provide fertile soil for the flourishing of a multitude of evangelical institutions. John Wesley's appointment of Francis Asbury and Thomas Coke as general superintendents of American Methodism in 1784 had already reflected both the national independence of the United States and the evolution of Methodism into a distinct denomination. Then, in January 1788, the movement gained a presence on the far-flung shores of New South Wales, with the arrival of the First Fleet and its evangelical chaplain, Richard Johnson, who on 3 February celebrated the first Christian service on the site of what was to become Sydney. Back in London, on 12 May 1789, William Wilberforce rose in the House of Commons to deliver his first speech calling for the abolition of the slave trade, initiating a moral and political crusade that became emblematic of the aspirations of evangelicals not only to save souls but to transform society, on a global stage as well as a national one. The campaign against the slave trade, and eventually slavery itself, was to lead to great successes but also bitter division from those evangelicals in the slaveholding communities in the American South.

Two months later, on 14 July 1789, the revolutionary crowd in Paris stormed the Bastille, the fortress prison that was regarded as a central symbol of the old regime in France. Its overthrow gave impetus to the chain of events that was to culminate in the abolition of the monarchy and the unleashing of wars that were to convulse Europe until 1815. On 2 March 1791, a very different kind of old order came to an end with the death of John Wesley, whose powerful personality and organisational genius had shaped the major part of the Methodist movement for more than half a century. Methodism without Wesley was to expand to a much greater extent than it had done in his lifetime, but it also experienced successive and sometimes disruptive internal conflicts. Finally, on 12 May 1792, William Carey published an *Enquiry into the Obligation of Christians to Use Means for the Conversion of the Heathen.* It was a pamphlet which, like many momentous things, initially only had a limited impact but in retrospect came to be seen as the inspiration for the foundation of the great missionary societies, including the Baptist Missionary Society (1792), the London Missionary Society (1795), the Society for Missions to Africa and the East (later the Church Missionary Society) (1799) and the American Board for Foreign Missions (1810). Carey himself was to play a pioneering role in bringing evangelicalism to India, while in the longer term, the nineteenth-century missionary movement was to sow the seeds that in the twentieth century bore fruit in the globalisation of evangelicalism. Moreover, all these developments were occurring against the background of the economic and social transformations characterised as the 'industrial revolution'. Of their very nature, these are not as precisely dateable as the events mentioned previously, but in Britain at least they were reaching a decisive phase in the last two decades of the eighteenth century, producing in the first half of the nineteenth century an increasingly populous, industrialised and urbanised society.

The chronological coincidence of all these developments has given rise to much historiographical debate, about the role of evangelicalism in the consolidation of revolution in North America and its avoidance in Britain, in the development of the new forms of work discipline and social structure in the emerging industrial society and in the more material impulses driving British overseas expansion.[1] The focus of this chapter, however, is on the remarkable expansion of evangelicalism itself, driven forward by the readiness of countless men and women to volunteer for the cause of advancing the 'kingdom of God'. The *Oxford English Dictionary* defines a volunteer as a 'person who spontaneously undertakes [a] task'. Such work may or may not be paid, but the essence of volunteering is a personal commitment to the endeavour in question, which is undertaken not under external constraint or primarily in the expectation of financial gain. The movement was indeed characterised by grassroots dynamism rather than by central direction, and although it profoundly influenced the state churches of the United Kingdom and Prussia, its advance owed little to government intervention. The word 'voluntaryism' has come to have a more specific application to religious activity independent of state control or finance, but in practice it also represents a much broader spirit among evangelicals, whose intense experiences of personal conversion and calling could take place in a moment but inspire an earnest activism that might be pursued self-sacrificially across a whole lifetime.

The progress of evangelicalism during the ensuing half-century was symbolised by the first international conference of the Evangelical Alliance, which met in

[1] See later in the chapter for a brief discussion of these issues.

London in August and September 1846. There were expressions of support from as far away as Agra, Cape Town and Hobart, Tasmania. Although this was still predominantly a North Atlantic movement, it was indeed edging toward becoming a truly global one. Moreover, it had a strong presence in all the major orthodox Protestant denominations: at the 1846 conference, there were Anglican, Baptist, Congregational, Presbyterian and Wesleyan Methodist contingents, as well as significant representation from Lutherans, and from other Methodist groups. This was a movement that was now conscious of its own numerical strength and considerable social and cultural influence.[2]

There were three main dimensions of evangelical expansion between 1790 and 1850. First, there was enormous growth in Methodism, the archetypal evangelical denomination arising from the eighteenth-century revivals; second, the evangelicalisation of existing denominations; and third, the growth of voluntary societies that complemented the work of the churches by promoting particular forms of mission and social engagement. In this chapter, those societies committed to overseas mission will receive particular attention because of their role during the early nineteenth century in extending the reach of evangelicalism far outside its primary North Atlantic heartland. Finally we shall outline the debate on the wider historical impact of evangelical zeal.

THE METHODIST SURGE

Although the number of Methodists grew substantially between 1760 and 1790, they were still a small minority. In Great Britain, there were 58,218 members of Wesley's Connexion, and even if allowance is made for an unknown number of Calvinistic Methodists (especially strong in Wales), they would have made up at most 1 per cent of an estimated national population of around 8 million. The 14,158 Irish members made up a similar proportion of that island's Protestant population.[3] In the United States, there were also approximately 58,000 Methodists in 1790, although these were already a rather larger proportion of a smaller 'national' population of 3.93 million.[4] The subsequent spectacular expansion of Methodism on both sides of the Atlantic evidenced the most dramatic manifestation of the evangelical voluntary spirit. During the following sixty years, membership in Great Britain increased to 94,000 in 1801, 227,000 in 1821 and 557,000 (including 52,600 Welsh Calvinistic Methodists) in 1851.[5] Growth in the United States was even more rapid. In 1770, there were fewer than a thousand Methodists, but by 1800, there already were 65,000,

[2] Wolffe, *The Expansion of Evangelicalism: The Age of Wilberforce, More, Chalmers and Finney*, Nottingham: Intervarsity Press, 2006, pp. 231–2.

[3] Robert Currie, Alan Gilbert and Lee Horsley, *Churches and Churchgoers: Patterns of Church Growth in the British Isles since 1700*, Oxford: Clarendon, 1977, p. 139.

[4] Mark Noll, *America's God from Jonathan Edwards to Abraham Lincoln*, New York: Oxford University Press, 2002, p. 169.

[5] Currie, Gilbert and Horsley, *Churches and Churchgoers*, pp. 140–1, 148.

increasing to 257,000 in 1820 and 1.185 million in 1850. These increases substantially outpaced very rapid growth in the overall population: in 1851, Methodist *members* made up 2.7 per cent of the population of Britain and 5.1 per cent of that of the United States.[6] These figures relate to *members*: in this period, *attendances* almost certainly substantially exceeded membership, probably by a factor of as much as three or four. In the 1851 religious census in Britain, there were nearly 2.75 million Methodist attendances,[7] nearly five times the size of membership at the time (although this figure includes significant double-counting of individuals who attended more than one service). By the middle of the nineteenth century, Methodism had become the largest single denominational group in the United States with more than 34 per cent of church members;[8] in England and Wales in 1851, 25.7 per cent of reported church attendances were Methodist ones, a proportion second only to the Church of England.[9] In 1833 Methodist membership in Upper Canada (modern Ontario) amounted to over 5 per cent of the total population,[10] a comparable proportion to that in the United States. By the time of the 1861 census their numbers had overtaken both the Anglicans and the Presbyterians, with 29.7 per cent of the Protestant population identifying themselves as Methodists.[11] Only in regions where historic Reformed Protestant faith was integrated with a regional identity (through, for instance, parish structures, or mass migration) did Methodism fail to take off. Little headway was made in Scotland, where much of the evangelical impulse was initially contained within the Church of Scotland; in Ireland in the nineteenth century, Methodism failed to maintain the momentum of its early expansion; and in the Canadian Maritimes, Methodists faced strong competition from Baptists as well as Presbyterians. Nevertheless, even in such areas of relative weakness, Methodism was still a dynamic minority presence.

Within both Britain and the United States, the regional distribution of Methodism was uneven. The 1851 religious census showed that it was strongest in the west, in Wales and Cornwall, and in the north-east, in Lincolnshire, Yorkshire and Durham. In all these regions, total Methodist attendances significantly exceeded

[6] Noll, *America's God*, p. 169; Wolffe, *Expansion of Evangelicalism*, p. 66.

[7] *Census of Great Britain 1851: Religious Worship, England and Wales – Report and Tables*, London: House of Commons Sessional Papers 1852–3, vol. 89, pp. clxxviii–clxxix; *Religious Worship and Education, Scotland*, London: House of Commons Sessional Papers 1854, vol. 59, pp. 2–3.

[8] John Wigger, *Taking Heaven by Storm: Methodism and the Rise of Popular Christianity in America*, New York: Oxford University Press, 1998, p. 3.

[9] B.I. Coleman, *The Church of England in the Mid-Nineteenth Century: A Social Geography*, Historical Association Pamphlet, General Series 98 (1980), pp. 40–1.

[10] In 1833, when the estimated population of Upper Canada was 295,554 (Statistics Canada, http://www.statcan.gc.ca/pub/98–187-x/4064808-eng.etm, accessed 9 April 2011), there were more than 16,000 Methodist members (Neil Semple, *The Lord's Dominion: The History of Canadian Methodism*, Montreal and Kingston: McGill-Queen's University Press, 1996, p. 86.

[11] Michael Gauvreau, 'Protestantism Transformed: Personal Piety and the Evangelical Social Vision' in George A. Rawlyk, ed., *The Canadian Protestant Experience 1760–1990*, Montreal and Kingston: McGill-Queen's University Press, 1990, p. 66.

Anglican ones, making them the largest denominational grouping. On the other hand, Methodism was much weaker in south-east England.[12] In the United States, Methodism was strongest in the eastern coastal states from Delaware southwards and in the West, and weakest in New England.[13] Nevertheless, in both countries it was successful in establishing a genuinely national presence (except in Scotland), ranging from significant minority to absolute majority.

Methodism's success was rooted in the readiness of its leaders at all levels to commit themselves voluntarily to tremendous labours in the cause of proclaiming the Gospel and supporting converts. The work of lay preachers and class leaders was entirely 'voluntary' in the sense of being unpaid; full-time itinerant preachers often received barely a living wage.[14] Francis Asbury, who led the Methodist Church in the United States from 1784 until his death in 1815, was exemplary in his relentless itinerancy. It has been estimated that during his career he travelled more than 130,000 miles on horseback and preached more than 10,000 sermons.[15] The leading English Methodist James Everett claimed to have covered 320,000 miles and preached 13,000 sermons over the course of a 60-year ministry. Such workloads were emulated by less famous preachers: in a single year – 1799 – Thomas Smith estimated that he travelled 4,200 miles in New Jersey and preached 324 times. Labours of this kind could lead to burnout and collapse even for the initially physically robust, and for many of those who survived, the responsibilities of marriage or a decline of energy with the passing years resulted in them ending or limiting their itinerancy.[16] Nevertheless, although the characteristic itinerant was young and single, others continued their ministry into old age: Asbury died in harness, still unmarried, at the age of seventy. Such sacrificial zeal on the part of the itinerants was only effective, however, because it was coordinated with the ongoing work of local preachers who sustained local chapels and class meetings between the visits of the full-time ministers and rooted these activities in a strong sense of community. Jacob Young's conversion in the late 1790s was stimulated by attending a class meeting in recently settled Kentucky, a gathering in which 'the congregation was melted into tears . . . and began to fall upon the floor like trees thrown down by a whirlwind'.[17] A few years later, when Young began to set up a new circuit, he was pleased to find a Methodist society already in existence, led by an African-American slave who, although illiterate, 'could preach a pretty good sermon'.[18] When another itinerant, Henry Smith, came to form a circuit in Ohio in

[12] John Wolffe, *The Religious Census of 1851 in Yorkshire*, York: Borthwick Institute, 2005, p. 5.

[13] Noll, *America's God*, p. 168; Wigger, *Taking Heaven by Storm*, p. 200.

[14] Wigger, *Taking Heaven by Storm*, pp. 23, 61.

[15] John Wigger, *American Saint: Francis Asbury and the Methodists*, New York: Oxford University Press, 2009, p. 3.

[16] Wigger, *Taking Heaven by Storm*, pp. 58–9; Michael Watts, *The Dissenters: Vol. II The Expansion of Evangelical Nonconformity*, Oxford: Clarendon, 1995, p. 152.

[17] Quoted Wigger, *Taking Heaven by Storm*, p. 53.

[18] Ibid, p. 22.

1799, he found no fewer than ten local preachers already at work along his route.[19] Women as well as men played an important role, sometimes as preachers, but often as hosts for cottage meetings and as 'mothers in Israel' who gave practical support to the itinerants. Young was aided by supportive women who gave him hospitality and made clothes for him. On one occasion, a female supporter even intervened to save him from assault by a man he had offended, by whipping the attacker 'with more severity with her tongue than he could me with his fists'.[20] On the other side of the Atlantic, at Hollington (near Derby) in the early nineteenth century, Elizabeth Gaunt drew on her personal experience of poverty, hard physical labour and family instability to inform her preaching, inspiring many, including Hugh Bourne, the founder of Primitive Methodism, with 'her pious and motherly conversation'.[21]

Methodism's regional concentrations were symptomatic of its capacity in this period to reach those on the margins of society, whether physically remote from other centres of population or places of worship – such as the settlers of the American frontier or the textile workers in new factory settlements in the north of England – or facing the stresses of dangerous and uncertain occupations, such as the miners of Cornwall or the fisherfolk of Newfoundland. The circuit system, together with small cottage and class meetings, was ideally suited for creating viable Christian communities in the initial absence of any purpose-built meeting house or chapel. In America, such regular activity was given a major boost in the summer by camp meetings, in which adherents from a wide area would gather at a central location for several days of preaching, exhortation and fellowship. It is estimated that by 1815 as many as a million people in the United States were attending such events every year.[22]

The camp meeting, however, was one touchstone of an important divergence between British and American Methodism which became increasingly apparent in the first two decades of the nineteenth century. Whereas Asbury enthused about the value of camp meetings in the United States, the British Wesleyan authorities were decidedly cool towards them. The most famous British camp meeting, which took place in 1807 at Mow Cop on the Cheshire-Staffordshire border, was the exception that proved the rule. It became a significant part of the prehistory of the most significant split in British Methodism, which took place in 1810 between the Wesleyans and the Primitive Methodists, with the latter taking a more positive view of camp meetings. The British Wesleyan dislike of such events reflected a denominational strategy of avoiding confrontation with civil authorities who, at a time when the country was fighting wars abroad and facing radical unrest at

[19] Ibid, p. 31.
[20] Ibid, pp. 159, 160, 166.
[21] Deborah Valenze, *Prophetic Sons and Daughters: Female Preaching and Popular Religion in Industrial England*, Princeton: Princeton University Press, 1985, pp. 38–9.
[22] Wigger, *Taking Heaven by Storm*, p. 97.

home, were liable to perceive unrestrained religious enthusiasm as subversive. In the United States, on the other hand, there were no such constraints.[23]

Methodists, alongside Baptists, were also instrumental in the widespread adoption of evangelical Christianity by black people in both the American South and the Caribbean between the 1780s and the 1830s. Whereas early Afro-Atlantic converts had been in a small minority, both among evangelicals and among their fellow slaves and free blacks, from the later 1780s movements of revival and Methodist and Baptist expansion had an extensive impact on blacks as well as whites. Indeed, the particular fervour with which black people, especially women, responded to evangelical preaching gave dynamism and intensity to the wider revival movements in the southern United States. For slaves, evangelicalism came to provide a crucial basis for the development of social and cultural community.[24] The Baptist George Liele, who had already been responsible for setting up and leading the First African Church in Savannah, moved to Jamaica after independence, and there formed the first Baptist Church in Kingston. By 1791, it already had 225 members and 350 adherents, predominantly black and coloured.[25] After the Methodists began systematic work in Jamaica in the same year, they also made rapid progress. The planters feared subversion, and in 1802, the island Assembly prohibited the 'preaching of ill-disposed, illiterate or ignorant enthusiasts' and enacted further repressive legislation in 1807. Nevertheless, Methodism continued to grow: in 1815, the Kingston society reported 2,700 members, and there were 15,220 in the West Indies as a whole. In the same year, there were more than 40,000 black Methodists in the United States, nearly a third of the total.[26]

The Wesleyan-Primitive split in Britain was one instance of the wider tendency of Methodism to internal division. Whereas the eighteenth-century division from Calvinistic Methodism had theological roots, later conflicts were essentially about issues of power within the organisation. The earliest such splits occurred in the 1790s. In the United States, the Republican Methodists (founded in 1794) objected to Asbury's assumption of episcopal authority, and in Britain, the Methodist New Connexion (1797) originated in lay objection to the concentration of power in the hands of ministers.[27] Other smaller and often short-lived groups in England resembled the Primitive Methodists in espousing a popular revivalistic enthusiasm distasteful to the Wesleyan authorities. The most substantial and long-lasting of these were the Bible Christians, concentrated in south-west

[23] Nathan O. Hatch, *The Democratization of American Christianity*, New Haven: Yale University Press, 1989, pp. 49–56.

[24] Sylvia R. Frey and Betty Wood, *Come Shouting to Zion: African American Protestantism in the American South and British Caribbean to 1830*, Chapel Hill: University of North Carolina Press, 1998, pp. 118–21.

[25] Ibid, p. 131.

[26] Ibid, pp. 134–8, 149.

[27] Wigger, *Taking Heaven by Storm*, p. 39; W.R. Ward, *Religion and Society in England 1790–1850*, London: Batsford, 1972, pp. 34–8.

England (and later spreading along Cornish migration tracks to places such as South Australia), whereas the Primitives were strongest in the Midlands and the North. In the United States, black Methodists, feeling the need for a distinct organisation that reflected their own religious culture, in 1816 formed the African Methodist Episcopal Church under the leadership of Richard Allen, and the separate African Methodist Episcopal Zion Church a few years later.[28] Further significant schisms occurred in 1828 in the United States with the formation of the Protestant Methodist Church, which rejected bishops and gave more influence to local preachers and settled ministers, and in 1849 in England, with the secession of the Wesleyan Reformers who were opposed to the perceived authoritarianism of the Wesleyan Conference.[29] Among the key leaders of the Reformers was the veteran itinerant James Everett,[30] an illustration of how the fissiparous tendency of Methodism reflected the movement's dynamism, and the intense commitment of dispersed volunteers who sought both empowerment for themselves and close engagement with their communities. In the long term, however, the more conservative factions, especially the British Wesleyan Methodists, moved away from their original popular base. The legacy of institutional fragmentation became problematic when expansion levelled off in the later nineteenth century and eventually turned to decline in the twentieth. In the early nineteenth century, however, Methodism was the most dramatically expansionist religious force on both sides of the Atlantic.[31]

RESHAPING THE TRADITIONAL PROTESTANT CHURCHES

From the earliest years of the mid-eighteenth-century revival, evangelicalism had a substantial impact on existing churches, with the enthusiastic adherence of individual ministers, sometimes in defiance of higher ecclesiastical authority, giving rise to tensions as inherited structures resisted the new impulse.[32] From the 1790s, however, this trend, like the parallel development of Methodism, moved into a qualitatively as well as quantitatively new phase. Evangelicals were no longer merely troublesome minorities, but were becoming dominant (or at least very numerous and influential) groupings which could no longer be ignored or marginalised.

In the Church of England, evangelicalism even began to become fashionable. In the mid-1790s, as revival in the textile and mining districts of Yorkshire led to the rapid growth of popular Methodism, William Wilberforce, who was one of the members of parliament for that county, was writing his first book. The work was eventually published in April 1797, with a lengthy title that summed up the content:

[28] Wolffe, *Expansion of Evangelicalism*, p. 65.

[29] Robert Baird, *Religion in the United States of America*, Glasgow: Blackie, 1844, pp. 595–6; Ward, *Religion and Society in England*, pp. 264–72.

[30] Oliver A. Beckerlegge, 'Everett, James', *DEB*, i.370–1.

[31] Cf. David Hempton, *Methodism: Empire of the Spirit*, New Haven: Yale University Press, 2005, especially pp. 11–31.

[32] See Chapter Two in this volume.

A Practical View of the Prevailing Religious Systems of Professed Christians in the Higher and Middle Classes of this Country Contrasted with Real Christianity. Wilberforce's intention was to appeal to élite social groups contemptuous or fearful of the Methodists, and to urge them too to accept 'real' (that is, evangelical) Christianity as a basis for bringing about general social, moral and spiritual transformation. Evangelicalism, in Wilberforce's view, was not only respectable, but essential to national well-being. The publication was timely in that it played to the insecurities of the British establishment in the face of war with revolutionary France and radical unrest at home, currents which seemed to converge alarmingly in naval mutinies at Spithead in the month of the book's publication and at the Nore a few weeks later. The book was reprinted five times in the course of 1797 and continued to enjoy steady sales throughout the early nineteenth century. American editions appeared in Philadelphia in 1798 and Boston in 1799. In the opinion of Daniel Wilson, then vicar of Islington, the *Practical View* was 'a mighty instrument in carrying forward the great work' of evangelical revival.[33] It was also something of a manifesto for the Clapham Sect, the grouping of influential evangelicals around Wilberforce and his close friend Henry Thornton, who were resident in the eponymous Surrey suburb at the turn of the nineteenth century. They campaigned for the abolition of the slave trade and for other religious and moral causes while modelling an ideal of upper-class evangelical family life which was empowering for women and had an abiding impact on the Victorians.[34]

Wilberforce's book was an effective catalyst because its dissemination coincided with the steady growth of evangelical structures within the Church of England. Whereas initially evangelical clergy often ministered as isolated individuals, by the early nineteenth century, networks such as the Eclectic Society in London and the Elland Society in Yorkshire were providing mechanisms for mutual support and, crucially, for nurturing and supporting the next generation.[35] As will be seen later in the chapter, organisations such as the Church Missionary Society and the Bible Society similarly served to bring evangelical Anglicans together and give them a growing sense of strength and collective identity. The *Christian Observer* magazine, which commenced publication in 1800, further assisted this process. Anglican evangelicals also developed strong influence and networks as a result of their work in education, led by men such as Joseph Milner at Hull Grammar School and John Hill at St Edmund Hall, Oxford.[36] Above all, there was Charles Simeon's work at the University of Cambridge. Simeon, who exercised a formative influence on

[33] John Wolffe, 'William Wilberforce's *Practical View* (1797) and its reception' in Kate Cooper and Jeremy Gregory, eds, *Revival and Resurgence in Christian History: Studies in Church History 44*, Woodbridge: Boydell, 2008, pp. 175–84.

[34] John Wolffe, 'Clapham Sect (act. 1792–1815)', *ODNB*.

[35] John H. Pratt, *Notes of the Discussions of the Eclectic Society, London, during the years 1798–1914*, London, 1856 (reprinted Edinburgh: Banner of Truth, 1978); John Walsh and Stephen Taylor, eds, *The Papers of the Elland Society, 1769–1828*, Woodbridge: Boydell, in press.

[36] J.S. Reynolds, 'Hill, John', *DEB*, i.551; Arthur Pollard, 'Milner, Joseph', *DEB*, ii.776.

evangelical clergy across two long generations, from the 1780s until the 1830s, tried to place his *protégés* in strategic posts, and ensured the continuance of evangelical ministries by 'buying up' patronage.[37] Meanwhile, although Wilberforce's hopes for a general espousal of evangelicalism by the British aristocracy remained unfulfilled, there were still significant and influential supporters. These included Spencer Perceval, prime minister from 1809 to 1812, and several members of the Ryder family, notably the Earl of Harrowby, Lord President of the Council from 1812 to 1827, and his brother Henry, who became Bishop of Gloucester in 1815.[38] Among younger aristocrats, the preeminent evangelical convert was Lord Ashley, later Earl of Shaftesbury, the leading advocate of factory reform in the 1830s and 1840s.[39] Charlotte Sophia, Duchess of Beaufort, exercised a significant influence on the next generation through the marriages of her numerous daughters who shared her evangelical faith.[40] Even the royal family was not untouched, with George III's third son, the Duke of Kent, father of the future Queen Victoria, and the king's nephew, the Duke of Gloucester, both known to be sympathetic to evangelicalism.[41] Volunteers of this kind operated in a different social universe from the miners of Cornwall or the farmers of the American frontier, but their involvement drew strength from a similar spiritual impulse to promote vital Christianity.

It is not possible exactly to quantify the strength of evangelicalism in the Church of England, but one plausible contemporary estimate suggested that in 1853, 5,800 of the church's 18,300 clergy (31.7 per cent) were evangelicals.[42] Moreover, in 1848, the appointment of John Bird Sumner as Archbishop of Canterbury had shown it was possible for an evangelical to rise to the very top of the Anglican ecclesiastical tree. In the late 1850s, under Lord Palmerston's premiership, the number of evangelical episcopal appointments was increased so as to achieve a rough proportionality with the strength of evangelicalism among the clergy.[43] With the Gorham Judgement of 1850 concluding that their doctrinal position was acceptable within the Church of England, it was clear that evangelicals had established a strong, enduring presence in the national church.

As evangelicalism gained ground in the Church of England, it also became more diverse. Tensions with Anglican evangelicalism developed particularly in the 1820s and 1830s because of a rising generation that perceived their elders as too ready to compromise in order to gain political and social influence. Their concerns were

[37] William Carus, *Memoirs of the Life of Charles Simeon*, London: Hatchard, 1847.

[38] Denis Gray, *Spencer Perceval*, Manchester University Press, 1963; John Wolffea, 'Harrowby, first Earl of', *DEB*, i.524–5; G.C.B. Davies, *The First Evangelical Bishop*, London: Tyndale, 1958.

[39] G.B.A.M. Finlayson, *The Seventh Earl of Shaftesbury*, London: Eyre Methuen, 1981.

[40] John Oakes, 'Somerset, Charlotte Sophia', *DEB*, ii.1033.

[41] Peter J. Lineham, 'Kent, Edward Augustus', *DEB*, ii.641; Ford K. Brown, *Fathers of the Victorians: The Age of Wilberforce*, Cambridge University Press, 1961, pp. 302, 311–5.

[42] W.J. Conybeare (ed. Arthur Burns), 'Church Parties', in Stephen Taylor, ed., *From Cranmer to Davidson*, Woodbridge: Boydell/Church of England Record Society, 1999, p. 357.

[43] John Wolffe, 'Lord Palmerston and Religion: A Reappraisal', *English Historical Review*, 120 (2005), 924.

focused particularly by the articulation of premillennial eschatologies, anticipating the imminent Second Coming of Christ after a period of global cataclysm. These contrasted with the postmillennial eschatology characteristic of the Clapham Sect generation, which implied ongoing spiritual and social advance would be achieved through human agency, with the Second Coming still in a remote future.[44] Premillennial ideas were developed at a series of conferences at Albury in Surrey in the late 1820s, with a subsequent Irish series at Powerscourt near Dublin in the early 1830s. Meanwhile, the dynamic and controversial ministry of Edward Irving at the Scottish Church in London drew Anglicans as well as Presbyterians and became a focal point not only for prophetic interest, but also for apparent manifestations of charismatic gifts. In 1833, Irving was tried for heresy and deposed from the Church of Scotland ministry, and died the following year. By that time he had had a profound impact on British evangelicals.[45]

During the 1830s, premillennialists moved in three different directions. Two groups left the Church of England. Those associated with Irving and Henry Drummond, who had hosted the Albury meetings, founded the Catholic Apostolic Church, which grafted elaborate ritual on to an originally evangelical theology, and taught that the Second Coming would appear within the lifetimes of its original leaders.[46] Meanwhile, John Nelson Darby, a leading figure in the Powerscourt conferences, advocated the secession of true believers from the Anglican Church, leading in the early 1840s to the emergence of the Brethren. Darby travelled widely in Europe and North America and was of considerable importance for the later history of evangelicalism because of his development of a distinctive version of premillennialism, known as dispensational futurism. Darby conceived of various spiritual ages (dispensations) in human history and anticipated the secret rapture of true believers, which would enable them to escape the disasters befalling the unregenerate before Christ returns. Darby's ideas eventually acquired widespread currency in the United States in the twentieth century.[47] A third group of premillennialists remained in the Church of England and formed the core of a hard-line evangelical constituency that became known as the 'Recordites', after *The Record* newspaper, which was a prominent advocate of their views. They were also characterised by strong Calvinism and a pronounced anti-Catholicism reinforced by their readiness to equate the Papacy with the biblical Whore of Babylon (Revelation 17).[48]

Outside England, the evangelical presence in the Anglican and Episcopalian churches was patchy. There was substantial growth in the evangelical movement

[44] David Hempton, 'Evangelicalism and Eschatology', *Journal of Ecclesiastical History*, 31 (1980), 179–94.

[45] Margaret Oliphant, *The Life of Edward Irving*, 2 vols, London: Hurst and Blackett, 1862.

[46] Columba Flegg, *Gathered Under Apostles: A Study of the Catholic Apostolic Church*, Oxford: Oxford University Press, 1992.

[47] Harold H. Rowdon, *The Origins of the Brethren 1825–1850*, London: Pickering and Inglis, 1967.

[48] John Wolffe, 'Recordites (*act.* 1828–*c.*1860)', *ODNB*.

in the Church of Ireland in the early nineteenth century, gaining the adherence of numerous clergy and of influential aristocrats such as Lord Farnham and the Earl of Roden.[49] In 1834, however, Anglicans only made up 10.7 per cent of the Irish population.[50] In Wales, although bishops such as Thomas Vowler Short (at St Asaph from 1846 to 1872) and Arthur Ollivant (at Llandaff from 1849 to 1882)[51] were regarded as sympathetic to evangelicalism, the initiative lay with the Nonconformists, and thus Anglicans were liable to react by asserting a more High Church identity. In Scotland, evangelicals were a minority within the small Episcopalian minority, with several of their churches seceding in the 1840s and seeking oversight from English rather than Scottish bishops.[52] In the United States, the Revolution initially had a catastrophic effect on the Episcopal Church, with its strong English associations. However, as it began to regroup from the 1790s onwards, an evangelical presence emerged and was to receive effective leadership from Charles Pettit McIlvaine, Bishop of Ohio from 1832 until 1873. In 1844, evangelicals were estimated to make up about two-thirds of an Episcopalian population of 700,000, although this was a church that made up less than 5 per cent of the total population of the United States.[53]

Presbyterianism had been quite receptive to evangelicalism in the eighteenth century, and although its impact had in some respects been divisive, there was still in 1790 a firm base for further expansion. In the Church of Scotland, Thomas Chalmers emerged in the 1810s as a pre-eminent evangelical leader, building his reputation on his endeavours, with the aid of numerous volunteers, to combat poverty and promote morality and spiritual growth in his Glasgow parishes.[54] In 1834, the evangelicals became the majority in the General Assembly and were able to push forward characteristic concerns, particularly the creation of new parishes and support for the right of parishioners to reject a patron's nominee as minister. However, their actions were eventually judged illegal by the civil courts, prompting 450 ministers to leave in the Disruption of 1843 to form the Free Church of Scotland. The Free Church proved to be a particularly striking manifestation of evangelical voluntaryism, relinquishing the resources of the state church and creating a competing nationwide ecclesiastical structure, including

49 Irene Whelan, *The Bible War in Ireland*, Madison: University of Wisconsin Press, 2005, pp. 108–18, 172–6.

50 Sean Connolly, *Religion and Society in Nineteenth-Century Ireland*, Dundalk: Dundalgan, 1985, p. 3.

51 A.R. Buckland, 'Short, Thomas Vowler (1790–1872)', rev. M.C. Curthoys, *ODNB*; O.W. Jones, 'Ollivant, Alfred (1798–1882)', *ODNB*.

52 Patricia Meldrum, *Conscience and Compromise: Forgotten Evangelicals of Nineteenth-Century Scotland*, Carlisle: Paternoster, 2006.

53 Baird, *Religion in America*, pp. 506, 600; Diana Hochstedt Butler, *Standing Against the Whirlwind: Evangelical Episcopalians in Nineteenth-Century America*, New York: Oxford University Press, 2005.

54 Stewart J. Brown, *Thomas Chalmers and the Godly Commonwealth in Scotland*, Oxford: Oxford University Press, 1982, pp. 91–151.

building 700 new churches by 1847.[55] In the meantime, the eighteenth-century secessions from the Church of Scotland had prospered and in 1847 merged to form the United Presbyterian Church.[56] Thus, by the middle of the century, Scottish Presbyterianism was split into three major groups, two of which were dominated by evangelicals, while the Church of Scotland retained a significant evangelical minority. In Ulster, by contrast, evangelical Presbyterian groups came together in the nineteenth century. In the 1820s, largely because of the assertiveness of the evangelical leader, Henry Cooke, the Synod of Ulster was persuaded to exclude those of Arian beliefs from the ministry, thus paving the way to reunion with smaller evangelical groups who had seceded in the eighteenth century, and the formation of the Presbyterian Church of Ireland in 1840.[57] On the other hand, in Canada and Australia, which retained close links to Scotland, the Church of Scotland–Free Church schism was directly replicated.[58]

Events in the United States followed a parallel course, shaped by the unfolding tension between popular revivalism and the conservative Calvinism of the socially respectable, historically predominant Presbyterians in the Middle Atlantic states of New York, New Jersey and Pennsylvania. In 1801, local Presbyterian ministers, led by Barton Stone, took a prominent role in the seminal camp meeting revival at Cane Ridge, Kentucky. In 1803, however, Stone and others seceded in the face of orthodox Calvinist disapproval to form a separate movement, initially calling themselves simply 'Christians' but eventually merging to form the Disciples of Christ.[59] In the mid-1820s, Charles Grandison Finney also emerged from within the Presbyterian tradition to become one of the leading revivalists of the century, achieving his greatest success in 1830–1 at Rochester, in western New York, but also having a substantial impact along the eastern seaboard, and eventually visiting England in 1849–51. Finney's success was founded, among other things, in his ability to present an intense Methodist-style evangelistic appeal in more élite social *milieux* inaccessible to the Methodists themselves, and in his development of a systematic methodology, published in his widely circulated *Lectures on Revivals of Religion* (1835). Wherever revival broke out among evangelicals for the next century and a half, Finney's *Lectures* would be close at hand.[60] The activities of this theologically untrained and initially unordained volunteer, however, were viewed with decidedly

[55] Stewart J. Brown, *The National Churches of England, Ireland and Scotland 1801–1846*, Oxford: Oxford University Press, 2001, pp. 190, 217–27, 358–9.

[56] Andrew L. Drummond and James Bulloch, *The Church in Victorian Scotland 1843–1874*, Edinburgh: St Andrew, 1975, pp. 43–4.

[57] Finlay Holmes, *Henry Cooke*, Belfast: Christian Journals, 1981; Peter Brooke, *Ulster Presbyterianism: The Historical Perspective, 1610–1970*, Dublin: Gill and Macmillan, 1987, pp. 143–53, 178.

[58] Mark Noll, *A History of Christianity in the United States and Canada*, Grand Rapids: Eerdmans, 1992, p. 274.

[59] Wolffe, *Expansion of Evangelicalism*, pp. 55–7, 89.

[60] For example see Richard Carwardine, 'The Welsh Evangelical Community and "Finney's Revival"', *Journal of Ecclesiastical History*, 29 (1978), 463–80.

mixed feelings by the denominational authorities, and would be a major factor contributing in 1837 to a split between the 'Old School' (conservative Calvinist) and 'New School' (pro-revival) factions in the U.S. Presbyterian Church.[61] On the other hand, evangelicalism, despite its institutionally divisive consequences, played a central role in the renewed numerical growth of American Presbyterianism after a period of stagnation around the turn of the nineteenth century.

The socially and theologically conservative Calvinism represented by Presbyterians in Scotland, Ireland, Canada and the Middle Atlantic United States, was represented by Congregationalists in New England. Here the persistence of state establishments into the early nineteenth century operated as a brake on evangelical voluntaryism. Evangelicalism did have prominent advocates among the Congregationalists, such as Timothy Dwight, president of Yale from 1795 to 1817, and his leading pupil, Lyman Beecher (1777–1863), who exercised enormous influence in successive pastorates, copious publications and the fathering of a numerous and eminent family.[62] Nevertheless, the relatively limited impact of evangelicalism on American Congregationalism was apparent in its comparatively slow growth: the number of Congregational churches only increased by a factor of three between 1790 and 1860, whereas the U.S. population grew by a factor of eight. In the same period, the number of Presbyterian churches grew by a factor of 8.8, thus keeping pace with the population, while the Methodists, with a growth factor of 27.9, greatly exceeded it.[63]

English and Welsh Congregationalism, untrammelled by civil obligations, proved more uniformly responsive to evangelicalism and hence expanded much more rapidly. Whereas in 1773 there were only around 300 churches in England and Wales (compared with 625 in 1770 in the American colonies), in 1851 there were 3,244 Congregational places of worship, compared with 2,234 in the United States in 1860.[64] In England, although the revival initially had its critics, by the mid-nineteenth century even ministers who retained a High Calvinist theology, such as Joseph Irons and Andrew Reed, were responsive to the prevailing evangelical ethos.[65] Two factors were especially significant in explaining Congregational success. First, in the expanding towns of early-nineteenth-century England, evangelical Congregationalism appealed to a growing industrial and commercial middle class for whom the Church of England was too socially exclusive and Methodism too populist.[66] It was this social group that was foundational to successful urban

[61] Wolffe, *Expansion of Evangelicalism*, pp. 69–76, 84–5, 89.

[62] Noll, *America's God*, pp. 276–81; Marie Caskey, *Chariot of Fire: Religion and the Beecher Family*, New Haven: Yale University Press, 1978.

[63] Noll, *America's God*, p. 166.

[64] Watts, *Dissenters*, p. 24; Noll, *America's God*, p. 166.

[65] R. Tudur Jones, *Congregationalism in England 1662–1962*, London: Independent, 1962, pp. 160–1; Ian J. Shaw, *High Calvinists in Action*, Oxford: Oxford University Press, 2002.

[66] Leonore Davidoff and Catherine Hall, *Family Fortunes: Men and Women of the English Middle Class 1780–1850*, London: Hutchinson, 1987, p. 81.

ministries such as that of William Roby in Manchester from 1795 to 1830 and John Angell James in Birmingham from 1805 to 1858.[67] They also supported the political and journalistic activism of men such as Edward Miall, who campaigned for the removal of the privileges of the Church of England, and the two Edward Baines, father and son, who controlled the *Leeds Mercury*, a major provincial newspaper, across much of the nineteenth century.[68] Second, like the New School Presbyterians in the United States, they were ready to apply Methodist techniques, notably the use of itinerant preachers, to develop congregations in hitherto unevangelized locations, a movement given direction by the Congregational Society for Spreading the Gospel in England, founded in 1797.[69] For example, Roby's church in Manchester was a centre from which members went out to hold services in smaller Lancashire towns, eventually leading to the formation of independent churches in places such as Rochdale, Oldham and Salford.[70] Congregationalism was also the largest non-Presbyterian evangelical denomination in Scotland, its growth originally attributable to a campaign of itinerant revivalism led by the brothers James Alexander and Robert Haldane in the 1790s and 1800s. Its profile was sustained in the nineteenth century by prosperous urban ministries on the English pattern, by men such as Ralph Wardlaw in Glasgow and William Lindsay Alexander in Edinburgh.[71]

The final major historic Protestant denominational grouping, the Baptists, also proved highly responsive to evangelicalism, on both sides of the Atlantic. In England and Wales, they followed a similar pattern of steady growth to the Congregationalists, making use of itinerants in rural areas. In English towns, they appealed to a growing middle-class constituency, tending to be more numerous where the Congregationalists were weaker, and vice versa. For example, in Leicester in 1851, 23.5 per cent of total attendances were at Baptist chapels and only 7.8 per cent at Congregational ones, whereas in Oldham in the same year, 20.5 per cent of attendances were Congregational and only 6.7 per cent Baptist. In South Wales, however, both groups were strong; for example, in Merthyr Tydfil, Congregationalists made up 30.6 per cent of attendances and Baptists 36.8 per cent. In North

[67] W.G. Robinson, *William Roby, 1766–1830, and the Revival of Independency in the North*, London: Independent, 1954; R.W. Dale, ed., *The Life and Letters of John Angell James*. London: Nisbet, 1861.

[68] D.W. Bebbington, 'Miall, Edward (1809–1881)', *ODNB*; Alan G. Crosby, 'Baines, Edward (1774–1848)', *ODNB*; J.R. Lowerson, 'Baines, Sir Edward (1800–1890)', *ODNB*.

[69] Deryck W. Lovegrove, *Established Church, Sectarian People: Itinerancy and the Transformation of English Dissent, 1780–1830*, Cambridge: Cambridge University Press, 1988.

[70] Tudur Jones, *Congregationalism*, pp. 158–9.

[71] James Alexander Haldane, *Journal of a Tour Through the Northern Counties of Scotland*, Edinburgh: Ritchie, 1798; Alexander Haldane, *Memoirs of the Lives of R. Haldane of Airthrey and his Brother J.A. Haldane*, London: Hamilton Adams, 1852, pp. 151–203; William Lindsay Alexander, *Memoirs of the Life and Writings of Ralph Wardlaw*, Edinburgh: Black, 1856; James Ross, *W.L. Alexander: His Life and Work*, London: Nisbet, 1887.

Wales, by contrast, Methodism predominated.[72] In the United States, the Baptist advance was particularly impressive, with an increase in membership from 1.6 per cent of total population in 1792 to 3.7 per cent in 1848, against the background of massive overall population growth.[73] Such success was second only to that of the Methodists. The dynamics of Baptist expansion still await the close historical attention accorded to Methodists, but it seems that they had a similar appeal to dispersed settler communities, which were independent of traditional authority, and readily engaged by an intense voluntaryist religious ethos. Also like the Methodists, they appealed to slaves and other African Americans, and indeed in some parts of the South appear to have been even more successful than the Methodists among the black population. The Baptists were the main denominational competitor not only to the Methodists in the southern and western states, but also to the Congregationalists in New England, where they offered a more democratic version of evangelicalism.[74] Further north, they also enjoyed considerable success in the Maritimes, where Methodism was relatively weak.[75]

By the middle of the nineteenth century there were few Protestant groups in the English-speaking world that had not been transformed by evangelicalism. The Society of Friends (Quakers) remained a small but influential group in which a significant proportion of members identified with evangelicalism. Continental migrants to the United States, including Lutherans and adherents to German and Dutch Reformed churches, were somewhat insulated by language and culture from the mainstream of Anglo-American evangelicalism, but still began to be influenced by it. These groups, together with theologically orthodox Quakers, were included in Baird's authoritative contemporary listing of evangelical denominations.[76] High Church Anglicans and Unitarians, who had theologies that were by definition non-evangelical, were not immune from assimilating something of the ethos of evangelicalism, both through contact with their evangelical neighbours and through the spiritual migration of former evangelicals, such as the Newman brothers, John Henry and Francis William, who moved respectively to Anglo- and eventually Roman Catholicism and to Unitarianism. Even where evangelicalism was rejected it still had an impact.

THE GROWTH OF EVANGELICAL VOLUNTARY SOCIETIES

Alongside the expansion of Methodism and the evangelicalisation of the existing denominations, a third major channel for evangelical growth was the plethora of voluntary societies that began to develop in Britain from the 1780s and in

[72] Coleman, *Church of England*, Table 4, pp. 40–1.
[73] Noll, *America's God*, p. 181.
[74] Ibid, pp. 168, 180.
[75] Gauvreau, 'Protestantism Transformed', p. 65.
[76] Baird, *Religion in America*, pp. 577–600.

North America from the 1810s. Five interrelated categories will be surveyed in this section: those promoting day or Sunday School education; those concerned with the publication and distribution of Bibles and other religious literature; home mission societies; those promoting particular moral causes; and finally those committed to the support of the poor. [77] A sixth category, societies concerned with mission abroad, will be considered in the next section.

Education Societies

The evangelical commitment to education stemmed from their sense of the liberating power of literacy, the *sine qua non* of Bible reading. The Society for the Support and Encouragement of Sunday Schools, set up in London in 1785, was the earliest significant evangelical voluntary society.[78] A few Sunday Schools were already in existence prior to 1785, but the emergence of an organisation dedicated to promoting them gave a significant boost to the movement, which grew rapidly in the ensuing years. In 1803, it was followed by the more practically orientated Sunday School Union, led by Nonconformists, which eventually superseded the Sunday School Society.[79] The Sunday School Union Society of Canada followed in the early 1820s and the American Sunday School Union in 1824, although there were already numerous Sunday Schools in North America before these organisations were formed.[80] By 1833, an estimated 45 per cent of English children were attending Sunday Schools, and although participation in the United States was substantially lower, there too rapid progress was being made.[81] In colonial settings like Australia and Canada, Sunday Schools were often the first educational institution of any kind in many localities. The central purposes of Sunday Schools were spiritual and moral: to teach children to read the Bible, to understand core Christian beliefs and to acquire 'habits of piety and virtue'.[82] The acquisition of basic literacy was a necessary ancillary.

Evangelicals were initially less central to the development of day schools, which were the responsibility of parishes in Scotland and in England and Wales that of

[77] This section summarises a fuller survey in Wolffe, *Expansion of Evangelicalism*, pp. 155–82.

[78] *Plan of a Society Established in London for the Support and Encouragement of Sunday Schools*, London: Sunday-School Society, 1787.

[79] William Henry Watson, *The History of the Sunday School Union*, London: SSU, 1853; Thomas Walter Laqueur, *Religion and Respectability: Sunday Schools and Working Class Culture 1780–1850*, New Haven: Yale University Press, 1976; Philip B. Cliff, *The Rise and Development of the Sunday School Movement in England 1780–1980*; Redhill: National Christian Education Council, 1986.

[80] *The Second Report of the Sunday School Union of Canada*, Montreal: Sparhawk, 1824; Anne M. Boylan, *Sunday School: The Formation of an American Institution*, New Haven: Yale University Press, 1988.

[81] Laqueur, *Religion and Respectability*, p. 44; Boylan, *Sunday School*, pp. 9–11.

[82] Jabez Bunting, *A Great Work Described and Recommended*, London: Richard Edwards, 1805, p. 9.

the High Church National Society for Promoting the Education of the Poor in the Principles of the Established Church, founded in 1811, as well as the Nonconformist and Liberal British and Foreign Schools Society (1814). In North America, common schools were set up by the civil authorities. In all these contexts, however, evangelicals actively sought to influence the curricula and ethos of schools, leading sometimes – for example, in both Liverpool and New York City in the 1830s – to heated local political conflict with Roman Catholics or other interest groups.[83] Meanwhile, in Ireland, evangelical provision of education through organisations such as the London Hibernian Society (1806) and the Irish Society (1818) reflected aspirations to secure the wholesale conversion of the Roman Catholic population.[84]

Bible and Tract Societies

The publication of religious tracts began as a matter of personal initiative, notably with Hannah More's *Cheap Repository Tracts* (1795–8), which were widely circulated on both sides of the Atlantic. In 1799, the Religious Tract Society was formed in London, with the purpose of distributing tracts, broadsheets and handbills to edify the 'thoughtless multitudes'. It had reportedly circulated 500 million such publications by 1849.[85] It was followed by tract societies in New York in 1812 and New England in 1814, which merged to form the American Tract Society in 1824.[86]

The British and Foreign Bible Society, one of the greatest and most enduring of evangelical voluntary societies, was founded in 1804. Its initial focus was on the provision of cheap Bibles (including Welsh and Gaelic translations) for circulation to the poor, distributing them 'without note or comment' so that its supporters were free to disagree about matters of interpretation. Later, however, translations into continental European and other foreign languages made up an increasing proportion of the Society's sales, around a third by 1850.[87] The American Bible Society followed in 1816, with a parallel concern to make the Scriptures available to settlers on the frontier who lacked other religious provision.[88] Globally, Bible societies acted to bring together denominationally divided evangelicals and because of their relative lack of doctrinal content could even attract support from colonial elites.

[83] Wolffe, *Expansion of Evangelicalism*, pp. 166–8.

[84] Whelan, *Bible War in Ireland*, pp. 92–107, 115–6.

[85] *A Brief View of the Plan and Operations of the Religious Tract Society*, London: RTS, 1828, pp. 5–9; Ian Bradley, *The Call to Seriousness: The Evangelical Impact on the Victorians*, London: Jonathan Cape, 1976, p. 42.

[86] Clifford S. Griffin, *Their Brothers' Keepers: Moral Stewardship in the United States, 1800–1865*, New Brunswick: Rutgers University Press, 1960, pp. 32–5.

[87] Leslie Howsam, *Cheap Bibles: Nineteenth Century Publishing and the British and Foreign Bible Society*, Cambridge: Cambridge University Press, 1991, p. 210.

[88] Charles I. Foster, *An Errand of Mercy: The Evangelical United Front 1790–1837*, Chapel Hill: University of North Carolina Press, 1960, pp. 104–16; Griffin, *Their Brothers' Keepers*, pp. 27–9, 46, 81–3.

Home Mission Societies

Initial home mission activities in the late eighteenth and early nineteenth centuries were directed towards the perceived geographical margins, the Scottish Highlands and Islands, Ireland, and settlers and Native Americans on the western frontier. More accessible populations were felt to be adequately served by the churches themselves, supplemented by the work of the tract and Sunday School societies.[89]

From the 1820s, however, there was a growing recognition that the burgeoning cities of the North Atlantic world presented distinctive evangelistic challenges. Thus in 1829, the New York City Tract Society moved from merely distributing literature to undertaking systematic visitation of poor families.[90] Meanwhile, David Nasmith, a Scot, had founded city missions in Glasgow in 1826 and Dublin in 1828, before visiting North America where he helped the Tract Society set up the New York City Mission in 1830. Nasmith then returned to Europe, where in 1835 he was responsible for the formation of the London City Mission, his most substantial and lasting achievement, bringing together Anglicans and Nonconformists and by 1850 employing 242 agents on house-to-house visitation. The exclusively Anglican Scripture Readers Association was founded in 1844, and by 1850 was employing a further 98 agents.[91] Also by 1844, fifty-three other British towns and cities had established similar urban missions.[92] A parallel Anglican evangelical initiative was the formation in 1836 of the Church Pastoral Aid Society which financed additional curates and lay workers in large, understaffed parishes.

Moral Reform

Wilberforce's creation of the Proclamation Society in 1787 initiated organised efforts to redress the moral deficiencies evangelicals saw around them. It was later superseded by the Society for the Suppression of Vice, founded in 1802, which sought to combat gambling, obscenity, prostitution, blasphemy and atheism. Sunday observance emerged as a particular concern, leading in 1809 to the formation of the Society for Promoting the Observance of the Christian Sabbath and in 1831 to the Lord's Day Observance Society, which campaigned for legislative restrictions on Sunday activities.[93] While the desire for such limitations might seem oppressive to non-evangelicals, they reflected wider concerns for the humanisation of industrial society through regulation of hours of work.

89 Wolffe, *Expansion of Evangelicalism*, pp. 161–4.

90 Carroll Smith-Rosenberg, *Religion and the Rise of the American City: The New York City Mission Movement 1812–1870*, Ithaca: Cornell University Press, 1971, pp. 70–96.

91 John Campbell, *Memoirs of David Nasmith*, London: John Snow, 1844, pp. 209–10, 260; Donald M. Lewis, *Lighten Their Darkness: The Evangelical Mission to Working-Class London, 1828–1860*, Westport, CT: Greenwood Press, 1986, p. 278.

92 Campbell, *Nasmith*, pp. 465–7.

93 Wolffe, *Expansion of Evangelicalism*, pp. 169–70.

In the United States, activities of this kind were slow to gather momentum, as they were apt to be perceived as unconstitutional interference with individual liberties. However, there were more localised efforts to reform manners and, in particular, to reclaim prostitutes and 'name and shame' their clients.[94] Americans, however, tended to lead the way in opposing the abuse of alcoholic beverages, with the formation of the American Society for the Promotion of Temperance in 1826, predating that of the British and Foreign Temperance Society in 1831. Early temperance campaigners merely opposed excessive drinking, especially of spirits, and continued to countenance moderate use of beer and wine. However, from the mid-1830s onwards, there was a growing teetotal movement which advocated complete abstinence from alcoholic beverages of all kinds. Teetotalism rapidly became a strong force in America, but – having roots which were not specifically Christian – had a more limited appeal among British evangelicals.[95]

Relieving Poverty

Much evangelical support for the poor was undoubtedly given in individual, unorganised and hence unrecorded ways, and by churches rather than societies. In 1796, however, the formation in London of the Society for Bettering the Condition and Increasing the Comforts of the Poor was indicative of endeavours to take a more strategic view. Nevertheless the Bettering Society (as it was known) itself operated by disseminating good practice rather than by directly organising relief activities. Indeed from the 1820s onwards, the influential ideas of Thomas Chalmers, who argued on the basis of his own pastoral experience in Glasgow that the solution for poverty lay not in the generosity of external benefactors, but in the mutual support of local communities, discouraged organised philanthropy of this kind. Where societies developed for this purpose, they normally focused their activities either on particular localities or specific groups facing particular hardship, such as widows and children.[96] Meanwhile in Britain, the evangelical Lord Ashley, who succeeded as Earl of Shaftesbury in 1852, took a leading role in promoting legislative measures to improve living and working conditions, notably by restricting child labour and promoting public health improvements.[97]

The aforementioned five categories of activity are useful for analytical purposes but need to be applied with caution lest they appear to separate things that were very much interconnected in the evangelical mind. Thus Sunday Schools and tract distribution were supported as instruments in the task of home mission; the moral improvement of the poor was perceived as an important means of equipping them

[94] Mary P. Ryan, *Cradle of the Middle Class: The Family in Oneida County, New York 1790–1865*, Cambridge: Cambridge University Press, 1981, pp. 116–23.

[95] Wolffe, *Expansion of Evangelicalism*, pp. 171–3.

[96] Ibid., pp. 173–6.

[97] Finlayson, *The Seventh Earl of Shaftesbury*.

to overcome their material deprivation. These mindsets and the societies they fostered, moreover, reflected the attitudes and circumstances of wealthy evangelicals, of the predominantly Anglican, Congregational and Presbyterian landed, professional and commercial classes rather than the lower-class Methodists of the Yorkshire mill towns or the American South. In major urban centres, above all London and New York, the annual spring meetings of the principal evangelical voluntary societies were to become the high point in the social calendar of the godly élite.[98] Such events were far removed from the world of less socially privileged evangelicals, for whom the local chapel community rather than the national or regional voluntary society was the natural focus for charitable and evangelistic activity. Nevertheless, the sheer diversity of evangelical structures and organisation ensured their widespread and pervasive presence, and their overlapping directorships assisted the maintenance of evangelical communal identities.

DEVELOPING A GLOBAL MISSION

The ultimate expression of evangelical volunteering was the readiness of a few to become missionaries to distant countries and unfamiliar cultures, placing themselves many months journey from home and family and exposing themselves to an increased risk of premature death from hardship and disease. Something of the spirit in which such missionaries embarked on their work is implicit in the tone of the letter in which Samuel Marsden, a *protégé* of the Elland Society who was soon to take ship for New South Wales, proposed to his future wife Elizabeth in March 1793.[99] Marsden made it clear that his commitment to overseas mission was non-negotiable: only if Elizabeth was prepared also to commit herself to that cause was he prepared to commit himself to her. Evidently, however, she was not deterred by Samuel's sense of priorities, and within four months of receiving his letter she was already married, pregnant and at sea on the way to Australia. The young couple was still at sea in uncomfortable conditions eight months later when the child was born, with Samuel himself serving as the only midwife.[100] In a similar spirit, four decades later, an older man, Daniel Wilson, left a comfortable post as Vicar of Islington in north London to become Bishop of Calcutta, inspired 'by a great desire to dedicate myself to this Missionary Bishopric, if the Lord would accept me.'[101] His sea voyage was less fraught than that of the Marsdens, but was also undertaken with a sense of absolute dedication to the cause and acceptance of permanent departure from all friends, family and interests left behind in Britain.[102]

[98] Cowie, 'Exeter Hall'; Wolffe, *Expansion of Evangelicalism*, p. 176.

[99] J.R. Elder, *The Letters and Journals of Samuel Marsden*, Dunedin: Coulls Somerville Wilkie, 1932, p. 22.

[100] Ibid., pp. 23–5.

[101] Josiah Bateman, *The Life of the Right Rev Daniel Wilson, DD*, 2 vols, London: Murray, 1860, i.280.

[102] Ibid., i.295–312.

Such self-sacrifice did not always achieve rapid results, but it sowed the seeds of the eventual transformation of evangelicalism from a North Atlantic and European movement to a global faith.

During the eighteenth century, missions were led on the one hand by the Methodists and Moravians, on the other hand by the predominantly High Church Anglican Society for the Propagation of the Gospel (formed in 1701). The primary focus had been the slaves in the West Indies, alongside white settlers in America.[103] The 1790s and early 1800s saw the formation of Baptist, evangelical Anglican, Congregational and Presbyterian societies, which gave new direction and breadth to the movement and helped to open up wider geographical horizons, particularly in India, southern and western Africa, Australia, New Zealand and the islands of the Pacific.

India, central to British imperial aspirations and the home of mature non-Christian cultures, was a particularly compelling challenge for evangelical missionaries. The distinguished historian of mission, Bishop Stephen Neill, would sum up the significance of William Carey's arrival in Calcutta on 11 November 1793 as follows: 'The day of the English-speaking peoples in overseas mission had begun.'[104] His words were well chosen. Christianity in India already had a very long history. The Syriac Churches of the south originated in the early centuries after Christ, and Catholic missionaries had been active in India since Francis Xavier's arrival in Goa in 1542. In the nineteenth century, Catholics in the sub-continent, albeit concentrated in the Portuguese and French enclaves of Goa and Pondicherry, still substantially outnumbered Protestants.[105] The first Protestant mission was established in 1706 at Tranquebar on the coast of Tamil Nadu by the Danish Lutheran Pietists Bartholomaus Ziegenbalg and Heinrich Plutschau. Between 1778 and 1798, another Lutheran, the German Christian Friedrich Schwartz, had a remarkable ministry at nearby Tanjore (modern Thanjavur). By adopting effective enculturation approaches, he exercised a strong influence on the local ruler and by the time of his death in 1798 there were an estimated 6,000 Christians in the region under the oversight of his disciples. Moreover, between 1795 and 1805, a grassroots movement around Tirunelveli, close to India's southern tip, brought about more than 5,000 conversions.[106]

Nevertheless, Neill was right to highlight Carey's arrival as a new departure. English-speaking missionaries extended Protestant endeavour to the north of India which, lacking the indigenous Christian traditions of the far south, was less prepossessing territory. Nevertheless, in the face of the hostility of the British East India

[103] Andrew Porter, *Religion versus Empire? British Protestant Missionaries and Overseas Expansion, 1700–1914*, Manchester University Press, 2004, pp. 15–38.

[104] Stephen Neill, *A History of Christian Missions*, 2nd edn, Harmondsworth: Penguin, 1986, p. 223.

[105] Robert Eric Frykenberg, *Christianity in India from the Beginnings to the Present*, Oxford: Oxford University Press, 2008.

[106] Neill, *Christian Missions*, pp. 194–200; Frykenberg, *Christianity in India*, pp. 152–68.

Company authorities, who feared missions would have a destabilising effect, the decision of Carey and his colleagues to base themselves not in Calcutta but in the small Danish colony of Serampore was indicative of the continuing importance of continental European networks in sustaining the missionary enterprise.[107] Indeed, in their early years, the British missionary societies relied heavily on recruits from the continent, such as William Ringeltaube, who worked in Travancore (modern Kerala) under the auspices of the London Missionary Society between 1803 and 1815, and Charles Rhenius, sent by the Church Missionary Society to work among the Tamils of the south-east in 1814. The Basel Missionary Society was especially important in supplying men for the CMS and was to begin its own mission at Mangalore on the west coast in 1834. Americans also established missions in the 1830s, the Presbyterians in the Punjab and the Congregationalists at the other end of India at Madurai in southern Tamil Nadu.[108]

In the meantime, Carey and his associates at Serampore, Joshua and Hannah Marshman and William Ward, developed a long term strategy for the diffusion of Christianity in India. It was observed of Carey that he never converted an Indian by his own preaching,[109] and in general the mission's achievements in terms of immediate conversions were limited. However, they invested enormous effort into translating the Bible into a variety of Indian languages. They also developed extensive educational provision, culminating in the foundation in 1819 of the Serampore College 'for instruction in Eastern Literature and European Science'.[110] By offering schooling to Indian youth in a manner that respected their cultural inheritance and did not force them to accept Christianity, they made a significant indirect contribution to the intellectual renewal known as the 'Bengal Renaissance'. Hindus and Muslims were not easily converted, but they often did acquire a sympathetic understanding of Christian belief. Education was similarly central to the strategy of the pioneer Church of Scotland missionary, Alexander Duff, who arrived in Calcutta in 1830 and set up a successful school. Duff's work also led to few conversions, although some of these were controversial at the time. Like Carey's group, however, his work was important in giving Christianity an enduring presence among the Bengal social élite and thus laying the foundation for an indigenous church.[111]

In 1813 the charter of the East India Company came up for renewal, and William Wilberforce and his evangelical friends took the opportunity to campaign for greater acceptance of missionary activity. Their efforts in parliament, supported by extensive petitioning, were successful insofar as the new charter required the

[107] Neill, *Christian Missions*, pp. 223–6.

[108] Ibid, pp. 231–5; Richard C. Blake, 'Rhenius, Charles Theophilus Ewald', *DEB*, ii.926–8.

[109] E. Daniel Potts, 'Carey, William', *DEB*, i. 198, citing funeral sermon by John Mack.

[110] Neill, *Christian Missions*, pp. 224–5; G. Smith, *The Life of Alexander Duff*, London: Hodder and Stoughton, 1879, i.171–6.

[111] Ibid, pp. 233–4.

company to assist those going to India to advance 'religious and moral improvement'.[112] In the following year, an Anglican bishopric of Calcutta was set up. The first incumbent was a High Churchman, and his immediate successors were short-lived. Following his appointment in 1832, however, Daniel Wilson survived for a quarter of a century. Wilson's efforts to establish episcopal authority led to difficult relations with missionaries on the ground and even his sympathetic biographer acknowledged that he was 'a man much spoken against'.[113] Nevertheless, his energetic ministry asserted the place of evangelical Christianity as a significant part of the ethos of British rule in India.

In 1851, the earliest date for which a plausible figure is available, there were reportedly 91,092 Protestants in the whole of India. However, more than half of these were concentrated in the far south, the only region in which evangelicalism had at this point achieved even an echo of the kind of popular appeal to the socially marginalized that had enabled the advance of Methodism in Britain and America.[114] Elsewhere, progress was slow. The frustrations were to be exposed in 1857 when the Indian Mutiny/First War of Independence broke out and was seen by critics of evangelicalism as confirmation of their fears that missionary zeal would antagonise predominantly Hindu and Muslim populations. In his history of the Serampore mission, published in 1859, John Clark Marshman, son of Joshua and Hannah, acknowledged that recent events appeared 'to countenance the doctrine that any attempt to interfere with the religious prejudices of the natives must be attended with imminent peril', but asserted that there was 'most conclusive evidence' that the mutiny was not caused by the missionaries.[115] Evangelicals themselves were indeed prone to see the rising as divine judgement on account of national maintenance of Hindu idolatry and failure to do more to evangelise India.[116] It would have been premature at this stage to judge evangelicalism to have failed in India, but its role remained contested and controversial.

In Australia, which was in its early years an imperial and ecclesial extension of India, evangelicals received little encouragement from the governing authorities, but otherwise the environment was a very different one. Richard Johnson, the chaplain who arrived with the First Fleet in January 1788, had only been appointed as something of an afterthought, as a result of Wilberforce's lobbying, and he faced an uphill task in ministering to a white community that initially largely consisted

[112] Brian Stanley, *The Bible and the Flag: Protestant Missions and British Imperialism in the Nineteenth and Twentieth Centuries*, Leicester: Apollos, 1990, p. 99.

[113] Neill, *Christian Missions*, pp. 227–8; Bateman, *Wilson*, ii.244.

[114] Neill, *Christian Missions*, p. 237.

[115] John Clark Marshman, *The Life and Times of Carey, Marshman and Ward*, London: Longman, 1859, i.v–vi.

[116] Brian Stanley, 'Christian Responses to the Indian Mutiny of 1857', in W.J. Sheils, ed., *Studies in Church History 20: The Church and War*, Oxford: Blackwell, 1983, p. 280.

of convicts and soldiers.[117] His successor, Samuel Marsden, was more persistent, but his confrontational style and success in establishing himself as a prosperous farmer did not lend themselves to effective evangelism.[118] Nonconformists from the London Missionary Society (LMS) first arrived in 1798 after retreating from Tahiti and had greater popular appeal among the free settlers, but all groups found the convicts usually to be spiritual stony ground.[119] The first Methodist missionary, Samuel Leigh, arrived in 1815, to be joined three years later by Walter Lawry. Although these two men were exemplars of the kind of dedicated itinerant ministry that was proving so successful in England and North America at the same period, the convict/command culture of early colonial New South Wales proved unreceptive, and in 1831, there were still only 112 Methodist members. Nor was there significant progress among the indigenous population. There were some transient attempts to 'civilise' and Christianise Aborigines: in 1789, Richard Johnson and his wife took an apparently orphaned girl into their home and gave her English and Christian instruction; in 1814, former LMS missionaries William and Elizabeth Shelley set up the Parramatta Native Institution which sought to educate orphaned children and prepare them for Christian marriage. It survived until 1823 before being relocated further west.[120] In general, however, the oppressive and degrading behaviour of many of the white population was hardly a convincing recommendation for their nominal Christianity. By the time when, in 1826, the LMS missionary Lancelot Threlkeld began the first serious missionary effort among the Aborigines around Lake Macquarie, they were already alienated and in catastrophic numerical decline. Following a similar strategy to the Serampore trio in India, Thelkeld spent years translating the Bible into the local language, only to find that there was now scarcely anyone left to read it.[121]

Although evangelicals thus found progress to be slow in New South Wales itself, they still looked to it as a springboard for further missionary advance into the Pacific. The cultural obstacles to mission there were initially too great, but in the longer term during the early nineteenth century, Polynesia saw mass conversions and the development of strong indigenous evangelical traditions.[122] Meanwhile, Samuel Marsden was not content with a settled family and pastoral life at Parramatta, west of Sydney, and between 1807 and 1809 travelled back to England in order to persuade the CMS to launch a mission to New Zealand. He believed that the

[117] Neil K. Macintosh, *Richard Johnson: His Life and Times 1755–1827*, Sydney: Library of Australian History, 1978, pp. 24–30, 49–59.

[118] A.T. Yarwood, *Samuel Marsden*, Carlton: Melbourne University Press, 1977.

[119] Allan M. Grocott, *Convicts, Clergymen and Churches*, Sydney: Sydney University Press, 1980.

[120] Amanda Barry et al., eds, *Evangelists of Empire? Missionaries in Colonial History*, Melbourne: University of Melbourne, 2008, pp. 87–102, 115–24.

[121] Piggin, *Evangelical Christianity in Australia*, pp. 22–3.

[122] Neill, *Christian Missions*, p. 251; Ian Breward, *A History of the Churches in Australasia*, Oxford: Oxford University Press, 2001, pp. 24–41.

Maori were 'a savage race . . . wholly under the power of the influence of the Prince of Darkness' who needed to be freed 'by the Gospel of a crucified Saviour'.[123] Once the mission was under way, he himself visited New Zealand seven times between 1814 and his death in 1838 and commenced a 'Maori seminary' in Parramatta.[124] In the medium term, evangelicals enjoyed significantly greater success with the Maori than with the Australian Aborigines: although they assimilated Christianity on their own terms, it is estimated that by 1845, about half of the population of New Zealand were regularly attending worship.[125]

It would be easy to multiply accounts of evangelical missionary volunteers such as Carey and Marsden, who permanently left homes in Britain, continental Europe and North America and committed their lives to long-term work in remote and initially inhospitable contexts. A further notable example on a different continent is that of Robert Moffat, a Scot who arrived in South Africa in 1817 and in 1824 established a mission village at Kuruman in the north of Cape Colony, not far from the border with what is now Botswana, remaining there until he retired in 1870.[126] Kuruman became an important base for mission further into the interior of southern Africa, most famously, David Livingstone's journeys in the 1840s and 1850s. However, the implicit 'centrifugal' model of mission as a movement outward from North Atlantic centres risks distorting a more complex reality in which, even in relatively early days, the impulse to proclaim the gospel carried men and women in numerous different geographical directions.

Furthermore, the direction of missionary flows within the North Atlantic world itself began to change in the early nineteenth century. As we saw in the previous chapter, evangelicalism had significant roots in the Pietist and Moravian churches of central Europe, driven westward to Britain and eventually North America both by the push of persecution and the pull of missionary calling. However, in late 1799, a young American, Lorenzo Dow, travelled *east* to Ireland, where he worked as an itinerant revivalist until early 1801. He returned to Britain and Ireland from 1805 to 1807 and again in 1818 and 1819,[127] the first of a succession of American evangelists to visit the United Kingdom during the course of the nineteenth century.

Anglo-American missionary interest also extended to continental Europe. In 1816, Robert Haldane, who had already played a key role in promoting evangelical expansion in Scotland, travelled first to Geneva and then to Montauban in south-west France, where he encouraged the further development of ongoing revival movements among local Protestant communities. In 1819, Haldane and Henry Drummond, another British visitor to Geneva, founded the Continental Society

[123] Elder, *Samuel Marsden*, p. 60.

[124] Stuart Piggin, *Evangelical Christianity in Australia: Spirit, World and World*, Melbourne: Oxford University Press, 1996, p. 15.

[125] Breward, *Churches in Australasia*, p. 46.

[126] Andrew C. Ross, 'Moffat, Robert', *DEB*, ii.779; Adrian Hastings, *The Church in Africa 1450–1950*, Oxford: Oxford University Press, 1994, pp. 207–9.

[127] Wolffe, *Expansion of Evangelicalism*, pp. 15–16.

to further the cause of evangelism and Protestant renewal in Europe.[128] American missionary interest in Europe developed slightly later, particularly under the pioneering influence of Robert Baird, who became the agent of the Foreign Evangelical Society when it was formed in the United States in 1839.[129] From 1846, the Evangelical Alliance was also centrally interested in Europe, promoting mission and advocating freedom of religion for scattered Protestant communities.[130]

Meanwhile, the networks associated with slavery, the slave trade and the campaigns for its abolition were an important further channel for evangelical expansion. For evangelical abolitionists, a fundamental argument against slavery was a missionary one. As Wilberforce put it in 1823, 'the almost universal destitution of religious and moral instruction among the slaves is the most serious of all the vices of the West Indian system.'[131] From the outset, Africans themselves played active roles in the process. A leading early opponent of the slave trade was Olaudah Equiano. Born in Benin in 1745 and kidnapped into slavery as a boy, he purchased his freedom in 1766 and experienced an evangelical conversion in 1774. His autobiography, published in 1789, was widely read and was a significant factor in turning British public opinion against slavery.[132] In the late 1780s, British abolitionists founded the colony of Sierra Leone in West Africa as a haven for freed slaves, especially those forced out of the American colonies because of their loyalty to Britain. It was also, in evangelical eyes, a potential bridgehead for the evangelisation of the continent. In the United States, evangelical abolitionists developed a parallel initiative, pursued by the American Colonization Society, founded in 1816, and leading to the foundation of Liberia in 1822.[133] Missionary connections also played an important role in turning public opinion in Britain towards the eventual freeing of the West Indian slaves, which parliament enacted in 1833. After the leading Baptist missionary William Knibb was forced to leave Jamaica by pro-slavery forces in 1831, on his return to Britain he gave evidence against slavery to parliamentary Select Committees and also spoke at numerous public meetings, proclaiming 'that God who has made of one blood all nations – the same God who views all nations as one flesh.'[134]

[128] Kenneth J. Stewart, 'Haldane, Robert', *DEB*, i.501; Timothy C.F. Stunt, *From Awakening to Secession: Radical Evangelicals in Switzerland and Britain 1815–1835*, Edinburgh: T&T Clark, 2000.

[129] Henry Martyn Baird, *The Life of the Rev. Robert Baird*, New York: Randolph, 1866, pp. 169–70.

[130] John Wolffe, 'British Protestants and Europe,1820–1860', in Richard Bonney and D.J.B. Trim, eds, *The Development of Pluralism in Britain and France*, Bern: Lang, 2007, pp. 217–23.

[131] William Wilberforce, *An Appeal to the Religion, Justice, and Humanity of the Inhabitants of the British Empire, in Behalf of the Negro Slaves in the West Indies*, London: Hatchard, 1823, p. 19.

[132] Olaudah Equiano, *Sold as a Slave*, London: Penguin, 2007.

[133] Lamin Sanneh, *Abolitionists Abroad: American Blacks and the Making of Modern West Africa*, Cambridge, MA: Harvard University Press, 1999.

[134] Quoted Catherine Hall, *Civilising Subjects: Metropole and Colony in the English Imagination, 1830–1867*, Oxford: Polity, 2002, p. 114.

Individual stories further illustrate the significance of such transatlantic networks. David George (1743–1810), a former slave converted by itinerating black preachers in Virginia in the early 1770s, subsequently had a remarkable career as a Baptist minister, moving first to Nova Scotia after the American Revolution, and then in 1792 to Sierra Leone, pastoring this pioneer colony of ex-slaves on the west coast of Africa.[135] The population of freed slaves grew substantially after the ending of the British slave trade in 1807, because it became the obvious place to land those released by the Royal Navy from ships that were illegally continuing to carry human cargo. Among such involuntary migrants was Samuel Ajayi Crowther, born in Nigeria around 1806 and resettled in Sierra Leone in 1822. In 1826, he went to London to complete his education at the CMS's training college in Islington and subsequently returned to Sierra Leone as a missionary. Crowther eventually, in 1864, became the first black African Anglican bishop, with responsibility for large parts of West Africa, including particularly the Niger delta, and a key figure in 'laying the foundation of Christianity as an African religion'.[136] A more obscure life story that further points up the diverse connections of missionary evangelicalism was that of Mary Hickson, an African woman from Sierra Leone. Sometime in the 1820s, she married a German CMS missionary, George Metzger, and emigrated with him first to Britain and then to the United States, ending her days in 1847 in Liverpool, Ohio, where her husband was at the time serving as minister of a German congregation.[137] Despite the slow pace of communication in an age when travel was still limited to the pace of the fastest horse or ship, evangelicalism was already becoming a global movement.

EVALUATING THE IMPACT OF EVANGELICALISM

The rapid expansion of evangelicalism in an era also characterised by major, and in some cases revolutionary, political and social change has naturally led historians to explore questions of cause and effect, and some have made strong claims for the socially and culturally transformative impact of the movement. Early in the twentieth century, the leading French historian Elie Halévy contrasted the relative stability of Britain in the later eighteenth and early nineteenth centuries with the turmoil of revolutionary France, and argued that the influence of evangelicalism in general and Methodism in particular played a crucial role in maintaining an orderly society. Later scholars have been reluctant to give unqualified endorsement to what has become known as the 'Halévy thesis', but it has nevertheless been

[135] Noll, *Rise of Evangelicalism*, pp. 161–6; Kidd, *Great Awakening*, pp. 213–33; Grant Gordon, *From Slavery to Freedom: The Life of David George, Pioneer Black Baptist Minister*, Hantsport, Nova Scotia: Lancelot Press, 1992.

[136] Sanneh, *Abolitionists Abroad*, pp. 126–8, 158 and passim; John Flint, 'Crowther, Samuel Ajayi (*c.* 1807–1891)', *ODNB*.

[137] Wolffe, *Expansion of Evangelicalism*, pp. 16–17.

very influential. Much attention has been given to refining and qualifying the original argument.[138] One particularly provocative development of Halévy's ideas was made by the British Marxist historian Edward Thompson in *The Making of the English Working Class*, first published in 1963. In Thompson's view, Methodism was crucially instrumental in the readiness of early industrial workers to accept the harsh discipline of the factory system and hence their own subordination. It offered them 'the chiliasm of despair', inducing them to accept hardship and oppression in this world in virtue of their confidence that there was a better world to come.[139] Hence not only did evangelicalism enable Britain to avert political revolution, but it facilitated its success in achieving 'industrial revolution'.

More recently, historians of North America have also become interested in the relationship between evangelicalism, revolution and democratisation after 1776. While recent scholarship has tended to play down the view that evangelicalism was a significant factor contributing to the American Revolution,[140] there is strong support for the converse argument, that the Revolution itself opened doors for evangelicalism to take a major role in shaping politics and society in the early republic. The idea that American democracy had strong roots in popular Christianity is by no means new, having been articulated by Alexis de Tocqueville as early as the 1830s.[141] The thesis has, however, been convincingly developed by Nathan Hatch through his examination of popular religious movements, including the Methodists, Baptists and Afro-Americans, leading him to the conclusion that 'America's non-restrictive environment permitted an unexpected and often explosive conjunction of evangelical fervor and popular sovereignty.'[142] It was a democratisation tinged with the radical authoritarianism of leaders who sought to realize their own vision of the kingdom of God,[143] but in the absence of equally dynamic alternatives, it played a central part in shaping American national identity and political culture in the northern and middle states. Elsewhere, in the southern United States and in Canada, as in Britain, the political impact of evangelicalism was more conservative, but amidst the revolutionary ferment following 1789 in France as well as 1776 in America, its widespread transformative effect was unmistakeable.[144]

[138] G.W. Olsen, ed., *Religion and Revolution in Early Industrial England: The Halévy Thesis and its Critics*, Lanham: University Press of America, 1990.

[139] E.P. Thompson, *The Making of the English Working Class*, Harmondsworth: Penguin, 1968, pp. 411–40.

[140] Noll, *America's God*, p. 78.

[141] Alexis de Tocqueville (trans. and ed. Harvey C. Mansfield and Delba Winthrop), *Democracy in America*, Chicago: University of Chicago Press, 2000, p. 275.

[142] Hatch, *Democratization of American Christianity*, p. 9.

[143] Jon Butler *Awash in a Sea of Faith: Christianizing the American People*, Cambridge, MA: Harvard University Press, pp. 286–8.

[144] Mark Noll, 'Revolution and the Rise of Evangelical Social Influence in North Atlantic Societies', in Noll, Bebbington and Rawlyk, eds, *Evangelicalism*, pp. 113–36.

A further line of argument, which developed particularly during the 1950s and 1960s, was to highlight the social and political changes achieved as a result of the work of evangelical voluntary societies and, in Britain, the efforts in parliament of men such as William Wilberforce and the Clapham Sect.[145] Thus evangelicalism was seen as bringing about substantial advances in fields such as education and the practical support of the poor, and with creating many of the institutions that make up what we now think of as civil society. At the same time, there were significant specific political achievements, such as the abolition of the slave trade in British dominions and ships in 1807, the result of nearly two decades of hard work by Wilberforce and others. Evangelicals were also credited with a major role in the later abolition of slavery itself in British colonies in 1833 and, through Lord Shaftesbury, in mid-century social reforms at home.

Alongside these specific organisational and legislative achievements, there is also the view that evangelicalism brought about major cultural change, leading to the ascendancy of the value systems characterised as 'Victorian' – a view articulated in G.M. Young's *Victorian England: Portrait of an Age* in 1936. According to Young, 'The Evangelicals gave to the island a creed which was at once the basis of its morality and the justification of its wealth and power, and, with the creed, that sense of being an Elect People which, set to a more blatant tune, became a principal element in Late Victorian Imperialism.'[146] Important developments of this line of argument include Boyd Hilton's *The Age of Atonement* (1988), which explores how the characteristically evangelical doctrine of substitutionary atonement came, in his view, to dominate social and economic thought in the first half of the nineteenth century. A different perspective is presented by Leonore Davidoff and Catherine Hall in *Family Fortunes* (1988), in which they argue that during this same period, evangelicalism shaped the value systems of the English middle class, especially their sense of masculinity, femininity and domesticity. Similar arguments have been made in relation to the United States by Mary Ryan and Nancy Cott, who argue that evangelical religion 'endowed women with a vital identity and purpose'.[147]

Finally, and most controversially, the overseas missionary movement, in which evangelicals played a central part, has been seen as spearheading the march of European imperialism, with zeal of missionaries for the spread of the gospel both placing them in the forefront of contact with indigenous peoples and providing an ideological rationale for their subjugation. Thus, on the lines of Gibbon's enlightenment criticism of Christianity in the Roman Empire, evangelicalism in the British Empire has been written about as a highly influential, but malign, force.

[145] Brown, *Fathers of the Victorians*; Timothy L. Smith, *Revivalism and Social Reform in Mid-Nineteenth Century America*, New York: Abingdon Press, 1957; Griffin, *Their Brothers' Keepers*; Bradley, *Call to Seriousness*.

[146] G.M. Young, *Victorian England*, London: Oxford University Press, 1936, p. 4.

[147] Ryan, *Cradle of the Middle Class*; Nancy F. Cott, *The Bonds of Womanhood: 'Women's Sphere' in New England 1780–1835*, New Haven: Yale University Press, 1977.

Such views were especially widespread in both religious and academic circles at the time of the anti-colonial reaction of the 1960s.[148] More recent years, however, have seen the development of a more nuanced understanding of the relationship between evangelicalism, missionaries and empire. Detailed analysis of particular cases shows a complex and chequered record, in which missionaries certainly sometimes advanced the cause of empire, but in other contexts could be vigorous critics of insensitive political and economic expansion.[149] Likewise, empires, whether British, French or German, could both advance and undermine the influence of evangelicalism. Although missionaries were no passive agents of imperial policy, they nevertheless played a crucial role in sustaining strong ties between colony and metropole.[150] Conversely, 'God's empire' of colonial churches 'was a house of many spiritual mansions, and was characterised by the variety and vigour of its competing religious forces.'[151] Herein are to be found the roots of the later development of indigenised forms of evangelicalism that asserted spiritual and political independence from European influences.

A detailed evaluation of such arguments is beyond the scope of this book, insofar as it would require a balanced consideration of other factors such as the parallel religious influence of Catholic revival, the cultural impact of Romanticism, the socio-economic pressures of an expanding industrialising and urbanising society, and the growth of secular political ideals of liberalism and democracy and the conservative reaction against them. It is nevertheless important that the history of a movement such as evangelicalism avoids the tunnel vision that gives an exaggerated impression of its importance. In terms of its wider influence, evangelicalism must be seen as merely one strand in a complex matrix of influences. It would be highly misleading to characterise, say, the eventual success of the British anti-slavery campaign or the growth of democracy in the United States as solely, or even primarily, the achievement of evangelicals. In reality, evangelicals existed in mixed societies where their own vision of the kingdom was inevitably distorted and compromised by other influences, but their intense commitment, activism and zealous voluntarism made them a major force in shaping the nineteenth-century world.

[148] Brian Stanley, *Bible and the Flag*, pp. 11–31.
[149] Ibid.; Porter, *Religion versus Empire?*, passim.
[150] Hall, *Civilising Subjects*, passim.
[151] Hilary M. Carey, *God's Empire: Religion and Colonialism in the British World, c. 1901–1908*, Cambridge: Cambridge University Press, 2011, p. 379.

4

The Kingdom Enlarged and Contested: 1840s to 1870s

In 1824, Thomas Chalmers, recently appointed to the Chair of Moral Philosophy at St Andrew's University, was aghast to discover a misprint in an article in the *Edinburgh Review*. It arose in the midst of his calculations for pauperism in England, his experimental treatment of which as minister of the industrial parish of St John's, Glasgow, was the basis for his somewhat contentious international reputation. For a mathematician, chemistry lecturer and now moral philosopher, this 'glaring inaccuracy' opened him up to 'discredit and derision . . . [in] many periodicals', just when he was building an academic reputation that would enable his social ideas to gain greater traction. The issues, as Chalmers knew, were deeper than the dropping of a 'zero', so that 100 became 10: sloppiness and inaccuracy in Christian thought was a primary critique of the rationalist enemies of public Christianity. Chalmers himself was not happy with systematised theologies which adopted only 'the form and aspect of a regular science'. Showing the adaptive power of evangelical thought, he looked to moral philosophy to unify faith and science.[1] This was the synthesis which had enabled evangelicalism to face the encroachment and professionalisation of new and multiplying disciplines of thought, and which would power it to unprecedented cultural dominance in the English-speaking world over the period between 1840 and 1870. Chalmers' saw the struggle to maintain a synthetic worldview – 'a place of enlargement' beyond 'mere theology', where science and faith were one – as leading 'on to the higher manifestations of Christianity'.[2]

What made Chalmers a key, even iconic, religious figure in the mid-nineteenth century was his leadership of a church facing the problems typical of all the European Reformation settlements. How did evangelicals retain the spiritual independence of the church in the face of the encroachments of modernising, totalising nation states? His leadership of the Disruption of the Church of Scotland in 1843 shows very clearly the interaction of religious revival with a secularising society. The Disruption was an attempt to have the spiritual church of Jesus Christ recognised as the 'true' Scottish national church, and a vibrant contributor to society

[1] Thomas Chalmers, *The Christian and Civic Economy of Large Towns*, Glasgow: Collins, 1826, pp. xiii; idem, 'On Natural Theology', in *Works of Thomas Chalmers*, Vol. 1, New York: Carter, 1840, pp. ix, x, xiii.

[2] Chalmers, 'On Natural Theology', p. xiv.

without being an extension of the state.[3] Their reform program was expressed in the reorganisation of church structure around 'five great schemes' ('Church Extension, Education, Foreign Missions, Colonial Churches and the Mission to the Jews'),[4] but ran into the brick wall of Tories antagonistic to religious enthusiasm, Radicals indifferent to denominational distinctives, and internal church division over voluntarism. Opposed in official circles, evangelicals reverted to their popular side. When banned from entering a number of parishes where patronage had become an issue, Chalmers and others revived the Covenanter and revivalist tradition of open-air preaching.

REVIVAL AND THE MILLENNIUM

While the crisis in the Church of Scotland deepened, revival broke out in Kilsyth in 1839 and quickly spread to other areas of the country. As we have already seen, the North Lanarkshire town had been a site of significant revival under James Robe in the 1740s. It became so again a century later under William Chalmers Burns, as resentment smouldered among miners at the repression of the Newport Chartist rising in Wales and the local population struggled with overcrowded accommodation.[5] Revivalism was not merely a response to local issues, however. The tensions between localism, nationalism and internationalism, and biblicism, intellectualism and mysticism are intensely evident in the relationship between mass revival movements and evangelical growth. Much of the literature about revival has focused either on 'revival as result' (i.e. of contextual causes), or 'revival as cause' (i.e. a popular or divine movement which changes circumstances.) For evangelicals in this period, it was both – divinely caused by God, materially needed by all people, and therefore a significant weapon in the evangelical armoury. The transatlantic society which emerged from the late 1600s had developed migration pathways marked, in part, by revival hotspots. Several areas were sites of recurrent revival between 1730 and 1859, particularly around the Celtic fringe (Scotland, Ireland, Wales, Cornwall and in their points of migration to the 'new worlds' of the United States, Australia, Canada, South Africa and South America).[6] The Kilsyth outbreak exemplified the interconnectedness of these locations.

William Chalmers Burns was at the time assistant minister to Robert Murray M'Cheyne at Dundee, a fervent evangelical whose flaming life and early death would leave him with the reputation of something of a Presbyterian saint. He and his friend Andrew Bonar were influenced both by Thomas Chalmers *and* by

[3] Stewart J. Brown, 'The Ten Years' Conflict and the Disruption of 1843' in Stewart J. Brown and Michael Fry, eds, *Scotland in the Age of the Disruption*, Edinburgh: Edinburgh University Press, 1993, p. 1.

[4] Ibid., p. 8.

[5] Alan B. Campbell, *The Lanarkshire Miners: A Social History of Their Trade Unions, 1775–1974*, Edinburgh: John Donald, 2003, p. 103.

[6] The Scoto-Irish soil, in Gibson's eyes, 'received in amplest measure the shower of blessing'.

Edward Irving – and so it is no mere coincidence that prior to the events at Kilsyth, Burns was preaching 'with increasing interest' at Dundee because M'Cheyne was absent in Palestine, making inquiry into appropriate means for undertaking missions to the Jews. The European political context of the 1840s had become increasingly propitious for Christian Zionism and the restoration of a Jewish state. Some evangelicals, such as Sir Culling Eardley or Ridley Haim Herschell, had close Jewish connections. The *Times* of London opined: 'It is not Jews only who anticipate [the rebirth of a Jewish state]; Christians are becoming equally impressed with the conviction, are . . . intently watching these coming events whose shadows are believed to be now passing over the political horizon'.[7]

Revivalism and Zionism were both fuelled by the premillennialism circulating in European Protestant circles through the influence of Albury and Powerscourt, Irving and Darby. It was further stimulated by the revolutionary turmoil in Europe in 1848, and later 'signs of the times' such as the Crimean War and the apocalyptic clash between industrial Prussian and industrialising French forces at Sedan in 1870.[8] Meanwhile, evangelical social concern and biblicism came together in attempts, from Lord Shaftesbury to Arthur Balfour, to restore the Jewish people 'to the Land of their Ancestors'.[9] 'If the Church of Scotland in these perilous times, "take hold of the skirt of the Jew,"' Bonar later wrote, 'God may remember her for Zion's sake' and bring revival.[10] In the premillennial vision, the conversion of the Jews and Holy Spirit revival were both signs of the return of Christ.

When M'Cheyne returned from Palestine, Chalmers Burns returned to his father's parish at Kilsyth to find people praying for 'the return of the time of revival'[11] and raising the spiritual temperature through visitation, prayer meetings, and cross-denominational action. On his arrival, Burns junior preached with dramatic effect at a communion meeting, leaving people desiring 'the speedy repetition of the solemnity'.[12] The following communion saw 'unwonted excitement' and 'visiters [sic] from all parts of the surrounding country'. On the 'fast day', many people suspended work and crowded into the church where they were addressed 'by the Rev. Mr. Brown, of Edinburgh; Dr. Malan, of Geneva;[13] and the

[7] *The Times*, 17 August 1840, quoted in Nicholas M. Railton, *No North Sea: The Anglo-German Evangelical Network in the Middle of the Nineteenth Century*, Leiden: Brill, 2000, p. 196.

[8] Ibid., p. 91.

[9] Donald M. Lewis, *The Origins of Christian Zionism: Lord Shaftesbury and Evangelical Support for a Jewish Homeland*, Cambridge: Cambridge University Press, p. 13.

[10] Viz. A.A. Bonar and R. M. M'Cheyne, *The Holy Land and Mission of Inquiry to the Jews*, Edinburgh: Oliphant, 1842, p. vi, p. 518.

[11] William Burns, 'Revivals of Religion: Kilsyth, 1839', *Evangelical Magazine*, 17 (December 1839), 601.

[12] *Evangelical Magazine*, 17 (December 1839), 551.

[13] Malan, who was a student of Haldane's, represented the earlier French and Swiss *Reveil.* Stunt depicts his group in Geneva as Calvinist Moravians (Timothy C.F. Stunt, *From Awakening to Secession: Radical Evangelicals in Switzerland and Britain 1815–1835*, Edinburgh: T&T Clark, 2000, p. 36).

Rev. Mr. Macnaughton, of Paisley'. The congregation soon overflowed into field preaching attended by up to 15,000 people, with innovations in other meetings such as moonlight gatherings and overflow tents: 'the impression, on the minds of young and old', noted the *Evangelical Magazine*, 'appears to have been eminently pentecostal'.[14] The longed-for revival had come. The meetings were lacking in 'extravagancies', although Burns reported 'meltings' and tears, and a radical transformation of the town's life which provided 'truly wonderful proofs of a most surprising and delightful revival'.[15]

Kilsyth was one of a series of religious revivals which sparked off each other in the early 1840s throughout the English-speaking world, from North Wales to New Zealand, in Presbyterian 'long communion' seasons and Methodist camp and prayer meetings.[16] In Australia, there was almost simultaneous revival activity in Parramatta, Windsor and Castlereagh (1840–41), Melbourne (1843), and Western Australia (1844).[17] The first of John Watsford's 'glorious gospel triumphs' was in a prayer meeting in Parramatta in 1840, convened 'for the outpouring of the Holy Spirit and the revival of God's work'.[18] Finney's *Lectures* (republished in London in 1839 in time for the Kilsyth Revival of that year) were ever present, as was a rising tide of transatlantic revival literature which followed exchanges of personnel, and circulated around the world through the significant (especially nonconformist) evangelical presence in the emerging colonial newspapers.[19] The year of the Scottish Disruption, 1843, also marked something of a climax in the revival movement in the United States, fuelled by the teaching of William Miller, who predicted the imminent return of Christ. The 'great disappointment' of the Millerites when 22 October 1844, the last of several dates they had calculated, passed without incident contributed both to a wider loss of revival momentum, and in America to a temporary discrediting of premillenialism.[20]

In New York City, Phoebe Worrall Palmer's 'Tuesday Meeting for the Promotion of Holiness' started among women, incorporated men, and multiplied and expanded the Palmers' ministry into pre-existing camp meeting and conference networks.[21] The 'holiness movement' would become a major institutional basis for

[14] *Evangelical Magazine*, 17 (December 1839), 552.

[15] Burns, 'Revivals of Religion', 605.

[16] Viz. Alison Clarke, '"Days of Heaven on Earth": Presbyterian Communion Seasons in Nineteenth-Century Otago,' *Journal of Religious History*, 26 (2002), 274–97.

[17] Stuart Piggin, *Evangelical Christianity in Australia: Spirit, World and World*, Melbourne: Oxford University Press, 1996, pp. 24ff.

[18] John Watsford, *Glorious Gospel Triumphs*, London: Charles Kelly, 1900, p. 21.

[19] In its July edition of 1840 (vol. 8) alone, the *Eclectic Review* reviewed six volumes on the revival of religion. See also Stuart Johnson, 'The Shaping of Colonial Liberalism: John Fairfax and the Sydney Morning Herald', PhD thesis, University of New South Wales, 2006.

[20] Ernest R. Sandeen, *The Roots of Fundamentalism: British and American Millenarianism 1800–1930*, Chicago: University of Chicago Press, 1970, pp. 53–5.

[21] Walter Hampel, 'Prayer Revivals and the Third Great Awakening', *Evangelical Review of Theology*, 31 (2007), 31.

the spread of later revivals. Palmer took her 'prayer revival' approach to Britain and especially Ireland in 1859, and when Irish Presbyterian leader William Gibson wrote his account of that revival (*The Year of Grace*), he wrote it specifically *for* 'the American Christian public'.[22] Palmer's influence, along with the rise of Catherine Booth, specifically tied revivalism and Holy Spirit freedom to the gender question.[23] Palmer had found the ground prepared for her in Britain and Ireland (by news of the 1857 New York Businessmen's revival, sparked by a convert of Finney's, Jeremiah Lanphier) and her success there would in turn be of great use to her when she returned to the United States. From New York, 'the Businessmen's revival' spread rapidly to Richmond, 'Boston, Springfield, Hoboken, and numerous cities throughout America.'[24] American Holiness evangelicalism would follow these revivalist pathways and construct enduring interdenominational institutions: colleges, newspapers, healing homes, social welfare agencies and the like.

By June 1858, Charles Spurgeon was mentioning these revivals in his sermons, having 'received continually fresh confirmations of the good news from a far country' that some 250,000 people had been regenerated in the previous 6 months.[25] His exposition was a fine example of the evangelical understanding of revival as an antidote for 'rationalism, popery and infidelity' in an industrial age. The Holy Spirit, he preached, righted man's reasoning and gave him the power to overcome circumstances. It put 'the right axle to the right wheel' and then added 'fire and steam' to give 'motive power... to move the whole'.[26] To Spurgeon, the result of revival was to make of the church a spiritual Stephenson's *Rocket*, a powerful presence in the steam age.

The revival train next steamed into Ireland, which had an Ulster revival tradition stretching back to at least 1625 (Six Mile Water Revival). Here, news of international revivals stirred a desire to see life amidst a people 'trained to reason, warm in party and cold in religion', supplying 'the power of the Spirit to impart... a vivifying energy' to evangelical ministries, particularly around Antrim.[27] Ulster newspapers reported conversions in the thousands, and public prayer meetings of 3,000, 5,000 and, on one occasion, 25,000. This phenomenon was 'reflexive'. Having been inspired by reports of American revivals, which in turn were impacted by Kilsyth, the Ulster revival re-entered the west coast of Scotland and set off a series of local revivals there and in Wales, and was transported around the world through

[22] Gibson, *The Year of Grace*, p. iii.

[23] Pamela J. Walker, *Pulling the Devil's Kingdom Down: The Salvation Army in Victorian Britain*, Berkeley: University of California Press, p. 26.

[24] Hampel, 'Prayer Revivals', 32.

[25] C.H. Spurgeon, 'The Outpouring of the Holy Spirit', in *Revival Year Sermons, Preached at the Surrey Gardens Music Hall during 1859*, London: Banner of Truth, 1959.

[26] Spurgeon, 'The Outpouring of the Holy Spirit'.

[27] Rev. J.A. Canning of Coleraine, in Gibson, *Year of Grace*, p. 10.

the Irish diaspora.[28] In 1859–60, in Wales alone, it was estimated that the full membership of Evangelical Alliance churches rose by more than 90,000.[29] In 1858, the Methodist Episcopal Church in the United States (which the previous year grew by 2 per cent) grew by 16 per cent, whereas the Regular Baptists in 1858 and the 'Old School' Presbyterian Church of the United States in 1859 grew by 12 per cent (as opposed to 4 per cent and 1 per cent, respectively, in the previous year).[30] As Holmes has pointed out, this was not a mystical retreat from the world, but an increasingly professionalised and intentional approach to problem solving by many evangelicals. The realm of the spiritual was, as Chalmers noted, as rational a place as science – the trick was not to let its attendant methodology lead it to becoming rational*ised*.[31]

In an age when mass migration was a 'way out' of Europe's intractable problems, revival also became a linked means of distilling local identities into transportable spiritualities. Evangelical revival was thus intrinsically internationalising, permitting disestablished Irish Protestants to reappropriate the 'faith of their fathers' in a living, immediate, powerful and personal way. The *Times* of London dismissed such revivals under the 'genus hysterical',[32] but even that attention contributed to the phenomenon's spread to new local places among migrant peoples. In far-away New Zealand, for example, Methodists prayed for a 'general revival of religion' and Presbyterians listened 'with great attention' to Thomas Macfarlane's stirring account of the emergence of celebrated lay evangelists, including the gentlemen preachers, Reginald Ratcliffe and Brownlow North, and the Shropshire Methodist Richard Weaver – a 'celebrated lay Revivalist . . . [who] is now the most successful preacher since the days of Whitfield'.[33] A generation of new itinerant preachers travelled the pathways of regional, then national and finally international mass-evangelistic networks in ways which became commonplace in the following period. Among them were some who became evangelical 'household names': William Carter, John Hambleton, Edward Usher, Henry Varley, Denham Smith, Henry Moorhouse,[34] Henry Grattan Guinness, William and Catherine Booth. Thousands of others carried on work of a more local character, the impact of which lasted long after the close of the period. These same networks became the pathways trod by temperance

[28] Kathryn Long, *The Revival of 1857–58: Interpreting an American Religious Awakening*, New York: Oxford University Press, 1998, pp. 5–9.

[29] Kenneth Hylson-Smith, *Evangelicals in the Church of England, 1734–1984*, Edinburgh: T. & T. Clark, 1988, pp. 188–9.

[30] Long, *The Revival of 1857–58*, pp. 144–6.

[31] See Janice Holmes, *Religious Revivals in Britain and Ireland, 1859–1905*, Dublin: Irish Academic Press, 2000.

[32] Quoted in *The Times*, 17 September 1859.

[33] *Daily Southern Cross*, XVII: 1460 (13 December 1861), 3.

[34] George Needham, *Recollections of Henry Moorhouse, Evangelist*, Chicago: Revell, 1881, pp. 14–15.

reformers and first-wave feminists in their campaigns to extend reform around the world and to define the 'place of enlargement' for evangelical effort.

THINGS FLY APART

The three decades from 1840 were among the most energetic in European history. While a European presence had already been planted in many parts of the globe, dynamic colonialisation largely dates to this period. 'Steam-shipping, telegraphs, and railways began to make a major impact.'[35] The number of Europeans working in India doubled between 1830 and the mid-1850s, as did average annual trade between the two regions. Sponsored mass migration to New South Wales and Canada and the activities of chartered companies in New Zealand[36] created a global economy and a new global politics. *Pax Britannica* took a leaf out of the Roman *res gestae* and settled its legionaries in different parts of the world.[37] In 1844, inaugurating the electronic communications revolution that would compress that world, the evangelical polymath Samuel F. B. Morse tapped out 'What hath God wrought!'[38] Active in the 'transformation' of empire – through the linked processes of revival and reform, crisis and continuous change – evangelicals found themselves in all the 'places of enlargement' that such processes formed. Revival and the pressure for definition and reform in the colonies made spaces for the various streams of evangelicalism to interact, to clash and so contribute to the emerging international culture.[39] The expansion into the world made this community of mutual recognition more variegated than it had ever been.

Events, however, also frequently punctured evangelical euphoria. In 1845, the potato blight – which had caused crop failures in the United States the previous year – decimated Irish crops and so ushered in a human tragedy to which British politicians failed adequately to respond. Millions died or migrated, and Irish

[35] D.A. Washbrook, 'India,1818–1860: The Two Faces of Colonialism' in W.R. Louis, A. Porter and A.M. Low, eds, *The Oxford History of the British Empire*, vol. 3, Oxford: Oxford University Press, 1999, p. 417.

[36] Chartered Companies remained powerful through the first half of the century, although shifting towards straight stockholder arrangements rather than as a direct arm of state policy. See Anatole Browde, 'Settling the Canadian Colonies: a Comparison of Two Nineteenth-century Land Companies', *Business History Review*, 76:2 (2002), 291ff.

[37] George Raudzens, *The British Ordnance Department and Canada's Canals, 1815–1855*, Waterloo: Wilfrid Laurier University Press, 1979, pp. 126–7; Richard Boast, *Buying the Land, Selling the Land: Governments and Maori Land in the North Island 1865–1921*, Wellington: Victoria University Press, 2008, p. 50.

[38] Daniel J. Czitrom, *Media and the American Mind: From Morse to McLuhan*, Chapel Hill: University of North Carolina Press, 1982, p. 188; for Morse's father's theology, see William Warren Sweet, *Religion in the Development of American Culture, 1765–1840*, New York: Scribner's, 1952, p. 194.

[39] Kevin Blackburn, 'Imagining Aboriginal Nations: Early Nineteenth Century: Evangelicals on the Australian Frontier and the "Nation" Concept,' *Australian Journal of Politics and History*, 48:2 (2002), 174.

grievances against Britain were reinforced: in the eyes of the nationalist John Mitchel, 'the Almighty indeed sent the potato blight, but the English created the Famine.'[40] As it receded in 1848, a commercial crisis further disrupted events. Traditional spiritualised responses seemed struck dumb before events of such scale: merely pointing to 'the sins of the nation' (a favoured trope of the religious press) seemed an impertinence.[41] John Mitchel 'noted bitterly that Britain had been prepared to spend £20 million to emancipate the black slaves of the West Indies (in Mitchel's words, "to turn negroes wild"), because it appealed to sentimental evangelicals, but it was unwilling to spend a fraction of this amount on famine relief in Ireland'.[42]

It would be a familiar and repeated criticism: in 1894, G. E. Morrison estimated that 3,000 Chinese had been converted by 1,500 missionaries at the cost of 'the combined incomes of the ten chief London hospitals.'[43] The bitterness of events began to weigh on the evangelical approach to public influence. In 1847, the conflicted world of Charlotte Brontë (in *Jane Eyre*) was a straw in the wind. Faith remained in the centre of the story while at the same time redefining social conventions. Brontë did not (unlike some Victorian novelists such as Charles Dickens, Thomas Hardy and George Eliot) 'lose, reject, or deny her faith'.[44] Jane's story, however, was an identification of a key evangelical characteristic – a powerful internal worldview which works in the world through an energetic ambivalence about the ability of the present to live up to the vision projected by the biblical text.

The obvious influence of evangelicals in the 'Age of Reform' created a problem for the movement: there emerged a stereotype of the 'imaginary evangelical' against whom public scorn could be directed. Yet, there was no such movement, at least not in any unitary sense. Rather, the demonstrable effectiveness (indeed, apparent inevitability) of social activism and reform (seen as moral 'do-goodism') was appropriated by progressive elites who transferred it into the heart of their societies. In his book *Making English Morals*, Michael Roberts traces this process of appropriation as evangelicals 'rebranded' their utility to British society, first as a way of meeting moral crisis, then of avoiding a mob-state through the creation of civil society and then of schooling the 'autonomous moral individual' in the

[40] Alvin Jackson, 'Ireland, the Union, and the Empire, 1800–1960' in Kevin Kenny, ed., *Ireland and the British Empire*, New York: Oxford University Press, 2004, p. 134.

[41] 'European Intelligence', *Evangelical Christendom* 2:1 (January 1848), 4; Peter Gray, 'National Humiliation and the Great Hunger: Fast and Famine in 1847', *Irish Historical Studies*, 32 (2006–7), 193–216.

[42] James Quinn, 'John Mitchel and the Rejection of the Nineteenth Century', *Eire-Ireland: A Journal of Irish Studies*, 38:3–4 (2003), 99.

[43] G.E. Morrison, *An Australian in China: being the narrative of a quiet journey across China to Burma*, London: Cox, 1895, chapter 1.

[44] Emily Griesinger, 'Charlotte Bronte's Religion: Faith, Feminism, and Jane Eyre', *Christianity and Literature*, 58:1 (2008), 31.

market society.[45] Likewise, Ian Tyrell sees in the 1850s and 1860s the birth period of what he would identify (from 1880) as 'America's moral empire'.[46]

Materialist historians and those with a tendency to conflate religion with its social context have often assumed that Victorian morality *was* evangelical religion, and vice versa. An interpretation which *totally* identifies evangelicalism with conventional piety is, however, largely the result of either prejudgement or ignorance. Such views ignore the vibrancy of Victorian intellectual elites, many of whom (such as J.S. Mill's circle) resisted being pressed into the 'manufacture of consent' necessary in the rapidly changing society. Some of the keenest critics of evangelicalism were themselves the children of evangelical families, who rightly felt an inadequate approach to the critical questions of the age, or a failure to satisfy the aesthetic drift in succeeding generations.[47] John Henry Newman among the Catholics, Samuel Wilberforce among the Anglicans, and Thomas Babington Macaulay among the Whig historians[48] were representative figures of this broader search.[49] The rise of the Anglican evangelical party's great global foe, Tractarianism, was directly linked to evangelical predecessors, and within evangelicalism itself, there was a proliferation of divisions out of the mainline Arminianism/Calvinism tension (from John Wroe to Brigham Young). Evangelicals did more than teach the world to behave; they taught other traditions to communicate, to adapt to modernity, to co-opt or bypass the artificial walls of status quo and state religion. Moreover, evangelicalism itself was not (as is often portrayed) static: this is an illusion which disappears rapidly on any closer look at the ferment in the movement during this time.

In fact, the great challenge for evangelicals in the period between 1840 and 1870 lay not in their disappearance into moralism, but in the enervating effects of having to keep running the vast array of causes which were the means of their impact on Victorian society. Exeter Hall played host to an ever-expanding range of new philanthropic bodies, which 'were founded at an average rate of six a year'.[50] 'The annual meeting of the fictitious Society for the Distribution of Moral Pocket Handkerchiefs (Secretary: Soapy Bareface, Esq. Committee members: the Rev. Augustus Cant and the Rev. Nasal Whine) was gleefully chronicled by a High Church journal in 1860.'[51]

[45] See M.J.D. Roberts, *Making English Morals: Voluntary Association and Moral Reform In England, 1787–1886*, Cambridge: Cambridge University Press, 2004.

[46] See Ian Tyrrell. *Reforming the World: The Creation of America's Moral Empire*, Princeton: Princeton University Press, 2010.

[47] Isaac Taylor traced this drift in his third-person account of his own experience. Isaac Taylor, 'Physical Theory of Another Life', *Edinburgh Review*, 71 (April 1840), 220ff.

[48] Terry Brotherstone, Anna Clark and Kevin Whelan, eds, *These Fissured Isles: Ireland, Scotland and the Making of Modern Britain 1798–1848*, Edinburgh: John Donald, 2005, p. 64.

[49] Wilson Smith, *Professors & Public Ethics: Studies of Northern Moral Philosophers before the Civil War*, Ithaca: Cornell University Press, 1956, p. 166.

[50] Bebbington, *Evangelicalism in Modern Britain*, p. 135.

[51] Ibid., p. 122.

Activism ('the word' in 'the world') could overpower reflective spirituality and intellection, leaving many parts of the movement running unreflectively on those models which had been so successful in the eighteenth century. The very prominence of revivalism was indicative of a paucity of other constructive responses to contemporary conditions. The fact that William Paton Mackay could write the lyrics to 'Revive us again' in 1863,[52] only a year after one of those great waves, illustrates the necessity of revival expectation to the regeneration of evangelical fortunes between successive generations. 'Systematic' approaches such as Finney's were central to mobilising a workforce for continued social and geographical extension.

As with any social movement, evangelicalism's very success in the period up to 1830 had – by establishing it as a permanent factor in transatlantic society – rendered it subject to identification with the 'normal', the mundane. Bebbington notes that not only did evangelicals lose public sympathy, and thus political power; they also lost intellectual traction: 'Practical work so occupied Shaftesbury, who had gained a first-class degree, that he "lost the art" of reading.'[53] Inevitably the best and the brightest became detached from the institutional centres of thought and reflection in the West, many of them isolated, and some in early graves out on the mission field. Evangelicals thus tended to miss the critical shift in modernist institutions, as represented in Darwin and German higher criticism. The result was loss of influence over those for whom the academic life was a preference, and thus over the traditional centres of clergy training for the established church. Between 1865 and 1900, for instance, only six outright evangelicals became bishops in the Church of England,[54] handing the domestic impetus within that church to contending traditions (particularly Tractarianism).

For most Britons and many Americans during this period, the key issues related to the expansion of the great industrial cities. Living conditions fluctuated for many along with patterns of mobility, and mortality rates increased among the labouring classes, despite the fact that *overall* mortality rates were decreasing.[55] By 1825, per capita income was increasing in Britain at a rate five times that experienced a century before, though it was woefully ill-distributed.[56] The demands of the European cities in large part drove the development of their colonies, which acted as relief valves for excess population. The growth of industrialisation in the northern United States created enormous tensions with the plantation culture of

[52] William Paton Mackay, *Abundant Grace: Selected Addresses*, London: J.E. Hawkins, 1886. See 'Memoir' by A. Macpherson.

[53] Bebbington, *Evangelicalism in Modern Britain*, p. 137.

[54] Ibid., pp. 146, 149.

[55] Richard Brown, *Society and Economy in Modern Britain, 1700–1850*, New York: Routledge, 1991, pp. 37, 39.

[56] Anthony Cooke and Ian Donnachie, 'Aspects of Industrialisation prior to 1850' in Anthony Cooke, Ian Donnachie, Ann MacSween and Christopher A. Whatley, eds, *Modern Scottish History, 1707 To the Present*, vol. 1, East Linton: Tuckwell, 1998, p. 131.

the South, and when the two went to war, it cut across the production/consumption relationships of those economies which were connected to Europe. By the end of the period from 1840 to 1870, that would include most of the world.

For evangelicals, such trends were both a curse and a blessing. On the one hand, they placed significant influence into the hands of those middling classes whose expanding wealth became a mainstay of evangelical influence.[57] Short-distance population migration facilitated the transmission of evangelical dissent and made trans-parochial churches more central as social institutions.[58] However, *long*-distance population migration altered the balance between types of evangelicals, resulting in differing evangelical cultures. In no small part, the division between 'establishment' and 'dissenting' churches assisted in the process of 'the colonies' becoming secular states. With relatively more influence, and plenty of potential allies against religious establishment, dissenting evangelicals found in the colonies the opportunity to undo the Reformation church monopolies under which they had suffered at home.[59] Alliances of enlightenment liberals, reformist Whigs, and dissenting antiestablishmentarians were able to use the new disciplines (such as economics) to undermine Canadian "Clergy Reserves" and the Australian 'Church and Schools Corporation'. The result – in the British world – was the effective breaking (between 1829 and 1854) of Anglican control over education and the 'co-establishment' of the major Christian denominations.[60] In Sydney, for example, while one Anglican colonial journalist was bemoaning the fact that he could suggest 'no solution' to divisions over education and privilege,[61] his dissenting evangelical colleague (John West) had already written a plan for resolving the impasse through constituting the Australian colonies into a separate, secular state.[62]

Such challenges opened up gaps in the Protestant armoury which, in Catholic circles, had been filled by central planning and religious orders.[63] Evangelicals were very aware of the requirements for spiritual formation, and set about trying to find a response to the problems of urbanisation. As an Irish commentator noted in the

57 Brown, *Society and Economy in Modern Britain*, p. 295.

58 See C.G. Brown, 'The Mechanism of Religious Growth in Urban Societies: British Cities since the Eighteenth Century' in Hugh McLeod, ed., *European Religion in the Age of Great Cities 1830–1930*, London: Routledge, 1994, pp. 239–62.

59 See John Lambton, *Report and Despatches of the Earl of Durham, on British North America*, London: Ridgways, 1839, p. 158.

60 John Dunmore Lang, *An historical and statistical account of New South Wales*, London: Longman, 1852, pp. 522–3.

61 Editorial, *Sydney Gazette and NSW Advertiser*, 20 February 1841, p. 2.

62 John West, *John West's 'Union among the Colonies'* (ed. Gregory Melleuish) , Kew: Australian Scholarly Publishing, 2001; Johnson, 'The Shaping of Colonial Liberalism', p. 3.

63 Some Protestant responses to urbanisation are equally clear, direct responses to Catholic innovations, e.g. Gore's urban missions, and Nightingale's early understanding of the work of the French Sisters of Charity (Lynn McDonald, *Florence Nightingale: An Introduction to Her Life and Family*, Waterloo: Wilfrid Laurier University Press, 2001, p. 29).

1830s, 'our large towns are . . . growing into hordes of heathen, after whom no man is looking, and of whom nothing can reasonably be expected but aggravated and increased depravity'.[64] In places like Belfast, Liverpool, Glasgow, and New York, industrialisation also saw large net inflows of Catholics – population shifts which were deemed a threat.[65] Migrant clergy – often pressed into missionary vocations by an overcrowded clerical marketplace at home – took these tensions with them out into the colonies. In Australia, for instance, Chalmers's former associate, John Dunmore Lang, energetically promoted the migration of Scots (and, when they were insufficient, Ulstermen) in order to avoid New South Wales becoming 'a province of popedom' through a seeming flood of Irish peasants. Lang was one of many to pursue evangelical agrarian utopias in the colonies, filled with people who were moral, educated, intelligent and skilled.[66] The Free Church of Scotland, in expansionary mode after Disruption, tapped into this utopianism and sponsored a new colony in Otago. The faithful Free Kirk Disruptionist Thomas Burns wrote that they would plant both 'the pure Gospel' and 'an independent Scottish race in the far south, which shall be equally distinguished with their kinsmen in the far north'.[67]

At home, mass societies required complementary forms of organisation. Evangelicals scrambled both to understand the emerging social situation and respond to it. Chalmers's 'moral philosophy' sought to find solutions to that 'most mischievous effect of the English pauperism, that it depresses the wages of labour.' He 'could not but regret . . . the outrage and the violence wherewith it was associated' as those marginalised by industrial change took matters into their own hands, forming 'combinations' which challenged the established order – and by implication, traditional evangelical approaches to reform and change.[68] Industrial society progressively rendered the evangelical leavening of elites (on the Clapham Sect model) less effective as a way of achieving social change. It was clear that evangelicals would not be able to grow fast enough to control the course of events through sheer numbers. In Ulster, evangelical growth rates 'evened off in the 1840s despite a temporary surge in the wake of the 1859 revival', providing enough leverage to 'establish evangelical voluntarism' as a catalytic force, but not as a mass party.[69] In Scotland, Chalmers proposed that the labouring classes seek 'the more excellent way' of education and training and self-help organisations such as Savings Banks

[64] David Hempton and Myrtle Hill, *Evangelical Protestantism in Ulster Society 1740–1890*, London: Routledge, 1992, p. 110.

[65] Ibid., p. 107.

[66] See John Dunmore Lang, *Queensland, Australia; a highly eligible field for emigration, and the future cotton-field of Great Britain*, London: Stanford, 1861.

[67] W. Cargill, *The Free Church Colony of Otago in New Zealand. . . . Letter from Capt. Cargill to Dr. Aldcorn, of Oban*, London: Waterloo, 1847, p. 12.

[68] Chalmers, *Christian and Civic Economy of Large Towns*, pp. v–vi.

[69] Hempton and Hill, *Evangelical Protestantism in Ulster*, p. 79.

and Mechanics Schools, while the church and the social elite should voluntarily seek to raise wages and work on the causes of pauperism.

Around the world, evangelicals were already interpolating themselves in the very institutions which Chalmers described as the means for the uplift of industrial populations. In South Africa, they joined with liberal newspapermen to form those voluntary societies which 'were increasingly perceived as central, not only to urban sociability, but also to public advancement and communal identity'.[70] For someone like John West – whose experience in ministry near Birmingham had given him an intimate knowledge of industrial radicalism and the need for reform – translocation to Tasmania resulted in a flurry of founding activity, including the mechanics institute, the city mission, a non-denominational high school, the local newspaper (the *Launceston Examiner*, 1842) and many others besides.[71] Evangelicals co-opted or cooperated with liberal ideals. Just as the economy was seen as 'an impersonal agent of moral law',[72] so society was a 'moral organism' in which one may 'serve [one's] own generation' under God.[73]

The expansion of empire gave rise to a further set of dilemmas. At times 'compelled to highlight the imperial benefits of evangelization to sustain their cause',[74] evangelicals came to different conclusions as to how to deal with the great facts of their day. The bloodbaths of the Crimean War and the Indian Mutiny demanded a sympathetic response, a response which varied according to the starting point of the believer. State church evangelicals could operate out of a tradition of 'the just war', a tradition which drew on Pauline texts (such as 2 Timothy 2:3) to produce the category of 'the good soldier'. Sentimental tracts portrayed the faith of public figures such as Sir Henry Havelock, 'The Christian Soldier', who married a daughter of missionaries (Hannah Marshman), embraced Baptist evangelicalism, and won 'glory' in death as a military leader in defence of Europeans under threat in the Indian Mutiny.[75] Less well known, but widely circulated, was the story of Hedley Vicars, whose Royal Engineer father had laid his 'dying hand . . . upon his head, with the earnest prayer "that he might be a good soldier of Jesus Christ, and so fight manfully under his banner as to glorify his holy name."'[76] Hedley's

[70] Saul Dubow, *A Commonwealth of Knowledge: Science, Sensibility, and White South Africa, 1820–2000*, New York: Oxford University Press, 2006, p. 27.

[71] Mark Hutchinson, 'John West, 1809–1874', *Australian Dictionary of Evangelical Biography*, Adelaide: EHAA, 1994, online at http://webjournals.alphacrucis.edu.au/journals/adeb/w/west-john-1809–1874/

[72] Jones, *An End to Poverty?*, p. 178.

[73] William Slayter, *A Funeral Sermon on the Life and Death of the Rev. John West*, Sydney: n.p., 1874, p. 7.

[74] Porter, quoted in William C. Barnhart, 'Evangelicalism, Masculinity and the Making of Imperial Missionaries in Late Georgian Britain, 1795–1820', *The Historian*, 67 (2005), 713.

[75] See John C. Marshman, *Memoirs of Major-General Sir Henry Havelock, K.C.B.*, London: Longman, 1860.

[76] Catherine Marsh, *Memorials of Captain Hedley Vicars, Ninety-seventh regiment*, New York: Carter, 1856, p. 14.

career as a soldier, his conversion in Canada, his spiritual activities in spreading evangelical faith among his fellow soldiers, association with Exeter Hall, actions among the cholera epidemic in the Crimea and his bravery in the trenches and mention in despatches before dying in the Siege of Sebastopol were enshrined in imperial folklore by Catherine Marsh as a paean to the influence of evangelical motherhood. The story of this relatively minor imperial soldier would be told and retold in the revivalist and holiness literature of evangelicalism for the rest of the century.[77]

None of this heralded the mere incorporation of evangelical opinion into the cultures of expanding empires. While wrestling with the seeming militarism of the Old Testament, for instance, such evangelicals as J.N. Darby came down on the side of the preponderance of the New. 'I quite understand that the sentiment of patriotism may be strong in the heart of a man,' he wrote in reaction to the Franco-Prussian War: 'I do not think that the heart is capable of *affection* towards the whole world. At bottom, human affection must have a centre.... One would sacrifice one's life – everything... for one's country, one's friends. But... the Christian, if consistent, declares plainly that he seeks a country–a better, that is to say, a heavenly country. His affections, his ties, his citizenship, are above.'[78]

Such separationism was extreme; it arose not out of humanitarian interest, but out of a return to biblical holiness through 'separation from the world', with which even Darby's contemporary, Edward Irving, would have disagreed.[79] After the abolition of slavery throughout the Empire in 1833, the British and Foreign Anti-Slavery Society (formed in 1839) actively promoted the use of the British military to end slavery outside the empire. Other evangelical traditions such as Quakers and Mennonites, however, held the 'peace testimony' to be absolute, even in pursuit of such good objectives.[80]

Evangelicals, therefore, were neither static nor uniform in their responses, and local experimentation meant even further divergence. In the liberal revolutions of 1848, for instance, evangelicals in countries with significant Catholic populations found it difficult to choose sides between their traditional enemies, 'Popery' (Catholicism) and 'Infidelity' (secular liberalism). After all, the liberals 'were the men who supported regimes that were willing to plunge the world into war not to make it safe for democracy... but to remake mankind, or to forge a new order, or to appropriate history in the name of a nation or a race.'[81] Evangelicals, in the

[77] Among those who would use Vicars's life as a vehicle were W.E. Boardman, William Conant and Robert Steel of Manchester.

[78] Quoted in Peter Brock, 'The Peace Testimony of the Early Plymouth Brethren', *Church History*, 53 (1984), 35.

[79] Ibid., 40.

[80] See, for instance, the thought of Thomas Gisborne, as discussed by Martin Ceadel, *The Origins of War Prevention: The British Peace Movement and International Relations, 1730–1854*, Oxford: Oxford University Press, 1996, p. 13.

[81] Christopher Coker, *War and the Illiberal Conscience*. Boulder: Westview Press, 1998, p. x.

main, could support assertiveness ('manliness') in their public figures, but any sort of political absolutism – liberal or conservative – combined with the increasing power of industrialised militaries to wreak havoc on masses of human bodies, was a frightening prospect. The practising of 'the most hateful intolerance and persecution' by Swiss liberals 'against the faithful witnesses of Christ'[82] would remain a symbol for evangelicals in other European countries of liberal illiberalism.

For Italian evangelicals, on the other hand, liberalism was seen less as a rationalist opponent and more as an ally which would assist in the establishment of religious freedom. The 'almost bloodless' revolutions in Italian city-states were seen as a significant opportunity for the Protestant faith to enter a previously closed area of Europe, and as 'victories of the King of Peace'.[83] When liberal Catholics such as Raffaello Lambruschini began to talk about freedom of religion as a necessary outflow of the neo-Guelph doctrine of Italian cultural leadership, evangelicals were necessarily divided.[84] Could liberalism be good in one country and bad in another? How did this reflect on political alliances, on the ability of evangelicals to identify their enemies and so construct their shifting alliances? Evangelical politics tended to develop as an extension of the movement's core pragmatism, differing from country to country.

HOLDING THINGS TOGETHER

Despite being the joint offspring of the transatlantic revival of the 1730s, American evangelicals often found their encounters with their British cousins difficult. When the first World Anti-Slavery Convention was hosted in London in 1840, American women were shocked to find themselves excluded from full participation. Cultural difference posed an early challenge to the powerful fusion of evangelicalism and feminism which saw 'Evangelical religion . . . [become] more important than feminism in enlarging [the] sphere [of women] during the nineteenth century'.[85] The anger of women such as the Quaker Anne Knight led directly to heightened agitation for women's suffrage and to the formation of competing associations. It was a claim which could not be ignored. As George Thompson noted to Knight, whether it was in missions funding or anti-slavery agitation, women were to the fore: 'Where [women's associations] existed, they . . . formed the cement of the whole Antislavery building.'[86] The same might have been said for missions and

[82] 'Switzerland', *Evangelical Christendom*, 2:1 (January 1848), 19.
[83] 'Italy', *Evangelical Christendom*, 2:1 (January 1848), 16.
[84] A. Gaudio, "Lambruschini Raffaello" in *Dizionario di scienze dell'educazione*, Leumann-Torino, Elle Di Ci - LAS - SEI, 1997, pp. 591–2.
[85] D. W. Bebbington, *Evangelicalism in Modern Britain: A history from the 1730s to the 1980s*, London: Unwin Hyman, 1989, p. 129.
[86] Clare Midgley, *Women against Slavery: The British Campaigns, 1780–1870*, London: Routledge, 1995, p. 44.

social welfare enterprises. Action led to reaction. In India, gender and caste definitions required the organization of 'women only' organisations, such as the Zenana missions, leading to the establishment of organisations entirely run, funded and staffed by women.[87] Flowing back in the other direction, 'colonial' women such as Pandita Ramabai, Cornelia Sorabji and Rukhmabai (to mention only names from India) became a regular part of the increasingly global philanthropic endeavour.[88] The same women were often activists for social work in Europe and Britain, India, America and Australia. The rise of the Deaconess orders, first in Germany and later, by adoption, in the English-speaking world, was one approach to formalising a female 'order' while organising response to social needs. The revivalist Antoine Vermeil de Sasie, for example, drew on the work of Elizabeth Fry and on German Pietism to establish the first French Deaconness Institute in Paris in 1840. This originally German movement would spread rapidly throughout the evangelical world and have a lasting influence on the shape of emerging health science disciplines and practice.[89]

Given that commerce was the new praxis, other evangelicals attending the 1840 Anti-Slavery Convention (such as Thomas Fowell Buxton) sought to baptise it as they had baptised much else. Reason, commerce and religion would go hand in hand into the world to create a 'moral space' where self-interest would not work against the common good. In the words of Cambridge scientist Adam Sedgwick, 'The office of spiritual religion is not to destroy the faculties of the mind and body, but to renovate them and restore them to their proper use, as obedient instruments in their Maker's service.'[90] Sedgwick was also clear, however, about the opposition faced by those who sought to maintain an evangelical middle ground. Facing resistance from traditional imperial elites and appropriation of their earlier approaches by Whigs and liberals, evangelicals used 'legitimate commerce' to temper power and oppression. What they did at home (in supporting, for example, amelioration of the Corn Laws) they also increasingly tried to do abroad (through the education for 'industrial usefulness' of indigenous peoples, so removing any argument for their enslavement and relocation). Evangelical ranks continued to include great political leaders, but increasingly became associated in the public mind with 'cross-over figures' such as Sedgwick's friend, David Livingstone. As 'H.M. Consul at Quilimane for the Eastern Coast and independent districts of the

[87] Eliza F. Kent, *Converting Women: Gender and Protestant Christianity in Colonial South India*, New York: Oxford University Press, 2004, p. 91; Alison Twells, 'Missionary Domesticity, Global Reform and "Woman's Sphere" in Early Nineteenth-Century England', *Gender & History*, 18 (2006), 266–84.

[88] Antoinette Burton, *Burdens of History: British Feminists, Indian Women, and Imperial Culture, 1865–1915*, Chapel Hill: University of North Carolina Press, 1994, p. 8.

[89] Viz. Zelie Jennings, *Some Account of Dettmar Basse, the Passavant Family and Their Arrival in America*, Zelienople Historical Society, 1988.

[90] Adam Sedgwick, *A Discourse on the Studies of the University of Cambridge*, London: Parker, 1850, p. 130.

interior, and commander of an expedition for exploring Eastern and Central Africa, for the promotion of Commerce and Civilization with a view to the extinction of the slave-trade', Livingstone encapsulated the evangelical fusion of utilitarianism and faith in the service of a higher cause.[91] By his own description, he went into 'darkest Africa' 'with the intention of benefitting both the African and my own countrymen' through 'the development of African trade and the promotion of civilization', thereby trusting 'the invisible hand' of 'free labour on the African soil [to] render slave labour, which is notoriously dear labour, quite unprofitable'.[92]

While Livingstone was involved in bringing to birth a more energetic fusion of faith, science and commerce in 'Darkest Africa', others were more concerned with the problems of Darkest Europe.[93] The associations described previously – such as the Sunday School networks – provided a ready starting point. In 1844, the future Lord Shaftesbury established a coalition (mostly evangelical) to reach 'a wild and lawless race' of street children through 'the Ragged Schools Union'. By 1854, the Union claimed 120 ragged schools in London alone, including 'nearly 14,000 scholars, taught by 221 paid, and 1,800 voluntary teachers.'[94] The 'schools' (often without formal buildings) also acted as bases for interdenominational services, and promoted the further multiplication of cooperative agencies such as the Missions to Seamen (1856) and the Evangelization Society (1864).[95] Apart from suspicions that they did not achieve much in the way of education,[96] however, such efforts could barely impact on the present need, let alone the burgeoning population of the great cities. For this, too, their ambivalent friends (such as Charles Dickens) and enemies (such as the secularisers) criticised evangelicals for their paternalist focus on the symptom rather than the disease.[97]

Again, evangelicals turned to revivalism in order to address the numbers problem. In 1865, the East London Christian Revival Society (soon renamed a 'Mission') was founded by two former Methodist evangelists, William and Catherine Booth. The Salvation Army (as they were renamed from 1878) was an attempt to shape radical evangelical conversion into popular cultural moulds (imperial military, music hall tunes, the idioms of popular entertainment) and to direct these aggressively at the 'Devil's domain'. Both of the Booths had rejected the deadening hand

[91] George Seaver, *David Livingstone: His Life and Letters*, New York: Harper, 1957, p. 308.

[92] Quoted in Seaver, *David Livingstone*, p. 308.

[93] William Booth would capture such concerns in his manifesto, *In Darkest England and the Way Out*; Richard Tames, *London: A Cultural History*, New York: Oxford University Press, 2006, pp. 32–3.

[94] *Monthly Christian Spectator*, 5:1 (January 1854), 63.

[95] Bebbington, *Evangelicalism in Modern Britain*, p. 128.

[96] F. David Roberts, *The Social Conscience of the Early Victorians*, Stanford: Stanford University Press, 2002, p. 210.

[97] Bebbington, *Evangelicalism in Modern Britain*, 125; Lydia Murdoch, *Imagined Orphans: Poor Families, Child Welfare, and Contested Citizenship in London*, New Brunswick: Rutgers University Press, 2006, pp. 5–6.

of Wesleyan Connexional denominationalism, where there was a creeping opposition to revivalism and to the freedom of women to minister.[98] By wrapping their members in uniforms, the Army transcended the gender and class barriers which bedevilled much charity work, and captured the energy of popular 'Holy Spirit' religion for social transformation. In the working-class areas of the Anglophone world (and less spectacularly elsewhere) the Army created communities of the physically, socially and spiritually redeemed, exhibiting many of the characteristics of what scholars would later call 'new social movements'.[99] In the Booths' battle for the nation's soul and social fabric, and against denominationalism, the Army's growth was dramatic: 'By 1879, it had 72 stations in London, the Midlands, the North, and the Northeast. A year later, it had 172 stations and 363 officers. By December 1886, it had 1,749 congregations, known as corps, with 4,192 officers in Great Britain, and 743 corps and 1,932 officers abroad.'[100] Its influence was expanded by the migration of members infected by its policy of 'developing lay leadership from within'[101] and by that keenest of flatteries – unsanctioned emulators among the Philadelphia Irish, black Methodists in Cleveland, on the Pacific American coast and among Adelaide tradesmen.[102] By the 1880s, the group could also be found in France, India and Australia,[103] their confrontational style ensuring newspaper coverage. In Wales, the South Australian *Advertiser* reported, 'the religious enthusiasts who compose what is designated the Salvation Army' had produced 'unwonted excitement' through a number of their leaders being 'committed to prison'. When they were released, 'at least twenty thousand persons assembled to welcome the discharged "captives"... with vociferous plaudits.'[104] The actual events in Wales were less important than the expectation created on the other side of the world. The fusion of the urban mission form with Holy Spirit revivalism, pragmatic Wesleyan theology and the emphasis on incarnational community was a powerful one. A generation later, it would act in many countries as the starting point for the emergence of global pentecostalism.[105]

While hopes for large-scale social transformation continued, and the Salvation Army mounted commando raids from their citadels in 'Darkest London', others sought to cooperate with the 'new world' dreams of imperialists in order to find

[98] Walker, *Pulling the Devil's Kingdom Down*, p. 13.

[99] See Steve Breyman's useful discussion of Melucci et al. in *Movement Genesis: Social Movement Theory and the 1980s West German Peace Movement*, Boulder: Westview, 1998, p. 22ff.

[100] Walker, *Pulling the Devil's Kingdom Down*, p. 42.

[101] Lillian Taiz, *Hallelujah Lads & Lasses: Remaking the Salvation Army in America, 1880–1930*, Chapel Hill: University of North Carolina Press, 2001, p. 21.

[102] Ibid., p. 20.

[103] Ibid., p. 13.

[104] *Advertiser* (Adelaide), 29 October 1879, p. 1.

[105] See entries in M. Hutchinson, ed., *Australasian Dictionary of Pentecostal and Charismatic Movements*, online, http://webjournals.alphacrucis.edu.au/journals/ADPCM/a_/armstrong-maxwell-1881–1959; B. Knowles, 'History of the New Life Churches in New Zealand', PhD thesis, University of Otago, 2003, p. 107.

more morally promising surroundings. Annie Macpherson's revulsion with regard to the oppression of the match industry led her to organise mass child migration to the colonies. She and fellow evangelical Thomas Barnardo sent tens of thousands of children to the dominions over the period between 1870 and 1900. Evangelicals such as Barnardo pioneered humane models for dealing with the children of the poor, such as the family-centred model at the Ilford Girls' Village Home.[106] Like many of their contemporaries, evangelical reformers did not entirely understand the sociological complexity of England's migrant urban populations. The opportunity to do good could lead to unforeseen consequences. As their charitable innovations were caught up (or copied) by the state, evangelicals found themselves involved in large-scale, paternalist social engineering which too often broke up poor families. A century later, several governments were to make public apologies to more than 150,000 children sent under the Children's Act 1948 alone to institutions, orphanages and foster care in Australia, Canada, New Zealand and elsewhere.[107]

In searching for explanations as to why the movement was not conquering all, the continuing divisions within the evangelical body itself was one form of data readily available to the forensic evangelical conscience. In Switzerland, Merle D'Aubigné grieved over Christian divisions: 'Brothers war with brothers and we weep and pray.'[108] William Toase in Paris was dismayed at both the ineffectiveness of evangelical witness and the self-involvement and disunity of European Protestants.[109] Evangelicals in the established Church of Scotland had sadly to inform the Venerable Company of Pastors in Geneva that they would not be attending the 300th anniversary celebrations of the Swiss Reformation because of 'the almost "universal contagion" of Neologian, Socinian, and Infidel tenets and opinions among the Reformed Protestant churches of the continent.'[110] Yet unity was a 'sign' of the greatly desired revival, and so was increasingly elevated in some quarters as a necessity. The proposal for greater cooperation and symbolic public unity which resulted in the Evangelical Alliance produced variant responses. For some in Protestant-minority countries, the call for unity was too much of an admission of *disunity*, which played into the hands of Catholic majorities. The Belgian Edouard Panchaud reported 'not much zeal' for the Alliance, as admission of disunity 'would needlessly put a stumbling block in the way of their flocks', many of whom were first-generation converts: 'it is better', he thought, 'to leave them to their own course of experience than to make them inquisitive into what is passing in other

[106] Murdoch, *Imagined Orphans*, p. 43.

[107] Australian Government, *Lost Innocents and Forgotten Australians Revisited*, Canberra: Government Printer, 2009, p. 13.

[108] *Evangelical Christendom*, 2:1 (January 1848), 2.

[109] Railton, *No North Sea*, p. 11.

[110] Quoted in 'Jubilee of the Reformation', *The Biblical Repertory and Theological Review*, VIII: 1 (1836), 137.

quarters'.[111] This was a subtle challenge for British evangelicals, used to explaining continental unresponsiveness by reference to the sin of *others*.[112] Unity had to be sought in the context of respect for conscience. Within the same decade, therefore, God could be praised for bringing reunion to the Relief and Secession branches of the Presbyterian Church in Scotland in the formation of the United Presbyterian Church (1847), and also for producing a new internal unity through the greatest division of the age: the Disruption of the Church of Scotland to form the Free Church. These divergent results were the product of the same powerful evangelical impetus for reform, as was the disestablishment movement in England which (organised from 1844 as the Anti-State Church Association and from 1853 as the Liberation Society), 'assumed the features of an Evangelical crusade'.[113]

HOMO SCIENTIUS

Failing to grasp the sociological complexities of the time was not an uncommon condition. It was not until 1840 that the word 'scientist' itself was coined and began to displace terms such as 'natural philosopher' and 'experimentalist' in common usage.[114] Individual sciences 'had little professional cohesion' and the general cultural role of science was not clearly defined. Indeed, some leading figures – such as Herbert Spencer – were dilettantes who lived on the edges of disciplines and entertained what would now be considered the most extraordinary 'quackery'. If an unorthodox religious innovator such as Henry James could 'expect science to enforce spirituality', and his more famous son William 'enter scientific school with that assumption intact', we should not be surprised at the continuing tendency of evangelicals to absorb emerging scientific thought into their pre-existing religious worldviews.[115]

Matters changed dramatically in the single generation between 1840 and 1870. In 1840, the conservative American Protestant scientific luminary Asa Gray had already begun to make the observations that would contribute to the theory of evolution.[116] By the end of the period, the theories of his scientific associate, Charles Darwin, had become the linchpin in the modernist doctrines seeking to sweep the religious explanations, which Gray himself retained, out of serious contention. The relationship between the physical and the *social* sciences was even more unclear. Darwin himself deliberately avoided the topic of humanity in *The Origin of Species* (1859) and only fully articulated his views in *The Descent of Man*

[111] E. Panchaud, 'Belgium', *Evangelical Christendom*, 2:1 (January 1848), 18.
[112] Spurgeon, 'The Outpouring of the Holy Spirit'.
[113] Bebbington, *Evangelicalism in Modern Britain*, 136; Stewart J. Brown, 'Preface' in Brown and Fry, eds, *Scotland in the Age of the Disruption*, p. viii.
[114] Paul Jerome Croce, *Science and Religion in the Era of William James*, Chapel Hill: University of North Carolina Press, 1995, p. 260.
[115] Ibid., p. 89.
[116] Ibid., p. 128.

(1871).[117] The change from the ruling Baconian empiricism towards the probabilism that underpinned British Darwinism and American pragmatism was slow and never fully complete.[118] Evangelicals in the period between 1840 and 1860 thus continued to 'feel' for the mainstream of social thought, accepting the reasonable and opposing those things associated with their traditional opponents. Here too, evangelicals were led into opposing positions depending on their social location, but a suggestion – prevailing among modern popularisers[119] – that evangelicals were absent or somehow in conflict with the rise of the sciences is not supported by the evidence.[120] The conflict, rather, was sharpest between (on the one hand) those defending Baconian empiricism and 'Common Sense' philosophy in order to retain perspicuity, and (on the other) those caught up in the institutionalisation of the sciences. Evangelicals found themselves on both sides of the debate, as the terms 'experientialism' and 'experimentalism' drifted apart from one another.

It is not *that* revelation played a central role in evangelical thought which mattered, but *how* it did so. The Bible (as a correspondent of the evangelical Anglican *Christian Observer* noted in 1839), 'ought not to be bended and conformed to philosophy, but more plastic science should rather be assimilated to . . . Scripture'.[121] Evangelicals treated revelation itself as a form of empirical data. It was not in Platonic abstractions that a man found the value of good policy, suggested Thomas Chalmers, but by the modification of 'the generalizations of abstract thought, by the demands of a felt and urgent expediency.'[122] In the work of Finney, even the 'enthusiasm' of revival was reduced to workable proportions. The preacher of the 1859 Ferryden revival, Hay Macdowall, for instance, made such precise calculations of the revival potential of a place that he was said to have 'computed the influence of the Holy Spirit in fractions'.[123] Revival itself was a quantum for observation, with regard to which 'no sane man . . . could think of denying it. There may be something of spurious excitement mixed up with it, but that good, lasting good, has been accomplished, no rational man can deny.'[124]

[117] Peter Dickens, *Social Darwinism: Linking Evolutionary Thought to Social Theory*, Buckingham: Open University Press, 2000, pp. 8, 14.

[118] Croce, *Science and Religion*, p. 90.

[119] Viz. Terry Eagleton, *Reason, Faith and Revolution: Reflections on the God Debate*, New Haven: Yale University Press, 2009.

[120] Levesque and Guillaume suggest it is more accurate to portray the opposition of science and religion as the *cause*, rather than the result, of literalist understanding of the biblical text. Paul J. Levesque and Andrea M. Guillaume, 'Teachers, Evolution and Religion: No Resolution in Sight', *Review of Religious Research*, 51 (2010), 349–65.

[121] Quoted in David Bebbington, 'Science and Evangelical Theology in Britain from Wesley to Orr' in David N. Livingstone, D.G. Hart, and Mark A. Noll, eds, *Evangelicals and Science in Historical Perspective*, New York: Oxford University Press, 1999, p. 121.

[122] Chalmers, *Christian and Civic Economy of Large Towns*, p. 183.

[123] David Bebbington, 'Contrasting Worldviews in Revival: Ferryden, Scotland, in 1859', *Evangelical Review of Theology*, 31:1 (2007), 44.

[124] Spurgeon, 'The Outpouring of the Holy Spirit'.

It was the recognition of evangelical activists that (in the words of Daniel Wilson, Bishop of Calcutta) 'the works of creation, wonderful as they are, are incapable of changing the heart.'[125] Such assessments were not about conflict between religion and science, but about the value of an individual's life and how it might best be spent. Evangelicals were too few and too busy *doing* in order to stop and speculate. To change a society, science had to turn itself into a religion (a teleological system of human meanings), which seemed to evangelicals to be counter-intellectual. 'Pure Science is but the glass, in which the God of Creation is reflected; and, had man to do only with God's creative attributes, then were Science man's true religion.'[126] They already *had* a religion – what was needed now were the levers to change society towards the good. It was this very process that left evangelicals increasingly on the back foot, as their modernizing opponents stereotyped them as remnants of a past rejected by 'advancing' humanity.[127] In fact, the story was more complex. When science showed itself to be useful, evangelicals warmly supported it, introducing it as supporting evidence into their writings and sermons.[128] Interpreters such as Chalmers were in regular contact with evangelicals of not inconsiderable scientific achievements: Sir David Brewster (principal of the University of Edinburgh); John Fleming (professor of natural history at King's College); Hugh Miller, the popularizer of geological investigation; and the Cambridge dons, Francis Wollaston and William Parish (successive occupants of the Jacksonian chair of natural and experimental philosophy), along with their colleague, Adam Sedgwick.[129]

An example of how this worked within the abolitionist worldview was the link between abolitionism and the founding in 1843 of the Ethnological Society. Reflecting the work of Quaker physician James Cowles Pritchard, the Society was committed to the 'single development track' (monogenism) for humankind.[130] Scientific monogenism fitted well with the conviction that all humans had been created by one God in a single historical act. The foundation of the scientific Ethnological Society was thus of a piece with political action towards the Slavery Abolition Act in 1833, with Thomas Fowell Buxton's Select Committee on Aborigines (British Settlements) and with social action towards the foundation of the British and Foreign

[125] Bebbington, 'Science and Evangelical Theology', p. 121. See Croce, *Science and Religion in the Era of William James*, p. 15.

[126] George W. Mylne, 'Science and Literature Considered in their Bearings on Divine Truth', *Evangelical Christendom*, 1 (October 1847), 289.

[127] Bebbington, 'Science and Evangelical Theology', p. 121. Cavanaugh notes the same tendency in politics: 'in what are called "Western" societies, the attempt to create a transhistorical and trans-cultural concept of religion that is essentially prone to violence is one of the foundational legitimating myths of the liberal nation-state' (William Cavanaugh, *The Myth of Religious Violence*, Oxford: Oxford University Press, 2009, p. 3).

[128] Bebbington, 'Science and Evangelical Theology', p. 123.

[129] Ibid., p. 123.

[130] Gregory D. Smithers, '"Black Gentleman as Good as White": A Comparative Analysis of African American and Australian Aboriginal Political Protests, 1830–1865', *The Journal of African American History*, 93 (2008), 315.

Aborigines Protection Society in 1837.[131] That Livingstone's economically inspired anti-slavery campaign in Africa emerges in his correspondence with his friend, Adam Sedgwick, Woodwardian Professor of Geology at Cambridge and an early teacher to Charles Darwin, therefore made more sense to nineteenth-century interpreters than it would to historians in the twentieth century.[132] Sedgwick refused to 'set... up natural religion in the place of revealed: I am no advocate of modern "Rationalism" nor have I once asserted... that man, as a religious being, can be converted from evil to good by the mere natural power of persuasion acting on the moral elements within his bosom, and without spiritual help.'[133]

Evangelicals maintained high visibility in reforming and educational institutions alike, and trod the same paths as other Christians to study in those German institutions where theology, sciences and social reformism were increasingly intertwined. Indeed, one of the great originators of sociology, Max Weber, would do his first quantitative research for the Evangelical Social Union in Germany, while many of those who would later oppose theological modernism (such as B.B. Warfield, R.A. Torrey, and J. Gresham Machen) studied in Germany.[134] Weber's earlier colleagues – Durkheim and Mauss in France, for example – relied heavily on evangelical missionaries to provide them with observations and materials on which to build their social theories.[135] Many of the same criticisms aimed at evangelicals – pragmatism, lack of respect for the particular in the general, intellectual disengagement – were as much a result of a culture shared by Comte and Spencer as the specific outcomes of evangelical religion. As the social sciences worked out their methodological issues, these too were absorbed into a variety of evangelical traditions 'as the essential equipment of the modern minister'.[136] Evangelicals would walk into the latter nineteenth century as both literalists *and* as modernist interpreters.[137] Not all could maintain the tension[138] – for those who remained in

[131] Ronald Rainger, 'Philanthropy and Science in the 1830's: The British and Foreign Aborigines' Protection Society', *Man*, new series, 15 (Dec. 1980), 702–17.

[132] Michael B. Roberts, 'Geological clerics and Christian geologists: Adam Sedgwick (1785–1873): geologist and evangelical', Geological Society, London, *Special Publications*, 2009; v. 310, pp. 155–70.

[133] Sedgwick, *Discourse on the Studies of the University of Cambridge*, p. 130.

[134] Lynn Mcdonald, *The Early Origins of the Social Sciences*, Montreal: McGill-Queens University Press, 1996, p. 242.

[135] As explored in Malcolm Prentis, *Science, Race & Faith: a Life of John Mathew, 1849–1929*, Sydney: Centre for the Study of Australian Christianity, 1998, and see Terry F. Godlove Jr., *Teaching Durkheim*, New York: Oxford University Press, 2005, p. 120.

[136] Michael Gauvreau and Nancy Christie, 'Toward a Christian Social Science in Canada, 1890–1930' in Livingstone, Hart and Noll, eds, *Evangelicals and Science in Historical Perspective*, p. 293.

[137] James Moore, 'Telling Tales: Evangelicals and the Darwin Legend' in Livingstone, Hart, and Noll, eds, *Evangelicals and Science in Historical Perspective*, p. 221.

[138] See, for instance, Vanderford's description of the 'regression to classic natural right theory in Virginia' in order to legitimize 'positive good' arguments for the retention of slavery (Chad Vanderford, 'Proslavery Professors: Classic Natural Right and the Positive Good Argument in Antebellum Virginia', *Civil War History*, 55:1 (2009), 8).

the evangelical camp, the 'war between science and religion' would be dealt with through a balance of intense internal personal spirituality and a sense of location in history.

WARS AND RUMOURS OF WARS

This dynamic relationship with emerging secularism and scientism was particularly evident in the great crises of the period. The Crimean War made Florence Nightingale a national hero but profoundly challenged her faith in the adequacy of good intentions.[139] For his part, the Cambridge mathematician John Colenso walked into a missionary setting where Africans, Boers and Britons struggled with one another for power, and emerged with a Zulu Bible depicting a higher critical Moses. The civil war in the United States brought about *both* the rise of a united country under a powerful civil religion and collapse in Protestant clerical authority.

The American Civil War was a brutal revelation of the tensions inside the evangelical synthesis. Evangelicalism and abolitionism remain closely associated in the popular imagination as 'causes' of the war. It was an impression strengthened by the fact that, when contemporaries thought about America in the 1850s, two names came to the fore: Abraham Lincoln and Harriet Beecher Stowe. The first was a great populariser of a rising American civil religion which used the language of evangelicalism to unite a fractured but expansionary nation. The latter was the evangelical author of *Uncle Tom's Cabin*, an abolitionist tale which long remained the best-selling novel in American history.[140] When the two met in the White House, Lincoln reputedly greeted Stowe with the words, 'So you're the little woman who wrote the book that made this great war.'[141] Stowe, however, was under no illusions as to the nature of the civil war, which she saw as being motivated less by abolition than by the problems of the social and economic order. It was for her a war 'for the rights of the working classes of mankind, as against the usurpation of privileged aristocracies', for the 'poor laborers of Birmingham and Manchester, the poor silk weavers of Lyons', against 'all aristocrats and holders of exclusive privileges'.[142]

Inevitably, it was a war – fratricidal, geographically extended, bloody – which would be fought in the pulpit as well as in parliaments. Religion provided the backbone to fissiparous, 'invertebrate America', providing institutions, press outlets, welfare support and public ideologies where all else was partial, absent or

[139] McDonald, *Florence Nightingale*, p. 29; Robert B. Edgerton, *Death or Glory: The Legacy of the Crimean War*, Boulder: Westview Press, 1999, p. 149.

[140] Harry S. Stout, *Upon the Altar of the Nation: A Moral History of the Civil War*, New York: Penguin, 2006, p. 1.

[141] Quoted in Herbert Mitgang, ed., *Abraham Lincoln, a Press Portrait*, Athens: University of Georgia Press, 1989, p. 373.

[142] Harriet Beecher Stowe, 'Abraham Lincoln', *The Watchman and Reflector* (1864), quoted in Mitgang, *Abraham Lincoln*, p. 374.

conflicted.[143] The Union was thus the most democratic, most profoundly Protestant nation of the age, and the first to resolve its inner demons by national mobilisation.[144] The novelised, journalistic evangelical preaching which Stowe adapted from her father Lyman Beecher's revivalism was a genre more broadly applied to the American search for redemptive purpose, filtered through writing and speaking and magnified in pulpits and from presses across the country. It not only shaped peoples' attitudes towards slavery, but connected earlier evangelical reforms to global human rights campaigns.

At the same time, Stowe (that 'female, evangelical Byron'),[145] demonstrated the problems which arose from the evangelical fusion of sentiment, intense spiritual motivation and public suasion. On one side of the Atlantic, British evangelicals sought a 'middle way' between Catholic 'idolatry' and totalising liberal rationalism, supporting human rights by steady, rational reform. While many British evangelicals held that British liberal institutions relied upon biblical Christianity, American evangelical clergy viewed their voluntaryist religion as essential to the success of the American experiment. Internationally, the two national theologies could (and did) conflict, with the American vision acting (even within the British Empire) as a counterweight to the older imperial narrative.[146] In Australia, for example, American voluntaryism became a major inspiration for Church of Christ and Baptist voluntaryism, a counter-model in Scots Presbyterian evangelical resistance to moderatism, and an influence in the anti-transportation campaigns of the 1850s.[147]

Stowe's romanticism encountered emerging manifest destiny on the killing fields which sprawled over 1,500 miles of the continent, from Harrisburg in the northeast to Galveston in the southwest. With more than a half a million dead, observers asked not only 'whose side is God on?' but 'whose side are the evangelicals on?' The answer was both – and neither. If the war resulted in increased Protestant influence in affairs of state, evangelical clergy – who were competing with the emerging professional sector for public influence[148] – were less clear on just what that influence should be. The American population presented an extreme case of the mobility emerging everywhere as a result of industrialisation. American clergy, therefore, were increasingly drawn into popularist dependence on their

[143] Allan Nevins, quoted in Randall M. Miller, Harry S. Stout and Charles Reagan Wilson eds, *Religion and the American Civil War*, New York: Oxford University Press, 1998, p. 5.

[144] Paul A. Cimbala and Randall M. Miller, eds, *An Uncommon Time: The Civil War and the Northern Home Front*, New York: Fordham University Press, 2002, p. 61.

[145] Molly Hiro, 'Transatlantic Stowe: Harriet Beecher Stowe and European Culture,' *Legacy: A Journal of American Women Writers*, 25 (2008), 335.

[146] See, for instance, John Dunmore Lang, *Freedom and Independence for the Golden Lands of Australia*, 2nd edn, Sydney: Cunninghame, 1857, pp. 310–11.

[147] See Mark Hutchinson, *Iron in Our Blood: A History of the Presbyterian Church in NSW, 1788–2001*, Sydney: Ferguson, 2001.

[148] Miller, Stout and Wilson, *Religion and the American Civil War*, pp. 112–13.

mediatorial position as *vox Dei vox populi*.[149] Abolitionism had previously been a minority interest among the American clergy, but in the 1850s, with an expanding frontier where the identity and economic interests of the North were at stake, a clear shift in evangelical opinions occurred. The Kansas-Nebraska Act (1854) seemed to breach the order on which the nation was founded,[150] making way for the extension of the evil of 'slave power'. 'Bleeding Kansas' fed the discourse of apocalyptic violence back to the eastern states, placing pressure on evangelicals as to the acceptability of coercion and war. Violence followed on its heels, even entering the American Senate, where a leading abolitionist given to 'scathing, intemperate speech'[151] was caned nearly to death by an honour-driven pro-slavery congressman from South Carolina. By the time the first shots were fired at Fort Sumter in 1861, people had been fighting and dying over abolitionism for nearly a decade.

At first, most of these were not evangelicals: Northern evangelicals tended to be either pacifists (in the tradition of William Penn), or against division in that higher spiritual good, the Union itself. It was not until war began that the majority of evangelical spokesmen in the North began to support coercive abolition. In the South, the 'authority' was the individual state rather than a higher Union, and the '"peculiar institution" of slavery was not only expedient but also ordained by God and upheld in Holy Scripture.'[152] Most Methodist Episcopal and other church leaders were slaveholders, and 'slavery was clearly part of the southern vision for an orderly and virtuous Christian America with limited central government.'[153] To Southerners, the war was God's punishment on the North for its nationalist idolatry.[154]

On both sides, churches were stripped of their young men, civil life disrupted, evangelical (and other) theologies bowdlerised and used as political props. In the end, the real religious winners were the respective civil religions of North and South, which incorporated evangelical passion and terminology into their own pantheons, the grand narratives which would have long-term, if divisive, effects on evangelicalism. In the eventually victorious North, 'the Union' effectively replaced God and became the organising point for subsequent American adventurism. In the battered South, civil religion morphed into a messianic catacombs religion, institutionalising continuing inequalities until the civil rights campaigns of the 1960s. Inevitably, there was even greater black-white division in the South *after*

[149] Ibid., p. 112.
[150] Thomas Goodrich, *War to the Knife: Bleeding Kansas, 1854–1861*, Lincoln: University of Nebraska Press, 2004, p. 8.
[151] Ibid., p. 119.
[152] Harry S. Stout, 'Religion in the Civil War: The Southern Perspective', http://nationalhumanitiescenter.org/tserve/nineteen/nkeyinfo/cwsouth.htm
[153] Michael O. Emerson and Christian Smith, *Divided by Faith: Evangelical Religion and the Problem of Race in America*, Oxford: Oxford University Press, 2001, p. 36.
[154] Miller, Stout and Wilson, *Religion and the American Civil War*, p. 120.

the war than there was before.[155] By the time the Jim Crow laws were reintroduced by traditional Southern Democrats returning to power in the 1870s, segregation was a social fact, in the North as effectively (if not as visibly) as in the South. More cogently, the 'Christian' interpreters of the war made comparatively little attempt (apart from a shrill minority of 'injudicious friends up North') to stop Southern official segregation from becoming a legal fact.[156] Meanwhile, when, in 1865, Edwin Stanton (the Union's Secretary of War) sought to meet with leaders of the African-American community to discuss emancipation, he found that most of them were evangelical pastors from Savannah's African churches.[157] From that point on, the black church would grow in strength as the centre of a freed 'nation within a nation'. White evangelicals had failed to match their performance to their public rhetoric. Protest against unfair racial restriction within white churches led in the Reconstruction period to African Americans leaving 'white churches *en masse* to form their own churches'.[158] Public confidence in Northern Protestant clergy declined, both in the long term as church leaders and in the shorter term as public commentators.[159]

CONCLUSION

This loss of authority took different forms depending on the context. It is certainly true that evangelicalism did rather better among the aspirational middling classes than among the elites – another indicator that it was associated with social aspiration and with *movement* rather than *stasis*. It was, at this time, the means, rather than the end, of *embourgeoisement*:[160] in non-crisis periods, 'evangelicals made good capitalists and liberals'. They shared the same core values (frugality, moderation, sobriety and hard work) and defined themselves against the same enemies (intemperance, sloth and Catholicism).[161] The general Protestant tone of Britain, Germany, Holland and the countries of European settlement to which they gave birth promoted a comfortable myth that the liberalising trend of society was to the detriment of superstition and to the advantage of 'reasonable faith'. By preaching morality and obedience, evangelicals thought, the kingdom of God would inevitably come by incremental transformation of the present society. Between crises (wars, depressions and revivals), 'postmillennialism was turning into a

[155] Emerson and Smith, *Divided by Faith*, p. 36.
[156] Ibid., p. 40.
[157] Andrew Billingsley, *Mighty Like a River: The Black Church and Social Reform*, New York: Oxford University Press, 1999, p. 26.
[158] Smith, *Divided by Faith*, p. 39.
[159] Smith, *Professors & Public Ethics*, p. 166.
[160] Bebbington, *Evangelicalism in Modern Britain*, p. 110.
[161] Piggin, *Evangelical Christianity*, p. 24.

theological analogue of the broader middle-class ideology of gradual moral and material progress.'[162]

Such evangelicals found themselves in conflict with 'irreligious influences' among the increasingly self-conscious industrial-trades classes. These included the proto-communism evinced by Marx and popular organisations such as the *Deutsche Bildungs-Gesellschaft für Arbeiter* (the German Workers Education Society), the 'social ideas' developing among workers[163] and their confluence with nationalist secularism. In this context, evangelicals inevitably moved towards support of the status quo; in Germany, for example, some evangelical clergy began to identify piety with pro-Prussianism, a trend which would have bitter fruit in the disappointment which followed the collapse of German missions after World War I.[164] Very few could, like William Guthrie Spence, respond to industrial problems with that evangelical genius for cultural appropriation which made him the innovative edge of the Australian trades union movement.[165] The failure of their vision for a 'reasonable', incremental millennium – as Railton demonstrates in the case of Marx's great supporter, Friedrich Engels – would be a contributor to the search for alternative, non-Christian millenial visions.[166] It was also a contributor to the swing towards premillennialism among many evangelicals under the linked hammer blows of intense revival experience and social dispossession.[167]

The internal alliances which made up the evangelical 'movement' were neither necessary nor monolithic. It was an age when transdenominational Bible Societies would have to consider criticism of entertaining Catholic Apostolics in their ranks, when Darbyite preachers redrew concepts of the millennium and challenged the church's compact with the world, when lectures on 'Apostolic Christianity, the Church's Lost Power' jostled with mesmerists, single taxers and 'electrolytic' healers in the advertisement columns of provincial papers.[168] Evangelicals grew tetchy with one another over perceived syncretism in increasingly plural settings. Railton, for example, points to the tensions between *Réveil* thinking and French evangelical criticisms of 'somnambulism' in German mystical evangelicalism.[169] There was – as the success of Anglo-Scots Irvingism in German settings exemplified – always a

[162] Miller, Stout and Wilson, eds, *Religion and the American Civil War*, p. 115.
[163] Railton, *No North Sea*, p. 101.
[164] Ibid., p. 86.
[165] Stuart Piggin, 'Australia's Christian Heritage: The Untold Story', Address to the NACL, Old Parliament House, Canberra, ACT, Australia, 26 November 2005. See also Melissa Bellanta, 'A Man of Civic Sentiment: the Case of William Guthrie Spence', *Journal of Australian Studies*, 32:1 (2008), 63–76.
[166] Railton, *No North Sea*, p. 114.
[167] Andrew Holmes, 'Millennialism and the Interpretation of Prophecy in Ulster Presbyterianism, 1790–1850' in C. Gribben and T.C.F. Stunt, eds, *Prisoners of Hope: Aspects of Evangelical Millennialism in Scotland and Ireland, 1800–1880*, Carlisle: Paternoster, 2005, ch. 7.
[168] *Argus* (Melbourne), 3 December 1910, p. 13.
[169] Railton, *No North Sea*, p. xviii.

mystical fringe with 'a special taste for speculations on apocalyptic and millenarian topics'.[170] This fringe would remain an important reservoir of alternative vision which refused to allow evangelicalism to settle down and become merely bourgeois, or nativist, or bombastically populist. The movement's core universalism (based on 'the Word' as 'good news for all mankind') militated against being swallowed by nationalism or a specific context. Continental evangelicals touched by the *Réveil* – such as, for instance, Jean Henri Dunant, later founder of the Red Cross – were impelled by their engaged humanitarianism to be present with suffering humanity at the nineteenth century's nation-forming wars.[171] There was no *single* evangelical response, then, but rather a range of responses which reflected biblicism and activism working out in particular locations.

As Western society reorganised itself, evangelicalism's emphasis on principled engagement would see it enter into temporary and often contradictory alliances with 'the World'.[172] In the 1830s and 1840s, American evangelicalism moved towards an alliance with nativism, whereas Australian evangelicalism allied with Richard Bourke's liberal reformism. In the context of aggressive majority Catholicism, evangelicals cooperated with the secular state. Where 'Tractarian' bishops resisted attempts to introduce new state-church relationships based on proportional funding, evangelicals promoted them. Where secular authorities excluded their missions from moving into Nigeria or North Africa, evangelicals opposed them. Expansionist internationalist evangelicalism in the 1840s and 1850s, therefore, found itself seeking effectiveness through affiliation with local and national identities. By 1870, much of the evangelical iceberg was below the water's surface, embedded in local communities and associations around the world, and invisible to its critics.

Such diversity threatened disintegration, but evangelicals adapted and found ways of countering it. They adopted new communications and transport technologies, created theological 'bridging' movements, undertook a deliberate strategy to 'hitch a ride' with expansionary forces such as commerce and scientific exploration, and developed their transportable spiritual theology (revivalism) on a massive scale. In the period under review in this chapter, these innovations were barely beginning to transform the theological life of those who self-identified as evangelicals. Their great upsurge as a truly global religion still lay in the future. In the interim, communities of evangelicals largely faced the local or news-mediated problems of the world as a matter of negotiating their distinctives (biblicism, crucicentrism, conversionism and activism) around what might be identified as three 'key problems'.

[170] Ibid., p. xviii.
[171] John F. Hutchinson, *Champions of Charity: War and the Rise of the Red Cross*, Boulder: Westview, 1996, p. 11.
[172] William M. Shea, *The Lion and the Lamb: Evangelicals and Catholics in America*, New York: Oxford University Press, 2004, p. 56.

The first of these was what to do with the individual-in-community – what was authentic community, the showing forth of the Kingdom of God? All agreed that the "true church" was probably not here among us.[173] Some Anglican evangelicals, however, continued to defend the establishment, others (such as Ryle) continued the fight for a purer expression within the broad tradition presaging the eventual appearing of the church spiritual, and yet others (such as Darby) considered the only defensible path to be withdrawal, gathering true believers together to await the appearing of Christ. Evangelicals responded to the rise of the liberal state by forming *both* new corporatist approaches to the visible church (e.g. the formation of the Evangelical Alliance) *and* by the proliferation of smaller, independent groups (such as the Brethren) which were often anti-establishment.

The second 'key problem' related to the traditional Christian tension of immanence/transcendence. Was the church in the world, or was it a spiritual reality only to be truly realised at the end of all things? This became critical in the mid-nineteenth century, because many evangelicals felt that transcendental crucicentrism made it impossible to live within a secularised established church once the demands of state connection conflicted with revivalism and biblicism. One result was the Scottish Disruption. The East London Christian Revival Society became essential for the Booths when the power of revivalism met the demand of industrial cities, requiring a new form for the Cross to become immanent in Darkest England.

The third key problem related to the question: 'Where are we in time?'. The sheer rapidity of change brought history to the fore in European societies at this time. The age of Buckle, von Ranke, Lecky, and Macaulay – the re-tellers of national stories – was also the age of the emergence of evangelical divisions over premillennialism. Counter to expectations, this premillennial belief was not the Anabaptist quietism of the English Civil War, but an activist strand producing (in the next period) a form of mainstream corporatism. It was a form of 'counter-history' not only to postmillennial confidence but also to the national appropriations of history which legitimised the state. This premillennial vision was aimed at creating end-times communities which would present the church as the 'spotless bride' to the soon-coming Christ. It had the advantage of being able to ask everything of its adherents, because by completing the missions mandate, the last (historical) prerequisite for the return of Christ would be fulfilled. The millennium would then usher in the time of rest, of the rule of the church. Evangelicals located themselves along the continuum producing wide variations in millennial understanding, from traditional postmillennialism, to the historical premillennialism of Müller and Guinness, to Darby's futurism.[174]

The interaction between the first individual-community axis and Bebbington's quadrilateral helps us to understand why 'things fly apart' in a proliferation of

[173] J.C. Ryle, *Holiness*, reprint, Lafayette: Sovereign Grace Pub., 2001, p. 136.
[174] Scott M. Gibson, *A.J. Gordon: American Premillennialist*, Lanham: University Press of America, 2001, pp. xxix–xxx, 74.

evangelical identities in this period. The emergence of corporatist activism saw, on the one hand, the emergence of the Evangelical Alliance, the Red Cross, the Ethnological Society and the Salvation Army, whereas, on the other hand, individualist activism underlay an upsurge of itinerant evangelistic ministries outside denominational structures. Incarnational activists pressed into the cities, while sectarian transcendentalists wandered the world opening new fields (and, more to the consternation of evangelical opinion makers, new theologies). Historicist premillennialists such as Spurgeon, Guinness and Müller built great institutions at the heart of the British empire, while the upsurge of dispensational premillennialism would go on to influence the growth of globe-spanning faith missions. Things flew apart because there was the space, the transportation and communications technologies, and the pressing social and ecclesial issues to push evangelicals out into the world. Between 1840 and 1870, evangelicals – pushed by revival and pulled by the opportunities opened up by the expansion of Western interests – seemed to have found Chalmers' 'place of enlargement' in which they could establish communities which would evince the 'higher manifestations of Christianity'.

5

A New Global Spiritual Unity: 1870s to 1914

When the vigorous anti-Catholic controversialist Hugh McNeile died, the *Times* of London (31 January 1879) felt safe enough to overreach itself by writing not only his obituary, but the obituary of that 'old Evangelicalism . . . whose influence has almost ceased to count in current controversies'.[1] An evangelical champion, J.C. Ryle, soon to be Bishop of Liverpool, replied tartly to the effect that rumours of evangelicalism's death were greatly exaggerated, and driven by attempts to expunge the evangelical voice from Western public conversations.[2] The exaggeration, however, carried force. The cost of Victorian-era success for evangelicalism was its popular association with all that made the age quotidian and bland. Having taught nations the lessons of the First Great Awakening and provided models for mobilising the mass voluntarist society, did it have anything further to give? Science and the stock market cast doubt on it. The world had once been explained in terms of 'divine interventions' (Newton) and the 'invisible hand' (Smith),[3] but these new titans now seemed increasingly sufficient in themselves. In an age where nationalisms projected themselves as semi-religious totalities embracing both private conscience and political behaviour, evangelicals were pushed to reconsider the architecture of their faith, to search for a new unity of external practice and internal conviction.

It was in part a matter of where the observer stood. By the 1850s, evangelicals could stand on a proud history of reform (seen in legislation for individual conscience and working conditions), public welfare (seen in schools, hospitals and charitable institutions) and the restraint of evil (abolitionism). For all their iconic successes, however, the postmillennial dream of the kingdom built on earth had not come to pass. Indeed, to some degree it had been absorbed and bypassed by the confident expansion of national states which sought to wrap claims to ultimate authority in the language of religion.[4] For Americans, the popular press promoted the idea of a 'manifest destiny to overspread the continent allotted by Providence

1 'The Death of Dean McNeile', *The Times*, 31 January 1879.

2 J. C. Ryle, 'Where are we?', *Churchman*, 1 (1879), 3.

3 I. Bernard Cohen and George E. Smith, eds, *The Cambridge Companion to Newton*, Cambridge: Cambridge University Press, 2002, p. 448. On Smith, see Elsie B. Michie, 'Austen's Powers: Engaging with Adam Smith in Debates about Wealth and Virtue', *Novel*, 34:1 (2000), 5–27.

4 Pt 1, Chapter 5: 'every earthly State should be, in the end, completely transformed into the Church and should become nothing else but a Church'.

for the free development of our yearly multiplying millions'.[5] While initially used to tidy up the American map, such claims were universalist at their base, and would be applied to global empire. On the other side of the Atlantic, British nationalist co-option of religion into the state progressed under the aegis of high imperialism towards disestablishment, Spencerian social Darwinism, public welfare and bureaucratization for imperial efficiency.[6]

Evangelicals found themselves divided by such trends, following mixed policies of accommodation, appropriation and separation.[7] Inevitably, variations between place and policy created internal strains when evangelicals attempted to meet as a community of faith. Within the Church of England, Ryle and others noted that merely sharing a location – for example, Exeter Hall, or the Mildmay Conference – was insufficient to create an effective unity. The radicalization of Tractarian and High Church movements (institutionalised in the English Church Union in 1859 and Keble College in 1870) and the confident appropriation of the middle ground by influential "Broad Church" modernisers (such as F.D. Maurice's Christian Socialism and the authors of *Essays and Reviews*, 1860) were both in part responses to the successes of earlier generations of evangelicals. Even non-evangelicals such as Bishop Tait of London had learned to use open-air preaching to reach an 'apostate' nation.[8] Others had revived the Anglican monastic tradition, developed a striking spirituality and aesthetic and found extensive media outlets for their form of engaged conservatism. Evangelicals would also need to adapt. The charge that evangelicals could field no theologians, and were seen as backward-looking dogmatists, was a serious one in 'the age of improvement'.

Ryle's own contributions were significant but limited. His friends, such as Edward Garbett, drew together local bodies of Anglican evangelicals into defensive organisations, from the Church Association (1865) to the National Church League (1906). Wycliffe Hall, Oxford (1877) and Ridley Hall, Cambridge (1881) were founded to train evangelical clergy, and wealthy evangelicals such as Alfred Peache funded 'red-brick' colleges such as St John's, Kilburn (1863).[9] Their purpose was specifically to counter Anglo-Catholic advances in Anglican theological training, 'to help to put down Popish and infidel teaching'.[10] This was not limited to England: Peache funded a chair of Divinity at Huron College (Ontario, Canada),[11]

[5] John Louis O'Sullivan, quoted in Robert W. Johannsen, et al., *Manifest Destiny and Empire: American Antebellum Expansionism*, College Station: A&M University Press, 1997, p. 8.

[6] See, for instance, John Wolffe, *God and Greater Britain: Religion and National Life in Britain and Ireland, 1843–1945*, London: Routledge, 1994, p. 129.

[7] Christopher P. Gilbert, *The Impact of Churches on Political Behavior: An Empirical Study*, Westport, CT: Greenwood, 1993, p. 5.

[8] Joseph S. Meisel, *Public Speech and the Culture of Public Life in the Age of Gladstone*, New York: Columbia University Press, 2001, p. 116.

[9] David Dowland, *Nineteenth-Century Anglican Theological Training: The Redbrick Challenge*, Oxford: Clarendon Press, 1997, p. 71.

[10] Ibid., p. 73.

[11] Ibid., p. 70.

while others (such as Wycliffe College, Toronto, and Moore College, Sydney) sought to contest Anglican churchmanship around the world. Their defensive nature ran against the public taste of the age. That 'acrimonious controversialist' Lord Grimthorpe led the Protestant Churchmen's Alliance, and the intransigence of the Church Association's attacks on ritualists reinforced public stereotypes of evangelicals as angular and difficult.[12] In Ireland these attitudes combined with the hostile Protestant response to Home Rule, to lay the basis for the transformation of 1870s British controversialism into 1920s 'fighting fundamentalism'. The Irish Protestant diaspora from William Dill Macky (1849–1913) to Thomas Chatterton Hammond (1877–1961) took this public style around the world.

Ryle himself was too much the pastor to provide intellectual leadership to the fractious movement: his sort of English Calvinist faith tended to retreat into vibrant local church cultures, centred on a 'great preacher'. Aided by the expanding popular press, this period would become 'the greatest era for religious oratory in British history'.[13] The 'prince' of this crop was not an Anglican, but a Baptist. Charles Haddon Spurgeon's roots in Calvinist Congregationalism, his conversion under the influence of Primitive Methodism, and his early call in 1854 to revive the fortunes of a failing urban chapel (New Park Street Chapel)[14] combined with considerable personal gifts into a synergistic fusion of 'Spirit, word and world'. Within a year, the previously failing New Park Street required expansion, causing the congregation to move to Exeter Hall during renovations. This larger space, too, was quickly filled, with 'the overflow clogging a major London thoroughfare, further advanc[ing] the Spurgeon phenomenon'.[15] Spurgeon resorted to preaching in an open field to an estimated 10,000 people. Although complaining that "scarcely a Baptist minister of standing will own me",[16] he achieved at the end of the nineteenth century what Methodists had done at the beginning: he turned preaching into an effective mechanism for reaching the "nation of shopkeepers" made up of the aspirational urban lower middle classes. In 1861, Spurgeon opened the 'Metropolitan Tabernacle', Southwark – not a church 'but a great preaching hall' combining aspects of the basilica, the theatre and the popular nineteenth-century lecture hall. There he preached (through multiple services) to an estimated 18,000 attendees a week, by ticketed entrance,[17] and became a standing London tourist attraction. 'The Tab's' influence was spread around the world through the training of Spurgeon's Pastor's College and through publications (such as the *Sword and the Trowel* and the *Metropolitan Tabernacle Pulpit*). By March 1863, more than

[12] L.C. Sanders, 'Beckett, Edmund, first Baron Grimthorpe (1816–1905)', rev. Catherine Pease-Watkin, *ODNB*.

[13] Meisel, *Public Speech*, p. 107.

[14] Lewis A. Drummond, *Spurgeon: Prince of Preachers*, Grand Rapids: Kregel, 1992, p. 186.

[15] Meisel, *Public Speech*, p. 128.

[16] Quoted in Lewis Drummond, 'The Secrets of Spurgeon's Preaching' *Christian History*, 10 (1991), 14.

[17] Meisel, *Public Speech*, p. 130.

8 million copies of Spurgeon's sermons had been sold worldwide.[18] The dominance of this first modern mega-church would remain long after his death.

While both Calvinists who warmly affirmed each other's work, Ryle and Spurgeon nevertheless differed in ecclesiology and application. To Spurgeon, Ryle wallowed 'in the darkness of ecclesiasticism' of that 'unclean thing', the Anglican Church,[19] whereas Ryle wished that Spurgeon had a more nuanced appreciation of Calvinism.[20] Again, such differences cried out for, in Ryle's words, a 'new unity'. When it came, however, it was from a source which he could not accept. It would come neither from mere reaffirmation of doctrine nor from better political organisation, but rather from a synergy of global movements combining populist energy with a greater emphasis on personal spirituality, a larger view of God's action in the world and demonstrable effectiveness. These movements were initially focused on the burgeoning midwestern American metropolis of Chicago and the small Lake District town of Keswick in northern England, but had roots and ramifications that spanned the globe, from Sierra Leone to Shanghai and from Maharashtra to Melbourne.

CHICAGO

Internal turmoil and the continuing internal opportunities for expansion would delay the emergence of the United States as a global *political* power until the end of the nineteenth century. By then, however, it had already emerged as an important global *economic* power, centred on great port cities (such as New York) and inland transportation hubs (such as Chicago). Unlike the legacy systems of European countries, American society was built on an expansive hope for new beginnings, for economic wealth and advancement, powered by the greatest migration wave in human history. In some decades, more than a quarter of a million people resettled in the United States every year, part of the outflow of the more than 55 million people who left Europe for other parts of the world across the latter half of the nineteenth century.[21] These newly teeming cities of mass consumption produced, ironically, fruitful seedbeds for faith. As early as the 1840s, British colonies such as Australia ('the future America of the Southern Hemisphere') were looking to the United States for alternative models of state-church relationship.[22] The subtle threat of 'the American option' would become a constant spur for religious innovation in Europe's extended dependencies. This was not through the export of an 'American

[18] Ibid., p. 132.
[19] Iain Murray, *The Forgotten Spurgeon*, London: Banner of Truth, 1973, p. 137.
[20] Viz. Michael Chavura, 'A History of Calvinism in the Baptist Churches of New South Wales, 1831–1914', PhD thesis, Macquarie University, 1994.
[21] Adam McKeown, 'Global Migration 1846–1940', *Journal of World History*, 15:2 (2004), 156.
[22] See J.D. Lang, *The Moral and Religious Aspect of the Future America of the Southern Hemisphere*, New York: van Norden, 1840.

gospel', as some scholars have sought to show,[23] but a more subtle shifting of the centre of Christianity away from state church and imperial norms towards 'new world' models. As Mark Noll has shown, American Christianity participated in a larger 'multi-centering' of Christianity globally, acting as an early and essential catalyst for postcolonial dreams, at the same time shaping and being shaped by the emergence of a global society.[24] This resulted in an enormous release of evangelical energy in the twentieth century.

The American 'hopeful society' was not a homogenously Christian one; the multicultural nation had forged between 1776 and 1865 a malleable but powerful civil religion which incorporated but did not privilege evangelical Christianity.[25] The potential amorality of powerful materialism was demonstrated by the rise of the 'railway barons'. Among these, the corrupt transport king Charles Tyson Yerkes was fictionalised in W.T. Stead's *If Christ Came to Chicago* and as Frank Cowperwood in Theodore Dreiser's *Trilogy of Desire*.[26] Such corruption was the 'flip side' of that dynamic pragmatism which, in the hands of American evangelicalism, converted money into a 'highly moral' force.[27] Transnational, interdenominational evangelicalism provided a moral location in which the transmutation of the material into the spiritual could take place across the church's walls, so that 'Mammon unrighteous all-holy may be'.[28] The 'hopeful society' symbolised by America was increasingly recreated around the world through commerce, education and reform movements. In this society, economic capital could become symbolic capital through the powerful convergence of 'Creation,' 'New Israel', 'People of God' and sacrifice myths which populated the nineteenth-century American cosmos. On the one hand, it could provide a welcome to the 'good works' of a great egotist such as Andrew Carnegie, whereas on the other, it could produce the evangelical philanthropy of America's largest 'gilded age' retailer, Joseph Wanamaker, or an oil magnate such as J. Howard Pew.

Growing up in the midst of family prayers in a strictly sabbatarian and evangelical yet fairly interdenominational Lutheran setting, Wanamaker's first 'big purchase' was 'a small red leather Bible about eight inches long and six inches wide . . . [for] $2.75 which I paid for . . . [from] my own money. . . . [It became] the foundation on which my life has been built, and it has made possible all that has counted most.'[29] In 1857, he became the first paid secretary of the Philadelphia Young

[23] See, e.g. Steve Brouwer, *Exporting the American Gospel*, New York: Routledge, 1996.

[24] M.A. Noll, *The New Shape of World Christianity*, Downer's Grove: InterVarsity, 2009.

[25] See Harry S. Stout, *Upon the Altar of the Nation: A Moral History of the Civil War*, New York: Penguin,2006,.

[26] See John Franch, *Robber Baron: The Life of Charles Tyson Yerkes*, Urbana: University of Illinois Press, 2006.

[27] John H. Hamer, 'Money and the Moral Order in Late Nineteenth and Early Twentieth-Century American Capitalism', *Anthropological Quarterly*, 71:3 (1998), 138.

[28] *The Church*, ix: ns 1 (June 1867), 166.

[29] Joseph H. Appel, *The Business Biography of John Wanamaker*, New York: Macmillan, 1930, p. 16.

Men's Christian Association (YMCA); in 1861, he began his own retail store which by 1880 was the largest retail establishment in the United States. Wanamaker exemplified the energetic American fusion of commercial drive and personal piety, which sought to improve the lives of people through commerce and Christian fellowship. His money fertilised mission societies, the YMCA, the international Sunday school movement, a Penny Savings Bank for marginalized urban workers, the campaigns of D.L. Moody and Billy Sunday and popular magazines from the *Sunday School Times* to the *Ladies' Home Journal.* Under his fellow Presbyterian, President Benjamin Harrison, he would serve as Post-Master General (1889–93). While Harrison was laying the basis for projecting American power into the Pacific, Wanamaker was pushing for prohibition and protection of the Sabbath at home. In the face of sneers about 'Honest John', Wanamaker attempted to reunify faith and secular vocation, and instantiate 'the Golden Rule of the New Testament... [as] the Golden Rule of business'.[30]

Wanamaker was not alone. Most countries of European settlement developed groups of wealthy, activist lay evangelicals. The first generation benefitted from the wealth of the 'gilded age', the second emerged in time to make an impression on the last period before the rise of global corporations erased the role of the individual. In Britain, landed generational wealth transitioned into mercantile and later corporate wealth. The role played by the Countess of Huntingdon in the mid-1700s was, by the 1880s, played by someone like Joseph Tritton of Barclay's Bank,[31] a key figure in the British YMCA and the Baptist Missionary Society. In Australia, the equivalent was the 'Venetian oligarchy', centred on newspaper magnate John Fairfax and retailer David Jones, which dominated Sydney's business life in the 1880s from the diaconate of Pitt Street Congregational Church. They and a small number of other successful merchants (such as John Hay Goodlet at Ashfield Presbyterian) funded churches, missions and charities out of their extensive business holdings while founding significant companies (such as the AMP Society, or John Fairfax and Sons).[32] For such men, as Rev. John Graham said of Fairfax, 'every faculty, affection, and influence we can exercise is a talent entrusted, and of which account must be given.... Faithful stewardship... implies personal service to God, in the service of men... [and] powers which we cannot delegate to agents and societies'.[33]

The larger-than-life energy of a 'railway baron' town like Chicago required a larger-than-life figure. Dwight Lyman Moody spoke to more than 100 million people, reputedly saw a million decisions for Christ and became 'one of the

30 Appel, *John Wanamaker*, pp. vii, xv.

31 Jessie Campbell, 'Tritton, Joseph Herbert (1844–1923)', *ODNB*.

32 Stuart Johnson, 'The Shaping of Colonial Liberalism: John Fairfax and the Sydney Morning Herald', PhD thesis, University of New South Wales, 2006.

33 Stuart Johnson, 'John Fairfax: "Busy for Both Worlds"', MCSI Newsletter, http://www.mcsi.edu.au/documents/Think_P March_03.pdf, accessed 30 December 2009.

best-known and most widely quoted men of the Gilded Age.'[34] A shoe salesman with only a fourth-grade education, Moody's energy and ownership of the American vision saw him succeed in business in Chicago. Caught up in the anti-slavery campaigns in Boston,[35] during the Civil War he served as a conscientious objector in the U.S. Christian Commission of the YMCA, finally entering Richmond with the army of Ulysses S. Grant. Returning to Chicago, he applied his business acumen to build the most successful Sunday School of his time, prompting the recently elected Abraham Lincoln to visit in 1860. He was pastor of the Illinois Street Church from 1864, but after 1866 began to work primarily with missions, as president of the YMCA, and as publisher of his own paper, *Heavenly Tidings*. The destruction of his church in the Great Chicago Fire (1871) sent Moody into an energetic round of fund raising – which, like Whitefield's tours in the previous century, resulted in a major mission. Raising $500 from his long-standing backer, John Farwell, and offering $100 a month to a musician, Ira D. Sankey, Moody set off with few prospects to England.

At first, the only splash Moody made in his starting point (York) was his own promotional copy, and the curiosity value of Ira Sankey's attractive singing.[36] Moody himself struck his hearers as being fairly ordinary, with a strange accent and poor grammar. A Mrs Curtis scoffed that Moody 'had no gift save common sense'.[37] He did know how to use media, however. Supporters raised enough money to send a three-month subscription of R.C. Morgan's paper, *The Christian*, to every one of the 40,000 ministers in the United Kingdom.[38] Morgan's 'publicity machine' made Moody and Sankey 'media personalities', creating the expectation which both encouraged the necessary citywide evangelical unity and created the popular groundswell which guaranteed success. 'Revivalism was Moody's business, and he saw to it with a businessman's attention to detail.'[39] He was not afraid of democracy: gatherings of the working classes were not, in America, read as a preface to insurrection. Moreover, just as he had been building on the results of previous awakenings in Chicago,[40] the mechanism of ecumenical 'invitation' by revival-oriented groups effectively drew this American layman along the pathway of previous revivals. Moving from northern England to Scotland to Ulster, Moody built ever-mounting support where the memory and effect of the 1859 revival still

[34] Bruce J. Evensen, *God's Man for the Gilded Age: D.L. Moody and the Rise of Modern Mass Evangelism*, New York: Oxford University Press, 2003, p. 3.

[35] William Revell Moody, *The Life of Dwight L. Moody*. New York, Chicago: Revell, 1900, p. 30.

[36] Evensen, *God's Man for the Gilded Age*, p. 19.

[37] Deborah Lavin, *From Empire to International Commonwealth*, Oxford: Clarendon Press, 1995, p. 6.

[38] Evensen, *God's Man for the Gilded Age*, p. 23.

[39] Ibid., p. 27.

[40] See J. Edwin Orr, 'A Call for the Re-Study of Revival and Revivalism', tss, Fuller Theological Seminary School of World Mission, 1981, p. 32.

burned.[41] Using the prayer meeting mechanisms of interdenominational champions such as Thomas Toye of Belfast,[42] and avoiding 'political Protestantism', Moody's campaign strategy turned expectation into a sense of active involvement in God's work as he headed south to Dublin, and then back to the major English cities of Manchester, Sheffield, Birmingham and Liverpool. When they arrived in London, Moody and Sankey were already a religious phenomenon, and their campaign in the capital attracted some 2.5 million attendees over a twenty-week period.[43]

Moody's British campaign of 1873–5, his subsequent related success in North America and his return to Europe in 1881 and again in 1891 and 1892 had profound effects. Moody became nearly omnipresent in the printed media, while Sankey's hugely successful printed choruses consolidated interdenominational evangelical commitment to evangelism through popular culture. What had been extraordinary in Spurgeon's Tabernacle – church as theatre, church as event – became through Moody a standard means for evangelical outreach into the twentieth century. Moody's approach mitigated British class antagonisms and European anti-Americanism,[44] facilitating the way for future cultural and theological exchanges and legitimising the already rising tide of revivalism throughout global British Empire connections. The imprimatur given to interdenominational mass evangelism by success in the Anglophone world's greatest city (London) also energised a whole generation of global evangelists (including F.B. Meyer, Rodney 'Gipsy' Smith, C.T. Studd and the 'Cambridge Seven', G. Campbell Morgan and even the less theologically evangelical Henry Drummond) and institution founders (including Wilson Carlile of the Church Army and Henry Montgomery of the Shankill Road Mission). It was at the urban crossroads of British global evangelicalism that energetic American voluntarism found its window onto the world.

KESWICK

The interdenominational dynamic unleashed by the revivals between 1839 and 1873 provided a cultural crucible from which such a new synthesis of Christian experience could emerge. From the Wesleyan perfectionist tradition, Phoebe Palmer, who had already played an important part in the revivals of 1859 and through the 1860s, brought the keystone of holiness and the methodology of the prayer

[41] David Hempton and Myrtle Hill, *Evangelical Protestantism in Ulster Society 1740–1890*, London: Routledge , p. 149.

[42] John Weir, *Irish Revivals: The Ulster Awakening, Its Origin, Progress and Fruit*, London: Arthur Hall, Virtue, 1860, p. 88.

[43] Evensen, *God's Man for the Gilded Age*, p. 45ff.

[44] William R. Hutchison, 'Innocence Abroad: The "American Religion" in Europe', *Church History*, 51 (1982), 73, 75.

circle.[45] Holiness influence also impacted on the English-speaking world through the spread of a growing number of books, particularly those by Asa Mahan (*Scripture Doctrine of Christian Perfection*, 1839 and *Baptism of the Holy Ghost*, 1870), William Arthur (*Tongue of Fire*, 1858); W. E. Boardman (*Higher Christian Life*, 1859) and Robert Pearsall Smith (*Holiness Through Faith*, 1870). While Moody carried the headlines, in 1873 Pearsall Smith was touring southern England and the continent, touching many with his personalist Quaker applications of evangelical holiness. Amid growing opposition from evangelical leaders committed to a slower, progressive model of sanctification, holiness meetings (Cambridge, 1874) became holiness camp meetings (Broadlands Park, Summer 1874), and then 'Union conferences' (Stroud, early 1874 and Oxford, 29 August to 7 September, 1874) and Conventions featuring thousands of people (Brighton, 29 May to 7 June 1875). Many people left these events with a variety of possible models for the 'continuation' of holiness activities on the local scale.

Whereas 8,000 people had descended upon Brighton, T. Harford Battersby, rector of the small Lake District town of Keswick, was thinking of the more limited, rural idyll of Broadlands Park when he circulated an invitation to a holiness convention in the grounds of his rectory. He was motivated by the 'higher Christian Life' that he had read about in Boardman's biographies, as well as a 'significant religious experience' he had encountered at the Oxford conference.[46] Although initial numbers were small (approximately 400), many of those who attended Keswick testified to experiences of the higher life.[47] By 1900, Keswick was surpassing the Brighton conference in numbers. More importantly, it acted as a model and resource base for the many imitators which sprang up around the world at the confluence points of Methodist holiness, Celtic itinerancy, and interdenominational global missions.

Moody's Northfield campus became an effective centre (to which he returned in 1875 to begin building schools, and later a seminary), as did the Geelong Convention in Victoria, Australia (where Keswick preacher George Grubb was sent in 1891), and its offspring at Upwey and Katoomba, while the Keswick 'Colony of Mercy' in New Jersey was founded by the Australian William Raws in 1897. On the European continent, a renewed German *Gemeinschaftsbewegung* tradition (organised in the Gnadauer Verband in 1888, and featuring leading German evangelicals such as Elias Schrenk and Otto Stockmayer) swept up older pietist prayer,

[45] Phoebe Palmer, *Four Years in the Old World*, New York: Foster & Palmer, 1867, pp. 686–7, quoted in Thomas C. Oden, ed., *Phoebe Palmer: Selected Writings*, New York: Paulist Press, 1988, p. 280.

[46] David Bundy, 'Keswick and Evangelical Piety' in Edith L. Blumhofer and Randall Balmer, eds, *Modern Christian Revivals*, Urbana: University of Illinois Press, 1993, p. 129.

[47] Bundy, 'Keswick and Evangelical Piety', p. 129.

teaching and missions circles and introduced – particularly through the teaching activities of Theodor Jellinghaus – thousands of laity and clergy to holiness teaching.[48] From 1886, Anna von Weling's Bad Blankenburg conferences provided thousands of German evangelicals with a continental Keswick option.[49] Robert Pearsall Smith's tours on the continent saw many of the leadership of the Evangelical Alliance – such as Adolphe Monod and his nephew Theodore – adopt holiness teaching in the categories of the French *Réveil*.[50] Influential evangelicals planted Keswick's name on institutions and geographical locations around the world: from Adelaide, Australia to Ontario, Canada; from Maryland, United States to Madurai, India. Wherever pious evangelicals went, Keswick iconography signalled broader attempts at transforming their environment.

Why was Keswick so successful? After all, its theology – a combination of previous streams – was hardly new. Francis Paynter, reputedly England's wealthiest clergyman, was captured by Keswick in 1882. He described the doctrine simply as:

> the life of peace, joy, and victory upon which Christians can enter, and in which they can be kept by full surrender and faith in Christ. It is summed up in the lines:
> "Christ without our safety,
> "Christ within our joy!"
> Not only Christ without, but Christ within. Col. i. 27, Eph. iii, 17. Christ within to apply to us by the Holy Spirit His finished work on the Cross; to manifest Himself in the study of the Word; to cleanse us from sin, and keep us cleansed; to fill us continually out of His fulness; to enable us to identify ourselves with Himself on the Cross; to keep self in the dust of death; to use us as, and when, and where He pleases.[51]

The metaphor (and experience) of enjoying 'spiritual rest' while the divine surgeon worked to cleanse, cure, reintegrate and direct along a singular path of calling was congruent with the broader therapeutic society in which these middling classes lived and placed their hope.[52] As Grant Wacker has said of the movement's younger sibling, pentecostalism, Keswick 'made life better.'[53]

On the social level, Keswick also chanced upon a sheer – but important – coincidence. Keswick's banner "All One in Christ Jesus" connected unity directly

[48] Ibid.; Paul Fleisch and Alwin Gottleib. *Die moderne Gemeinschaftsbewegung in Deutschland*, Leipzig: H.G. Wallmann, 1912; Harold S. Bender, "Gemeinschaftsbewegung." *Global Anabaptist Mennonite Encyclopedia Online*, 1956, http://www.gameo.org/encyclopedia/contents/G4537.html, accessed 28 December 2009.

[49] Nicholas M. Railton, 'German Free Churches and the Nazi Regime', *Journal of Ecclesiastical History*, 49 (1998), 93.

[50] Bundy, 'Keswick and Evangelical Piety', p. 130.

[51] Charles F. Harford, ed., *The Keswick Convention: Its Message, Its Method and Its Men*, London: Marshall, 1907, p. 35.

[52] These are themes explored by Philip Rieff (*Triumph of the Therapeutic*) and T. Jackson Lears (*No Place for Grace*). Viz that archetypical tourist, Robert Louis Stevenson in his *Essays of Travel*, London: Chatto & Windus, 1905, p. 62.

[53] This is the unitive theme of Wacker's *Heaven Below: Early Pentecostals and American Culture*, Cambridge MA: Harvard University Press, 2003.

to ecclesial and imperial concerns, concerns which the middling classes had made their own. Held in a holiday period, in a location increasingly associated with English tourism, Keswick – which was a place where there was 'something to see'[54] – also captured and spiritualised contemporary bourgeois concerns about physical rest and health. It was no coincidence that the modern culture of 'experiencing' place with a guide book in one's hand should converge on this favourite haunt of the Romantic poets, where the spiritual concerns about the experiential self of the English middle classes were being explored.[55] Indeed, through Thomas Cook evangelicalism provided a major stimulus to the development of organised tourism from the pilgrimage and 'Grand Tour' forms it had previously taken.[56] As he would show by his presence at the Grindelwald Conferences twenty years later, Battersby had an uncanny knack for spiritual experience in spectacular locations.[57] Under the tents in Battersby's garden, the Keswick convention united the Methodist camp meeting form with Cook's inexpensive, salutary holidays: good for the spiritual, the social and the physical self of the masses. 'Our desire', wrote Battersby, 'is to let those speak to us and lead us . . . whom God has manifestly led into the secret of the Divine Life, and who are willing to be nothing and let Him speak through them'.[58]

The result was thus necessarily experiential, interdenominational and dynamic. Early speakers came from a wide range of traditions, but the underlying themes established by recent revivals increasingly pressed the perfectionist message into the background[59] and emphasised a second, empowering experience of being filled again and again with the Spirit by 'walking in the light'. In David Martin's terms, it was a mechanism which allowed for 'downward mobilisation' of marginalised peoples.[60] It would not long stay locked up in the comfortable European bourgeoisie, although even there this technology of spiritual activation had all the marks of a quiet revolution.

Almost immediately, Keswick connected itself to the media. Marshall Brothers Ltd, for instance, was located in Keswick House on Paternoster Row, producing dozens of Keswick-related titles (including the *Life of Faith* and the *Keswick Week*) and a wide range of journals for missionary agencies such as the Church of England Zenana Missionary Society, Prayer Union for Egypt, and the Central Asian Pioneer Mission. During the Convention, Marshall Brothers organised bookstalls,

[54] Stevenson, *Essays of Travel*, p. 60.

[55] Rudy Koshar, *German Travel Cultures*, Oxford: Berg, 2000, pp. 1ff.

[56] Piers Brendon, *Thomas Cook: 150 years of popular tourism*, London: Elek, 1990, and his 'Cook, Thomas (1808–1892)', *ODNB*.

[57] Christopher Oldstone-Moore, 'The Forgotten Origins of the Ecumenical Movement in England: The Grindelwald Conferences, 1892–95', *Church History*, 70 (2001), 73ff.

[58] Quoted in A.T. Pierson, *The Keswick Movement in Precept and Practise*, New York and London: Funk & Wagnalls, 1903, pp. 46–7.

[59] Bundy, 'Keswick and Evangelical Piety', pp. 130–1.

[60] David Martin, *Pentecostalism: The World Their Parish*, Oxford: Blackwell, 2002, p. 30.

distributing the profits to the movement,[61] circulating their publications around the empire in advance of Keswick messengers, providing copy to colonial newspapers and taking advantage of the reading publics which emerged in their wake.[62] From 1886, with the renewed interest in the link between holiness and missions, Keswick publications, conferences, and teachings became almost synonymous with mainstream evangelicalism.[63]

Birthed among the English bourgeoisie, Keswick spirituality was made to order as a missionary motivator. It made the difficult seem easy – the 'rest in faith' and indwelling of the Spirit wedded personal faith to an activist absolute assurance. Faith missions – those radical interdenominational forerunners of a post-Eurocentric Christianity – in particular acted as vectors for the Keswick teaching. It was no coincidence that the Student Volunteer Movement commenced at Moody's North American base for Keswick at Northfield and the Australian branch of the CMS through the Geelong Convention.[64] They produced a missionary force dominated by the bright, the privileged, and the mobile, and which would lay the basis for the global student recruitment and organisation of John Mott, Howard Guiness and their successors in the twentieth century.[65] It was at Keswick that Amy Carmichael was inspired by the speaking of James Hudson Taylor, founder of the China Inland Mission (CIM), to make her decision to become a missionary, leading eventually to her establishment of the Dohnavur Fellowship in South India. It was through Keswick that such organisations as the Japan Evangelistic Band, The Faith Mission, Africa Evangelistic Band and La Mission-Foi-Evangile were founded and many others resourced and strengthened. In 1880, Hudson Taylor – who actively encouraged the union of CIM organisation and Keswick practices – asserted that two-thirds of the missionaries serving in the CIM were there because of Keswick.[66] Keswick may not have been representative of what all evangelicals were *thinking*, but it was intrinsically integrated into what evangelicals around the world were *doing*.

Faith missions such as the CIM were perhaps the most energetic outflow of the biblicist, premillennial activism which was empowered by the revivals of the 1850s and 1860s.[67] Founders such as Hudson Taylor did not originally intend to establish

[61] Harford, *The Keswick Convention*, p. 13.

[62] Ibid., p. 138.

[63] Ignatius, 'The Spiritual Exercises', quoted in Walter J. Stohrer, 'Descartes and Ignatius Loyola: La Flèche and Manresa Revisited', *Journal of the History of Philosophy*, 17:1 (1979), 19.

[64] Darrell Paproth, 'Hussey Burgh Macartney Jr: Mission Enthusiast', p. 11, Conference paper, ANZ Missionaries, at Home and Abroad, 1st Biennial TransTasman Conference, Australian National University, Canberra, 8–10 October, 2004.

[65] Valentin H. Rabe, *The Home Base of American China missions, 1880–1920*, Cambridge, MA: Harvard University Press, 1978, pp. 94–6.

[66] Alvyn Austin, *China's Millions: The China Inland Mission and Late Qing Society, 1832–1905*, Grand Rapids: Eerdmans, 2007, p. 187.

[67] Klaus Fiedler, 'Edinburgh 2010 and the Evangelicals', *Evangelical Review of Theology*, 34 (2010), 322–3.

separate missions – they often began with denominational missions, became frustrated with their political politeness, and were energized to do something about it. Taylor commenced the China Inland Mission when his entreaties for existing mission societies to work in the interior of China fell on deaf ears. The son of 'an earnest and successful [lay Methodist] evangelist at home',[68] Taylor was *influenced* by the missional practice of medical missions and the Plymouth Brethren, and *driven* by a sense of calling to China and the need to give account to God. As a medical student in Hull, for example, he started his lifelong practice of going through his house and ensuring that he had no more possessions than were useful to God. 'The effect of this blessed hope was a thoroughly practical one. It led me to look carefully through my little library to see if there were any books there that were not needed or likely to be of further service, and to examine my small wardrobe, to be quite sure that it contained nothing that I should be sorry to give an account of should the MASTER come at once.'[69] He determined to 'have no claim on any one for anything; my only claim will be on GOD . . . and to move man through GOD . . . by prayer alone'.[70] This was the spiritual outlook that led to the idea of the China Inland Mission. Taylor originally joined Karl Gutzlaff's Chinese Evangelization Society, but on discovery that Gutzlaff was largely misled in his understanding as to the openness of China, he left to become a medical missionary in Ningbo. Returning to England due to illness, Taylor tirelessly promoted (as the title of his first book noted) *China's Spiritual Need and Claims* (1865). That same year, he and W. T. Berger founded the CIM in Brighton, accepting in its first year twenty-one missionaries and raising more than £2,000, before Taylor returned to China in 1866. By 1883, his mission had grown to oversee 225 missionaries and 59 churches, fuelled by careful self-promotion through holiness circles and the establishment (with H. Grattan Guinness and his wife Fanny) of a dedicated faith missionary training home in east London (The East London Training Institute, or ELTI). By 1914, the CIM fielded more than 1,000 missionaries, with a Chinese constituency of some 85,000.[71]

Taylor's narrative successfully joined British high imperial 'boy's own' spiritual adventures with the allure of the Far East, while at the same time avoiding association with imperial*ism*. It was a methodology which worked, successfully institutionalising for the first time the principles of cross-cultural missions at organisational level. Around the ELTI, similar faith missions proliferated in order to apply Taylor's faith methodology to other locations, particularly Africa (Livingstone Inland Mission, founded in 1878, the North Africa Mission, 1881, the Qua Iboe Mission, 1887 and the Congo Balolo Mission, 1889). The approach also quickly found imitators across the Atlantic (particularly in the work of A.B. Simpson's

68 James Hudson Taylor, *A Retrospect*, London: Morgan, 1894, chapter 2.
69 Ibid.
70 Ibid.
71 D.B. Barrett, *World Christian Encyclopaedia*, Oxford University Press, 1982, p. 233.

Christian and Missionary Alliance and A.T. Pierson's *Missionary Review of the World*), in Europe (with the formation of the Svenska Missionsfürbundet, 1885) and around the British Commonwealth. These missions were international, interdenominational (organised by statement of faith rather than denomination), staffed not by employees but by 'members' who received no salary, did not require high levels of training or even ordination, included women and wives as full members (including as isolated pioneer missionaries), identified as far as possible with the culture of their host country (including dress, diet and language), expected sacrifice and suffering, emphasised itinerant work and were directed by those in the 'field' rather than by Home Councils.[72]

In 1910 these faith missions were still the junior partner in the missionary enterprise – it may even be argued that their greatest influence in this period was not in the numbers converted abroad, but in their reflex influence on Western churches. Faith mission organisations were not only supported by holiness constituencies, but had a significant impact in reinforcing sense of vocation, effectiveness and identity on the 'home front'.[73] They also acted as a vector for the return to prominence of miracle narratives in Western Christian discourse, an evidential basis used (as Theodore Christlieb did in his *Modern Doubt and Christian Belief*, published in 1874) to counter the rise of modernism in the Western church.[74] Over the longer term, however, their deliberate self-inculturation would become a powerful means for the indigenisation of Christianity in the majority world. Even more than the convention movement as such, faith missions entrenched Keswick spirituality in the global village.

GLOBAL CONNECTIONS

Inevitably, the context in which they needed to act influenced local and regional evangelical approaches to community formation and engagement. Canada and Australia, for example, were big countries with relatively small populations and fewer concentrated resources than the United States. As a consequence, evangelicals in the dominions dealt more with paternal 'big governments',[75] were less able to develop independent subcultures and were much more 'British', with a smaller range of church denominations and traditions. Although Canadian and Australian evangelicals were active politically across the period between 1880 and 1900, the *type* of evangelical politics in the age of steamships and telegraphs was moderate and not

[72] Klaus Fiedler, *The Story of Faith Missions*, Oxford: Regnum, 1994, p. 33.
[73] Dana L. Robert, 'The Influence of American Missionary Women on the World Back Home', *Religion and American Culture*, 12:1 (Winter 2002), 5.
[74] Gary B. McGee, 'Miracles and Mission Revisited', *International Bulletin of Missionary Research*, 25:4 (October 2001), 152.
[75] D.R. Jones, 'The Art of Philanthropy', *Eureka Street*, September 2004, p. 39.

yet ready to recede into fundamentalist subcultures.[76] Where communal survival was at stake, however – as it seemed to be in Ulster when, from the mid-1880s onwards, Home Rule came on to the mainstream political agenda – evangelicalism could be co-opted into a nationalist fundamentalism which undermined the broad, cooperative liberality more typical of evangelical action through the nineteenth century. Such attitudes were transmitted around the empire by the Irish Protestant diaspora.

Although invited, Moody never made it to Australia. Melbourne had to be satisfied with his successors, Reuben Archer Torrey and Charles Alexander. Having taken over Moody's campaigns after the big man's collapse in Kansas City in 1899, Torrey had already made a mark as a writer and teacher on prayer, the Bible and the Holy Spirit. As head of the Chicago Evangelisation Society (later Moody Bible Institute), he took advantage of the invitation to Australia to visit the Society's missionaries in Japan. The ease of travel was startling: what in 1863 took Hunter Corbett six months and caused injury to his health, in 1902 now took weeks, and 'any one can do it'.[77] Torrey's mastery of Moody's revivalist methodology was complete. Intensive preparation, multiple services and multiple locations culminated in meetings in the 8,000-seat Melbourne Exhibition Building where 15,000 people per night struggled to gain entrance. Half the population of the city attended a service, and the month-long Melbourne campaign led to six months of campaigns in Australia and New Zealand, which gained international coverage as 'the Melbourne Revival'.[78] Some 20,000 people made commitments and dozens of candidates volunteered for training for missionary service. Having already visited China and Japan, on returning through India, Germany, England, Scotland and Ireland, the Torrey party's success saw them touch most of the underlying nodes of the global evangelical faith mission and holiness network (with the exception of Africa).[79]

Unknown to Torrey, a graduate of his own Bible Institute had slipped into Melbourne from India to witness the campaign. Minnie Abrams brought with her Manoramabai, the daughter of leading women's rights, literacy and anti-poverty campaigner Pandita Ramabai. A product of the Hindu scholarly resurgence in the nineteenth century, Ramabai's conversion to Christianity in 1883 had been something of a cause célèbre in a country where her reforming activities and achievements had won her the highest honours. 'Social reformer, scholar, visionary,

[76] Lydia Bean, Marco Gonzalez and Jason Kaufman, 'Why Doesn't Canada Have an American-Style Christian Right?', *Canadian Journal of Sociology*, 33 (2008), 899 ff.

[77] Arthur J. Brown, 'Changing Conditions in Eastern Asia' in *Students and the Present Missionary Crisis*, New York: Student Volunteer Movement for Foreign Missions, 1910, p. 57.

[78] Darrell Paproth, 'Revivalism in Melbourne from Federation to World War I: The Torrey-Alexander-Chapman Campaigns' in Mark Hutchinson and Stuart Piggin, eds, *Reviving Australia*, Sydney: Centre for the Study of Australian Christianity, 1994, pp. 143–69.

[79] Billy Graham Centre Archives, Wheaton College, Wheaton, Illinois: Collection Guide, Ephemera of Reuben Archer Torrey Senior – Collection 107.

diplomat and Christian saint',[80] her establishment of famine and women's rescue missions were, like her faith and writings, implicitly critical of both Indian society and the West.[81] Already famous in evangelical missionary and social reforming circles, her Mukti Mission at Kedgaon in Maharashtra was also a centre for YWCA and WCTU activities in India. Ramabai managed both to engage and critique her international friends, fundraising going hand in hand with revival interest and her insistence on a truly Indian Christianity. As her introductory letter noted, Manoramabai's purpose in Australia was to capture the revival spirit in Melbourne in order to fire up indigenous Indian evangelism.[82] Three years later, the same Mukti mission would – among those indigenous Bible women – become an originating point for global pentecostal revival.[83]

Conditions outside the Anglophone world varied immensely, adding to the complexity of the evangelicalism which would emerge in the twentieth century. 'Success' for evangelical attempts to associate their faith with national identity in the West could cause simplistic associations when that faith was transported elsewhere. In some locations (as in parts of Kenya), evangelicalism became associated with the elites; in others (as in Japanese-dominated Korea), with the oppressed. Some societies (such as Ghana) which were tracking towards engagement with the emerging global economy embedded evangelical religion in their growing national aspirations. In Korea, where religious competitors were tainted with anti-nationalism or irrelevance, evangelicalism became a dynamic and popular force. On the other hand, where elites became associated with retreating imperialism, churches, missions and social welfare agencies could become the targets. In China, this would eventually lead, on the one hand, to attacks on indigenous Christians and the expulsion of missionaries, and on the other to cultural appropriations into popular shamanism.[84] The progressive disaster of the Taiping rebellion in China (1850–64) – leading to the deaths of some 20 million people – placed Western evangelicals on alert with regard to the danger of indigenous nationalist appropriations of Christianity while projecting into the Chinese future a model of religious nationalism. The Boxer Rebellion, at the end of the century, specifically targeted

[80] Ruth Vassar Burges, 'Pandita Ramabai: A Woman for All Seasons', *Asian Journal of Pentecostal Studies*, 9:2 (2006), 183.

[81] Pandita Ramabai (trans. Meera Kosambi), *Pandita Ramabai's American Encounter*, Bloomington: Indiana University Press, 2003, p. 19.

[82] 'Mission Work in India,' *The Advertiser*, 26 September 1902, p. 6.

[83] Gary B. McGee, '"Latter Rain" Falling in the East: Early-Twentieth-Century Pentecostalism in India and the Debate over Speaking in Tongues', *Church History*, 68 (1999), 656; Jay R. Case, 'And Ever the Twain Shall Meet: The Holiness Missionary Movement and the Birth of World Pentecostalism, 1870–1920,' *Religion and American Culture*, 16:2 (Summer 2006), 125–60.

[84] Wang Gungwu, *Anglo-Chinese Encounters since 1800: War, Trade, Science, and Governance*, Cambridge: Cambridge University Press, 2003, p. 75.

Christian missionaries and converts as 'second class devils'.[85] The lessons learned created hesitation about emerging indigenous forms. Many of those who might have assisted in building bridges between the cultures – such as Brahmo Samaj reformer Keshub Chunder Sen – were left confused by the spectacle of European missions abroad and European secularism at home, between a gospel of love and an alien culture given to 'traducing our [Indian] nationality and national character, and . . . distrusting and hating Orientalism'.[86] The class assumptions and the cultural and educational origins of the more motivated missionary constituencies also often reinforced cultural dislocation.[87]

For their part, many colonial administrators[88] resorted to 'covert forms of official resistance to missionaries',[89] ranging from administrivia to redrawing national boundaries (such as in the Sudan and Nigeria) in order to control missionary expansion. Evangelical missionaries needed, first, to break out of the dual trap of paternalism and Eurocentrism, which sought to protect indigenous converts, and then from the increasingly expensive 'social service' ghetto (both ideological and organisational/ financial) into which missions were pressured by the apparent ineffectiveness of preaching, as well as colonial demands for a 'useful' church.[90]

In Africa, the 'most considerable and confident Christian community' was to be found in the states which were to make up Nigeria. Despite (or perhaps because of) the perceived British Anglican betrayal of the first African bishop (Samuel Crowther), the spread of a particularly Yoruba form of Christianity escaped the boundaries of the Yoruba mission and spread inland. It became the first major non-Western culture to realize Henry Venn's dream of a church which was 'self-propagating', as well as theoretically 'self-supporting and self-governing'.[91] The appointment of African Methodist ministers on the Gold Coast also led to rapid indigenization under the guidance of Thomas Birch Freeman.[92] The result was the development of a 'rather pan-African culture of the wider coastal world with its "civilized" and Christian emphases'. By 1870, all the leaders of the Fante

[85] 'Address on India', *The Mercury*, 27 May 1915, p. 3; Michael H. Hunt, *The Making of a Special Relationship: The United States and China to 1914*, New York: Columbia University Press, 1983, p. 186.

[86] 'Jesus Christ: Europe and Asia' in *Keshub Chunder Sen's Lectures in India*, pp. 33–34, quoted in Theodore De Bary, Stephen N. Hay, Royal Weiler, and Andrew Yarrow, eds, *Sources of Indian Tradition*, New York: Columbia University Press, 1958, p. 615.

[87] Robert E. Frykenberg and Alaine Low, eds, *Christians and Missionaries in India: Cross-Cultural Communication since 1500*, Grand Rapids: Eerdmans, 2003, p. 22.

[88] Hunt, *The Making of a Special Relationship*, p. 161.

[89] Frykenberg and Low, *Christians and Missionaries in India*, p. 56.

[90] Wang, *Anglo-Chinese Encounters*, p. 77.

[91] Jehu Hanciles, *Euthanasia of a Mission: African Church Autonomy in a Colonial Context*, Westport: Praeger, 2002, p. 25.

[92] Adrian Hastings, *The Church in Africa 1450–1950*, Oxford: Oxford University Press, 1994, p. 341.

Confederation (which formed in 1868 to seek self-rule) were 'Ethiopianist' Methodists – 'people successfully merging African political aspirations of a modern sort with a measure of traditional culture as well as of Christian commitment'.[93] In China, the appropriation of imperial power by missionaries against a coherent Middle Kingdom drove the emergent state towards an areligious (even secular) approach on the Japanese model.[94] In India, British pressure forced the emergence of an Indian nationalism based on a resurgent indigenous religion. In Africa, by way of contrast, the more fragmented tribal settings produced situations where it seemed natural for state building to include an indigenised Christian component.

The entry of an expansive United States into world politics destabilised old colonial establishments and inserted 'free market' themes which were caught up by missionaries and indigenous Christians alike. American anti-colonialism would determine many of the tensions in the global twentieth century,[95] beginning with the formal release of millions of Afro-American slaves after the Civil War. The resulting multidirectional migrations carried with them 'a resilient form of Judeo-Christian faith fused to an African base' which became self-organising among 'Negro Methodists' and 'Negro Baptists' in the New World,[96] and helped drive the emergence of the 'Black Atlantic'.[97] In Sierra Leone, fiercely independent Nova Scotian settlers laid the basis for the indigenous African spirituality now commonly referred to as 'ethiopianism', leading to the foundation of an independent West African Methodist Church.[98] This stratum of opinion laid the basis for later generations to begin to agitate for a more truly indigenous church and nation, under the leadership of rising African middle-class professionals such as James Beale Horton (educated at Fourah Bay, King's College, London, and Edinburgh University) and Samuel Crowther's grandson, Herbert Macaulay. The first was a major intellectual contributor to British thinking about self-determination, and the second is still widely considered the father of Nigerian nationalism.[99] Both had their roots in evangelical action and both contributed to the shape of the world in which evangelicalism would need to work.

The entry of increasingly wealthy protagonists of indigenous evangelicalism made the Eurocentrism of evangelical missions apparent. As Ian Welsh notes, Chinese evangelists such as Cheok Hong Cheong – who came to Australia for

[93] Ibid., p. 342.

[94] Wang goes so far as to call the Japanese influence on China's modernization 'a kind of conversion' (p. 79); '... a secular conversion did take place between the years 1901–1910' (p. 81).

[95] William Roger Louis, 'American Anti-Colonialism and the Dissolution of the British Empire', *International Affairs*, 61 (1985), 395–420.

[96] Tiffany R. Patterson and Robin D.G. Kelley, 'Unfinished Migrations: Reflections on the African Diaspora and the Making of the Modern World,' *African Studies Review*, 43:1 (2000), 13.

[97] Ibid.

[98] Hanciles, *Euthanasia of a Mission*, p. 152.

[99] Ibid., pp. 152ff; Hakim Adi and Marika Sherwood, eds, *Pan-African History: Political Figures from Africa and the Diaspora since 1787*, New York: Routledge, 2003, p. 86.

economic reasons but were converted and trained in Australia – often found themselves depicted as 'fractious' or unstable because they opposed white-dominated decision making. 'Disobedient' behaviour by non-European converts was seen as evidence of syncretism – in the case of Chinese ministers, the lingering effects of Confucianism, nationalism or 'low racial characteristics'.[100] Cheong dealt with this by participating in his father's business, by switching church allegiances (so using his relatively rare linguistic skill set to his advantage) from the Presbyterian to the Anglican Church, and by positioning himself as the English-language spokesman for China's interests in Victoria and Australia.[101] A Sinophile, Cheong's success in church life led to a greater Australian awareness of Chinese issues – not only did he found two Chinese-language training programs for ministers, but he was also prominent in political movements seeking reform in China, and reform of Western attitudes towards China. He pointed out the patent hypocrisy of the West which preached a gospel of self-denial but sold opium into China.[102] Chinese Christian mercantile communities in the world's gateway cities (e.g. Vancouver, Toronto, New York, San Francisco and Los Angeles) resisted absorption in a society typified by racist attitudes and legislation.[103] When Western migration laws began to change around the world between 1960 and 1980 (exclusion in the United States ended in 1943), such communities would become an important basis for mission to the growing Chinese and Asian populations in the newly multicultural societies.

RETHINKING MISSION STRATEGIES

As the 'spearhead' of 'Western knowledge culture, and power',[104] evangelical missionaries often 'saw' the issues arising in culture contact situations before their sending agencies and societies. A key concern was the growing discontinuity between the religiously-integrated world of the peoples among whom they lived and the religious disintegration of the West from which they came. Growing evangelical disappointment with the latter was one reason why premillennialism – as a sort of 'tao' of dispossessed evangelical fatalism, and as a means of distancing themselves from their sending cultures – began to take hold in evangelical and missionary ranks. Government involvement in 'mission' school curricula, they saw, effectively usurped the institution's raison d'être. As Rev. R. Thackwell, of the

[100] See Hunt, *Making of a Special Relationship*, pp. 295ff. for how this played out with regard to the Lien-chou massacre of Presbyterian missionaries in Kwangtung in 1905.

[101] Ian Welch, 'Cheok Hong Cheong, 1851–1928', *St Mark's Review*, 171 (Spring 1997), 23.

[102] Welch, 'Cheok Hong Cheong', 24. See also Huping Ling, 'Reconceptualizing Chinese American Community in St. Louis: From Chinatown to Cultural Community', *Journal of American Ethnic History*, 24:2 (Winter 2005), 65–101; Hunt, *Making of a Special Relationship*, p. 26.

[103] Emily Aronson and Robert B. Kent, 'A Midwestern Chinatown? Cleveland, Ohio in North American Context, 1900–2005', *Journal of Cultural Geography*, 25:3 (2008), 306.

[104] Jehu Hanciles, 'Migration and Mission: The Religious Significance of the North-South Divide' in Andrew Walls and Cathy Ross, eds, *Mission in the 21st Century: Exploring the Five Marks of Global Mission*, Marynoll: Orbis, 2008, p. 120.

American Presbyterian Mission in Umbala, Haryana, complained to the Punjab Missionary Conference, Lahore in 1858, no matter how 'much the missionary may be anxious to keep the Bible in the foreground . . . his pupils, seeing that it is proficiency in the secular branches of learning only, that leads to preferment, will pay more attention to those branches than to the Bible.'[105] Nationalism and secularism combined were powerful tools for the emergence of a divinised nation state.

Evangelicals were less united on the degree to which science and modernism posed a threat. Although *The Origin of Species* had been published in 1859, its impact was less an explosion than a gradually percolating set of adaptations. 'Particular religious communities, in particular space-time settings, developed particular tactics for coping with particular evolutionary theses.'[106] At first, the issue was the conflict between Darwin's method and the Baconian presuppositions of the day, leading to criticisms of Darwin's 'unscientific assumption against the supernatural'.[107] Protestant leaders of widely varying theological persuasions (including advanced thinkers such as Congregationalist Horace Bushnell, moderates such as Episcopalian Phillips Brooks and conservatives such as Presbyterian Charles Hodge) united in rejecting Darwin's transmutation hypothesis as simply bad science.[108]

Conservative Protestants such as Asa Gray argued with his friend Darwin that the theory of evolution did not void God's providence and maintenance of the world.[109] As crusaders such as Thomas Huxley preached the reductionist form of Darwin's theory in such a way as to divorce faith from knowledge,[110] however, the general confidence underpinning both the evangelical doctrinal consensus and the socio-religious compacts of the late-nineteenth-century West began to come undone. Again, evangelicals responded in different ways. Some took it as an assault on biblical authority – and therefore on the human social condition. From 1878, the Presbyterian John I. Duffield held that Darwinianism was 'irreconcilable with what the Scriptures teach as to man's original and present spiritual condition'. Other conservatives defined a form of theistic evolution, allowing them to affirm evolution within the boundaries of historic Christian doctrines. Yet others saw a new synthesis based on scientific naturalism (such as Herbert Spencer's Social

[105] *Report of the Punjab Missionary Conference at Lahore, in December and January, 1862–63*, Lodiana: American Presbyterian Mission Press, 1863, p. 47.

[106] David Livingstone, 'Situating Evangelical Responses to Evolution' in David N. Livingstone, D.G. Hart, and Mark A. Noll, eds, *Evangelicals and Science in Historical Perspective*, New York: Oxford University Press, p. 194.

[107] Quoted in Andrew R. Holmes, 'Biblical Authority and the Impact of Higher Criticism in Irish Presbyterianism, ca 1850–1930', *Church History*, 75 (2006), 355.

[108] Mark Noll, *The Scandal of the Evangelical Mind*, Grand Rapids: Eerdmans, 1995, p. 179.

[109] Asa Gray, 'The Origin of Species by Means of Natural Selection', in his *Darwiniana: Essays and Reviews Pertaining to Darwinism*, New York: Appleton, 1888, p. 67.

[110] Paul White, *Thomas Huxley: Making the "Man of Science"*, Cambridge: Cambridge University Press, 2003, p. 102.

Darwinist sociology) as the foundation for inquiry into the religious quest.[111] Despite James Bashford's warning at the great Missions conference in Edinburgh in 1910 that five years previously, by defeating the Russian fleet, Japanese battleships had sent comfortable Spencerian myths of European superiority to the bottom of the Tsushima Straits,[112] Social Darwinism could still be found informing the missiologist Julius Richter's descriptions of 'the primitive races.'[113]

As we shall see, the presence of Richter, Meinhof, Mirbt, Berner and Warneck at Edinburgh in 1910 was symbolic of another ongoing evangelical concern: the spreading influence of 'the German theology'. Evangelical missionaries ran into it among, for instance, Japanese students and thinkers returning from German universities. From 1885, the German Allgemeiner Evangelisch-Protestantischer Missionsverein specifically advocated liberal theology and higher criticism in its missions work. The growing coolness on the part of Asian (particularly Japanese) elites towards Christianity reinforced the suspicion of missionaries towards liberal theology, and began to cause splintering of the missionary comity.[114] In Africa, J.W. Colenso's translation of the Bible into Zulu led him (originally on the grounds of German philology absorbed as a student at Cambridge) to doubt the efficacy of treating some Old Testament accounts as historical. His book, *The Pentateuch and the Book of Joshua Critically Examined*, became a target for the reactions which had already been building against the incursions of *The Origin of Species* and Jowett's assertion in *Essays and Reviews* (1860) that the Bible should be read like any other book.[115] The absorption of 'Tubingen School' secularist presumptions collapsed the long-accepted unity between the evangelical clergyman and science. Over time, rationalist-Christian approaches would impact on Japanese appropriations of Christianity into Confucian settings.[116] Elsewhere, some would absorb and attempt to apply the 'scientific' approaches to scriptural interpretation. Others, such as R.A. Torrey, would build their authority on the fact that they had mastered the German theology (in his case at Leipzig and Erlangen) and rejected it for the 'pure' word of God.[117]

German evangelicals, however, were not readily co-opted. The German Pietist tradition had its own historical relationship to 'evangelische' Lutheranism,

[111] Quoted in Noll, *Scandal of the Evangelical Mind*, p. 180.

[112] World Missionary Conference, *The History and Records of the Conference*, Edinburgh: World Missionary Conference, Oliphant, Anderson & Ferrier, 1910, p. 247.

[113] Julius Richter, 'The Decisive Hour in the History of Protestant Missions' in Student Volunteer Movement, *Students and the Present Missionary Crisis*, New York: SVM, 1910, p. 119.

[114] Mark R. Mullins, *Handbook of Christianity in Japan*, Boston: Brill, 2003, p. 42.

[115] Ronald L. Numbers, '"The Most Important Biblical Discovery of our Time": William Henry Green and the Demise of Ussher's Chronology', *Church History*, 69 (2000), 257–76.

[116] E.g. the addition of neo-Confucian content to the canon of the Bible by The Way. Mullins, *Handbook of Christianity in Japan*, p. 156.

[117] R.A. Torrey, ed, *The Higher Criticism and the New Theology, Unscientific, Unscriptural, and Unwholesome*, New York: Gospel Publishing House, 1911.

to a different and ultimately contending form of imperialism,[118] a commitment to university education and scientific engagement and its own missionary tradition. The historical reliance of Anglican and Presbyterian Churches on Pietist and Moravian missionaries in new frontiers only reinforced their sense of efficacy.[119] The Europeans were suspicious of Anglophone dominance and American enthusiasm, which (they felt) could lead to the boiling-down of the faith to a lowest common denominator. Warneck in particular had already criticised the premillennialist drive behind much of the American missionary push, taking aim at Mott's battle cry, 'The evangelization of the world in this generation' (also known as 'the watchword'), at the 1897 international missions conference. In 1900, he (and most of the German delegates) had refused to attend the Ecumenical Missionary Conference in New York, sending a message that warned against the rashness and quantity-mindedness of the watchword, and against an Anglo-American propensity to export Western language and culture along with Christianity. 'Our Lord did not command anything sounding like "Go ye and teach English to every creature."'[120] A decade later at Edinburgh, Carl Theodor Mirbt (University of Marburg) reminded his American and English audience that mission studies in German universities took place in a purely secular and scientific environment: 'in a German university, missions can only become a subject of teaching on condition that they are treated in a truly scientific way. Our notion of universities would not allow the treatment of the subject in a merely practical or edifying manner. Lectures are not sermons. We are convinced that missions can stand scientific enquiry, and that they will profit by it.'[121]

There was a large difference between theological discussion over modernism within church bureaucracies and its impact in the pews. It was not until World War I that such 'external threats' impacted widely on the expansive network of evangelical missionary societies, conferences, voluntary societies, churches and seminaries. Mildmay, Keswick and their international network of conventions and prayer circles, Moody's Northfield, Halle – all progressed and indeed continued to grow energetically. The warning signs might, however, have been read in the growing number of local conflicts – particularly in American Baptist and Presbyterian theological colleges – over modernist or doctrinal issues. In 1878–9, Alexander Winchell and Crawford H. Toy resigned for the same reason from their respective institutions (Methodist Vanderbilt University and the Southern Baptist Seminary

118 Christopher M. Clark, *Iron Kingdom: The Rise and Downfall of Prussia, 1600–1947*, Cambridge, MA: Harvard University Press, 2006, p. 131ff.

119 Felicity Jensz, 'Imperial Critics: Moravian Missionaries in the British Colonial World', History Conference and Seminar Series, University of Melbourne, no. 18 (2008), online version, http://www.msp.unimelb.edu.au/eoe/index.php/missions/article/view/15, accessed 8 January 2010.

120 Hutchison, 'Innocence Abroad', 79–80.

121 Carl Theodor Mirbt, 'The Extent and Characteristics of German Missions', in World Missionary Conference, *History and Records of the Conference*, p. 212.

at Louisville): 'questionable' teaching on the subject of Genesis.[122] Of more importance were accusations of heresy regarding the Christian intelligentsia, whose works contributed directly to the training of ministers and evangelical engagement with the world. When William Robertson Smith, Professor at the Free Church College in Aberdeen, was 'libelled' in 1876 for his historical-critical approaches to Scripture, it was a direct challenge to the idea of a biblical/evangelical science.[123] Despite his dismissal in 1881, the schisms of 1892 and 1900, resulting in the Free Presbyterian Church and the continuing Free Church of Scotland, showed that the issue had not gone away.[124] The case involving Charles Augustus Briggs (1891) pointed to divisions within denominations (in his case, between the wealthy, privileged Presbyterian foundations at Union Theological Seminary and Princeton Theological Seminary), problems with the concept of 'revelation' (particularly the biblical text) in a modern context and the issue of individual rights with regard to corporate conscience.[125] The first reflex was to preserve unity. The ageing D.L. Moody asked rhetorically, 'Couldn't they [the critics] agree to a truce and for ten years bring out no fresh views, just to let us get on with the practical work of the kingdom?'[126] For Glenn Atkins, 'the ten or fifteen years before the war were, controversially, a kind of Truce of God.'[127] It was, however, a truce based on functional separation: the critics would do the thinking while the evangelicals would do the preaching; the critics could have the theological colleges, while evangelicals increasingly emphasised their Bible institutes, conventions and their extensive missions networks. It was not an arrangement which could last, precisely because the aspirations of both were global and dependent on local church support.

For evangelicals, the failure to 'Christianise' a rising Japan and stirring China threatened a view of the world held since the 1790s. Moreover, simply replicating the West throughout the world threatened to spread the contagion of materialism, secularism and nationalism in such a way as to silence the evangelical voice. For historical premillennialists (such as H. Grattan Guinness), the closing of doors to worldwide evangelization would be a roadblock to the return of Christ. 'It is,' Robert Speer regretted, 'in the weakness of our faith that these hindrances bar the speedy coming of the day of His triumph.'[128] Such a thing was unthinkable. Added to the threat of the 'great civilisations' of the East was the (to evangelicals) frustratingly resistant culture of Islam. Since Byzantine times, it had been an alien threat, and more lately, the Ottomans were the 'sick man of Europe'. Islamisation spreading across Africa was a threat to Christian missions south of the Sahara,

[122] Marsden, *Fundamentalism and American Culture*, p. 103.
[123] Livingstone, 'Situating Evangelical Responses to Evolution', p. 197.
[124] Wolffe, *God and Greater Britain*, pp. 165–6.
[125] Mark Massa, *Charles Augustus Briggs and the Crisis of Historical Criticism*, Minneapolis: Fortress, 1990.
[126] Quoted in Marsden, *Fundamentalism and American Culture*, p. 33.
[127] Ibid., p. 106.
[128] World Missionary Conference, *History and Records of the Conference*, p. 153.

particularly among the Hausa in Nigeria. At the battles of Khartoum (1885) and Omdurman (1898), Islamic messianism had written itself into the British imperial chronicle. As Samuel Zwemer noted in 1910, even if a 'Christian Far East' were realised, Islam would still present a 'great, central, unsympathetic, alien, and hostile wedge' between Europe and the East 'exhibiting to God and man not merely a seam, but a rent, from top to bottom, in the seamless robe of the great Catholic Church.'[129] The challenge was a great one. Even liberal evangelicals such as Methodist Episcopal Bishop J.W. Bashford sought for spiritual power to meet the pressing needs of the present. 'Not since the days of the Reformation, not indeed since Pentecost, has so great an opportunity confronted the Christian Church,' he told the delegates at Edinburgh in 1910. 'Oh that out of this Conference may come the spiritual power for the evangelisation of the Orient!'[130]

Conservative evangelicals were less inclined to believe that a conference or a state would provide the answer, but were themselves divided as to how history could be expected to move next. Experimental Calvinist postmillennialism was much more plausible in the period of strong church, weak secular state, and expanding frontiers. The emergence of a strong secular state, an increasingly marginal church and the decreasing openness of the frontiers favoured its early-nineteenth-century competitor, premillennialism. What had been a minority theological position, marginalised by expulsion and schism in the 1840s, was by the 1870s a significant force, with its own networks, institutions and demonstrable global effectiveness. When in 1910 Karl Kumm stood up at Edinburgh to report the advances of Islam in Africa, it was at the weakness of hazy liberal postmillennialism that he directed his critique. He was echoing the concerns of the humble and the marginalised in the great Protestant bureaucratic churches who held the transatlantic high ground. As Dyson Hague noted with regard to William Robertson Smith, although many of the leading higher critics were 'of deep piety and high spirituality',[131] many of the questions they asked were the questions of Western intellectuals caught up in an age of increasing individualism and disciplinary redefinition. 'How can Christianity be freed from restraining doctrines?' was not at the top of the list of questions being asked by Indian peasants, Chinese merchants or evangelical missionaries.[132]

By 1910, evangelical missions administrators were still bewailing the lack of missionary sensitivity to the way that Chinese and Indian peoples *received* the

[129] W. H. T. Gairdner, *Edinburgh 1910: An Account and Interpretation of the World Missionary Conference*, Edinburgh: Oliphant, Anderson and Ferrier, 1910, p. 75.

[130] G. R. Grose, *James W. Bashford: Pastor, Educator, Bishop*, New York, Cincinnati: The Methodist Book Concern, 1922, p. 51.

[131] Dyson Hague, 'The History of Higher Criticism', *The Fundamentals*, vol. 1, Chicago: Testimony Publishing Company, 1910, p. 37.

[132] Thomas Ice, 'Craven, E. R.' in M. Crouch, ed., *Dictionary of Premillennial Theology*, Grand Rapids: Kregel, 1997, p. 74.

gospel. The Edinburgh Missions Conference of that year was an interdenominational, Protestant meeting to marshal the resources to carry out the great task of evangelising the world.. One in a series of such conferences, the attraction of Edinburgh for evangelicals was its promise as a solution to their continued global search for unity, a search which had achieved extraordinary focus at the 1893 World Parliament of Religions in Chicago, and which would shortly be torn to shreds by World War I. As a search, however, it was better at raising the key questions than answering them. Evangelicals (and Edinburgh 1910 was not purely an evangelical event) were very broadly confident that progress had been made. Casting his eye over a century's work in foreign missions the year before, Arthur Brown had noted: 'Taking a broad view of the non-Christian world today, two million converts have been enrolled, and the number actually added last year was 167,674, an average of about 450 a day.'[133]

Progress there had been, but the consistent tone of publications was a sense of perpetual confidence in the midst of motivating crisis. For William Gairdner, the motivating crisis for the 1910 Edinburgh Missionary Conference was external – the victory of an Asian power over a European power in the Russo-Japanese War of 1905, and the release of violent nationalisms around the world.[134] The manner in which the Conference could bring together 1,200 'missionary specialists' indicated the degree to which evangelical missions had become bureaucratised and made into a business where effectiveness was a key value. Inevitably, the larger the professional cadre dedicated to solving problems, the more problems there seemed to be to solve. As one contemporary noted of the first meeting, 'the past hundred years of missionary campaigning has brought to light an almost endless number of problems and difficulties about which these missionary workers – both those at the front and those administering the enterprise at home – have good reasons to hold divergent opinions.'[135]

The Conference's concerns were both a reflection on the missionary challenge ahead and an admission that approaches to the gospel in so-called sending societies would need to change. With speakers limited to seven minutes per communication, any real progress made by the Conference was a result of the work of the publicity and the preparation/continuation committees which met before and after. Most of the concerns, however, were distillations of missionary experience which – posed in practice – had already achieved a range of solutions in those localities to which World Missionary Conference questionnaires were sent by the preparatory committees in 1909. The concerns were thus a window on missionary concerns as they developed through the vast expanse of Protestant effort from 1870 onwards,

[133] Brown, 'Changing Conditions in Eastern Asia', p. 57.

[134] Gairdner, *Edinburgh 1910*, pp. 11–12.

[135] Charles Clayton Morrison, 'The World Missionary Conference', *Christian Century*, July 7 1910, online reprint.

seeking to respond to perceived world 'crisis' through A.T. Pierson's formulaic 'Men, Money and Methods'.[136]

It was not a moment of intellectual breakthrough. Contributors continued to talk about 'Animism' or 'Hinduism' as monolithic systems and to regard Sufi 'sciences' as pantheism or charlatanism.[137] The inability to finish the task in 'the cultured nations of the East' (considered more 'mature' and therefore more capable of engaging the high point of human spirituality, European Christian doctrine) continued to block extension into 'unreached people groups' in the 'animist' world.[138] It was typical of such conferences that, even while warning the West of the complexity and difference of 'Asian' cultures, Julius Richter would reify them into monolithic blocs, subject to a singular Whig process (the 'one great and coherent evolution of the religious genius of mankind').[139] As noted earlier, some German evangelicals also felt that the 'global missionary project' merely consolidated the dominance of English and 'the image of a growing and heedless Anglo-American, but increasingly American, domination'.[140] They were suspicious both of them and of the 'cosmopolitan' evangelicalism represented by 'Free Church' German evangelicals with international links.[141] Despite being a 'conference of "foreign" missionaries',[142] delegates from the majority world were regarded by some cash-strapped mission societies as a 'dubious and expensive luxury'.[143] Even though the official account of the Conference opened with a glorious vision of a united world, the national background of those agencies still counted. The vision of a 'non-spatial' [i.e. spiritual] Christianity was not yet possible:[144] the traditional mental maps still organised the missionary priorities of many agencies.[145] Effective inculturation, as seen in Hudson Taylor's emphasis on national dress and language learning, or the attempt by Scandinavian missionaries to create a Santal national church, still tended to come from experiential immersion in their surroundings

[136] Quoted in William Lawrence Svelmoe, *A New Vision for Missions: William Cameron Townsend, the Wycliffe Bible Translators, and the Culture of Early Evangelical Faith Missions, 1896–1945*, Tuscaloosa: University of Alabama Press, 2008, p. 3.

[137] Richter, 'The Decisive Hour in the History of Protestant Missions', p. 121.

[138] Ibid., p. 121.

[139] Richter, 'The Decisive Hour in the History of Protestant Missions', p. 122.

[140] Frykenberg and Low, *Christians and Missionaries in India*, pp. 159, 246; Hutchison, 'Innocence Abroad', 80.

[141] Railton, 'German Free Churches and the Nazi Regime', 85.

[142] Kevin Ward, 'Review: *The World Missionary Conference, Edinburgh 1910*', *International Bulletin of Missionary Research*, 33:4 (October 2009), 216.

[143] Brian Stanley, *The World Missionary Conference*, Edinburgh 1910, Grand Rapids: Eerdmans, 2009, p. 142.

[144] Gairdner, *Edinburgh 1910*, pp. 5, 6.

[145] Brian Stanley, 'Defining the Boundaries of Christendom: The Two Worlds of the World Missionary Conference, 1910', *International Bulletin of Missionary Research*, 30:4 (October 2006), 171.

rather than from conferences.[146] Edinburgh, in short, raised the questions for which Keswick and Northfield were providing the answers.

CONCLUSION

Despite – or perhaps because – of the fact that they were so despised, premillennialist faith missionaries such as Kumm and his father-in-law, Henry Grattan Guinness, were people of influence. After all, they offered precisely what conferences such as Edinburgh were calling for: faith, motivation and results. Guinness was the archetype of the revivalist, scientific theorist of premillennialism. His book, *The Approaching End of the Age* (1879), attempted to establish – through calculations so exhaustive that he was elected a Fellow of two Royal Societies – a 'divine system' of times and seasons which united 'History, Prophecy, and Science'. Being a single system of faith, experience and scientific authority, its historicist premillennialism would have a significant impact on social activists and evangelicals alike.[147] Predicting through Bible prophecy that the world would see around 1917 both the reestablishment of Israel and a global conflagration, Guinness calculated that the Christian missionary force was totally inadequate: 'The non-Christian nations number over a thousand millions. To give no more than one missionary to every ten thousand of these we should need a hundred thousand missionaries.There are at present only six thousand in the entire field - men and women, all told.'[148] No church or institution could meet this need – it would have to come from a spiritual movement of God: the 'Church cannot create such labourers; only He who made the world can make a true missionary'.[149] Between 1873 and 1920, Guinness's East London Institute for Home and Foreign Missions produced hundreds of missionaries working towards the great goal that he himself had projected.

The key, Guinness considered, was mobilisation and spiritual empowerment. Keswick provided the spark and the method and laid the basis for later innovations. The greatest single evangelical missionary upsurge of the period began in 1886 at D.L. Moody's Mount Hermon School at Northfield, Massachusetts as an inter-campus conference for 251 undergraduate students. Ninety-nine students signed a commitment: 'We are willing and desirous, God permitting, to become

[146] Marine Carrin and Hakald Tambs-Lyche, 'The Santals, Though Unable to Plan for Tomorrow, Should Be Converted by the Santals' in Frykenberg and Low, *Christians and Missionaries in India*, p. 274.

[147] See, for instance, Tim Larsen's account of the book's influence on Christabel Pankhurst: Timothy Larsen, *Christabel Pankhurst: Fundamentalism and Feminism in Coalition*, Woodbridge: Boydell, 2002, p. 37.

[148] H. Grattan Guinness, 'The Training of Missionaries', an address given by Rev H. Grattan Guinness, on the first day of the General Missionary Conference, June 1888, http://theologicaleducation.org/2010/09/29/the-training-of-missionaries-by-grattan-guinness-june-1888 , accessed 5 Sept. 2011.

[149] Ibid.

foreign missionaries.' Building on the model of the 'Cambridge Seven', who had emerged from Moody's 1884 university mission, delegates (led by Robert Wilder, and later by John Mott) were sent out to other universities; by the end of 1887, some 2,200 volunteers had signed up for missionary service in meetings which featured all the emotional technique of a Moody crusade. The next year (1888), the mission was formalised at a YMCA conference at Northfield, as the Student Volunteer Movement for Foreign Missions (SVM), an interdenominational voluntarist auxiliary designed to provide candidates to the major missionary organisations. After its first formal conference in 1891, the SVM's numbers climbed dramatically. It would remain difficult to estimate their eventual impact, given the desire of denominational boards not to have their thunder stolen, as well as criticism from both liberal and conservative ends of the church as to the SVM's unthinking haste. Some indication may be drawn, however, from the SVM claim at its 1936 conference that the movement held the names of 13,000 serving missionaries who had found their vocation as its volunteers.[150] While the denominational boards would remain key players, the impetus created by such organisations made Protestant missions abroad a disproportionately evangelical activity. Between 1880 and 1900, evangelicalism made important steps towards becoming a global force, outside the countries and religious traditions which had spawned it. Its secret lay in its ability to motivate by providing a unified, experiential religious worldview built around a personal sense of calling to ultimate ends. That unity was the coming together of evangelical experience from India to Chicago, the end product of evangelical experimentalism, whereby a doctrinal core was freed from European origins by being associated with the mobile personal self, attached to a historical imaginary which gave the believer a sense of safety, wherever they might be. This global evangelicalism was a mobile, bounded spirituality based on the Keswick synthesis, made flexible through its experimental nature.

Keswick's commitment to non-material empowerment, global replication, missionary outcomes and avoidance of 'well-known speakers' made it a natural form for those outside the power structures of the denominations. When George Grubb thrilled the first Keswick Convention in Australia with his preaching on 'Can we have apostolic power today?', his aim was to empower his evangelical hearers (such as H.B. Macartney) and release people into missions (which he did successfully, some fifty committing to 'go' at his missionary meeting of 1891). What he did not expect was that when he preached on 'Pentecostal Christianity, and how it may be ours', some of his hearers might go back to the Book of Acts and appropriate it directly. It is possible that in his audience was James Moore Hickson, who in the 1920s would become a globally known advocate for the restoration of gifted

[150] Rabe, *Home Base of American China Missions*, p. 92. By 1936, Moody Bible Institute alone had produced 'nearly 12 percent of the reported total North American Protestant force' (Joel A. Carpenter, *Revive Us Again: The Reawakening of American Fundamentalism*, New York: Oxford University Press, 1997, p. 30).

Christianity and for divine healing.[151] It was at an offshoot of the Geelong Convention some years later that, during a prayer meeting, 'a young woman named Fraser was praying for the fullness of the Spirit when she spoke in tongues.... Jessie Ferguson, who was to become a missionary, received the Spirit later.... These manifestations caused a furore.'[152] In the uncontrolled world of the camp meeting and the convention, the Keswick genie got out of the box. In the period from 1893 to 1910, indeed, it would get out of the box in separate locations all over the world in a new phase of revival that was to give rise to the pentecostal movement.

By the end of the 1870–1914 period, evangelical Christians had encountered and developed a variety of solutions for the challenges posed by the industrialising West and their movement's need for generational change. It had developed or expanded upon new institutional forms (training colleges, new forms of evangelical press, the convention as an interdenominational, extra-ecclesial and replicable space, a greater emphasis on united evangelical moral reform movements, etc), new approaches to public outreach (particularly through the organisational appropriation of revivalism) and greater presence in global networks of communication and transport. This latter essentially unified the concerns of Atlantic evangelicals and provided global reach for new theological and spiritual movements by including formerly distant British dominions, colonies and outstations in the missions/evangelism/lecture network. The most significant development, however, was the growth of a new global spiritual unity through the development of a body of confident, transportable spiritual technique, as symbolised by Keswick and all it stood for. This development empowered the trends commenced in the pragmatic steps towards evangelical unity of the 1840s, helping evangelicals (particularly those from Free Church or fringe traditions) to sidestep the growing entanglements of nationalism, secularism, modernism and their related bureaucratic forms. Entangled in their denominational struggles, many denominational evangelicals were yet to understand how radical this shift had been. By moving out of national forms into international and even emerging transnational forms, it seemed to many that the very term 'evangelical' had lost its meaning, that they had avoided ossification in Europe only to be drowned in the great realities of a globalising world. A good many identified this state of seeming perpetual crisis with a soon coming 'End of all things',[153] to which the horrors of 1914 to 1919 would provide painful plausibility. In fact, the new beginnings hidden in the successful transnationalisation of evangelicalism were just beginning to sprout.

[151] M. Hutchinson, 'The Worcester Circle: An Anglo-Catholic attempt at Renewal in the 1920s' in *ReVeal*, 2010, http://webjournals.alphacrucis.edu.au/journals/reveal/2010/worcester-circle-anglo-catholic-attempt-renewal-19/, accessed 8 July 2011.

[152] Barry Chant, 'The Spirit of Pentecost: Origins and Development of the Pentecostal Movement in Australia, 1870–1939', PhD thesis, Macquarie University, 1999, p. 192.

[153] Larsen, *Christabel Pankhurst*, p. 37.

6

Fighting Wars and Engaging Modernity: 1900s to 1945

The seemingly boundless optimism and eschatological expectation that characterised the Edinburgh World Missionary Conference of June 1910 met its stark nemesis a little more than four years later. In August 1914, the German invasion of Belgium initiated a worldwide conflict that cost many millions of lives, profoundly changed the existing world order, and cast a long traumatic shadow on the twentieth century. The conflicts of the period from 1914 to 1945, which have been called 'the second Thirty Years War', echoed around the world,[1] impacting most of the places where evangelicals had scattered their missions, churches, and communities over the previous 150 years. The first Thirty Years War in the seventeenth century saw 'Christendom' broken up and absorbed into single states of religious profession; this second one saw the emergence of the technocratic, secular state and the deterritorialisation of religion in the West. It also saw the ascendancy of nationalism as a quasi-religion, leading to the virtual deification of the nation-state – a trend that reached its most extreme manifestations in Nazi Germany and Fascist Italy, but was also very much apparent in the English-speaking world. The result for evangelicals was a set of catalytic experiences leading to crises of conscience, disruption to communities and adaptation to new circumstances.

At the same time, evangelicals faced the less brutal but eventually equally pervasive challenges of ideological and cultural change. The ramifications of Charles Darwin's theories on human origins and Karl Marx's on human society continued to reshape the intellectual and political worlds, even as the dissemination of the ideas of more recent thinkers such as Friedrich Nietzsche (1844–1900), Sigmund Freud (1856–1939) and Émile Durkheim (1858–1917) presented further radical alternatives to traditional frameworks of belief and understanding. The advance of technology not only transformed warfare with devastating results, but also profoundly changed peacetime life in developed societies. The advent of motorized road transport, the aeroplane, radio, cinema and eventually television transformed long-distance travel and communication and made the world much more interconnected. For evangelicals, the central dilemma was when to translate the literal warfare that dominated the age into a metaphorical warfare against

[1] Philip Bobbitt, *The Shield of Achilles: War, Peace and the Course of History*, New York: Anchor Books, 2002, p. xxi.

mere innovation, and when effectively to engage modernity and turn it to their own ends.

In the history of evangelicalism, as in general world history, the Great War looms not as an even barrier, but as an erratic mountain range indented with deep valleys of continuity and steep ridges of abrupt change. Alongside the apparently seamless continuation of nineteenth-century developments, the first decade of the twentieth century saw the origins of important new movements that were to assume greater significance on the other side of the watershed of 1914. Accordingly the chronological range of this chapter overlaps with the preceding one.

THREE EVANGELICAL APPEALS

Evangelicals in 1900 were well used to organising public pressure to obtain social and religious gains, and so it is instructive to compare three attempts to bring their influence to bear in the first years of the century. In 1901, when King Carlos I of Portugal was visiting London, he received a deputation from the Evangelical Alliance, who pressed the claim of religious liberty in his country. Carlos, who needed British support to consolidate Portuguese colonial boundaries in Africa, received them warmly and promised to 'ensure that it was carried out'.[2] It was, seemingly, a significant victory: Portugal, for evangelicals, was a side-door not only to Europe, but one through which they could challenge the Roman Catholic supremacy in South America, an area in which – despite the vast expansion of British investment in that continent during the 1880s and from 1902 to 1912 – they had been having only limited success.[3] The exclusion of Latin America from consideration by the Edinburgh Missionary Conference in 1910 indicated what a touchy subject this 'Catholic continent' would continue to be.[4] There were evangelical migrant communities already in Latin America,[5] and many of the faith missions which were not represented at Edinburgh were already working in or on the continent's fringes. Gaining improved access was a priority.

In 1900, another delegation from the Evangelical Alliance – comprising 'a large number of clergymen' – had waited on the Ballarat City Council, in rural Victoria, Australia, expressing their concern over Sunday band performances at the local sporting oval.[6] This deputation too had larger motives. On the one hand, Sabbatarianism was a well-entrenched principle (particularly among the more than commonly Scots-based migrant society of rural Victoria). The ministers,

2 'The King of Portugal', *The Argus*, 9 February 1901, p. 13.

3 James F. Rippy, *British Investments in Latin America, 1822–1949*, Oxford: Oxford University Press, 1959, p. 11.

4 Kurt Fiedler, 'Edinburgh 2010 and the Evangelicals', *Evangelical Review of Theology*, 34 (2010), 326.

5 Harding Stricker, 'Pilgrims under the Southern Cross', *International Congregational Journal*, 9 (2010), 31.

6 *The Argus*, 30 October 1900, p. 7.

however, saw the sporting oval itself as a key element of the hedonistic colonial society, a cult of Hermes against which these Hebraists were struggling for cultural supremacy. Not surprisingly, evangelical churches found it more difficult to draw males than females to church, a position which diminished their public influence in a masculinist society, and made (in the absence of the main breadwinner) the financial support of denominations more difficult. Philip Pond's sermon in Sydney's Erskineville Church of Christ on 'Why men don't go to church' was one of many on the theme.[7] Adapters ever, evangelicals such as the cricketer and missionary C.T. Studd (1860–1931) were able to absorb some of the attributes of Charles Kingsley's muscular Christianity.[8] It was, however, an endeavour that required the sort of delicate balance that was easier to achieve in elite public schools in Britain than it was among the relatively well-paid, politically conscious working classes in the colonies. Evangelicals disliked the externality and thoughtlessness of the muscular tradition, as well as its liberal and Christian socialist associations, and were suspicious of anything which could be promoted as an end in itself. In the long run, their fear that sport would become a vehicle for secularisation proved to be justified.[9]

About the same time that Carlos I was receiving the Evangelical Alliance delegation in London, the evangelical Bishop of Liverpool Francis Chavasse responded to an appeal to British Christians from the clergy of the Evangelical Church in Switzerland, alleging that British conduct of the ongoing war in South Africa against the Boer republics was 'inhuman, oppressive and unrighteous'. The irregular nature of the war had indeed resulted in widespread repression, internment and what today would be called 'war crimes' on both sides.[10] The most systematic was under the command of Lord Kitchener: more than 27,000 Boer civilians died in concentration camps largely of malnutrition and disease.[11] The war raised painful dilemmas for some evangelicals: they recognised a strong religious cousinage to the Boers and the Dutch Reformed Church, and a vociferous minority of prominent British Nonconformists, such as John Clifford and Silvester Horne, opposed British policy on moral grounds.[12] Chavasse, however, had been recently appointed a bishop by the Conservative government responsible for the war, to preside over a diocese characterised by robustly patriotic Protestantism.

The aftermath of the three appeals was to be telling. The apparent success of the delegation to Carlos I seemed ephemeral when the king was killed by a

[7] *Sydney Morning Herald*, 1 August 1914, p. 3.

[8] Jim Parry, *Sport and Spirituality: An Introduction*, New York: Routledge, 2007, p. 87.

[9] Dominic Erdozain, *The Problem of Pleasure: Sport, Recreation and the Crisis of Victorian Religion*, Woodbridge: Boydell, 2010.

[10] *The Times*, 23 August 1901, p. 3; 'Evangelical Intercession', *The Register*, 17 August 1901, p. 7.

[11] Alexander B. Downes, *Targeting Civilians in War*, Ithaca: Cornell University Press, 2008, p. 161.

[12] Richard Elphick and Rodney Davenport, *Christianity in South Africa*, Oxford: Currey, 1997, p. 128; D.W. Bebbington, *The Nonconformist Conscience*, London: Allen & Unwin, 1982, pp. 123–4.

republican assassin's bullet in 1908. Then the war of 1914–18 brought a decisive end to the effective power of monarchs in most major European states. Although the interwar period was to see a significant advance of Protestantism among the socially influential classes in modernizing Brazil, this growth was not the result of the Alliance's traditional approach to diplomacy.[13] For the delegation of evangelical ministers of Ballarat, the City Council provided cold comfort: as a public institution, it needed to be open to all requests for its public spaces. The consequence of this division of the (leisured, secular, mass) public from the (serious, religious, élite) private was more subtle than the collapse of royal houses, but nonetheless significant. Chavasse, for his part, denied there was a problem. He defended the camps as a regrettable but necessary response to wartime conditions. The charges against Britain, he claimed, were based on 'seriously defective information', and in making them unjustly, the Swiss risked doing 'serious spiritual harm to the cause of Evangelical Christianity throughout the world.' He robustly affirmed: 'The great mass of Evangelical Christians in Great Britain, of all shades of political opinion, support and will continue to support the policy of their Government, because it involves the integrity of the British Empire, the complete civilization of South Africa, and the evangelization of the native races.'[14] In Europe and its dependencies, it would take some time for evangelicals who had become embedded in their national cultures to see moral issues apart from the national frame and to 'make war on war.'[15]

REVIVAL AND GLOBALISATION

The widespread revivals of the nineteenth century had tended to be North Atlantic in focus, with broader networks established through missionary, Keswick, Bible teaching and other associations. A list of early-twentieth-century evangelical revivals, by way of contrast, demonstrates the rapid emergence of a global evangelical culture. As Allan Anderson points out, there were 'many Jerusalems' both in and beyond the West during the early twentieth century: Melbourne (1902, see chapter 5), Wonsan, Korea (1903), Wales (1904), Mukti, India (1905), Los Angeles (1906), Pyongyang, Korea (1907), The Heart of Africa Mission in the Belgian Congo (1914), Ivory Coast and Ghana (1914–15); Shandong, China (1930) and Gahini, Rwanda, in East Africa (1936).[16] These outbreaks were linked by migrant Christian workers

[13] Paul Freston, *Evangelicals and Politics in Asia, Africa, and Latin America*, Cambridge: Cambridge University Press, 2001, p. 11.

[14] *The Argus*, 24 August 1901, p. 13; A.G. Sheill, *Briton versus Boer: A Letter to the Clergy of the Evangelical Church in Switzerland in Reply to the Bishop of Liverpool*, Brighton: Smith, 1902, p. 84.

[15] 'Bogatsky', *Evangelical Christendom*, 3 (1849), 107.

[16] Allan Anderson, 'Writing the Pentecostal history of Africa, Asia and Latin America,' *Journal of Beliefs & Values*, 25 (2004), 143.

such as Joseph Smale in Los Angeles,[17] Ellen and James Hebden in Toronto, Canada,[18] Joseph Marshall in rural Victoria, Australia,[19] W.W. Simpson in Gansu, China[20] and *trans*migrant workers such as Pandita Ramabai in Mukti, India. What later became known as 'pentecostal' revival did not, as is conventionally supposed, radiate outwards from events at the Azusa Street mission in Los Angeles in April 1906, but broke out almost simultaneously in different corners of the world. The degree of disconnection between the individual events supports David Martin's observation that this was a convergence of global (particularly Methodist) evangelicalisms. Each was discovering the solution to intractable problems in elites and establishments through the downward mobilisation of the Spirit in mass movements.[21] Although under-organised and resourced in the period covered in this chapter, early pentecostals posed significant questions to their evangelical contemporaries. What was the place of healing in Christian practice? If power followed experience rather than doctrine, what was the role of doctrine in 'defining' evangelicalism? More importantly, pentecostals challenged many of the establishment norms which evangelicals used to exert influence. Azusa Street crossed the 'race bar' which, despite the abolition of slavery, was entrenched in American churches. Early pentecostals tended to come from the socially active arm of the church, and so could fall foul of those evangelicals who (since the 1880s) had sought to defend evangelical doctrines against liberal and social gospel advocates.[22] Pentecostal insistence on the continuity of prophecy antagonised the intellectual core of Reformed evangelicals, whose biblicism depended on a closed canon. It also raised painful memories of the public spectacles that had attended the ministry of Edward Irving and (more recently) John Dowie.

The initial reactions of evangelicals should not be overstated. Pentecostalism was not yet a mass movement, and there were many greater challenges at hand. Nevertheless, it drew both support and fire from its evangelical seedbed. Some mainstream leaders, such as A.B. Simpson of the Christian and Missionary Alliance, saw the movement's continuity with Keswick and the Healing movement. Having already been burnt by his support for the restoration of the gifts in the 1890s,[23] Simpson would not commit his movement to pentecostalism, but

[17] Cecil M. Robeck, *The Azusa Street Mission and Revival*, Nashville: Nelson, 2006, p. 58.

[18] Adam Stewart, 'A Canadian Azusa? The Implications of the Hebden Mission for Pentecostal historiography' in M. Wilkinson and P. Althouse, eds, *Winds from the North: Canadian Contributions to the Pentecostal Movement*, Brill: Leiden, 2010, p. 19.

[19] Chant, 'Spirit of Pentecost', p. 131.

[20] Michael D. Wilson, 'Contending for Tongues: W. W. Simpson's Pentecostal Experience in Northwest China', *Pneuma*, 29 (2007), 285.

[21] Martin, *Pentecostalism*, pp. 30–1. As Pentecostalism is the subject of a companion volume by Edith Blumhofer, it does not receive a detailed discussion here.

[22] D.F. Ottati, *'Foreword', in Walter Rauschenbusch, Christianity and the Social Crisis*, Louisville: Westminster/John Knox Press, 1991.

[23] Gary B. McGee, 'Shortcut to Language Preparation? Radical Evangelicals, Missions, and the Gift of Tongues', *International Bulletin of Missionary Research*, 25 (2001), 119.

acknowledged it as 'a' (not 'the') sign of the infilling of the Holy Spirit.[24] Benjamin Warfield at Princeton, however, fighting against higher criticism and the weakening of doctrines of biblical inspiration, saw it as one of a succession of 'counterfeit miracles', not merely misleading but demonic. Of the orientation towards charismatic gifting which could be seen in great preachers such as Wesley, Warfield concluded: 'To such apparent lengths is it possible to be carried by the mere enthusiasm of faith.'[25] The early impulse of pentecostalism was outwards, along missionary and itinerant lines: while it stayed there, the debate would be restrained. Inevitably, however, the return of missionaries, the division of local churches and the planting of new pentecostal churches from the late 1910s brought the theological cousins into conflict. During the 1920s, most Keswick conventions (and finally the world body) rejected pentecostal manifestations and doctrine,[26] as did William Bell Riley's World Christian Fundamentals Association. Eventually, this division, and in the United States the inclusion of pentecostals in the National Association of Evangelicals after World War II, would prove a key dividing point within conservative evangelicalism.[27] In the period before World War I, however, Warfield and his colleagues were more concerned about the disappearance of the evangelical academy.

THE GREAT WAR

In July and August 1914, when Russia mobilised in defence of Slavic Serbia, and Germany responded in aid of Germanic Austria, there were few doubts as to the seriousness of affairs. In capital cities throughout the world, 'special prayers for peace [were] being offered.'[28] English-speaking evangelical churches varied widely on the theology of war: what brought them together was an effective theology of empire. Irish evangelicals often saw an imperial war as not only a duty, but as necessary to British success against Home Rulers in Ireland. The co-involvement of many of the latter in anti-Catholic Protestant defence and Loyal Orange Lodge movements made a positive response to the empire's war almost inevitable.[29] The shape of the response, however, was far from uniform. For some, one's duty to country and to Christ needed to be served on the front line in arms. One of these

[24] David R. Reid, 'Towards a Fourfold Gospel: A.B. Simpson, John Salmon, and the Christian and Missionary Alliance in Canada' in George A. Rawlyk, ed., *Aspects of the Canadian Evangelical Experience*, Montreal and Kingston: McGill-Queen's University Press, 1997, p. 277.

[25] Benjamin B. Warfield, *Counterfeit Miracles*, New York: Scribner's, 1918, p. 129.

[26] Randle Manwaring, *From Controversy to Co-existence: Evangelicals in the Church of England, 1914–1980*, Cambridge: Cambridge University Press, 2002, pp. 167–8.

[27] See Edith Blumhofer, *Restoring the Faith: the Assemblies of God, Pentecostalism, and American Culture*, Urbana: University of Illinois Press, 1993, p. 186.

[28] *The Sydney Morning Herald*, 3 August 1914, p. 1.

[29] John Wolffe, 'Anti-Catholicism and the British Empire, 1815–1914', in Hilary M. Carey, *Empires of Religion*, Basingstoke: Palgrave Macmillan, 2008, pp. 43–63.

was Everard Digges La Touche (1883–1915), an Ulsterman of Huguenot descent, who developed a significant reputation as an evangelical theologian and controversialist. In 1912, he moved to Australia to lecture at Moore College in Sydney. At the outbreak of war, he unsuccessfully sought a position as an army chaplain, but enlisted in the ranks, despite his bishop's disapproval. L.B. Radford, recently elected as Bishop of Goulburn and no friend to Sydney evangelicals, remembered him with warmth:

> We did not all approve of a priest taking the sword, but nobody could discuss the question with Digges in his tent without realising that whether he was right or wrong in his reading of the Bible, he had settled this question for himself with his Bible open before God.... Priest and officer in one, he carried his Lord's presence and power right into the heart of camp life and work.[30]

Arriving at Gallipoli on 5 August 1915, he was wounded almost immediately in the stomach and died twelve hours later.[31]

Another, more fortunate, Australian was John G. Ridley, a sergeant at Fromelles who survived being shot in the throat. He would draw sermon illustrations and write books for the next six decades, as he rose to become one of the best-known evangelists in the southern hemisphere.[32] For others, their obligation would not stretch to the carriage of arms: stretcher bearing, message running or headquarters work was often no less dangerous, but more conformable to the message of the Prince of Peace. In every arm of every service, Australian evangelicals volunteered to serve, sometimes with unexpected results. 'Fighting' William McKenzie of the Salvation Army so lived and bled with the troops on Gallipoli and the Western Front that when this Military Cross–winning chaplain returned home to Australia, 'tumultuous crowds greeted him in every state capital, and many smaller cities.'[33] Only a few such as the Baptist Francis Clemens in Melbourne, the (mainly Quaker) Australian Freedom League and the majority of pentecostals felt that conscientious objection on the grounds of Christian pacifism was their only option.[34] Methodists critiqued the war, but (with a background in activism and the language of the church militant) often ended up sending disproportionate numbers of their sons into battle.[35]

The dynamics were similar in Britain. Bishop John Taylor Smith, a former missionary who served as Chaplain-General to the Forces from 1901 to 1925, personified a close identification between evangelical Christianity and the war effort.

[30] Quoted in *The Burra Record*, 15 September 1915, p. 2.

[31] F.W. Taylor and T.A. Cusack, *Nulli Secundus. A History of the 2nd Battalion, A.I.F. 1914–19*, Sydney: New Century, 1942, p. 128.

[32] Robert D. Linder, *The Long Tragedy: Australian Evangelical Christians and the Great War, 1914–1918*, Adelaide: Open Book, 2000, pp. 20–1.

[33] Ibid., p. 133.

[34] Ibid., pp. 74–5.

[35] Ibid., p. 75.

Taylor Smith was untroubled by theological and moral complexities and vilified by Anglo-Catholics, who perceived him as narrow-minded and partisan. His primary concerns were pastoral and evangelistic, reflected in his exhortation to a chaplain joining the British Expeditionary Force in 1914 to 'take to all your comrades in the service (regardless of rank) a loving message, by life and by lip, of Jesus Christ, a personal Saviour'.[36] Although the moderate High Church Bishop of London Arthur Winnington-Ingram was the most prominent episcopal cheerleader for uncritical Anglican supporters of the war, leading evangelicals such as Bishop Chavasse and Henry Wace, the Dean of Canterbury, maintained a similar tone. Chavasse hoped the war would lead to a 'regenerated England and a regenerated Empire'.[37] Wace judged Germany to have become 'a moral outlaw' under the influence of 'false philosophy and an extravagant [biblical] criticism' and believed that the war was 'working out for our nation and Empire, and for the world at large, the establishment on a firmer basis than ever of true Christian civilization'.[38] A diffused evangelical influence was also very much apparent in the upper echelons of the army, notably in the deep Protestant piety and providential beliefs of Douglas Haig, commander-in-chief of the forces in France from December 1915, who was strongly influenced by his Presbyterian chaplain, George Duncan.[39] Meanwhile, Noel Chavasse, an army medical officer and son of the bishop, who himself held strong evangelical convictions, was the only man in the war to be awarded the Victoria Cross twice, for his bravery both at the Battle of the Somme in 1916 and at the third battle of Ypres, where he was mortally wounded in August 1917.[40] Nonconformist evangelicals too rallied behind the war effort: it was symbolic that the veteran Baptist leader John Clifford believed the British cause in the First World War to be morally justified on the same grounds of justice to small states that had led him vigorously to oppose the Boer War.[41]

Evangelical support for the war was not unqualified: Clifford opposed conscription as an infringement of liberty of conscience,[42] and there were other, more equivocal, voices such as that of Bishop Handley Moule of Durham, who saw the war as a 'righteous cause' but above all as an 'earnest warning' from God who

[36] E.L. Langston, *Bishop Taylor Smith*, London: Marshall, Morgan and Scott, 1938, p. 124. For radically divergent assessments of Taylor Smith, see Manwaring, *From Controversy to Coexistence*, pp. 4–5, 8–9, and Alan Wilkinson, *The Church of England and the First World War*, London: SPCK, 1978, pp. 124–6.

[37] J.B. Lancelot, *Francis James Chavasse Bishop of Liverpool*, Oxford: Blackwell, 1929, p. 196.

[38] Henry Wace, *The War and the Gospel*, London: Thynne, 1917, pp. 52, 58.

[39] Michael Snape, *God and the British Soldier: Religion and the British Army in the First and Second World Wars*, London: Routledge, 2005, pp. 62–72.

[40] Lancelot, *Chavasse*, pp. 199–204; Selwyn Gummer, *The Chavasse Twins*, London: Hodder and Stoughton, 1963, pp. 58–61.

[41] John Clifford, *Our Fight for Belgium and What It Means*, London: Hodder and Stoughton, 1918, pp. 4–5.

[42] James Marchant, *Dr John Clifford CH: Life Letters and Reminiscences*, London: Cassell, 1924, p. 226.

'bids us turn from our evil ways'.[43] And amidst the horror of the trenches, Wilfrid Owen, like Noel Chavasse the child of an evangelical home, reached a very different conclusion about where Christ stood in relation to the war:

> Near Golgotha strolls many a priest,
> And in their faces there is pride
> That they were flesh-marked by the Beast
> By whom the gentle Christ's denied.[44]

But Owen's lines, unpublished in his lifetime, point up the pervasiveness of the consensus he was questioning.

In the post-war mindset, it is difficult to recapture the calculus applied by churchmen encouraging their parishioners to go off to the meat grinder of the Western Front. This is the value and peril of hindsight. In the early part of the war, most clergy had little idea of its potential cost and were deeply invested in the society which provided them with legitimacy and influence. After the long period of urbanisation and change, many welcomed the conflict as a chance finally to do something that would match the heroic diction of their church traditions. In the United States, this connected to the desire to recapture the idealised Republic on the other side of the Civil War; for British volunteers, to build the godly empire overseeing the extension of civilisation and the gospel; for Methodists, the chance to do something which lived up to the exploits of Wesley or Asbury.[45] One South Australian newspaper remembered that 'an old-fashioned divine of the ultra-evangelical type said that revival meetings were much more successful in time of calamity than in halcyon days; and his remark contained a good deal of what the Americans call sound horse sense.'[46]

For most, it was an investment in the church's influence, which they expected to be paid back after the war in sound legislation and access to the decision makers. At the very least, it would enable clergy to stand before a younger generation made more masculine by the trials of war and (like John Ridley) speak to them with greater effectiveness because of their common experience. For the same reason that they had supported cadet groups in schools, the Boy Scouts, and similar boys' organisations with a military bent, they now supported the war in the belief that it would discipline the population from 'irreligion and drink' and cause men finally to face up to 'the big questions'.[47] Like Harry Amoss's 'Padre Who Was Born Again' (and so saw in the sacrifice of soldiers 'the glory of a thousand Christs') evangelists

[43] Quoted Manwaring, *From Controversy to Coexistence*, p. 13.

[44] 'At a Calvary near the Ancre' (1917/18), E. Blunden, ed., *The Poems of Wilfred Owen*, London: Chatto and Windus, 1931, p. 108.

[45] Jonathan Ebel, 'The Great War and the American Fighting Man', *Church History*, 78 (2009), 106.

[46] *The Register*, 8 September 1914, p. 4.

[47] Callum Brown, 'Piety, Gender and War in Scotland in the 1910s' in Catriona M.M. Macdonald and E.W. McFarland, eds, *Scotland and the Great War*, East Linton: Tuckwell, 1999, p. 173.

such as Rodney 'Gipsy' Smith went so far as to equate sacrifice in war with a sanctifying virtue.[48]

The after-effects of the war varied, although across the West there was a sense among the churches that it had not been for the good. Simplistic, consensual Christian socialism was undermined, as the working classes moved to the left and the churches 'lurched to the right'. In Canada, A.E. Smith, a long-standing Methodist minister, after a period as a Labour Church missionary, joined the Communist Party in 1925.[49] Nearly 40 per cent of Canadian Methodist Chaplains who served in the War 'resigned their orders upon returning to Canada and over a quarter disappeared altogether, choosing to have no further contact with the church'.[50] In Scotland, the churches moved in a conservative direction in the face of defections of their members to organised socialism; in Australia, the conscription debates and the subsequent realignment of the Labor Party saw the purging of many evangelicals.[51] It had been the enthusiastic supporters of the 'good empire' who disproportionately sent their sons to the war. It resulted in the death or maiming of many potential future evangelical leaders, the disruption of families in a family-centred movement, and the disillusionment of many who had held to a positive eschatology prior to the conflict. In many parts of the world, hundreds of thousands of people (Africans and Indians in particular) were uprooted by being drafted into service. They returned home after having been given a view of the world and the conflicts surrounding the emergence of an international global order that would inform their own views of Christianity and nationalism. 'From remote jungle villages', wrote a YMCA 'association man' in 1917, 'recruits have been obtained, the mission areas have been drained of boys able to act as interpreters and boss boys, every industry employing native labour is practically at a standstill and the whole life of the East African negro is passing through a reconstruction [sic].'[52] The injustice he saw in the drafting of large numbers of Africans into a European war resulted in a Baptist minister, John Chilembwe, sparking a short-lived but symbolically important military uprising in Malawi in 1915.[53]

The carnage of the war heightened many pre-existing divisions in ecclesial bodies and produced two, diametrically opposed effects on international relations. On the one hand, the post-war response to modern warfare and revulsion at the

[48] Jonathan F. Vance, *Death So Noble: Memory, Meaning, and the First World War*, Vancouver: University of British Columbia Press, 1997, p. 71.

[49] See Tom Mitchell, 'From the Social Gospel to "the Plain Bread of Leninism": A.E. Smith's Journey to the Left in the Epoch of Reaction After World War I,' *Labour / Le Travail*, 33 (1994), 125–151.

[50] Vance, *Death So Noble*, p. 71.

[51] Brown, 'Piety, Gender and War', p. 175; and see R.D. Linder, 'The Methodist Love Affair with the Australian Labor Party, 1891–1929', *Lucas* 23 & 24 (1997–8): 35–61.

[52] David Henry Anthony, 'Max Yergan, Marxism and Mission during the Interwar Era', *Social Sciences and Missions*, 22 (2009), 262.

[53] R.I. Rotberg, 'John Chilembwe: Brief life of an Anticolonial Rebel: 1871?–1915', *Harvard Magazine*, 107 (2005), 36.

punitive terms imposed on the Central Powers at Versailles produced a powerful orientation toward church involvement in social reform and the organs of international peace.[54] For some evangelicals, particularly those attached to international networks (such as the professions, universities, the military, media and globalising industries such as oil and automobiles), the war produced an internationalism of a different type. Godfrey Buxton, a great-grandson of the abolitionist Thomas Fowell Buxton, was one of those too wounded to enter missionary service. Instead, he became a mainstay of British student evangelicalism, and of missionary training institutions such as All Nations College and the Japan Evangelistic Band.[55] These two internationalisms would be intensely competitive with one another from the 1920s until the 1980s, when the decline of the Student Christian Movement in most Western institutions made the competition irrelevant. These movements, however, were matched among conservative sectarians by an increasingly activist *anti*-internationalism, aimed at refusing cooperation with non-Christian states, advancing the truth claims of orthodox Christianity in public policy, elevating (among Americans) the United States as an exceptionalist, Christian 'unilateral enforcer of right dealing', and a critique of all those who (they considered) had bartered their Christian heritage for international prestige.[56] Increasingly in the West during the 1920s and 1930s, evangelical doubts as to the fruits of that great example of internationalism, the Edinburgh 1910 Conference, grew into antagonism towards both the Faith and Order Movement and the formation of national councils of churches.[57]

FUNDAMENTALISM

The growing divisions between and within the churches in which evangelicals originated might have remained a passing phase of mobilisation by political opportunists if it had not converged with a longer-simmering, more profound division. The division emerged in different ways in different places. In Anglican contexts, where local bishops had a significant say in what was taught and practised at parish level, the conflict often broke out over matters of appointment or ritual. In the United States, on the other hand, with its large Baptist and Presbyterian seminaries, the fight took the form of divisions within educational institutions where liberal theological influences had gained the ascendancy before the First World

[54] Dana L. Robert, 'The First Globalization: the Internationalization of the Protestant Missionary Movement between the World Wars', *International Bulletin of Missionary Research*, 26 (2002), 50ff.

[55] C.D. Harley, 'Buxton, Barclay Godfrey' in Gerald H. Anderson, ed., *Biographical dictionary of Christian missions*, Grand Rapids: Eerdmans, 1999, p. 105.

[56] Markku Ruotsila, *The Origins of Christian Anti-Internationalism: Conservative Evangelicals and the League of Nations*, Washington: Georgetown University Press, 2008, pp. 3ff.

[57] Ian Randall, 'Evangelicals, Ecumenism and Unity: A Case Study of the Evangelical Alliance', *Evangel*, 22 (2004), 62–3.

War.[58] Reaction came with the printing and circulation between 1910 and 1915 by A.C. Dixon and R.A. Torrey (supported by Texas oil money) of a twelve-volume set of articles under the generic title *The Fundamentals: A Testimony to the Truth.* Originally meant as a conspectus of orthodox Christianity by leading scholars, the collection became a manifesto for the popular convention movement. In the words of populist preacher W.B. Riley, they were the twentieth century's ninety-five theses for 'the rise of a new Protestantism'.[59] The contents of its first volume in particular demonstrated the transatlantic nature of fundamentalism, and its specific foci became the defining points of evangelical agreement. Contributors included James Orr, professor in theology at the Free Church College, Glasgow, on the Virgin Birth; B.B. Warfield from Princeton on 'The Deity of Christ'; and G. Campbell Morgan, the influential pastor of London's Westminster Chapel, on 'The Purposes of the Incarnation'. R.A. Torrey, at Bible Institute of Los Angeles (Biola), wrote on 'The Personality and Deity of the Holy Spirit'; A.T. Pierson provided an apologetic piece on 'The Proof of the Living God'; and Dyson Hague at Wycliffe College, Toronto, wrote on the 'History of the Higher Criticism'. The volume ended with 'A Personal Testimony' by the leading surgeon Howard Atwood Kelly of Johns Hopkins Hospital in Baltimore, one of the founders of modern gynaecology.[60] His presence in the book, alongside theistic evolutionists such as Orr and Warfield,[61] demonstrates the tenor of the work. It was a position piece by respected public figures, issued on the assumption that public discourse was, first, still open, and second, open to a Christian orthodoxy identified with traditional evangelicalism.

By the early 1920s, however, the intellectual and cultural climate had become much more polarised. On the one hand, liberal voices such as the journal *Christian Century* became increasingly strident, with an explicit agenda of eradicating 'defective' religious conservatism. On the other, the Great War and its aftermath stirred a profound sense of cultural crisis in the United States and a heightening of pre-millennial pessimism among evangelicals. Against this background, in May 1919, William B. Riley and others convened the first conference of the World's Christian Fundamentals Association in order to confront the 'Great Apostasy... spreading like a plague through Christendom'.[62] This was a much more hard-edged and combative fundamentalism, and during the next few years, the major American denominations, especially the Baptists and Presbyterians, were bitterly divided in

58 Marsden, *Fundamentalism and American Culture*, p. 105.

59 W.W. Wiersbe, 'Introduction' in R. A. Torrey, Charles Lee Feinberg, and Warren W. Wiersbe, eds, *The Fundamentals: the Famous Sourcebook of Foundational Biblical Truths*, Grand Rapids: Kregel, 1990, p. 13.

60 Thomas Dormandy, *Moments of Truth: Four Creators of Modern Medicine*, Chichester: Wiley, 2003, p. 398; 'The Four Founding Physicians', http://www.hopkinsmedicine.org/about/history/history5.html.

61 Harriet Harris, *Fundamentalism and Evangelicals*, Oxford: Clarendon, p. 33.

62 George Marsden, *Fundamentalism and American Culture*, 2nd edn, New York: Oxford University Press, 2006, pp. 141–58.

a serious trial of strength with self-identified liberals. Matters came to a head in May 1922, when the leading Baptist, Harry Emerson Fosdick, preaching at First Presbyterian Church in New York, affirmed the liberal position and characterised the fundamentalists as intolerant conservatives. At the subsequent 1922 Northern Baptist Convention, Riley attempted to tie the denomination to a fundamentalist creed that would have unchurched Fosdick, but was outmanoeuvred by the liberals. The Presbyterian General Assembly in 1923, on the other hand, voted, in effect, to condemn Fosdick.[63] Before the Assembly met in 1924, however, the faculty of Auburn Theological Seminary in New York issued what came to be known as the Auburn Affirmation, in order to counter 'persistent attempts to divide the church and abridge its freedom'. According to this statement, the Westminster Confession was self-declaredly not infallible, and the 'Supreme Standard' of the church was the Bible. It continued:

> Some of us regard the particular theories contained in the deliverance of the General Assembly of 1923 as satisfactory explanations of these facts and doctrines. But we are united in believing that these are not the only theories allowed by the Scriptures and our standards as explanations of these facts and doctrines of our religion, and that all who hold to these facts and doctrines, whatever theories they may employ to explain them, are worthy of all confidence and fellowship.[64]

In other words, unity could only be accepted on the basis of liberty of conscience, an historically tricky compromise that depended on general goodwill. Crucially, the numerous signatories to the Auburn Affirmation included not only liberals but also moderate evangelicals who wanted to uphold unity and perceived militancy as counterproductive. Its effect was to marginalise the fundamentalists and divide them from other evangelicals, who, they believed, had betrayed the cause of truth.

The Scopes trial in July 1925 was an additional defining event.[65] The defence lawyer, Clarence Darrow, ably assisted by the brilliant atheist journalist H.L. Mencken, who reported on the trial for the *Baltimore Sun*, succeeded in humiliating Bryan and typecasting the fundamentalists as obscurantist and persecuting backwoodsmen. 'We are marching backwards to the glorious age of the sixteenth century', Darrow declared, 'when bigots lighted fagots to burn men who dared to bring any intelligence and enlightenment and culture to the human mind.'[66] According to Mencken, populist evangelical reversions to law were manifestations of 'that poisonous spirit which usually shows itself where Christian men gather to defend the great doctrines of their faith,' typical of a thousand years of Christian crusading,

[63] Ibid., pp. 171–5.
[64] *An Affirmation Designed to Safeguard the Unity and Liberty of the Presbyterian Church in the United States of America*, Auburn, 1924.
[65] See also Chapter 1 in this book.
[66] Edward J. Larson, *Summer for the Gods: The Scopes Trial and America's Continuing Debate over Science and Religion*, New York: Basic, 1997, p. 241.

witch burning and oppression.[67] Partisan though such comments were, they established a persistent stereotype of fundamentalism, subsequently reinforced by Sinclair Lewis's novel *Elmer Gantry* (published in 1927), which ignored its scholarly origins and closed the public space to further debate.[68]

Subsequent struggles over orthodoxy at Princeton Seminary assumed particular importance because of its intellectual standing in the globalising Reformed network.[69] Members of its faculty, notably A.A. Hodge and B.B. Warfield, were important contibutors to the fundamentalist synthesis which J. Gresham Machen articulated in *Christianity and Liberalism* (1923).[70] These were not, however, people who sat well with the populist movement that fundamentalism became. 'Do you suppose, gentlemen,' wrote Machen, a German-educated, orthodox Southern gentleman, in 1926,

> that I do not detect faults in many popular defenders of supernatural Christianity? Do you suppose that I do not regret my being called, by a term that I greatly dislike, a 'Fundamentalist'? Most certainly I do. But in the presence of a great common foe, I have little time to be attacking my brethren who stand with me in defense of the Word of God. I must continue to support an unpopular cause.[71]

The Princeton elite sat even less well with liberal modernism which, they considered, dissolved Christianity into mere morals and was dishonest, presumptuous and mere sentimentalism.[72] Machen controversially posited that 'modern naturalistic liberalism' was 'a totally diverse type of religious belief, which is only the more destructive of the Christian faith because it makes use of traditional Christian terminology.'[73] While they could, fundamentalists fought for reform inside their denominations, even as their populist co-belligerents (such William Bell Riley) were opting for secession. In the mid-1920s, however, much of their support was being reorganised in alternative institutions. In 1922, L. E. Maxwell opened Prairie Bible Institute in Alberta; in 1924, Lewis Sperry Chafer opened Dallas Theological Seminary; in 1927, the Baptist Bible Union took over the failing Des Moines University in Iowa, and Bob Jones established the college in Florida that would bear his name. In 1929, Machen himself withdrew in the face of the theological

[67] Ibid., p. 164. Mencken's articles on the trial have been reprinted in *A Religious Orgy in Tennessee*, Hoboken: Melville House, 2006.
[68] Larson, *Summer for the Gods*, p. 226; Marsden, *Fundamentalism and American Culture*, p. 188.
[69] See Mark Hutchinson, 'The Globalization of Presbyterian Identity, 1880–1900', *Lucas: An Evangelical History Review*, 31 (2002), 7–32.
[70] John D. Hannah, 'An Uncommon Union: Dallas Theological Seminary and American Evangelicalism', tss.
[71] Machen, quoted in Ned. B. Stonehouse, *J. Gresham Machen: A Biographical Memoir*, Grand Rapids: Eerdmans, 1954, pp. 337–8.
[72] Paul Kjoss Helseth, '"Re-imagining" the Princeton Mind: Postconservative Evangelicalism, Old Princeton, and the Rise of Neo-Fundamentalism,' *Journal of the Evangelical Theological Society*, 45 (2002), 427.
[73] J. Gresham Machen, *Christianity and Liberalism*, Grand Rapids: Eerdmans, 2009, p. 2.

reorganisation of Princeton Theological Seminary to found Westminster Theological Seminary in Philadelphia.[74] Existing institutions such as Wheaton College in Illinois were elevated in standing as centres for separatism, a safe place to send the children of fundamentalist families. In many cases, separate institutions led to separate ecclesial organisations. In 1936, Machen and his followers left his denomination to form the Orthodox Presbyterian Church, and thousands took advantage of the planting of new churches in Baptist and pentecostal denominations to move house.

These patterns were played out elsewhere, but with important differences. In Australia and Canada, fundamentalism did not have the institutional roots or population base from which to create a populist movement. Therefore, even though there was an efflorescence of separatist Bible Colleges in the 1920s and 1930s, these were mainly vocational colleges oriented towards the support of interdenominational missionary and convention movements. Rather than 'splitting', conservative evangelicals in mainstream denominations (such as the Sydney Diocese of the Church of England in Australia and the Presbyterian Churches of Australia and Canada) concentrated on forming alliances to retain the coherence of their movements. A rump of seventy-nine Presbyterian ministers decamped after unsuccessfully defending the 'continuing' cause in the church union debates in Canada, to 'reconstitute' under Ephraim Scott.[75] A Presbyterian Church Defence Association under J.L. 'Larry' Rentoul successfully postponed Union in Australia until the 1970s.[76] While, in both settings, identity and traditionalism were key factors in resistance to union, the objections of evangelicals to coercion and 'visible unity' at the cost of theological coherence, and their upholding of the Bible and the Westminster Confession as guards against human abuses of power over individual conscience were also decisive.

Developments in Britain showed significant parallels, but also marked differences from those in the United States. As early as 1910, the Cambridge Intercollegiate Christian Union (CICCU) had disaffiliated from the umbrella Student Christian Movement primarily in order to uphold a conservative view of the inspiration and authority of the Bible.[77] In 1913, George Jackson, a prospective professor at the Didsbury Methodist College, was attacked in the Wesleyan Conference for his openness to biblical criticism. Jackson's opponents lost the immediate argument, but formed the Wesley Bible Union (WBU) as a vehicle for their views. In 1922,

[74] Marsden, *Fundamentalism and American Culture*, p. 192.

[75] Kenneth J. Munro, *First Presbyterian Church, Edmonton: A History*, Victoria: Trafford, 2004, p. 131.

[76] Stewart D. Gill, 'Preserving the Presbyterians: Links between Canadian and Victorian Anti-Union Forces in the 1920s', *Lucas*, 29 (2001), 39–60.

[77] Justin Thacker and Susannah Clark, 'A Historical and Theological exploration of the 1910 disaffiliation of the CICCU from the SCM', unpublished paper presented to 'Evangelicalism and Fundamentalism in Britain Project', 2008, downloaded 13 July 2011 from http://www.eauk.org/efb. Thacker and Clark refute the widely held view that the atonement was the pivotal issue.

a conservative minority seceded from the CMS because of its readiness to accept recruits with a less than hard-line theology of Scripture and formed the Bible Churchmen's Missionary Society.[78]

Nevertheless, Britain did not see the kind of entrenched polarisation that occurred in the United States, nor was there any British counterpart to the high-profile legal theatrics of the Scopes trial. A Baptist Bible Union was formed in 1919, but in striking contrast to its American counterpart, which split its denomination, it failed to gain traction and disbanded in 1925.[79] The Wesley Bible Union survived as an irritant to Methodist modernisers, but by revising doctrinal standards to allow greater latitude of belief within the denomination, they rendered its efforts counterproductive. Subsequently, the WBU loosened its specific ties with Methodism and in 1932 changed its name to the British Bible Union. By renaming its journal *The Fundamentalist*, it nailed its colours emphatically to the mast, but it remained a small group on the extreme fringe of British evangelicalism.[80] Conservatives in Britain might hold theological views quite close to those of American fundamentalists, but in general, not wishing to 'contend for truth at the expense of charity',[81] they pointedly avoided use of the word 'fundamentalist' and preferred low-key local and private witness to public confrontation.

The most influential fundamentalist in the interwar United Kingdom was an Ulsterman, William Patteson Nicholson (1876–1959). During the First World War, he worked as an evangelist for the Presbyterian Church in the United States, and between 1918 and 1920 was on the staff at Biola, where R.A.Torrey was dean. He thus had direct links to American fundamentalism. In 1920, Nicholson returned to an Ireland in turmoil, facing extensive insurgency and the immediate prospect of partition and independence for the South. Against this backdrop, between 1920 and 1923, he held a series of missions in major towns in the North, presenting a clear-cut and dogmatic gospel that drew a powerful response from the Protestant working class. Arguably, Nicholson turned them away from violence, but reinforced their sense of a Protestant identity that legitimated partition. Nicholson also conducted missions elsewhere in the English-speaking world, notably at Cambridge University in 1926, where he was instrumental in reinforcing the conservative standpoint of the CICCU, and in Australia, South Africa and New Zealand, where many future evangelical Anglican leaders would trace their conversion to his missions.[82]

[78] D. W. Bebbington, *Evangelicalism in Modern Britain: A history from the 1730s to the 1980s*, London: Unwin Hyman, 1989, pp. 217–8.

[79] Ibid., p. 220.

[80] Martin Wellings, 'Methodist Fundamentalism before and after the First World War', unpublished paper 2008, downloaded from www.eauk.org/efb, 13 July 2011.

[81] Quoted Bebbington, *Evangelicalism in Modern Britain*, p. 222.

[82] Finlay Holmes, 'Nicholson, William Patteson (1876–1959)', *ODNB*; Steve Bruce, *Paisley: Religion and Politics in Northern Ireland*, Oxford: Oxford University Press, 2007, pp. 14–15; Mavis Heaney, ed., *To God be the Glory: The Personal Memoirs of Rev. William P. Nicholson*, Belfast:

Nicholson's success was indicative of a continuing strongly anti-Catholic orientation in British evangelicalism, which helped to fuel explicitly Protestant political action not only in Northern Ireland, but also in Liverpool, Glasgow and Edinburgh.[83] Similar attitudes were manifested in parliament in 1927 and 1928 when the Church of England's proposed revised Prayer Book was twice rejected by the House of Commons because of its perceived Romanising tendencies. Crucial to this unexpected evangelical triumph were, on the one hand, the influential parliamentary leadership of William Joynson-Hicks, the home secretary, and Thomas Inskip, the solicitor general, and on the other, the widespread support of Nonconformists who, although dissenting from the Church of England, feared a compromise of its Protestant identity.[84] Indeed, a further reason for the muted nature of British fundamentalism may well be that Rome and romanisers were still seen as a greater danger to the faith than were modernisers.

The year 1928 also saw the foundation of the Inter-Varsity Fellowship (later Universities and Colleges Christian Fellowship), a culmination of the chain of events that had started with the CICCU's split from the SCM in 1910. The first Inter-Varsity conference was held in 1919, in the shadow of the recent war and the ongoing influenza epidemic. A general committee formed in 1923. The key figures involved pointed to the confluence of traditions imposed by evangelical university work and the rising dominance of the professional classes. Norman Grubb was the son of an Anglican clergyman, wounded in the recent war, who after his conversion had married the daughter of the CICCU hero-missionary to Africa and representative of muscular Christianity, C.T. Studd.[85] Douglas Johnson and Howard Guinness were medical students, in the tradition of the medical missionaries who had built and staffed the institutions of the faith missions from 1870. Francis Noel Palmer, chair of the Oxford Intercollegiate Christian Union (OICCU), went on to become a Christian and Missionary Alliance pastor in Canada. Hugh Rowlands Gough, the IVF's first chairman, was the well-connected son of a CMS India missionary. In all, the rise of the IVF might be seen as the revenge of international evangelical missions on liberalising home elites. The variegated nature of the movement would, however, lead to constant internal friction, particularly with regard to views on the role of the Holy Spirit. In the United States, meanwhile, it was the tension over liberalisation inside the Student Volunteer Movement and the YMCA's Inter-Seminary Alliance (paralleling those in the denominations), which from 1920

Ambassador, 2004. See David Price, 'A Life of Service: Leonard E Buck (1906–1996)', *Lucas*, 21 & 22 (1996), 129.

[83] P.J. Waller, *Democracy and Sectarianism: A Political and Social History of Liverpool 1868–1939*, Liverpool: Liverpool University Press, 1981: Steve Bruce, *No Pope of Rome: Anti-Catholicism in Modern Scotland*, Edinburgh: Mainstream, 1985.

[84] John Maiden, *National Religion and the Prayer Book Controversy, 1927–1928*, Woodbridge: Boydell, 2009.

[85] See Stewart Dinnen and Marie Dinnen, *Faith on Fire: Norman Grubb and the Building of WEC*, Fearn: Christian Focus, 1997; and John Stott, *The Cross of Christ*, Downers Grove: InterVarsity, 2006, pp. 14–15.

proved the catalyst for division.[86] In 1925, those who would later be involved in the conflicts at Princeton acted under the leadership of J. Gresham Machen to form the League of Evangelical Students (LES),[87] establishing largely defensive chapters in key Protestant seminaries in 1929 and 1930.

In 1928, Norman Grubb returned to England just as the Inter-Varsity groups were formalising their national framework under the leadership of Douglas Johnson. Grubb challenged them to respond to the decay of evangelicalism among Canadian universities and called for a 'missionary' initiative. Whereas Hugh Gough was ordained and after the Second World War became Vicar of Islington, Bishop of Barking and eventually Archbishop of Sydney,[88] Howard Guinness began a lifetime of travelling the globe, starting and encouraging student groups in universities in Canada, South Africa, India, Australia and New Zealand. In some places there were pre-existing groups which Guinness could connect to the emerging international network: Auckland College Student Bible League, founded by returned medical missionary William Pettit in 1927, was one of these.[89] The work rapidly also developed high school and grammar school extensions – the Inter-School Christian Fellowships and Crusaders groups. In countries where there were longer summer school vacations, particularly in Canada, but also in the United States, Australia, and elsewhere, Christian camping became another influential form of outreach.[90] As Guinness travelled and founded, others followed in his footsteps. His first tour of Australia, for instance, would project C. Stacey Woods and Vincent Craven into the international work of student missions, providing the Inter-Varsity Fellowship with two of its major international footsoldiers.[91] Woods would, with former LES member Charles Troutman, establish the Intervarsity Fellowship throughout the United States and extend Guinness's work in Canada, along with Keswick one of the few cases of the adoption of a successful British Commonwealth transplant at the heart of American evangelicalism.

BACK TO THE FRONTIER

The polarisation of evangelicals between liberalism and fundamentalism, disillusionment with the traditional denominational form and the exit of thousands of Christian believers into the more fluid world of interdenominational conventions,

[86] Keith Hunt and Gladys M. Hunt, *For Christ and the university: the story of Intervarsity Christian Fellowship-USA, 1940–1990*, Downers Grove: InterVarsity, 1992, p. 54.

[87] Ibid., p. 60.

[88] Obituary by M.L. Loane, *Independent*, 29 November 1997.

[89] Nick Duke, 'The Origins of Evangelical University Work in Australia and New Zealand with Special Reference to Howard Guinness', tss; Peter J. Lineham, 'Pettit, William Haddow 1885–1985'. *Dictionary of New Zealand Biography*, updated 22 June 2007, accessed 20 July 2011, at http://www.dnzb.govt.nz/.

[90] John G. Stackhouse, *Canadian Evangelicalism in the Twentieth Century: An Introduction to Its Character*, Vancouver: Regent College, 1999, pp. 91–3.

[91] A. Donald MacLeod, *C. Stacey Woods and the Evangelical Rediscovery of the University*, Downers Grove: Inter-Varsity, 2007, p. 40.

organisations and missions provided a significant opening for both more sectarian forms of evangelicalism and more diversity on the religious fringe. Some evangelicals continued to engage with the ecumenical movement but now needed to work out how they related to their own traditions and to find new ways of thinking about 'the social' and of overcoming the 'public sin' of disunity. Individuals from 'catholic' traditions and with sufficient distance from the centre (such as Hendrik Kraemer, or many German evangelicals) continued to find themselves in association with all these streams well into the 1960s. Others, such as David Du Plessis from South Africa, would emerge to bridge the diverging worlds at critical junctures.[92]

In the United States, as contemporary commentators on the Scopes Trial noted, evangelical groups in mainline American denominations *seemed* to collapse between 1925 and 1929 and to disappear from the political process, but 'they didn't seem unwilling to go.'[93] Although evangelicals achieved local dominance in states such as North Carolina, owing to their internal pluralism and fragmentation they were unable to resist national trends in socially progressive legislation.[94] During the 1920s and 1930s, evangelical fragmentation was commonly read as a prelude to disappearance. The dominance of this view could still be heard in the puzzled comments of journalists two generations later when evangelicalism re-emerged as a politically powerful mass movement. Where did it go in the interim?

Recent studies suggest that evangelicalism went back to 'the frontier'.[95] Pressed out of mainline institutions, denominational and faith missions (and their support organisations, such as Bible Colleges) became far more central to the movement. In some places, such the southern United States, there was a physical migration: northwards, leading to the 'Baptistification' of American religion,[96] and westwards, to the vibrant melting pot that was California.[97] An example of the latter was Aimee Semple McPherson who settled in Los Angeles in 1923, where she founded Angelus Temple, appropriated the entertainment techniques and emerging technologies fitted to reaching mobile populations, and built a global denomination, the International Church of the Foursquare Gospel (ICFG).[98] This trend would become accentuated during the Great Depression, and with evangelicals gravitating towards centres of mass job creation in the re-industrialisation attending the onset of the Second World War in 1939. In later years, two of

[92] Vinson Synan, *The Holiness Pentecostal Tradition: Charismatic Movements in the Twentieth Century*, Grand Rapids: Eerdmans, 1997, p. 225.

[93] Larson, *Summer for the Gods*, p. 242.

[94] Grant Wacker, 'A Tar Heel Perspective on the Third Disestablishment,' *Journal for the Scientific Study of Religion*, 30 (1991), 521.

[95] For example Darren Dochuk, *From Bible Belt to Sun Belt: Plain-Folk Religion, Grass Roots Politics and the Rise of Evangelical Conservatism*, New York: Norton, 2010.

[96] Wacker, 'Tar Heel Perspective', 519.

[97] John Schmalzbauer, 'Route 66 Evangelicals', *Evangelical Studies Bulletin*, 78 (2011), 1.

[98] Edith Blumhofer, *Aimee Semple McPherson: Everybody's Sister*, Grand Rapids: Eerdmans, 1993, pp. 232ff.

Australia's more famous conservative religious figures (Joh Bjelke-Petersen and Fred Schwarz) would emerge from a similar trend in Queensland.[99] In short, like their forebears, evangelicals headed for the frontiers, both internally and externally.

The concentration in the literature on the materialism of the 'Roaring Twenties' can miss the fact that it was also a period of intense religious experimentation. On the 'inner frontier', spiritualism experienced a resurgence on the back of the massive casualties during the First World War. Technology, spirituality and science converged. After the 1918–19 influenza pandemic, there was intense interest in spiritual healing, resulting in the remarkable 'healing missions' of James Moore Hickson and the rise of African independent healer/prophets such as Simon Kimbangu (Congo) and Engenas Lekganyane (South Africa).[100] In the very different milieu of elite youth at Oxford and Cambridge universities, Frank Buchman, an American Lutheran minister converted at Keswick in 1908, advocated 'soul surgery', or collective confession of sins, as a means to spiritual rebirth, consecration of lives to God, and openness to divine guidance. Buchman's movement, which became known as the Oxford Group in 1928 and Moral Rearmament in 1939, had a major impact in Britain, North America, Scandinavia, Africa and elsewhere. Its methods divided evangelical opinion but helped to prepare the ground for later charismatic renewal.[101] Scattered independent churches, as well as new formal evangelical networks, were linked by conferences, journals and the new media. In consolidating these new communities, evangelicals were early adopters of radio, impacting an expanding community of listeners in the United States, Canada,[102] Australia[103] and (increasingly) around the world. Aimee Semple McPherson's pioneering use of radio significantly enhanced her impact and celebrity. When *Hoy Cristo Jesus Benedice* (HCJB Radio) began in a cow shed in Ecuador in 1931, it became the first missionary radio station in the world. It would grow to have worldwide reach and spawn many imitators.[104] Outside the confines of creedally defined communities

[99] See John Harrison, 'The religious culture of Queensland: Pietism in religious practice, congregationalism in ecclesial polity', University of Queensland ePublications, http://espace.library.uq.edu.au/view/UQ:8021, accessed 29 June 2011; and Rae Wear, *The Lord's Premier*, St Lucia: University of Queensland Press, 2002.

[100] See Pamela E. Klassen, 'Radio Mind: Protestant Experimentalists on the Frontiers of Healing,' *Journal of the American Academy of Religion*, 75 (2007), 651–83.

[101] Garth Lean, *Frank Buchman: A Life*, London: Constable, 1985; Bebbington, *Evangelicalism in Modern Britain*, pp. 235–42; Phillip Boobbyer, 'Moral Re-Armament in Africa in the Era of Decolonization' in Brian Stanley and Alaine Low, eds, *Missions, Nationalism and the End of Empire*, Grand Rapids: Eerdmans, 2003.

[102] Bob Burkinshaw, 'Conservative Evangelicalism in the Twentieth-Century "West": British Columbia and the United States', in George A. Rawlyk and Mark A. Noll, eds, *Amazing Grace: Evangelicalism in Australia, Britain, Canada, and the United States*, Montreal: McGill-Queen's University Press, 1994, p. 318.

[103] Bridget Griffen-Foley, 'Radio ministries: Religion on Australian Commercial Radio from the 1920s to the 1960s', *Journal of Religious History*, 32 (2008), 50.

[104] Eloy H. Nolivos, 'Hermeneutics and Missions in the Land of the Equinox', *Evangelical Review of Theology*, 35 (2011), 45.

with professional interpreters, this sort of shotgun evangelicalism was (like its sixteenth- and nineteenth-century forebears) a recipe for innovation.

A good example of this trend is the career of the Australian Baptist pastor William Lamb. By the 1920s, premillennialism, particularly through the influence of the Scofield Reference Bible[105] and its related correspondence courses, had established itself strongly in the global network of faith missions, in regional networks of churches and the growing pentecostal movement. Lamb had commenced publishing on advent themes with the booklet *Dark Days and Signs of the Times* during the First World War, and followed it up with the establishment of a regular journal, *The Advent Herald.* The war remained a prophetic warning to all who would hear, and fuelled millennialism in evangelical papers.[106] Lamb built up a national reputation in Australia for end-times preaching and writing. In 1927, he left his settled pastorate at Burton Street Tabernacle in Sydney to pursue an international ministry. Lamb held that 'a salutary dread' of the second coming was 'a motive for every duty, and as a magnet to draw men to Jesus Christ'.[107] Over a long ministry, he became a vector into Australia and its region for the teachings of Moody Bible Institute, Harry Ironside, A.J. Gordon and others. His ministry was a constant balancing act of placing himself on the frontier but not *over* it into the imaginary wilds of heresy and extremism.[108]

Perhaps Lamb's greatest legacy, therefore, was one he could not acknowledge. It was through Lamb's Burton Street church that Smith Wigglesworth held his first healing crusade in Sydney, and through his ejection (along with the Duncan family) that the Assemblies of God in New South Wales was born.[109] Even though Lamb rejected 'faith healing' and the racism of 'Anglo-Israelism', his brand of adventism found him regularly advertised in the same sections of public newspapers as the Rosicrucians, British Israel and Bible prophecy interpreters. It was no coincidence that Australasian Baptist and pentecostal circles would be riven by British Israelite teaching in the 1930s and 1940s, with the success of A.H. Dallimore in New Zealand and the expulsion of Cecil and Leo Harris from the Assemblies of God in Australia.[110] This sort of ambivalence between premillennial movements

[105] This annotated version of Bible, the work of Cyrus Scofield, first appeared in 1909 and gave considerable currency to dispensational premillennialist readings of the text.

[106] For example, Stanley Frodsham, 'What Shall Be the Sign?', *Good News*, 19:7 (1 July 1928), pp. 5–6.

[107] John G. Ridley, *William Lamb: Preacher and Prophet*, Glebe: Australian Baptist Publishing House, 1944, p. 72.

[108] Ibid., p. 53.

[109] See P.B. Duncan, *The Charismatic Tide*, Sydney: P. Duncan, 1978.

[110] See Mark Hutchinson, 'Cartledge, David Frederick (1940–2005)', *Australasian Dictionary of Pentecostal and Charismatic Movements*, Online, http://webjournals.alphacrucis.edu.au/journals/ADPCM/a-to-d/cartledge-david-frederick-1940–2005/, accessed 29 June 2011; and Laurie Guy, 'One of a Kind? The Auckland Ministry of A. H. Dallimore,' *Australasian Pentecostal Studies*, 8 (2008).

and their offspring was common to marginal evangelicals. Defining where they stood with regard to the frontier was always an important issue of identity.

THE WIDER WORLD

Cultural difference gave rise to even more challenging frontiers around the world. Whereas many evangelicals in India sweated away as 'sahibs', others learned from the enculturation techniques developed in Asia by the China Inland Mission.[111] The story of Henry Richards's 'Pentecost in the Congo' was an application of Hudson Taylor's dictum that the gospel needed to be stripped of its European accretions and repackaged in the spiritual clothing of the locale.[112] The 1920s and 1930s saw the proliferation of indigenous Christian groups. In the Indian subcontinent, for example, these ranged from K.E. Abraham's Indian Pentecostal Church of God (1924), to the Ceylon Pentecostal Mission (1927), to the tiny Dipti Mission (1925). Some, such as Kandiswamy Chetti's Fellowship of the Followers of Jesus (Madras, 1933–1943), were movement-critiques of European Christianity, and entirely indigenous. John Sung, who left his American education (and clothing) behind to prosecute power evangelism in China and among the Chinese diaspora in Southeast Asia, also incorporated a running critique of European/American 'domination'.[113] By the 1930s, Chinese conversion to Christianity was becoming a 'problem' for Dutch evangelical missions organisations in Malaya and Indonesia. How was an indigenous Christianity to be developed among a people who were not indigenous ('children of the soil', or *peranakan*)?[114] India, increasingly sensitive to issues of indigeneity, provided a melting pot for frustrated evangelicals, liberals and high churchmen alike. In both India and China, the 1920s were the high point for medical missions and building colleges, in part as a response to social gospel understandings that such work was 'inherently evangelistic'.[115]

With the traditional intellectual support bases for Christian action now largely in liberal or secular hands, the major missiological publishers tended to undermine traditional evangelical approaches. When W.E. Hocking produced a book entitled *Re-Thinking Mission: A Laymen's Inquiry after One Hundred Years* (1932), Hendrik Kraemer replied in *The Christian Message in a non-Christian World* (1938) that the

[111] Susan Billington Harper, *In the Shadow of the Mahatma: Bishop V. S. Azariah and the Travails of Christianity in British India*, Grand Rapids: Eerdmans, 2000, p. 205.

[112] Bengt Sundkler and Christopher Steed, *A History of the Church in Africa*, Cambridge: Cambridge University Press, 2000, p. 309.

[113] Lyall, *A Biography of John Sung*, p. xxiv; Hwa Yung, 'The Integrity of Mission in the Light of the Gospel: Bearing the Witness of the Spirit', *Mission Studies: Journal of the International Association for Mission Studies*, 24 (2007), 169.

[114] See Hendrik Kraemer's 1933 report in *From Missionfield to Independent Church. Report on a Decisive Decade in the Growth of Indigenous Churches in Indonesia*, London: SCM, 1958, p. 151.

[115] Jeffrey Cox, *The British Missionary Enterprise since 1700*, New York: Routledge, 2007, p. 218.

Harvard philosopher's book contained 'no authentic Christianity.'[116] Hocking's search for a 'new rootage' for a purged Christianity, a new verification of mystical Christian truth in experience, was not the faith of Jesus so much as an American pragmatist's response to German idealism.[117] Many evangelicals were also puzzled as to why the huge effort at institution building produced so few converts – another symbol (for them) of the fruitlessness of liberal theology. At Kobe College, Japan, for example, the 'persistent difficulties' in producing both cosmopolitan and Christian values among the school's alumni increasingly meant an emphasis on the former.[118] Those at the grassroots turned instead to popular dispensaries and healing missions.

Speaking at Edinburgh 1910, the leading Indian Anglican V.S. Azariah, noted the huge disparity between the missionary input and the vast need which, with population growth, outstripped the 'supply' of missionaries by a larger margin every year. He called for attention to the 'problem of race relationships', for mutual acceptance and help to become the norm rather than the 'happy exception'.[119] A new pragmatic literature emerged, notably in the works of the Englishman Roland Allen, addressing missions experience through the template of the biblical text, establishing a tradition which would, after its rediscovery in the 1960s by leading missiologists such as Lesslie Newbigin, profoundly influence evangelical thinking about culture.

There were increasing numbers of people willing to take up Azariah's challenge through innovation. Samuel Stokes, for example, developed with Sundar Singh the idea of a 'Brotherhood of the Imitation of Jesus', which would plant in India a startling innovation: 'a life of literal obedience and the detailed imitation of Christ'. The idea's Franciscan parallels struck a chord with high churchmen, while its biblicism appealed to low churchmen and nonconformists hungry for a 'sympathetic' approach to enculturating Christianity.[120] Whereas CMS administrators were concerned about such 'a man who has had very direct and unusual intercourse with God', their missionaries on the ground knew that it was precisely this sort of spirituality that was needed in the Indian philosophical marketplace. The explosion of interest in the West with regard to Sundar Singh's life and spirituality pointed to the uncomfortable reality both that there was also a real hunger for

[116] Ibid., p. 236. On Hocking, see Leroy S. Rouner, *Within Human Experience: the Philosophy of William Ernest Hocking*, Cambridge, MA: Harvard University Press, 1969.

[117] Hendrik Kraemer, *World Cultures and World Religions: The Coming Dialogue*, Cambridge: James Clarke, 1960, p. 341.

[118] Noriko Kawamura Ishii, *American Women Missionaries at Kobe College, 1873–1909*, New York: Routledge, 2004, p. 183.

[119] V.S. Azariah, 'The Problem of Co-operation between Foreign and Native Workers', *World Missionary Conference*, vol. 9, Edinburgh: Oliphant, Anderson & Ferrier, 1910, p. 306.

[120] William Emilsen, '"The Great Gulf Fixed": Samuel Stokes and the Brotherhood of the Imitation of Jesus' in Geoffrey A. Oddie, ed., *Religious Traditions in South Asia: Interaction and Change*, Richmond: Curzon, 1998, p. 101.

direct experience of God in the West, and that the possession of such an experience was one of the few sources of transferable authority in the East.[121]

Azariah himself was a leading example of overcoming the 'gulf' between Indian and European perceptions of the gospel. He was the first (and, until his death in 1945, the only) Anglican of Indian extraction to be made a bishop. He came from a Nadar family converted under CMS missionaries (amid tales of healing and exorcism more reminiscent of Martin of Tours than 'modern, educated Englishmen') in Megnanapuram, Madras Presidency.[122] He founded an indigenous Indian Missionary Society on CIM lines. Inspired by China missionary Hudson Taylor and revivalist Charles Grandison Finney, Azariah was a further demonstration that Indian churches could (as Henry Venn had dreamed) become self-supporting, self-propagating and self-governing. Unlike many American evangelicals, Azariah remained a committed internationalist, one of the minority of delegates to the Edinburgh 1910 Conference to come from the non-Western world. His call for 'friendship' on equal terms rather than 'condescending love'[123] challenged the patriarchy implicit in the 'sending' mentality of the West.

The development of faith missions provided people like Azariah with alternative modes of operation in the increasingly difficult inter-war period. Rising anti-colonialism directly challenged the European presence in the non-Western world. In 1919, Indian National Congress opposition was fanned into flame by the Amritsar Massacre, where hundreds were killed by British troops. In China, as the Guomindang nationalist government strove under a failing Sun Yat-sen to unite the country, labour unionists and students protested aggressively against the British and Japanese presence, also resulting in the resort to violence.[124] The late 1930s saw the definitive rise of anti-colonialist forces in China, with Mao declaring missionaries, schools and study abroad to be part of the 'cultural aggression' of the West. Meanwhile, Japanese occupation of large parts of China led to the introduction of mandatory Shinto worship, to which evangelicals had particular objections.[125] In such settings, grassroots evangelicalism was not as much an option as a political and social necessity.

As noted earlier, the traditional denominational missionary strategy had been to confront 'the great civilizations' (particularly India and China). Contemporary events fed evangelical doubts as to cooperation with Western states, and pushed them towards a more pragmatic concentration on those areas that produced the greatest returns. Consequently, British missionary effort shifted away from China, and to a lesser extent from India, towards Africa: by the late 1930s, there were

[121] Robert Eric Frykenberg, *Christians and Missionaries in India: Cross-Cultural Communication since 1500*, Grand Rapids: Eerdmans, 2003, p. 227.

[122] Harper, *In the Shadow of the Mahatma*, pp. 16–17.

[123] Azariah, 'The Problem of Co-operation', p. 308.

[124] Cox, *British Missionary Enterprise*, pp. 236–7.

[125] Scott Summers, 'Missionaries, Opium and Imperialism' in Wei-ying Ku, ed, *Authentic Chinese Christianity: Preludes to its Development*, Leuven University Press, 2001, p. 20.

nearly 3,000 British missionaries in sub-Saharan Africa.[126] In addition to the large flow of white Americans who became Student Volunteers in mainline and faith missions between 1880 and 1930, an increasing number of African Americans also turned their attention to Africa,[127] both as missionaries and as extensions of American educational and social concern for African advancement. Institutions like the Achimota School on the Gold Coast and Fort Hare in the Eastern Cape, the older mission school networks and foreign interests such as the Phelps-Stokes Fund were to have a significant influence on the emergence of national leaders in sub-Saharan Africa.[128] Meanwhile, independent sects and churches, many without form or structure, were a seedbed for militant political movements.[129] Elsewhere in sub-Saharan Africa, this period saw numerous revivals and the rapid growth of independent forms of African Christianity, deriving inspiration from evangelicalism while blending it with indigenous cultural and spiritual traditions. Such movements were launched by William Wadé Harris in Liberia and Ivory Coast in the 1910s and by Simon Kimbangu in the Congo and the Aladura ('praying people') in Nigeria in the 1920s.[130]

This period also saw the beginnings of significant growth in two very different regions of the world that had hitherto been little touched by evangelicalism, but were to become dynamic centres of the movement in the later twentieth century: Korea and Latin America. The first Protestant missionaries did not arrive in Korea until the 1880s, and initial growth in the Methodist and Presbyterian churches that they planted was steady rather than spectacular, with 20,914 church members in 1905. Under the impact of the Pyongyang revival of 1907, however, there was then a rapid growth to 144,242 by 1910, with numbers of Protestants overtaking those of the longer-established Catholic community. Korean evangelicals became prominent in the nationalist campaign against Japanese rule: in 1919, sixteen of thirty-three signatories to the declaration of independence were Protestants and 18.2 per cent of those questioned by the police following pro-independence demonstrations were Methodists or Presbyterians, at a time when they made up barely 1 per cent of the total population. Such associations increased their popular appeal, and although they remained a small minority in a still predominantly Buddhist country in the 1920s and 1930s, the foundations for their impressive post-war expansion were being laid.[131]

[126] Cox, *British Missionary Enterprise*, p. 237.

[127] Sylvia M. Jacobs, 'Give a Thought to Africa: Black Women Missionaries in Southern Africa' in Nupur Chaudhuri and Margaret Strobel, eds, *Western Women and Imperialism: Complicity and Resistance*, Bloomington: Indiana University Press, 1992, p. 208.

[128] See Shoko Yamada, '"Traditions" and Cultural Production: Character Training at the Achimota School in Colonial Ghana,' *History of Education*, 38:1 (2009), 29–59.

[129] James T. Campbell, *Songs of Zion: The African Methodist Episcopal Church in the United States and South Africa*, New York: Oxford University Press, 1995, p. 179.

[130] Hastings, *Church in Africa*, pp. 443–5, 505–18.

[131] Donald Baker, 'Sibling Rivalry in Twentieth-Century Korea: Comparative Growth Rates of Catholic and Protestant Communities' in Robert E. Buswell and Timothy S. Lee, eds, *Christianity in Korea*, Honolulu: University of Hawaii Press, 2006, pp. 289–96.

Meanwhile, the tiny evangelical minorities in overwhelmingly Catholic Latin American countries were also growing. In Brazil, in contrast to Korea, Protestantism was liable to be deemed unpatriotic, and was initially largely limited to expatriates, missionaries and immigrant communities such as German Lutherans and slaveholders who left the southern United States after the Civil War. Indigenous churches were planted in the late nineteenth century, but initially only grew very slowly. By the time of the Second World War, however, significant communities had developed: in the 1940 census, more than a million Protestants, amounting to 2.61 per cent of the population, were reported. As yet, only a small proportion of these were pentecostals.[132] A similar pattern of modest growth was apparent in Central America, where Protestant membership numbers increased from 10,442 in 1916 to 41,188 in 1936.[133] In Chile, where there were 55,000 Protestants in 1920 and where pentecostalism established itself rather earlier than in Brazil, there were, however, indications that numbers were taking off as the annual Protestant growth rate increased in the 1930s from 1.46 per cent to 6.45 per cent.[134] It was a sign of things to come.

THE GREAT DEPRESSION

When the world economy collapsed, the evangelical response was characteristically more practical than theological. Most continued to consider the problem to be personal sinfulness and public disobedience to God rather than mere economics. The World Evangelical Alliance opened 1929 with its regular 'Universal Week of Prayer', with an emphasis on 'a spirit of new adventure in Christian unity'.[135] Evangelical social action was often done in non-evangelical settings, even though its activism was expressed in a remarkable outpouring of social and cultural engagement after 1929. The contribution of evangelicals has therefore been largely obscured because, as with many of their reformist forebears, when they acted they tended to do so under other flags. In Canada, the idiosyncratic Bible preacher William Aberhart fomented a political movement of remarkable tenacity. Weaving together monetary theory, elements of the Communist Manifesto, training in public speaking skills and the reach of his popular radio, Radio Sunday School, and a newspaper preaching program, in 1933 Aberhart convened the first Social Credit Study Group at his Prophetic Bible Institute in downtown Calgary.[136] He then multiplied these groups across the city, capturing Labor supporters from their normal fare of socialist lecturers, railway workers in heavily unionised workshops, working-class

[132] Emilio Willems, *Followers of the New Faith: Culture Change and the Rise of Protestantism in Brazil and Chile*, Nashville: Vanderbilt University Press, 1967, pp. 59–67.
[133] Wilton M. Nelson, *Protestantism in Central America*, Grand Rapids: Eerdmans, 1984, p. 56.
[134] Willems, *Rise of Protestantism*, p. 68.
[135] As reported in *The Advertiser*, 1 August 1929, p. 16.
[136] Stackhouse, *Canadian Evangelicalism*, p. 39.

women from their houses, unemployed men from the dole queue, and drought-stricken farmers in the hinterland.[137] The Depression had made all of these the 'victims of financial powers in Ottawa, Toronto, Washington and New York'.[138] The study group movement became a political party, won a resounding victory in the 1935 provincial elections and held power in Alberta until 1971. Present in most local communities through overlapping networks of denominational, faith mission and missionary organisations, evangelical churches not only provided immediate care (shelter, food), but showed the ability to innovate in the provision of job retraining, labor communities, and so forth. In the heart of evangelical Sydney, R.B.S. Hammond built Hammond's Social Services into 'one of the largest social service providers in Sydney', predating government-funded social welfare payments and support.[139] Despite the relative minority status of evangelicals in Australia, and the decline of other socially active forms of Christianity over the years, Australia came (through such endeavours) to have a greater dependence on Christian charities for delivery of social services than any of its sending countries (England, Wales, Scotland or Ireland).[140]

In Canada's United Church, Hugh Wesley Dobson noted that the Depression sparked greater 'favour toward evangelical Christianity' as people sought meaning to their suffering and greater integration between theology and practice.[141] The 1930s would be a decade of gospel campaigns as well as soup kitchens and job creation schemes, a time of necessary (if unavoidable) disciplines. A variety of renewal streams emerged, which attempted to tie renewed spirituality with practical change. Entertainment-led approaches, mass baptisms and rapid expansion of Foursquare churches across New South Wales and Queensland indicated a strong religious response to Depression conditions. In 1933, the Oxford Group made its way across Canada, drawing large crowds.[142] The mystical wholeness movement, Camps Farthest Out (founded by Glenn Clark in 1930), emerged in Minnesota and was replicated across the United States, teaching 'the practicability of finding the Kingdom of Heaven in the practical world of men'.[143] In Christchurch, New Zealand, and Melbourne, Australia, the Salvation Army saw remarkable street conversions reminiscent of its earliest years. Many of the resulting members would

[137] Larry Hannant, 'The Calgary Working Class and the Social Credit Movement in Alberta, 1932–35', *Labour/Le Travail*, 16 (1985), 97ff.

[138] Stackhouse, *Canadian Evangelicalism*, p. 42.

[139] Brian Lucas and Anne Robinson, 'Religion as a Head of Charity' in Myles McGregor-Lowndes and Kerry O'Halloran, eds, *Modernising Charity Law: Recent Developments and Future Directions*, Cheltenham: Edward Elgar, 2010, p. 189.

[140] Ibid., p. 190.

[141] David Plaxton, '"We Will Evangelize with a Whole Gospel or None": Evangelicalism and the United Church of Canada' in Rawlyk, ed., *Aspects of the Canadian Evangelical Experience*, p. 112.

[142] Ibid., p. 114.

[143] Patricia Faith Appelbaum, *Kingdom to Commune: Protestant Pacifist Culture between World War I and the Vietnam Era*, Chapel Hill: University of North Carolina Press, 2009, p. 118.

later find their way into leadership in the pentecostal movement. In the Sydney inner-city district of Redfern, Philip Duncan's Jubilee Pentecostal Temple claimed that none of its members were unemployed, and the church grew almost continuously despite the surrounding misery. A contemporary newspaper advertisement suggests why: 'You will enjoy the old story told in a simple straightforward manner and the excellent power under which this preacher [C.L. Greenwood from Melbourne] ministers makes [sic] the promises of the Gospel real and living. Bright singing. Everyone welcome.'[144] The other evangelical institutions in Sydney were playing a similar tune, preaching the fundamentalist Gospel on Sundays and supporting charity works during the week. Soup kitchens, such as those run by the Peoples' Evangelistic Mission in in Toowoomba and Brisbane, were opened for the unemployed.[145] With middle-class supporters usually suffering less economic hardship and therefore able to maintain funding for such activities, the Depression thus gave evangelicals significant opportunities for linked mission and social engagement.[146]

THE SECOND WORLD WAR

While at war with one another in the Anglophone world, both liberals and evangelicals were wrong-footed by the challenges presented by the rise of Nazism. In Germany itself, the *Land* churches in the dysfunctional Weimar Republic not only 'whole-heartedly endorsed the government of Adolf Hitler', but 'campaigned to align the organization, theology, and practice' of their churches into a single, Nazi-certified Reich church. It was all the provincial churches could do to delay electing Hitler's adviser on church matters (Ludwig Müller) as supreme *Reichsbischof*.[147] A very large percentage of the missionary force dispossessed by the Versailles arrangements, and their supporters back at home, had already swung significantly to the right before Hitler came to power.[148] Some of those not purged in the Gleichschaltung of 1933 became supportive, occasionally enthusiastic, Nazis. International organisations, such as Life and Work, equivocated between the two parts of the divided German church until late 1935.[149] At the level of leadership, the Faith movement and Confessing Churches opposed accommodation with the Nazi regime, and its leaders (most famously, Dietrich Bonhoeffer) suffered for it

[144] *Sydney Morning Herald*, 18 July 1931, p. 15.

[145] *Brisbane Courier*, 15 October 1932, p. 19; M. Hutchinson, 'Brawner, Mina Conrod Ross' in *Australasian Dictionary of Pentecostal and Charismatic Movements*, online, http://webjournals.alphacrucis.edu.au/journals/ADPCM/a-to-d/brawner-mina-conrod-ross-1874–1960/, accessed 1 July 2011.

[146] Manwaring, *From Controversy to Co-existence*, p. 50; *The Advertiser*, 4 February 1930, p. 19.

[147] Kenneth C. Barnes, *Nazism, Liberalism, & Christianity: Protestant Social Thought in Germany and Great Britain, 1925 – 1937*, Lexington: University Press of Kentucky, 1991, p. 94.

[148] Ibid., p. 9.

[149] Ibid., p. 92.

in ways ranging from expulsion to imprisonment and even death.[150] For his part, the neo-Orthodox theologian Karl Barth traced the rise of the German Christians to the errors of theological liberalism: 'the last, most perfected and ugliest progeny of the neo-Protestantism' of Harnack and Troeltsch. 'The whole proud heritage of the eighteenth and nineteenth century', he proclaimed, 'proved incapable of resistance [to Nazism], obviously because it contained nothing that had to resist and could not give away.'[151] Barth's *Theological Existence Today* (1933) 'fundamentally changed the church situation', helping to polarise opinion and consolidate the opposition which came together around the Barmen Declaration (1934). Barth, Bonhoeffer and the Confessing Church were not just opposing Nazism; they were opposing what they considered to be an equal danger: the importation of 'alien principles' into the creedal basis of the German Evangelical Church, leading to its dissolution.[152] In contrast to Barth, Bonhoeffer's resistance was activist rather than purely intellectual, growing from a determination to live a life 'characterised by discipline and the constant knowledge of death and resurrection'. His involvement in resistance, and the plot to kill Hitler, resulted in his execution in April 1945 shortly before the end of the war. There were many evangelicals who saw the inside of a gaol cell under Fascist regimes in Germany, in Italy (under Mussolini's Concordat with the Roman Catholic Church) and in Vichy France. Few, however, had the impact that Bonhoeffer had on those post-war experiential evangelicals who encountered his prison writings and saw in his biography something of the spirit of nineteenth-century missionary saints.

Evangelical responses to the Second World War were more mixed than to the First. Addressing British Christians from Switzerland, Karl Barth, equating Hitler with an 'evil spirit', affirmed that it was 'a righteous war, which God does not simply allow, but which He commands us to wage'. It was to be fought 'unequivocally in the name of Jesus Christ'.[153] In Britain and America, however, it was, in general, not religious but political leaders who most straightforwardly characterised the war as a spiritual crusade in defence of Christian civilization and the free world. It was true that such language was echoed by Cyril Alrington, the Dean of Durham, in a pamphlet entitled *The Last Crusade*, published in 1940, but this was not well received in the churches.[154] In the United States, the prevalent emphasis of sermons was to portray the war not as holy, but rather as 'a tragic manifestation of sin'.[155]

[150] Eberhard Bethge, *Dietrich Bonhoeffer: A Biography*, trans. Eric Mosbacher et al., Minneapolis: Fortress, 2000, p. 178.

[151] Arne Rasmussen, 'Deprive Them of Their Pathos: Karl Barth and the Nazi Revolution Revisited', *Modern Theology*, 23 (2007), 370.

[152] Hubert G. Locke (ed. and trans.), *The Church Confronts the Nazis: Barmen Then and Now*, New York: Mellen, 1984, p. 21.

[153] Quoted Alan Wilkinson, *Dissent or Conform? War, Peace and the English Churches 1900–1945*, London: SCM, 1986, p. 202.

[154] Robert Jewett, *Mission and Menace: Four Centuries of American Religious Zeal*, Minneapolis: Fortress Press, pp. 238–40; Snape, *God and the British Soldier*, p. 184.

[155] Jess Yoder, quoted Jewett, *Mission and Menace*, p. 241.

Indeed, awareness of the very enormity of the struggle could enhance a sense of transcendent perspective: Christopher Chavasse, son of Francis and twin brother of Noel, who had been appointed Bishop of Rochester on the eve of the war, wrote that whereas in the First World War 'we looked to God for assistance in our righteous cause', in the Second 'it is God who is calling for *our* assistance in His cause of righteousness against devilish forces of evil'.[156] In Britain, however, historically evangelical denominations, especially Brethren and Methodists, were substantially over-represented among conscientious objectors.[157]

Nevertheless, amidst the danger and turmoil of war, there were some signs of religious revival. On the home front in Britain, this was not necessarily more than 'diffusive and discursive Christianity and . . . air-raid shelter spirituality', but it still helps to explain a modest increase in churchgoing and widespread receptivity to Billy Graham's message in the decade after the war.[158] In the armed forces too, there were moments of awakened spiritual interest, notably in the U.S. military in the months after Pearl Harbor and among British prisoners of war held by the Japanese in the Far East.[159] The war years also proved fertile for new initiatives that were of importance for the future. In 1943, the National Association of Evangelicals, which was to play a major role in bringing together the divided moderate and fundamentalist wings of American evangelicalism, was founded at a convention in Chicago. In 1944, large-scale Youth for Christ rallies began to gather momentum in cities across the United States, one of them addressed by a then-unknown young pastor named Billy Graham.[160] Across the Atlantic in 1945, a church commission led by Bishop Christopher Chavasse launched a substantial report, *Towards the Conversion of England*, which was path-breaking in its advocacy of the use of modern media as evangelistic tools. It unexpectedly proved to be a bestseller.[161]

In the short term, the two world wars disrupted overseas missionary activity and in particular cooperation between the German- and English-speaking arms of evangelicalism. Following the First World War, Germany had been stripped of most of her overseas colonies, leaving German evangelical missionaries *persona non grata*. In 1920, German New Guinea, for example, became an Australian-mandated territory. Even those who stayed (such as Karl Emil Schiller in Japan) faced the collapse of agency funding, first by isolation and then by the ruin of many of those firms (such as that of philanthropist Johann Karl Vietor, which failed in 1931) which depended on the colonies and had funded the missions. In East Africa, Johann Traugott Bachman's translation of the Bible into Nyika was stopped when he was

[156] Quoted Gummer, *Chevasse Twins*, p. 134.
[157] Wilkinson, *Dissent or Conform?* p. 291.
[158] Stephen Parker, *Faith on the Home Front: Aspects of Church Life and Popular Religion in Birmingham 1939–1945*, Bern: Peter Lang, 2005, p. 215.
[159] Jewett, *Mission and Menace*, pp. 240–1; Snape, *God and the British Soldier*, pp. 171–7.
[160] Joel A. Carpenter, *Revive Us Again: The Reawakening of American Fundamentalism*, New York: Oxford University Press, 1997, pp. 141, 166–8.
[161] Gummer, *Chavasse Twins*, pp. 160–9.

interned in 1916; Ernst Jakob Christoffel was expelled from Turkey after the First World War and interned by the British during the Second World War; Johannes R. A. Stosch of the Gossner Evangelical Lutheran Church was repatriated by the British from India in the First World War and interned in the Second World War, before being repatriated again in 1947.[162] In both wars, overtly German communities in countries of British settlement suffered repeated internship and institutional closure.[163] English-speaking missionaries also faced considerable difficulties. At the outbreak of the Second World War, almost all male missionaries were withdrawn from Morocco – only a veteran female missionary, Maude Carey, and three other single women remained behind to run things. Canadian Presbyterians James and Lillian Dickson left Formosa during the First World War, as did all Bethel Temple Missionaries when the Japanese invasion reached Indonesia.[164] Mabel Francis, a Christian and Missionary Alliance missionary in Japan, refused to be evacuated as she considered Japan to be her home. She spent the war under house arrest in a Catholic convent. Nor did British authorities appreciate too much missionary interest in strategically sensitive areas: facing invasion by the Japanese, numbers of missionaries who had developed sympathies with the Indian nationalist movement were excluded from the country.[165]

Nevertheless there were longer-term gains. The enforced withdrawal of missionaries from Asian countries resulted in a radical need for evangelicalism to undergo crash indigenisation.[166] Shortly before his death, Chinese evangelist John Sung 'revealed that God had showed him that a great revival was coming. But the western missionaries would all have to leave first.'[167] For Westerners who had given their lives to China, a painful loss led to new opportunities. Moreover, the war produced a global consciousness among many Western evangelicals. Not only did they read about the wider world in their newspapers, but millions served overseas. A Methodist soldier in the British army led prayer meetings in the desert before the battle of El Alamein, and another stimulated a small revival among his comrades in north-east India.[168] Among the more than a million American servicemen who visited Australia prior to MacArthur's great push into the Pacific were many evangelical chaplains and servicemen, who left their mark on the churches and

[162] See the relevant entries in A. Scott Moreau, Harold A. Netland, Charles Edward van Engen, David Burnett, et al., eds, *Evangelical Dictionary of World Missions*, Grand Rapids: Baker, 2000.

[163] For example, see John B. Koch, 'Nickel, Theodor August Friedrich Wilhelm (1865–1953)', *Australian Dictionary of Biography*, vol. 11, Carlton: Melbourne University Press, 1988, p. 28.

[164] See Mark Hutchinson, 'The Latter Rain Movement and the Phenomenon of Global Return' in Michael Wilkinson and Peter Althouse, eds, *Winds from the North Canadian Contributions to the Pentecostal Movement*, Leiden: Brill, 2010.

[165] Relevant entries in Moreau et al., *Evangelical Dictionary of World Missions*.

[166] S. Grypma, 'Withdrawal from Weihui: Chinese Missions and the Silencing of Missionary Nursing, 1888–1947', *Nursing Inquiry* 14:4 (2007), 318.

[167] Hwa Yung, 'The Integrity of Mission in the Light of the Gospel', p. 172.

[168] Snape, *God and the British Soldier*, p. 171.

denominations they visited. This would become a mechanism for rapid Americanisation of some Australian denominations (particularly the Queensland Baptists) during the 1950s. Military authorities found ex-missionaries useful in the information services in particular. Kenneth Grubb from the Worldwide Evangelization Crusade, for example, spent the Second World War first as director of the Latin American section and later as Overseas Controller of the Ministry of Information, before going on to head the Church Missionary Society.[169] This sort of information, in turn, would inform strategic decisions by evangelical leaders in the post-war period. According to Joel Carpenter, 'It is hard to overstate the war's role in reviving the idea of "global conquest" among evangelical missions promoters. The very scale of the conflict was suggestive to those who dreamed of world evangelization.'[170]

CONCLUSION

On V.J. Day in August 1945, Bishop Christopher Chavasse preached the sermon at a service of thanksgiving at Rochester Cathedral attended by Field Marshal Montgomery. Earlier in the year, Chavasse had rejoiced at victory in Europe, but the circumstances that had led to victory over Japan 'sickened and saddened him beyond anything he had experienced in his life'. He denounced the mass slaughter of non-combatants at Hiroshima and Nagasaki, feeling that by acquiescing in the indiscriminate use of the atom bomb, 'the England he loved had let him down' and that 'we are a nation of arch-hypocrites'. The advent of the nuclear age now starkly exposed the dangers of the uncritical equation of faith and patriotism that Chavasse's father had maintained in 1901, and for which his beloved twin brother had died in 1917.[171] Subsequently, as awareness grew that the Nazis had taken the British invention of concentration camps to unparalleled levels of horror and had engaged in the systematic extermination of Jews and other perceived undesirables, the capacity of modernity to foster evil of a seemingly apocalyptic depth was all too painfully apparent. The post-war world was to be a chastened and insecure one, which called for radical reassessment of many past patterns of thinking. Herein lay both profound challenge and exciting opportunity for evangelicals.

During the preceding troubled decades, evangelical engagement with modernity had been an uneven and fragmented process. At one extreme was the initially uncritical acceptance of the modern nation-state in all its destructive power; at the other, the polemical fundamentalist rejection of scientific and historical theories that were gaining mainstream acceptance. In the middle reaches of the spectrum were uneasy responses to new patterns of leisure and sporting activity, along with

[169] P.R. Clifford, 'Grubb, Kenneth George' in Anderson, ed., *Biographical Dictionary of Christian Missions*, p. 265.

[170] Carpenter, *Revive Us Again*, p. 178.

[171] Gummer, *Chavasse Twins*, pp. 158–9.

selective adoption of technological advances and new channels of communication. Modernity's crises – the hardship of economic depression and the trauma of war – caused some to reject traditional faith, but also gave rise to renewed evangelical social engagement and revivalistic energy. Sometimes seduced by modernity, sometimes fighting against it, evangelicals were nevertheless finding ways of turning it to their advantage.

7

Towards Global Trans-Denominationalism: 1945 to 1970s

As the guns stopped firing in the Pacific, and the millions who could travel left behind those who would never travel again, crowding onto the available means of transport back to their homes, the world turned to the problem of post-war reconstruction. Politicians, economists and denominational churchmen imagined external forms for a new age of cooperation and peace. For both traditional evangelicals and their younger successors, however, the prospect of a new age of merely human effort was greeted with ambivalence. The growing problems with the institutional church meant to them a growing commitment to the 'church invisible'. Speaking just before the outbreak of the Second World War, nineteenth-century holiness icon Catherine Booth-Clibborn had taken her respectable Sydney audience to task: 'How can you expect to bring peace when you ignore the Prince of Peace?'[1] Her successors (such as Billy Graham) would focus on change through inner experiences of grace, which motivated redemptive effort in the world. The promises of corporate cooperation appeared to have collapsed in the secular ruin of the League of Nations and its religious equivalents (such as the Interchurch World Movement).

For Graham and his contemporaries, the post-war world was an ambivalent place. The war was over, the antichrists had been conquered, but Jesus had not yet returned, despite the prophetic 'fig tree' seeming to blossom in the establishment of the state of Israel.[2] Faced with a global challenge in the context of a universal struggle, they wanted 'to do something really big for God' before Christ's expected return. 'Oh, Lord – let me do something,' Billy Graham implored his Saviour in 1948. 'Trust me just to do something for you before you come.'[3] The evangelical message was the same – Christ, the Word and energetic effort. But how should that effort be spent in the face of Russian apostasy and the threat of creeping Communism? In the shadow of the D-Day heroes, techniques had to change in order to restore to evangelicals something of their former effectiveness. Graham would be the best-known, but not a unique, representative of this activism which expressed itself in evangelical 'crusades' ranging from small-scale local revivals to global campaigns like the Assemblies of God's 'Global Conquest' (commenced in

[1] *The Sydney Morning Herald*, 16 June 1936, p. 10.
[2] Timothy Weber, *On the Road to Armageddon*, Grand Rapids: Baker, 2004.
[3] David Aikman, *Billy Graham: His Life and Influence*, Nashville: Nelson, 2007, p. 61.

1959). Across the board, evangelicals sought to cooperate with the energies released by war and reconstruction in order to remake the religious face of the world. In the period between 1945 and 1970, evangelicals may be seen responding to the dual impulses of defending and promoting 'a gospel which works' among masses of individuals. Along the way, both its formal organisations and its grassroots communities would learn new ways of relating to one another, as well as to broader social realities.

CONTENDING FOR THE PUBLIC SPHERE

The key challenge for evangelicals in the post-war period was to find alternatives to the institutional influence lost in the dual struggle with secularism and modernism in the period from 1870 to 1930. There were those traditional areas – such as newspapers and schooling systems – where they once had influence, and now no longer did. Where evangelical merchant princes such as John Fairfax and George Brown had once held sway over the most influential news organs of the anglophone world, and intellectuals such as Warfield held their own, most Western public institutions followed the path that Marsden describes in the subtitle of his grand study of American universities: 'From Protestant Establishment to Established Nonbelief'. In the world inhabited by the Toronto *Globe and Mail* and the *Sydney Morning Herald*, the arc of organs founded by evangelicals could be described, first, in the loss of their evangelical connections, then of their principled reformism, and finally – through corporatisation – the claim to being somehow fundamental to the national public spheres that they had helped to create. Such retrenchment limited the projection of the evangelical voice. In other words, the evangelical withdrawal was not (as has been suggested) just a problem of ideas – it was a fundamental lack of means. As such institutions as newspapers, universities and schools were gatekeepers to social influence, simply withdrawing into the sort of fundamentalist ghetto created by the proliferation of Bible colleges in the 1920s and 1930s was insufficient over the longer term. Whereas some fundamentalists hunkered down awaiting the return of Christ, others recognised the need to re-establish connection with the increasingly secularised public sphere. This meant, in the first wave, co-option of new technical media to promote the traditional, ungarnished 'preached word' and, over the longer term, new types of organisation with transformative goals for their surrounding cultures. Both waves grew directly out of the same nineteenth-century missions and convention movements. Nowhere is this more clearly seen than in the figure of Billy Graham.

Born four days before the Armistice brought the First World War to a fitful (though ultimately unfruitful) halt, Billy Graham was the grandson of Scots-Irish southerners shaped by the iconic American ethos of frontier, church and Civil War. His grandmother was a poor but proper North Carolina Presbyterian, and his grandfather a 'sometime Klansman and a full-time whiskey-drinking hell-raiser',[4] whose strongest contribution to his son (Frank Graham) was a determination not to take after him. Frank properly fulfilled this determination by being converted in a Methodist revival at the age of eighteen. The Graham household, based around the work on their dairy farm, was thus disciplined, biblical and (through their church associations) 'rock-ribbed Calvinist' – good morals met good business sense.[5] To this the Depression period added dispensationalism and revivalism – amidst which Billy Frank Graham was converted in 1933. 'I didn't have any tears, I didn't have any emotion.... But right there, I made my decision for Christ. It was as simple as that, and as conclusive.'[6] Conversion under a fiery preacher left Graham in the quandary as how to marry his moderate character to this new faith. He was shaped by itinerant evangelists who stayed in their home, by the institutions of the fundamentalist subculture (Bob Jones College, Florida Bible Institute and Wheaton College) and by his experience as a salesman (like Moody, but selling brushes rather than shoes) where his contemporaries acknowledged that he had 'a voice that appeals'.[7] From the start, he combined intense belief in the inspiration of the Bible and single-minded personal preparation with self-promotion, 'sanctified entertainment' and effective rhetoric. The American South taught him to preach; his transfer to the North provided him with a market and new technologies. At Wheaton he met, and later married, the daughter of Keswick medical missionaries to China (Ruth Bell), took over a church, connected with the wealthy and powerful (including industrialists such as R.G. Le Tourneau and pastoral leaders such as Torrey Johnson), launched a radio career and gained access to publishing networks. In the American West, Biola graduate Charles Fuller had (since 1925) already forged a similar approach through his 'Old Fashioned Revival Hour', as would, within a few years, Oral Roberts, a pentecostal holiness campaigner and faith healer. From 1943, emerging ministries committed to a more engaged evangelicalism found a common voice through the National Association of Evangelicals, and a mass base built on the large itinerant populations of soldiers mobilised for the war by such interdenominational organisations as Youth For Christ (YFC). In 1945, Graham (who, using a credit card provided by his wealthy backers, logged 135,000 miles, becoming United Airlines' top civilian passenger) and his colleagues presented YFC's 'evangelical vaudeville' and unvarnished appeals for public commitment to Christ every Saturday night to a cumulative total of nearly a million people. By 1947, YFC and Graham were in Europe, overcoming cultural resistance and anti-Americanism through new approaches to citywide evangelism, combining organisational techniques with ways of mobilising divergent cultures and approaches to authority. Like Moody

[4] William Martin, *A Prophet with Honor: The Billy Graham Story*, New York: Harper Perennial, 1992, p. 56.

[5] Ibid., p. 59.

[6] Ibid., p. 64.

[7] Ibid., p. 66, 70.

before him, Graham also had a private experience of the Holy Spirit (mediated by Welshman Stephen Olford) which others felt gave him a 'largeness and authority' not seen in his preaching before.[8] All of this was a preparation for what was to come.

In 1949, Graham's growing profile elicited an invitation to lead the interdenominational 'Christ for Greater Los Angeles' campaign. It had been forty-three years since that city had been surprised by the sudden outbreak of the Azusa Street Revival (1906). Since then, it had become better known as the home base of America's archetypical press baron, William Randolph Hearst, than for spirituality. Hearst, however, could smell a story. All Graham's organisation and charismatic presence could have not lifted him above the level of his contemporaries more effectively than the two-word missive sent by Hearst to his Los Angeles papers: 'Puff Graham'.[9] YFC appealed to Hearst: it reinforced traditional American values, and its promise of revival sold newspapers. Graham's anticommunist politics placed Hearst's editorial stance in a larger, millennial framework. Communism was, he believed, 'a religion that is inspired, directed, and motivated by the Devil himself, who has declared war against Almighty God,' and a sign of the sooncoming final conflagration and judgement on the world's sin, a conflagration which, after Hiroshima, had a specifically nuclear configuration.[10] Hearst's papers turned Graham's flagging three-week campaign into a blockbuster eight-week phenomenon, ultimately drawing a total attendance of more than 350,000. It was picked up in leading magazines such as *Time* (run by 'missionary kid' Henry R. Luce) and *Life*, with coverage which specifically drew parallels between Graham and D.L. Moody, Billy Sunday and Aimee Semple McPherson.[11] Billy Graham had made the transition from private religion to public icon. He moved on to Boston, where (unexpectedly for both the press and Christian leaders like Harold J. Ockenga) success on the brash West Coast was translated to the more conservative east. Twenty-five thousand people attended the final night service. The next stop, Columbia, South Carolina, saw a crowd of 40,000 on the final night. Invitations to pray at the opening of state houses began to come his way – and when Communist forces invaded the southern part of Korea in 1950, millennial projections, nuclear fears, private representations and the Graham charisma led to a personal meeting with President Truman. The development of electronic media saw his ministry expand into radio and, from 1951, television and film, with corresponding expansion of the staff directly employed by the newly formed Billy Graham Evangelistic Association (BGEA). The advent in 1951 of the World Evangelical Fellowship – established as a post-war revival of the original international Evangelical Alliance

[8] Ibid., p. 86.
[9] Ibid., p. 117.
[10] Ibid., p. 115.
[11] Marshall Frady, *Billy Graham: A Parable Of American Righteousness*, New York: Simon and Schuster, 2006, p. 255.

vision, and a counter to the World Council of Churches – provided Graham with a natural milieu in which to act.[12] His method depended upon united action, and the WEF aimed to 'foster that unity of the Spirit, which already exists between all true believers and is something infinitely deeper than the outward form of union which the World Council has brought into being'.[13] In return, Graham provided resources, impetus and method. The wealthy and powerful in the evangelical community gathered behind Graham, who was now a national figure. A campaign in Washington drew bipartisan political support (except from Truman himself, whom Graham had offended on his first visit), including his new, close and controversial friends, Richard Nixon and Lyndon Johnson.[14] He met Dwight Eisenhower, promoted his election as president,[15] and prayed at his inauguration. He would thereafter be seen internationally as a sort of religious ambassador for the United States.

This status was a double-edged sword. In Britain, Graham's Haringey campaign reportedly drew the largest crowd in British religious history. Cultural faux pas drew criticism and educated Graham's team on cross-cultural differences even within the same language. Graham would, over the years, progressively adapt his mode of address – dropping the word 'crusade' after a campaign in heavily Muslim parts of Africa, and calling for America to jettison 'the embarrassment' of racist segregation as likely to 'weaken [America] to the point where communism will gain the ultimate victory'.[16] In Germany and France, and at whistle-stop tours of other European cities, they discovered the depth of difference created by hundreds of years of Christian state-church theology, anti-Christian revolution, and their appropriations in local cultural identities. The Haringey success opened up the old British Empire links; Jack Dain, an Anglican missionary to India who was later assistant bishop in Australia, sketched for Graham a map of India on a napkin, and outlined the problems he would face.

Dain would later be closely associated with Graham in most of those global enterprises, including the Sydney Crusade (1959) and the organisation of the Lausanne Congress (1974), which bridged British and American cultures. The connection made the Graham organisation truly global and produced results previously unseen. It would require a shift in thought and cultural approach. In the post-colonial era, 'indigenous . . . missions found that, unless there is a social dimension to their evangelistic message there is little real response to their mere

[12] Mark Silk, 'The Rise of the New Evangelicalism: Shock and Adjustment' in William R. Hutchison, ed., *Between the Times: The Travail of the Protestant Establishment in America, 1900–1960*, New York: Cambridge University Press, 1990, p. 282.

[13] Ian Randall, 'Evangelicals, Ecumenism and Unity: A Case Study of the Evangelical Alliance', p. 6; http://www.eauk.org/, accessed 12 October 2010.

[14] Martin, *A Prophet with Honor*, pp. 144–5.

[15] Frady, *Billy Graham*, p. 255.

[16] Martin, *A Prophet with Honor*, pp. 175ff; Steven P. Miller, *Billy Graham and the Rise of the Republican South*, Philadelphia: University of Pennsylvania Press, 2009, p. 85.

preaching.'[17] The social impulse so embedded at Lausanne reflected developments in evangelical thought in the 1960s. This shift in evangelical consciousness expanded rapidly during the 1970s (for instance, the 1979 Madras Declaration), finding new forms of social agency (such as The Evangelical Alliance Relief Fund, or TEAR Fund, launched in 1968) and cultivating fundamentally different evangelical attitudes towards social engagement and mission.[18] Over time, therefore, evangelicals self-consciously stepped away from an 'American gospel', incorporating local and social elements rejected by their fundamentalist forebears. Graham's campaigns in India, Taiwan, the Philippines, Japan and Korea in 1956, the 'safari for souls' across Africa in 1960 and campaigns in several Iron Curtain countries in the 1960s prepared the way for this sort of development. The Southern Cross Crusade which took in Australia and New Zealand saw nearly 3.25 million attendances (equivalent to 25 per cent of the entire population of both nations), of which 150,000 'decided for Christ', an average response rate of 4.6 per cent (more than double Graham's average response rate).[19] BGEA publications (such as *Decision* Magazine), books, film, radio and television circulated around the world, and offices were opened in Australia, Canada, France, Germany, New Zealand, Spain and the United Kingdom.

The effectiveness of these campaigns was only as good as the church networks behind them. In Sydney, Jack Dain's follow-up scheme was reputedly 'so effective that a year later eighty per cent of the Anglicans who went forward were involved in their local churches.'[20] In London after the 1954 crusade, by contrast, the disappointing retention rates were such as to cause resistance among the clergy to 'American methods' in the nine successive UK campaigns. Thus, while millions of people responded to Graham's appeals over the more than sixty years of his active ministry, Graham's real success was in his direct impact on existing evangelical communities and clergy, and his indirect influence on the standing of evangelicalism around the world. Graham mobilised American industrial and middle-class wealth, brought the techniques of the fading revivalist tradition into the twentieth century through the co-option of modernist techniques and technologies and used his credibility and contacts to provide new organisational forms and pathways for the tacit trans-denominational networks of evangelicalism which had – in many cases – come into existence prior to the advent of his ministry. When 2,700 delegates from 150 nations met in Switzerland in 1974 for the Lausanne Congress, 'possibly the widest-ranging meeting of Christians ever held', Jack Dain made explicit what everyone already knew: 'Our presence here [he said] is, under God, the result of

[17] Colin Blair, 'Christian Mission in India: Contributions of Some Missions to Social Change', PhD thesis, Simon Fraser University, 2008, p. 1.

[18] 'Tear Fund: Silver Jubilee', *Third Way* (October 1993), 8.

[19] Stuart Piggin, *Evangelical Christianity in Australia: Spirit, World and World*, Melbourne: Oxford University Press, 1996, p. 168.

[20] Mark Hutchinson, 'Dain, Arthur John 'Jack' (1912 – 2003)', *Australian Dictionary of Evangelical Biography*, online.

the vision, the evangelistic passion, and the dedication to world evangelization of Dr. Graham. Although the resulting work has obviously been shared by many, the initiative and the essential undergirding has come from Dr. Graham.'[21]

Graham drew evangelicals into spheres of common action which downplayed their denominational differences and histories; his managerial techniques cut through pietist cultures and fostered a new pan-evangelical pragmatism. While this created resistance among more traditional evangelical forms (particularly in Germany), he helped to create a form of evangelicalism no longer dependent on the national states and identities. The effect was to create an evangelicalism increasingly ambivalent about its sectarian status.

Graham's inclusivism, however, came at a cost within his own constituency. His links to pentecostal healers in the 1950s, the charismatic movement in the early 1960s and the Jesus People and youth culture during the later 1960s, made the 'establishment' nervous – as much for the potential impact on middle-class funding as upon the theological issues such associations suggested.[22] Graham saw these as extensions of the need for 'all culture' to be redeemed. His fundamentalist constituency saw them as opportunities to regain the moral high ground. Some picketed his meetings, or attacked him in the Christian press. In New Zealand, Inter-Varsity founder William Pettit resigned from the Scripture Union because Graham's campaign was sponsored by the National Council of Churches. Graham succeeded by tapping the available energies of the moment: the sources of energy on the sawdust trail in the 1930s would not suffice for the post-war boom or the culture change of the 1960s and 1970s. In turn, his efforts legitimised and released forces in post-war evangelicalism which continued to act well beyond the well-organised confines of the campaign ground. At the end of the 1920s, the fundamentalists had been at the centre of evangelicalism and pentecostals were on the fringe; by the 1970s, however, the fundamentalists were heading for the edge of the movement, with the pentecostals rapidly taking their place.

PROMOTING GLOBAL REVIVAL

As Graham's work extended beyond the Atlantic societies, his success became increasingly dependent on the local forms evangelicalism had taken in its previous expansions. In East Africa, for instance, there had been an ongoing revival (largely explored in the literature as a maturing of Keswick spirituality) since 1929. Hunger for authentic spirituality in the context of mission settings where the teaching of the gospel had produced a widespread but largely nominal Christianity resulted in an increased emphasis on prayer and the doctrines of 'the deeper life'. Dissatisfaction

[21] A.J. Dain, 'Welcoming Remarks', International Congress on World Evangelization in Lausanne, Switzerland, 1974, transcript, Billy Graham Center Archives, Wheaton, IL.

[22] Larry Eskridge, quoted in Chris Armstrong, '"Tell Billy Graham the Jesus People Love Him." How Evangelism's Senior Statesman Helped the Hippies Tune in, Turn on to God.', *Christianity Today*, December, 2002.

with the controlled and conventional nature of the missionary church also played a role,[23] as did contextual factors, such as the failure of the rains in 1928, leading to famine and a refugee crisis. In reading together Scofield's notes on the Holy Spirit, a British missionary doctor (Joe Church) and the chief health officer in the Ugandan government (Simeon Nsibambi) discovered that they were seeking the same thing: a sin-quenching 'Victorious Life' in the individual, which would flow over into their institutions and societies.[24] Beginning in a localised way at the Gahini missionary hospital in Rwanda, and taking off more dramatically from the 1935 Kabale convention, the revival was 'an unlikely blend of Wesleyan-Anglican theology, Pentecostal fervor and African passion'.[25] The convention form married precursor tribal spiritualities, public confession and intense prayer meetings, which began to spread rapidly through Uganda, Rwanda, Burundi, Kenya and Tanzania. While under the influence of the Holy Spirit, people wept for hours, let out deep pain, confessed to fears in their lives and showed a spontaneous open expression of emotion. Fear of emotionalism was swept away under the waves of the Holy Spirit. People became radiant, full of joy and filled with a sense of awe at the holiness of God and the power of the work of the cross.[26]

Large numbers of people – over the longer term, in their millions – were certainly strongly influenced by the revival. There were significant 'social righteousness' and physical healing outcomes – but it is the long-term impact that makes it of interest. As late as the Rwanda genocide (1994), scholars have noted that the 'best of the Revival (Balokole) tradition' had undeniable long-term political consequences.[27] Through spokesmen such as Festo Kivengere, this international, indigenous revival stimulated others, such as the Galiwink'u revival among Aboriginal communities in Australia from 1979, and opposed dictatorial regimes in East Africa.[28] Revival was more than simply an absorption of African spirituality; it was also a claim to ecclesial leadership.[29] Kivengere would play a prominent role in the 1974 Lausanne Congress and gain significant exposure through his adoption by the Graham network.

Africans, Asians, Europeans and Americans were all changed by the encounters. The rapid indigenisation of Christianity through these means sharpened a deeper problem: having often been dispossessed in their own intellectual centres, what

[23] T.O. Beidelman, *Colonial Evangelism: A Socio-Historical Study of an East African Mission at the Grassroots*, Bloomington: Indiana University Press, 1982, p. 108.
[24] Richard MacMaster and Donald Jacobs, *A Gentle Wind of God: The Influence of the East Africa Revival*, Scottsdale: Herald, 2006, p. 28.
[25] Mark Noll, *The New Shape of World Christianity: How American Experience Reflects Global Faith*, Downers Grove: InterVarsity, 2009, p. 178.
[26] Emmanuel M. Kolini and Peter R. Holmes, *Christ Walks Where Evil Reigned: Responding to the Rwandan Genocide*, Colorado Springs: Authentic, 2008, p. 62.
[27] Kevin Ward, 'Africa' in Adrian Hastings, ed., *A World History of Christianity*, Grand Rapids: Eerdmans, 1999, p. 230.
[28] Viz. John Blacket, *Fire in the Outback*, Perth: Khesed Ministries, 2004.
[29] Beidelman, *Colonial Evangelism*, p. 108.

did Western evangelicals have to offer the rest of the world? Western evangelicals had tended to send overseas their worker-missionaries rather than their theologians. Their faith in the sufficiency of the cross also meant that Africans, Asians and others needed to work out for themselves what being a Christian in *this* place actually meant. In return, Westerners who encountered this new dynamism were challenged to the core as to how to deal with their own Eurocentric, Enlightenment traditions. Firsthand experience of the miraculous and the movement of the Holy Spirit in Argentina and China created considerable cognitive dissonance: 'I am trying to be discerning now about the Enlightenment,' reflected participant Donald Jacobs. 'Certainly that movement moved forward Western culture in some areas, but its insistence on human logic as the final arbiter of truth produced an anthropocentric worldview that was closed to any alternative view.'[30] World events (such as the Rwanda genocide in 1994) would be a significant blow to those pre-Lausanne forms of evangelicalism which emphasised evange*lism* for individual conversion only. Jack Dain was proved right: evange*lisation* – with its vision for social transformation – would be essential to the continuing evangelical presence in the world.

The organised, 'respectable' revivals engaged by public evangelicalism, however, were only part of the story. As majority world revivals, such as those in East Africa, South America and Pakistan, gained in influence through Anglican and Keswick networks, the same networks were responding to itinerant ministries, publications and indigenous growth. In China, the few remaining external links brought back news that the church had not been destroyed by the Communist government's repeated purges, but had put down strong roots. Cyclical college revivals in the United States – such as that which broke out at Wheaton College in 1950 – received national attention.[31] In Canada in 1948, under pressure from the institutionalisation of Canadian pentecostalism, another revival broke out at Sharon Orphanage and Schools in North Battleford, Saskatchewan, which rapidly spread through restorationist networks. While opposed and eventually driven out of the larger pentecostal denominations in North America, this 'New Order of the Latter Rain' lodged in West Coast locations and their related missionary networks. These took the new teachings of the restoration of apostles and prophets, the laying on of hands, and the associated biblicist theologies back to mission churches in Asia, Africa and the Pacific Rim (including, most importantly for the global charismatic movement after the 1980s, New Zealand).[32] Whereas the movement

[30] Donald R. Jacobs, 'My Pilgrimage in Mission', *International Bulletin of Missionary Research*, 16:4 (October 1992), online version, EBSCO.

[31] Richard Riss, 'The New Order of the Latter Rain', *Assemblies of God Heritage* (Fall 1987), 15.

[32] Brett Knowles, '"From the Ends of the Earth we Hear Songs": Music as an Indicator of New Zealand Pentecostal Spirituality and Theology', *Australasian Pentecostal Studies*, 5/6 (2002); Mark Hutchinson, 'The Latter Rain Movement and the Phenomenon of Global Return' in M. Wilkinson and P. Althouse, eds, *Winds from the North: Canadian Contributions to the Pentecostal Movement*, Brill: Leiden, 2010.

was submerged between 1950 and 1970, it proved – beyond expectations, given the seeming dominance of organised evangelicalism during the 1950s – sufficiently flexible to take on new forms more adapted to the mobile, fragmented 1980s and 1990s. Each of these revivals represented an occasion for an evangelical spirituality to respond to local need and embed itself in local identities. The division between organised and marginal evangelical expressions replayed the traditional tension in the movement between its denominational and grassroots forms.

The bridge between the evangelical margins (which were rapidly becoming centres in their own right) and the more established centres (which were rapidly becoming marginalised in their own cultures of origin) came from another sort of margin. In the shorter term, Graham's movement through and beyond big-tent evangelism was an encouragement to those who did not have his respectability. The pentecostal holiness Oklahoma farmer, Oral Roberts, started as part of a father-son team after his reported healing from tuberculosis in 1934. Roberts and W.M. Branham became the leading figures in what has become known as the Healing Revival of the 1950s. Coordinated through the *Voice of Healing* magazine (edited by J. Gordon Lindsay, a healing revivalist whose family had roots in the divine healing tradition of J.A. Dowie), this disparate group followed post-war American expansion all over the world, finding in the majority world an acceptance for their brand of naïve Holy Spirit evangelism which remained marginal in the West. Whereas Oral Roberts famously struck difficulties in Australia, the 1957 Mombasa campaign by T.L. Osborne provided significant traction for pentecostal Christianity in East Africa. Tommy Hicks's 1954 campaign in Argentina is credited with laying the basis for the pentecostal growth which would eventually become the South American revival,[33] a movement which (as David Martin has pointed out) has since had a global impact.[34] Such campaigns were less important for their Americanism than for their catalytic affect in wedding emerging indigenous streams of Christianity to the emerging global charismatic movement. Osborne, for example, developed a social mobilisation model which by 1964 was running in 80 countries involving more than 8,000 native missionaries.[35]

His pentecostal background aside, Roberts shared many attributes with Graham. They were both physically impressive and had intellectual ability and an eye for the strategic. When in 1947 he (like Graham) incorporated his ministry as the Oral Roberts Evangelistic Association, he followed Graham's relocation to Chicago by also moving to a more central location, in Tulsa, Oklahoma. Roberts's background in pentecostal holiness linked his evangelism with faith healing, albeit increasingly wrapped in a holistic philosophy ('Abundant Life') of 'healing the whole man'.

33 Allan Anderson, *An Introduction to Pentecostalism*, Cambridge University Press, 2006, p. 59.

34 Martin, *Tongues of Fire.*

35 Grant Lea, 'T. L. (Tommy Lee) Osborne', *Renewal Journal*, 1995, http://www.renewaljournal.com; David Edwin Harrell, *All Things Are Possible: The Healing and Charismatic Revivals in Modern America*, Bloomington: Indiana University Press, 1975, pp. 65ff.

Roberts followed Graham into film and television and, in a long ministry involving more than 300 crusades on 6 continents, would visit many of the places the better-known evangelist also went. With the establishment of his own University in Tulsa (1965), Roberts achieved something which Graham had long considered but from which he had drawn back in order to maintain a concentration on evangelism. The 1966 World Congress on Evangelism in Berlin, organised by the Graham-inspired journal *Christianity Today*, brought Roberts out of his 'honorary leper' status into the mainstream and resulted in Graham dedicating that university at its official opening.[36] In the face of criticism from traditional evangelical delegates, an Anglican bishop, R.O.C. King of Jamaica, rose to his feet and testified that many of his parishioners had been healed as a result of Roberts's radio ministry.[37] It did not solve the theological issues. As Carl Henry, editor of the sponsoring journal and later lecturer in theology at Fuller Seminary, noted, the mainstream still objected to 'glossolalia and healing, if these are made to be central and indispensable facts of normative Christian experience'.[38] The evangelical pragmatists of the Graham type, however, knew energy when they saw it. For his part, Roberts declared himself 'conquered by love' at this unparalleled global meeting which saw himself, a pentecostal evangelist, sit down to lunch with the Bishop of London.

'THE BOOKS THAT WILL CHANGE THE WAY PEOPLE THINK'

While the Graham-Roberts relationship had predated Berlin, Graham's fascination with universities was common among evangelicalism's post-war leaders. While crowds filled football stadia around the world to respond to the evangelical appeal, none of the neo-evangelicals forgot that 'the fundamentalist problem' had essentially been a battle between scholars, a struggle for the mind of the West, which they had lost. Even in retreat, however, no one had declared the war over. The genius of the effective rapprochement between the two poles of transatlantic evangelicalism after the war was that, instead of pursuing either British integralism or American sectarianism, different evangelical subcultures adopted either or both strategies depending on the situation and the protagonists. Whereas American students had the choice of a wide range of Christian institutions for academic preparation, in the Commonwealth welfare states the public universities dominated and there were comparatively few private options. In Britain, Australia and Canada, development of the sectarian option was restrained by a relative lack of private evangelical concentrations of philanthropic wealth, lack of a general 'going

[36] David Harrell, *Oral Roberts: An American Life*, Bloomington: Indiana University Press, 1985, p. 201.

[37] Harrell (pp. 202–3) also reports significant support from the South American delegates and from India.

[38] Ibid., p. 199.

to college' culture, and an Anglican integralism which still saw public universities as the preferred place for scholarship.

Although similar issues were faced at pre-tertiary levels, there state sponsorship was often available. Post-war mass public education meant that welfare states around the world were often forced to sponsor those private institutions which their public education acts in the late nineteenth century had been designed to displace.[39] Starting from the 1950s, and growing rapidly in the 1960s and 1970s, Christian schooling from kindergarten to age eighteen thus became a feature in many Western societies. This was strongest where the secular state education system was most comprehensive and state financial support was available, and where migration allowed the construction of self-aware communities of difference. In Australia, for instance, its growth was a result of the failure of the state system to adapt to rapid population growth, by the strength of the NGO sector as a silent partner with the welfare state and by the presence of a large number of Reformed migrants from Europe. By 1990, the combined Christian schooling system had grown larger than the total education systems of some states and territories, and its funding was becoming an issue in national elections. There was lower overall demand in the United States. Christian options there filled the gaps left by the public system: either traditional church 'grammar schools' for the elite or mission-centred, welfare-oriented elementary Christian schools serving 'the needs of urban minority children'.[40] The decay of evangelical confidence in American civil religion, however, may be measured by the fact that, whereas between 1920 and 1960, only 150 separatist day schools were founded, since the mid-1960s, as many as 12,000 have been set up, to which must be added the 'hidden' numbers of parents who have opted in favour of homeschooling for their children.[41] Internationally, as national state governments replaced colonial regimes in Africa and Asia, Christian schools were often co-opted into national systems. The Chinese mission school experience – which saw many of the graduates of schools and colleges become leaders in the anti-Christian movements of the 1920s – reinforced evangelical opinion that Christian institutions *should* remain centred on the specifically Christian function of witnessing for Christ.[42]

The new generation of university graduates emerging from para-church organisations such as the Inter-Varsity movement would provide the audience for – and later the academic thrust behind – evangelical responses to modernism and modernity in the 1950s, 1960s and 1970s. Evangelical writing at the time was fascinated

[39] See Mark Hutchinson, 'A Riveder le stelle: Gough Whitlam and the Origins of a University in Western Sydney', *The Whitlam Legacy*, no. 1, Paramatta: Whitlam Institute, 2011.

[40] 'African-American Christian Schools: An Interview', *Christian School Education Magazine*, http://www.acsi.org/Resources/PublicationsNewsletters/ChristianSchoolEducation, accessed 26 August 2011.

[41] James C. Carper and Thomas C. Hunt, 'The Christian Day School Movement' in idem, *The Dissenting Tradition in American Education*, New York: Peter Lang, 2007, p. 203.

[42] Oi Ki Ling, *The Changing Role of the British Protestant Missionaries in China, 1945–1952*, Madison: Fairleigh Dickinson University Press, 1999, p. 206.

with achieving 'the best' and 'most rigorous' scholarship. One source of this lay in evangelicalism's high emphasis on the facticity of the Scriptures – a reflection of the movement's pragmatism. The new institutional foundations of the 1940s and 1950s were also impelled by the need to respond to the American market. Writing to Wilbur Smith in 1946 as he was promoting the foundation of what would become Fuller Theological Seminary, Charles Fuller declared: 'if this school is to be, it should be the best of its kind in the world. It should stand out first, as being absolutely true to the fundamentals of the faith and second, as a school of high scholarship . . . particularly the study of the atoning work of Christ.'[43]

The primary reason – the need to counter liberal scholarship in the most convincing way possible – interacted with the second: American college education was essentially a pathway to respectability. The best affordable scholarship was essential to attracting students, and therefore the survival of the college. To sustain a university ministry, however, answers were needed to the secular orthodoxies which abounded. It would take the sectarian institutions decades before a viable research culture could develop. In the interim, church-based ministers from the Reformed traditions played an important role in encouraging the new generation of scholars. Harold Ockenga at Park Street Congregational Church in Boston would nurture many, as a founder both of the National Association of Evangelicals and of Fuller.[44] This would lead to the publication of defences of the 'new evangelicalism' in Bernard Ramm's *The Christian View of Science and Scripture* (1954), Edward Carnell's *The Case for Orthodox Theology* (1959), and Carl Henry's multi-roled career as theologian (*The Uneasy Conscience of Modern Fundamentalism*, 1947; *God Revelation and Authority*, 6 volumes, 1976–83) and editor of the Graham circle's counter-modernist journal, *Christianity Today* (founded in 1956). It was from Fuller Theological Seminary that W.R. "Bill" Bright emerged in 1951 to found – on the Graham model – Campus Crusade for Christ. Bright's success lay in his co-option of culture: his 'Four Spiritual Laws' tract has been circulated in the billions, while by the time of Bright's death in 2003, the organisation was claiming that their 'The Jesus Film' (launched in 1979) had 'been seen by more than 5.1 billion people in 234 countries'.[45] As with other elements of the evangelical post-war expansion, success bred conflict – as often as not with other evangelicals. For its part, the IVCF saw Campus Crusade as being un-, if not anti-, intellectual.[46]

[43] Charles E. Fuller to Wilbur M. Smith, October 7, 1946, quoted in G. Marsden, *Reforming Fundamentalism: Fuller Seminary and the New Evangelicalism*, Grand Rapids: Eerdmans, 1995, p. 13.

[44] Garth M. Rosell, *The Surprising Work of God: Harold John Ockenga, Billy Graham, and the Rebirth of Evangelicalism*, Grand Rapids: Baker, 2008.

[45] Obituary, Bill Bright, *Charity Wire*, http://www.charitywire.com/charity31/03386.html, accessed 25 October 2010.

[46] John G. Turner, *Bill Bright & Campus Crusade for Christ: The Renewal of Evangelicalism in Postwar America*, Chapel Hill: University of North Carolina Press, 2008, p. 71.

Evangelicals, however, continued to find themselves locked out of the research universities. The search for a sustainable, top-rank, evangelical research institution would remain a troubling element in the waters of American evangelicalism: the vast amounts spent on the expansion of Baylor University in Texas would become a symbol of this aspiration.[47] British institutions, meanwhile, came to play a disproportionate role in generating and giving credentials to evangelical scholarly literature for a worldwide public.[48] While still at Caius and Gonville College, Cambridge, the Brethren biblical student F.F. Bruce built a reputation for careful biblical inquiry from an evangelical perspective, which saw him (by 1959) rise to the position of Rylands Professor of Biblical Criticism and Exegesis at the University of Manchester. Making the most of archaeological and textual discoveries to reject higher criticism, he mocked its self-proclaimed victory 'against the traditional theories. It only remains to fix the amount of the indemnity.'[49] Instead, Bruce showed that (as with the Chester Beatty Papyrii), 'no point of Christian faith or practice is affected by these textual questions. Every fresh discovery helps to confirm the general reliability of our New Testament text.'[50] Bruce's major case for this stance would emerge in his *Archaeology and the New Testament* (1947).

The rise of this sort of evangelical scholarship reflected a new 'space' for such ideas, opened up through the rise of neo-orthodoxy,[51] the decline in reputation of liberal German theologians because of their connections with the Nazi regime,[52] and the archaeological findings of W.F. Albright.[53] In 1942, Max Warren of the CMS convened an Evangelical Fellowship for Theological Literature within the Anglican Church. In 1944, Bruce combined with the IVF-UK's Biblical Research Committee to form the Tyndale Fellowship for Biblical Research,[54] in order 'to consider how best the reproach of obscurantism and anti-intellectual prejudice might be removed from Evangelical Christianity in England'.[55] It was a deliberate attempt to change culture by separating 'evangelicalism' from 'that polite theological swearword . . . "fundamentalism"'. It did so at the nexus of subjectivism and objectivism – on

[47] See Jeannie Keaver, 'Baylor Regents Dismiss President', *Houston Chronicle*, 25 July 2008.

[48] Mark Noll, *Between Faith and Criticism: Evangelicals, Scholarship and the Bible in America*, San Francisco: Harper and Row, 1986, p. 137.

[49] F.F. Bruce, 'Old Testament Criticism and Modern Discovery', *The Believer's Magazine*, 49 (1939), 242.

[50] F.F. Bruce, 'The Chester Beatty Papyrii', *The Harvester*, 11 (1934), 164.

[51] Ned B. Stonehouse, '1957 Presidential Address: "The Infallibility of Scripture and Evangelical Progress"', *Bulletin of the Evangelical Theological Society*, 1.1 (Winter 1958), 9–10.

[52] Gary J. Dorrien, *Idealism, Realism, and Modernity, 1900–1950*, Louisville: Westminster John Knox Press, 2003, p. 433; idem, *The Barthian Revolt in Modern Theology: Theology without Weapons*, Louisville: Westminster John Knox Press 2000, p. 136; Susannah Heschel, 'When Jesus was an Aryan: The Protestant Church and Antisemitic Propaganda' in Robert P. Ericksen, ed., *Betrayal: German Churches and the Holocaust*, Minneapolis: Fortress, 1999.

[53] Noll, *Between Faith and Criticism*, p. 92.

[54] F.F. Bruce. 'The Tyndale Fellowship for Biblical Research', *The Evangelical Quarterly*, 19:1 (January 1947), 52–61.

[55] Ibid., 52.

the one hand declaring the evangelical bias in its contributors just as it was aware of the bias in its opponents, while on the other positioning itself as 'no friend of the irrationalism in some modern theological circles'.[56] Summer schools and annual lecture series prefaced the establishment of Tyndale House (1944) as a residential research centre which rapidly began to draw postgraduate scholars from all over the world and re-established Cambridge as a significant hub for evangelicalism. This hub was a scholarly endeavour with an international public which enabled it to sidestep the established university elites. The energetic Douglas Johnson established (with Ronald Inchley) a literature division which grew into Inter-Varsity Press (IVP). IVP's emerging global network sidestepped traditional publishers by direct address to evangelical students in seminaries, Bible colleges and universities around the world. Global distribution enabled the small British press to have a disproportionate influence. When F.F. Bruce's *Acts of the Apostles* was printed by IVP-USA in 1951, I. Howard Marshall declared the event 'the decisive date in the revival of evangelical scholarship in its recognition by other scholars'.[57] The *New Bible Commentary* series emerged with an unparalleled first print run of 30,000 copies, 22,000 of which were pre-ordered and partly paid in advance by American networks (especially the Michigan-based Dutch Calvinist publisher, W.B. Eerdmans, and the IVCF itself).[58] IVP-USA also had the advantage of being able to locate itself near the cluster of publishing-related missions agencies which had already gathered around Wheaton College.[59]

The Tyndale network emerged just in time to take advantage of the post-war expansion of universities, when its ability to draw private funding and international students gave it credibility, and in the relative absence of American alternatives. One of the early wardens of Tyndale House (1960–63) was Leon Morris, an Australian scholar whose book, *The Apostolic Preaching of the Cross* (1955), was a key biblical defence of the doctrine of substitutionary atonement. A fellow emerging scholar, J.I. Packer, greeted it as 'a book of the first importance'. By way of contrast, American evangelical scholarly organisations were closely dependent on conservative evangelical colleges, and so continued to define the role of evangelical scholarship as defensive. From the 1950s until the early 1990s, therefore, Morris and his fellow British Commonwealth scholars (particularly F.F. Bruce and I.H. Marshall) 'account[ed] for more of the books which shape the judgements of American evangelical scholars than any American authors'.[60] When the Britons were already a decade into the realisation of Bruce's agenda, Ned Bernard Stonehouse of Westminster was still defining 'progress' to the U.S.-based Evangelical

[56] Ibid., 60.

[57] Noll, *Between Faith and Criticism*, p. 103.

[58] Andrew T. Le Peau and Linda Doll, *Heart, Soul, Mind, Strength: an Anecdotal History of InterVarsity Press, 1947–2007*, Downers Grove: InterVarsity, 2006, p. 27.

[59] Ruth Tucker, *From Jerusalem to Irian Jaya: A Biographical History of Christian Missions*, Grand Rapids: Zondervan, 2004, p. 365.

[60] Noll, *Between Faith and Criticism*, p. 128.

Theological Society (founded in 1949) as the defence of the infallibility of the Scriptures.[61] While philosophers such as the Northern Baptist Warren C. Young pushed the envelope and challenged the 'cold textualism' of fundamentalism, such organisations were more adept at controlling expression than releasing scholarship. It would be some decades – and after more than a little cultural conflict – before American evangelical organisation and finance would begin to translate into viable intellectual alternatives.

There was, moreover, an underlying contradiction within the internationalising Graham synthesis: Reformed biblicism and evangelical experientialism were living in an unresolved tension, largely held together by the charisma of success and post-war optimism.[62] 'Evangelicalism' expanded on the back of a general concern for 'evangelism' among all churches, regardless of their attitudes to biblical authority.[63] Rob Warner suggests that this defensive Reformed dominance in evangelical thought (and, by extension, its experiential alliance) lasted into the mid-1960s, when it 'finally collapsed under an excess of mutually exclusive certainties'.[64] Again, it was a British evangelical scholar who gave clearest expression to the problem. In his *Fundamentalism and the Word of God* (1958), James Packer (then teaching at Tyndale Hall, Bristol) outlined the neo-evangelical position in the apologetic context. Much of the debate, he noted, was based on a confusion of ideas, or a misreading of church history.[65] Evangelical Christianity was not, he pointed out, an inwardly turned, anti-modernist innovation as had recently emerged in populist fundamentalism. Rather, it was apostolic Christianity based on the revelation of the Son of God, Jesus, in the only text which could provide a sufficient basis, the Bible. Its great enemy was not science or reason, but subjectivism, particularly as this emerged in liberal modernism.[66] Packer and his contemporary, John Stott, were particularly important for the new evangelical scholarly surge, as they bridged the work of serious scholars with the practice of students who went into ministry around the world. Their application of biblical truth was to find them at the centre of the founding of evangelical institutions internationally. Packer's small 'occasional' piece sold 30,000 copies in the first year and 'moulded the thinking of evangelical students in the 1950s and early 1960s,'

[61] Stonehouse, '1957 Presidential Address'.

[62] Warren C. Young, '1958 Presidential Address: "Whither Evangelicalism?"' *Bulletin of the Evangelical Theological Society*, 2:1 (Winter 1959), 5–16.

[63] See Brian Stanley's account of this in the Anglican communion, 'Post-War British Evangelicalism: Shifting Identities and Global Trajectories', tss, Evangelical Alliance, United Kingdom, http://www.eauk.org/efb/uploads/Post%20War%20British%20Evangelicalism_Stanley.doc, accessed 26 August 2011.

[64] Rob Warner, *Reinventing English Evangelicalism 1966–2001: A Theological and Sociological Study*, Milton Keynes: Paternoster, 2007, p. 25.

[65] James I. Packer, *Fundamentalism and the Word of God: Some Evangelical Principles*, Leicester: InterVarsity, 1958, p. 10.

[66] Packer, *Fundamentalism*, p. 170.

resulting in 'a significant growth in self-confidence within evangelicalism'.[67] As Paul Helm was later to write, Packer's book was a revelation: 'it fortified me for what lay ahead, and also acted as something of a model for how one should write about Christianity, and especially how to write about Christian doctrine.'[68] It was a very firm foundation for Packer's later rise to star status in the evangelical firmament.

On their own, however, improvements in scholarship and clerical effectiveness were insufficient. Supporting and releasing evangelical resurgence was a reconnection within evangelicalism between its elites and its key laity in the formation of effective new institutions. From the core Inter-Varsity networks proliferated hundreds of new 'fellowships' and missions which populated the evangelical world with acronyms. Norman Grubb, one of the original forces, went on to formalise Studd's work into the World Evangelization Crusade (WEC), spreading its work all over the world. A self-conscious inheritor of the Student Volunteer Movement, the IVCF in the United States commenced a triennial foreign missions conference at the University of Illinois-Urbana, which at its first convention in 1951 drew 1,600 students. It met at precisely the time when Western nations teemed with returned soldiers, some of whom turned their wartime experience into an impulse for moral and social service. As Piggin notes, this 'returned soldier' bulge would create its own problems.[69] The growth, however, realigned evangelical global priorities. The Urbana conference (at its peak) drew over 17,000 participants annually, projected tens of thousands of American students into international missionary work (particularly into related missionary associations such as the Latin American Mission [LAM]) and replicated itself in missionary conferences in Europe and Australia.[70] There was a seemingly ever-growing list of graduate fellowships, nursing fellowships, medical fellowships (CMF, ICMDA), fellowships for lawyers, historians,[71] scientists – anything which would support faith in secular university and professional environments where today's students could go on to become tomorrow's thought-leaders. 'Science groups' began within a few years of each other on either side of the Atlantic: the American Scientific Affiliation in 1941, the IVF-UK Science Group in 1944. From their ranks would come such figures as John Polkinghorne (subatomic particle physics), Francis Collins (Human Genome Project), J. Laurence Kulp (carbon-14 development and geochemistry) and others

[67] A. E. McGrath, quoted in MacLeod, *C. Stacey Woods*, p. 167.

[68] '*Fundamentalism and the Word of God* – Fifty years old! Text of a lunchtime lecture to be given at the Evangelical Library on Monday 10th March, 2008', Helm's Deep, http://paulhelmsdeep.blogspot.com/2008/03/fundamentalism-and-word-of-god-fifty_01.html, accessed 23 October 2010.

[69] Piggin, *Evangelical Christianity in Australia*, p. 325.

[70] B. Gordon Olson, *What in the World Is God Doing?: The Essentials of Global Missions: An Introductory Guide*, Cedar Knolls: Global Gospel Publishers, 2003, p. 159.

[71] See D.G. Hart, 'History in Search of Meaning: The Conference on Faith and History' in Ronald A. Wells, ed., *History and the Christian Historian*, Grand Rapids: Eerdmans, 1998.

who would maintain an evangelical voice in areas which, as the century progressed, would become areas of critical concern to humanity, but in which clerical voices were increasingly seen to be compromised. This proliferation of targeted forms captured and directed lay energy. Its weakness was that few ever reached self-sustainability in terms of finance or governance, and after the initial generation often required revitalisation or bypassing. Supported by trans-denominational networks, and engaged in the 'rough and tumble' of the religion-science debate, interdenominational evangelicals in intellectual vocations also inevitably found themselves in tension with their denominational and church-based brethren.

These divisions became very clear with the resurgence of 'Young Earth Creationism' from 1961 (with the publication of Henry M. Morris' *The Genesis Flood*). As Ronald Numbers suggests, 'organized creationism in North America appeared to be all but dead during the second quarter or so of the twentieth century,'[72] despite a continuing residual presence in sectarian, and particularly in fundamentalist, communities. From the 1960s, however, 'flood geology' emerged from the adventist subculture as a plank of the fundamentalist resistance to broader secularising trends. It drew away the support of a significant proportion of the laity and churches and provided the proponents of methodological atheism with a 'straw man' used in public debates. All evangelicalism became typified as naïve, six-day creationism. Its acceptance by the populist fundamentalist end of the evangelical compromise did more than embarrass those who – since Bernard Ramm's *The Christian View of Science and Scripture* (1954) – had been seeking for re-engagement with the public sphere.[73] Over the period from 1960 to 2000, evangelical thought on the science/religion debate splintered, with the emergence of a variety of positions and counterpositions; on the issue of origins alone, 'young earth', 'old earth', and progressive creation parties vied with 'theistic evolution' (or 'neo-Darwinist'), intelligent design, and more recently the concepts of the Biologos Foundation promoted by Francis Collins. Such divisions emerged in dynamic relationship to a resurgent, militant atheism which rejected the 'accommodationism' normally associated with the British academy. Critics like Richard Dawkins found a ready market in the conflict-driven media for absolute declarations that the scientific world was not a plural space.[74] The collapse of evangelical consensus and the rise of anti-accommodationism of the pre-Dawkins type contributed directly to the rise of fundamentalist politics. By the beginning of the 2000s, religion and science had once again become a key apologetic flashpoint, at least as important as biblical inspiration had been in the 1950s.

[72] Ronald L. Numbers, *The Creationists: The Evolution of Scientific Creationism*, Berkeley: University of California Press, 1993, p. 158.
[73] See Amos Yong, 'God and the Evangelical Laboratory: Recent Conservative Protestant Thinking about Theology and Science', *Theology and Science*, 5:2 (2007), 204.
[74] Numbers, *The Creationists*, p. 158.

Among open evangelicals (who may be defined as those who, like the alumni of the Inter-Varsity networks, were committed to engaging the questions of the time), informal and formal networks provided the demand and human resources for new types of institution. In speaking about the motivations behind evangelical innovation in higher education in the 1960s, James Houston has noted that the founders were motivated less by a search for spiritual theology and more by the need to respond to the concerns arising from the Cuban Missile crisis, the student revolts of 1968, and the turmoil associated with Vietnam: 'We were looking for connectedness and life. The technocratic mindset and the impact of living with science and scientism – there was a strong reaction to that. Their reductionism was cheating us.'[75] Although not always able to obtain formal recognition in the public sphere, residential colleges attached to universities often provided supportive bases for research centres and forums. Graham Kings (foundation director of The Henry Martyn Centre at Westminster College, Cambridge, and later Bishop of Sherborne), Denis Alexander (Director of the Faraday Institute at St Edmunds College, Cambridge) and Stuart Piggin (foundation director of the Centre for the Study of Australian Christianity at Macquarie University) are all examples of this sort of organised, research-led approach at the edge of the public sector emerging from 1950s and 1960s evangelicalism. The increasing dominance of research-led practice in higher education has driven even formerly sectarian institutions to develop similar institutions, while others fused the Bible college and evangelical network models. In Canada, Regent College was founded in Vancouver by a group of Brethren businessmen in 1968 as 'the first graduate school of theology in North America to make education of the laity its central focus'.[76] Here too, Inter-Varsity links were powerful: Ward Gasque and other Brethren delegates developed the idea through conversations at the Urbana missions conference in 1964.[77] First preferences for a founding Principal lay between two British Inter-Varsity activists, F.F. Bruce and James Houston. Under the latter, and with the later addition of Jim Packer, Regent would have significant influence in funnelling British influences into American evangelicalism and developing a worldwide network of graduates (on the IVCF model). Regent's influence is such that commentators (such as Maier) are often puzzled by the contradictions apparent in the development of a city (Vancouver) which 'is paradoxically one of the nation's most secular and evangelical urban areas'.[78] Close attention to the city's revivalist past, its function as a

[75] James M. Houston, quoted in Mark Filiatreau, 'Honouring our Elders: Dr. James Houston, Founder of Regent College,' *Canadian Christianity*, 21:6 (June 2001), http://canadianchristianity.com/cgi-bin/bc.cgi?bc/bccn/0601/supelders, accessed 23 August 2011.

[76] http://www.regent-college.edu/about_regent/introduction/history.html, accessed 25 Oct. 2010.

[77] Brian J. Fraser, *The Study of Religion in British Columbia: a State-of-the-art Review*, Waterloo: Wilfrid Laurier University Press, 1995, p. 21.

[78] Harry O. Maier, 'The Familiar Made Strange: An Orientation to Biblical Study in Vancouver', *Teaching Theology & Religion*, 10:2 (April 2007), 81.

communications node for faith missions such as the CIM and the disproportionate Christian element in Asian migration to North America would suggest that the paradox is more apparent than real. Combined with Fuller Theological Seminary (Pasadena), Westmont College and the proliferation of West Coast church-based ministries, Regent is a further indicator of the degree to which evangelical initiative had passed to the melting pots of the world – in this case, where East meets West, on the Pacific coast of North America.

Colleges like Regent were outside, but connected to, the traditional transatlantic axis. They not only provided higher education to the majority world, but fed evangelical influence back into other Western institutions, particularly as public academic institutions fell victim to economic rationalism, and so gained a new appreciation for the global public which evangelicals could attract. Wycliffe Hall, Oxford, an evangelical theological college founded in 1877,[79] which by the 1940s was unable to respond to calls for 'unhyphenated evangelicalism',[80] was gradually brought back to the engaged conservative centre. This trend would extend well beyond the period covered in this chapter: in 1996, Alister McGrath attached the Hall to the University specifically to 'enable evangelicalism to have a place in mainstream university life'.[81] Oak Hill Theological College in north London, conservative from its foundation in 1932, became a centre for the global interests of Reformed evangelicals based in Sydney and New York. Such colleges took a particular interest in developing candidates from the majority non-Western world towards higher academic training. John Stott's Langham and Evangelical Literature Trusts and the Australian-based Leon and Mildred Morris Foundation were specific attempts to channel the income resulting from the global expansion of evangelical media after the Second World War back into higher education. Over time, Inter-Varsity faded from being *the* evangelical presence on campuses around the world to becoming *a* presence among others, sometimes absorbed into a particular, locally powerful strain of evangelicalism. By then, however, its emphasis on penetration of the professions and education had seen its vision become successfully institutionalised into sustainable centres, connected to extensive networks.

CHARISMA AND INDIGENISATION

Such centres were sustainable because of the continuous growth of evangelicalism in the majority world. Regent absorbed the Commonwealth links, Fuller boomed in

[79] Andrew C. Atherstone, 'The Founding of Wycliffe Hall, Oxford', *Anglican and Episcopal History*, 73 (2004), 78.
[80] H.R. Gough, ed., *Evangelical Essentials*, London: Church Book Room Press, n.d. [1947], pp. 13–14.
[81] Alister McGrath, 'Theological Education and Global Tertiary Education: Risks and Opportunities', presented 19 August 2003 at the ICETE International Consultation for Theological Educators, High Wycombe, United Kingdom, tss.

the convergence of California's Hispanic missions and demand for graduate training for the emerging leadership from Latin America, Southern Baptist Colleges and missions expanded (particularly Southwestern Baptist Theological Seminary, which grew to become the largest Protestant seminary in the world) on the back of managerial effectiveness and its position as the 'Catholic Church of the South'.[82] As the evangelical front which had successfully met the challenges of post-war reconstruction came into the 1960s, it confronted the consequences of its own success. While burgeoning in the majority world, evangelicalism faced increasingly fragmented and fractious realities, in the context of its own vast diversification. Graham's 'politics of decency' was a reflection of 1950s values – values which collapsed in the West in the 1960s in ways well described by Callum Brown's phrase 'The Death of Christian Britain'. Traditional modes of reaching youth – particularly Sunday Schools, a mainstay of evangelicalism from the late eighteenth century – declined seriously from the late 1960s, leading Hugh McLeod to project their virtual annihilation in Scotland by the second decade of the twenty-first century.[83] (Robin Gill stated the trend more bluntly still: 'Sunday Schools have collapsed.')[84] In this process, evangelical communities tended to be less affected than liberal ones. Ironically, therefore, secularisation in the West increased the influence of evangelicalism on and within the mainstream of Western Christianity. This was particularly the case in the United States, with its larger base evangelical population, and essentially meant a fragmentation of evangelical trend data. As will be seen in Chapter 8, three major models appeared: American exceptionalism (with a large evangelical population largely resistant to secularisation), broader Western decline (with the slow collapse of traditionally evangelical denominations, particularly in the British Commonwealth) and rapid expansion of 'new evangelical' communities in the majority world and (by migration) to diasporic communities in the West. With their rise into visibility, evangelicals could no longer escape the problems affecting the wider society: widespread technological consumerism, generational differentiation, the impact of widespread secular public education, the boom-and-bust cycle of capitalist societies, the challenges of the Cold War. Evangelicalism faced these challenges in five revivals and a funeral. The funeral was hidden from no one. In 1965, with the closing of the Second Vatican Council, Tridentine Catholicism (ill for some time) died. The *aggiornamento* of Catholic doctrine and practice came at a critical juncture for evangelicals who, by the Berlin Congress of 1966, were

[82] Joseph E. Early, ed., *A Texas Baptist History Sourcebook*, Denton: University of North Texas Press, 2004, p. 217; Corrie E. Norman and Don S. Armentrout, eds, *Religion in the Contemporary South*, Knoxville: University of Tennessee Press, 2005, p. 78.

[83] The decline was sporadic in fundamentalist heartlands (L. David Cunningham, *A History of Florida Baptist's Sunday School* [Longwood]: Xulon Press, 2005, p. 38), but catastrophic across all mainstream churches in Britain (Hugh McLeod and Werner Ustorf, *The Decline of Christendom in Western Europe, 1750–2000*, Cambridge: Cambridge University Press, 2004, p. 32).

[84] Robin Gill, *The Empty Church Revisited*, Aldershot: Ashgate, 2003, p. 147.

positioning themselves as a 'third force' in world Christianity. From that point, the revivals – of charismatic phenomena and evangelical indigenisation in the majority world, of Reformed evangelical separatism, and of youth engagement and communalism – developed in the context of the collapse of the ecclesiastical Berlin Wall which had existed between global forms of Christianity since the Reformation.

The first two of these revivals – a double, interactive revival combining charismatic renewal and indigenisation – were global in scope and demonstrated the interplay between organised and grassroots evangelicalism. While the history of charismatic renewal is often traced to the outbreak of charismatic gifts in Dennis Bennett's Van Nuys Episcopalian congregation in 1959, missionaries from Latin America, Asia and Africa returning to nearby Fuller Theological Seminary had been experiencing similar outbreaks for some time – particularly in mainline Methodist and Baptist congregations. It is easy enough to trace 'genetic' links between continuing healing, prayer and pentecostal revival activities and those elements of renewal which eventually became caught up into charismatic organisations. The Healing Revival and its worldwide campaigns – in conjunction with networks such as Full Gospel Businessmen International, and those which emerged around key actors such as Agnes Sanford and the Order of St Luke, Camps Farthest Out, David Du Plessis and Harald Bredesen – had brought hundreds of thousands of mainline believers into 'spirit baptism'.[85] The 'problem' of charismatic origins, however, is largely an artefact of the terms used. Just as Methodism had thrown up intense indigenous 'return to pentecost' movements on the Celtic fringe in the 1830s and 1850s, on the American frontier in Methodist bush bowers and in Presbyterian long communions, so it also produced visions, dreams and manifestations in non-Western areas of Christian expansion in the 1920s, 1950s and 1960s–1970s. Where these emerged in the context of the struggle for authority, mainstream denominations often wrote them off as syncretism, so excluding them from official memory. With the emergence of new nations and the move towards national churches from the 1950s, however, there was a tendency to see such events as continuous with the life of the church rather than as an aberration. So Methodist/Anglican prophet William Wadé Harris was to some a revolutionary; his followers in the 1960s became the founders of a new nationalism.[86] In the 1910s, T.W. Ratana was to some a syncretist Maori pagan revivalist; after the visits of Tommy Hicks in the 1950s, he became more recognisable as a forerunner for self-governed charismatic Christianity. In the 1930s, evincing Holy Spirit manifestations was sufficient to spark a purge of the Sydney University Evangelical Union – yet by the 1980s, it was a recognised form of Anglican ministry, affecting 'most

[85] See entries on each of these figures in S. Burgess and E. Van der Maas, eds, *The New International Dictionary of Pentecostal and Charismatic Movements*, Grand Rapids: Zondervan, 2002.

[86] Sheila S. Walker, *The Religious Revolution in the Ivory Coast: The Prophet Harris and the Harrist Church*, Chapel Hill: University of North Carolina Press, 1983, p. 17.

missions and churches in Melanesia'.[87] The 'origins' of the charismatic movement therefore depend on who is telling the story. In both cases, the dividing point of opinion relates to the political ramifications of their ministries: anti-colonialism in Harris' case, and social reform and promulgation of the Treaty of Waitangi in the case of the Ratana movement.[88] While the literature has restored their position as nationalists, however, there has been comparatively little attempt to rewrite the history of the charismatic movement from the perspective of indigenisation (at least in part because of its oral nature).

The importance of the charismatic revival – which renewed some, antagonised others, and influenced most churches in the West – was not so much its local impact as its emergence in the period between 1960 and 1990 as a global culture linking together proliferating new forms of energetic, indigenised but interlinked Christianity.[89] Just as the recovery of a holistic life-organising spirituality was a pathway to broader respectability for healing evangelists such as Oral Roberts,[90] it was even more powerfully so in the majority world where holism engaged with the 'shamanist ground' of the non-Western world rather than Western materialism.[91] Such churches and communities were well established by the end of the 1960s, and exploded by spreading interdenominational links in the 1970s. The contemporary effects of these changes will be explored in Chapter 9, but examples from Nigeria and Korea here will help to clarify the process.

Contact with a pentecostal church in Ibadan led to the spread of Holy Spirit Baptism in the Christian Union at the University of Ibadan in 1970, leading to the formation of a 'World Action Team for Christ' (WATC) which spread the influence through other campuses: 'By 1975, all the six Nigerian universities at the time felt the touch of the revival,' leading to 'a startling proliferation of churches and ministries.'[92] By 1974, at least 10 charismatic organisations had been established by graduates, expanding by 2000 to more than 5,000 independent groups and churches.[93] By the early 2000s, such churches were so large, they were a noticeable element in the Nigerian economy; these Holy Spirit children of the evangelical revival were a significant mission force in Africa and along the lines of the

[87] Allison Griffiths, *Fire in the Islands: The Acts of the Holy Spirit in the Solomons*, Wheaton: Shaw, 1977; John Barr, 'A Survey of Ecstatic Phenomena and "Holy Spirit Movements" in Melanesia', *Oceania*, 54:2 (December 1983), 109–32.

[88] Kayleen M. Hazlehurst, *Political Expression and Ethnicity: Statecraft and Mobilisation in the Maori World*, Westport, CT: Praeger, 1993, p. 11.

[89] Karla Poewe, ed., *Charismatic Christianity as a Global Culture*, Columbia: University of South Carolina Press, 1994, p. xii.

[90] See Harrell's discussion, *Oral Roberts*, p. 130.

[91] Martin, *Pentecostalism*, pp. 26–8.

[92] Peter Nlemadim Domnwachukwu, *Authentic African Christianity: An Inculturation Model for the Igbo*, New York: Peter Lang, 2000, p. 85.

[93] Mathews A. Ojo, 'Extending Faith Frontiers: The Trans-nationalization of Nigerian Protestant Missionary Enterprises' in P. Freston, ed., *History and Sociology of the Protestant Missions Movement from the Global South* (forthcoming).

diaspora, and were beginning to influence the church on a global scale.[94] Although still only just founded when Billy Graham flew into Australia for his Southern Cross Crusade, Yonggi Cho's Assemblies of God-linked 'Full Gospel Central Church' in Seoul, Korea already had about 1,000 members in 1961. By the time students took to the streets in Paris in 1968, Seoul Full Gospel had grown to 8,000 members. When the Tenth Pentecostal World Conference met in the church five years later, it had grown to an estimated 18,000, and more than doubled every five years thereafter, expanding to more than three-quarters of a million (claims were made of a million or more members before Cho's retirement), projecting itself as an increasingly global denomination and missions-sending force in Korean and majority-world settings. The Korea which Billy Graham had urged President Truman to protect from communism in 1951 had, by the 1990s, become a celebrated (albeit not always uncontroversial) source of evangelical energy, its capital Seoul hosting, respectively, the largest pentecostal, Presbyterian and Methodist congregations in the world. Two things link Nigeria and Korea: both were settings in which post-war (civil war in the one case, Korean war in the other) foreign aid in reconstruction provided credibility for religious change,[95] and both were modernising settings where a Spirit-fired Protestant evangelicalism helped to integrate life-worlds towards engagement in the emerging global culture.[96] The result in both countries was an energetic, indigenous Christianity centred on 'faith which works'.

These interlinked revivals created significant conflict within evangelical denominational and interdenominational structures. Fundamentalist circles had rejected pentecostalism in the 1920s and tended to respond in the same way in the 1960s and 1970s, alternating between resting on their traditional cessationism (a consequence of their defensive stance on biblical inspiration) and aggressive counterattacks often based on stereotyped accounts of charismatic extremes.[97] In Sydney, the American South and other locations subject to strong Brethren or Calvinist influence, charismatic renewal and interdenominational discussions sparked a parallel third revival, of Reformed separatism. Such developments, many Reformed evangelicals

[94] For instance, in 2007–8, 'big evangelical churches attracted over 15 million people to their retreat grounds generating N90 billion (approximately $890 million) during [a] seven-day holiday period. . . . The "Holy Ghost Congress" at Ibafon, near Lagos, of the Redeemed Christian Church of God [RCCG] attracted over 3 million people from 34 countries – 14 African and 20 non-African countries.' http://www.eturbonews.com/752/mega-churches-stir-tourism-nigeria, accessed 25 October 2010.

[95] Domnwachukwu (p. 68) notes that response to the charismatic movement in the universities was mediated by the association between evangelical aid agencies and conclusions as to the failure of traditional religion.

[96] Veli-Matti Karkkainnen, *The Spirit in the World: Emerging Pentecostal Theologies in Global Contexts*, Grand Rapids: Eerdmans, 2009, pp. 46–7.

[97] Leading Biola graduate and Calvinist dispensationalist John F. Macarthur's book, *Charismatic Chaos*, was a contemporary version of this; a cruder diatribe by R. Carroll Stegall played a similar role in the disruption of Oral Roberts' 1956 Melbourne campaign (Harrell, *Oral Roberts*, p. 74).

felt, compromised the gains of the Reformation, were indifferent to theological truth and threatened the doctrine of the inspiration of Scripture. Although, as Grayson Carter has pointed out, this sort of division was not new to Anglican evangelicalism,[98] Reformed evangelical consolidation provoked global divisions within Anglicanism in response to church decline in North America, and over Southern Baptist efforts to clarify identity.[99] The emergence of Nine Marks, Sovereign Grace and Founders groups in the Southern Baptist Convention, as well as the Reformed Evangelical Protestant Association in Sydney Anglicanism, were reflections of the breakdown of consensus and return to older identities. Reformational traditions were particularly threatened by the links which grassroots charismatic ecumenism encouraged between Protestants and Catholics (later formalised in long-running theological discussions such as Evangelicals and Catholics Together, or the International Catholic-Pentecostal Dialogue). Reformed evangelicals responded with often stinging critiques of sloppiness in charismatic theology and practice and fears of a creeping Romanism in broader open evangelicalism, which would betray the Reformed heritage.[100]

Denominational pentecostals evinced a range of responses to the renewal – from disbelieving rejection, to cautious optimism, to wholesale embrace, sometimes by the same people over a period of time. 'Pentecostals wrestled with the conundrums presented by alcohol-imbibing, dancing, "worldly" Lutherans and Catholics speaking in tongues and being slain in the Spirit.'[101] The role of mediators such as David Du Plessis, and the pentecostal holiness background of Oral Roberts, proved influential. Norman Armstrong, who was disaffiliated from the Australian Assemblies of God in the 1950s for his activities with the Oral Roberts Evangelistic Association, found himself a charismatic leader in the 1970s and the symbol of pentecostal orthodoxy in the 1990s.[102] Where charismatics found resistance, they tended to go underground or to leave and set up their own networks. Ultimately, many of these (particularly those which encountered the Latter Rain movement) were later the organising centres for independent mega-churches, prayer networks, or 'post-evangelical' forms described in Chapter 9.

[98] See Grayson Carter, *Anglican Evangelicals: Protestant Secessions from the Via Media, c. 1800–1850*, Oxford: Oxford University Press, 2001.

[99] David S. Dockery, *Southern Baptist Consensus and Renewal*, Nashville: B & H Academic, 2008, p. 2.

[100] Paul Barnett and Peter Jensen, *The Quest for Power: Neo-Pentecostals and the New Testament*, Sydney: Anzea, 1973; John F. Macarthur, *Charismatic Chaos*, Grand Rapids: Zondervan, 1992.

[101] Larry Eskridge, 'Slain by the Music', *Christian Century*, 123:5, 3 July 2006, online, http://www.religion-online.org/showarticle.asp?title=3326, accessed 23 July 2011.

[102] D. O'Keefe, 'Armstrong, Norman Lloyd (1917–)', *Australian Dictionary of Pentecostal and Charismatic Movements*, online, http://webjournals.alphacrucis.edu.au/journals/ADPCM/a/armstrong-norman-l-1917-/, accessed 23 July 2011.

RE-INDIGENISING EVANGELICALISM IN THE WEST

The export of post-war American global influence was balanced by many imports. On the back of consumerism and the long economic boom of the 1950s, the export of blues music along with motor cars in the 1950s brought back with it the Beatles, the Rolling Stones, nihilist philosophy and the conscientisation of a generation in the 1960s. As Robynn Stilwell notes, 'the convergence of music history, socio-political history, and technological and economic development in the case of rock and roll is particularly volatile, even more so than at the similar birth of jazz some half a century earlier.'[103] The parallel with jazz it is apt – just as the 'planned spontaneity' of pentecostalism was born as a form of jazz evangelicalism in the early twentieth century, so the fragmentation of identities in the music industry of the 1960s provides a good description for the meeting of evangelicalism and youth culture leading to a final pair of revivals, of youth engagement and communalism. That the connection is stronger than mere metaphor has been pointed out by students of worship cultures, such as Larry Eskridge: 'The raw power of Gospel provided the emotional – and no small part of the musical – muscle that fueled both rock 'n' roll and R & B as it evolved into soul.'[104] In turn, folk and pop music (as commercialised media of private choice) became vehicles for re-indigenising evangelical worship. Meanwhile the great black migration into the American industrial north in the post-war period created the preconditions for the civil rights movement and broke down the class and aesthetic barriers which had protected white middle-class evangelicals from having to apply their faith to the immediate problems of a deeply divided nation. Billy Graham's mixed-race campaigns and discussions with Martin Luther King Jr. over civil disobedience posed evangelicals with a profound challenge. After all, their resurgence in the 1950s had been on the back of relatively narrow claims to (biblical and spiritual) authenticity. Now a whole culture asked questions about authenticity on a much broader front.

Inevitably, the dapper middle-class cultural ambivalence of white evangelicals – acting locally and explaining transcendentally – was read in youth culture as hypocrisy. With the failure of consensus, the methods relying on consensus – particularly the crusade as a form of mass evangelism, and so as a symbol of evangelical success – began to fade, provoking a frantic search for alternatives.[105] Having rejected the social gospel in the 1920s, the fissiparous nature of evangelicalism meant that it could not easily present a univocal response to key issues.

[103] Robynn Stilwell, 'Music of the Youth Revolution: Rock through the 1960s' in Nicholas Cook and Anthony Pople, eds, *The Cambridge History of Twentieth-Century Music*, Cambridge: Cambridge University Press, 2004, pp. 418–9.

[104] Eskridge, 'Slain by the Music'.

[105] James A. Patterson, 'Cultural Pessimism in Modern Evangelical Thought: Francis Schaeffer, Carl Henry, and Charles Colson', *Journal of the Evangelical Theological Society*, 49:4 (2006), 809.

Some felt that variant church responses to Vietnam, for instance, exposed the fiction of 'evangelicalism' as a single entity. On the one hand, 'the most prominent self-described evangelical in the post–World War II military', General William K. Harrison Jr, dismissed anti-war protests as 'sincere but erroneous', as 'wars will continue until man's rebellion runs its full course, terminating in . . . the second coming of the Lord Jesus Christ.'[106] The opposition to the war by evangelicals such as H.E. Hughes and Mark O. Hatfield was that of a vocal minority,[107] and arose because the association between conservative politics and evangelical faith was not yet nearly as tight as it would become. A small group, centred on Jim Wallis, at Trinity Evangelical Divinity School, fended off attempts to expel them while they protested against the war, racism and inequality of all types, expressing their ideas in the radical, biblical magazine entitled *The Post-American.* It would later be renamed *Sojourners* and become a standard of an increasingly visible 'evangelical left'. The initial title might have puzzled some older evangelicals; it certainly created concern in post-McCarthy America.[108]

A number of overlapping responses thus fed into the second pair of revivals, often known through the 1960s as the 'Jesus Revolution', but in fact representing a form of indigenisation in the first world through youth engagement and counter-individualism. It was an experience of civil rights language which restored a very Puritan priority of the human conscience, the communitarianism of the hippies and a generation-specific form of worship music sourced in Gospel but interpreted through rock and folk protest music. The appearance of folk singers like Barry McGuire (whose version of P.F. Sloan's apocalyptic 'Eve of Destruction' appeared in the same year as the Byrds' adaptation of *Ecclesiastes* in 'Turn, Turn, Turn', and was an anthem of the youth revolution)[109] in each of the Youth, Jesus People and later Contemporary Christian Music circles is an indicator of the common milieu which united them. It was a milieu foreign to many evangelicals, some of whom responded with the traditional dismissal that 'rock'n'roll is of the devil'.[110] Evangelical pragmatists, however, applied the lessons of nineteenth-century faith missions to the new situation. Suppressing 'a strong desire to "shave them, cut their hair, bathe them, and then preach to them"', Billy Graham disguised himself in dark glasses, old clothes, ball cap and a false beard and mingled with demonstrating

[106] Randall Balmer, *Encyclopedia of Evangelicalism*, Waco: Baylor University Press, 2004, p. 325.

[107] Fredrik Logevall, 'A Delicate Balance: John Sherman Cooper and the Republican Opposition to the Vietnam War' in Randall B. Woods, ed., *Vietnam and the American Political Tradition: The Politics of Dissent*, New York: Cambridge University Press, 2003, p. 237.

[108] Robert H. Krapohl and Charles H. Lippy, *The Evangelicals: A Historical, Thematic, and Biographical Guide*, Westport, CT: Greenwood Press, 1999, p. 60.

[109] Don Cusic, *The Sound of Light: a History of Gospel Music*, Bowling Green: State University Popular Press, 1990, p. 112.

[110] Stephanie Bennett, 'Going Digital with Contemporary Christian Music' in Quentin J. Schultze and Robert Woods, eds, *Understanding Evangelical Media: The Changing Face of Christian Communication*, Downers Grove: Inter-Varsity, 2008, p. 111.

youth at City University in New York.[111] He would later emerge at a Miami rock concert featuring the Grateful Dead and Santana, telling the crowd they could 'get high without hang-ups and hangovers'. Larry Eskridge has explored the course of Graham's relationship with the Jesus people in detail,[112] and concludes that his pragmatic decision to follow the cultural energy provided the affirmation which the Jesus People subculture needed in order to build an essential 'bridge of return' for thousands of young people who survived the subsequent crash of the counter-culture in the 1970s.[113]

The longer-term significance of this bridge into the youth revolution was greater than just the few thousand of Jesus People. It was to condition the direction of evangelical practice into the twenty-first century and spill over into variant forms of Christian community which detached themselves from geographic and local identities and reoriented themselves around mission and purpose. Examples of this process are legion (and often unusual). Arthur Blessitt, who was present at the conversions of both Barry McGuire and George W. Bush Jr, was inspired to carry a 12-foot cross on a 60,000-kilometre walk around the world.[114] Converted during an LSD trip, Lonnie Frisbee started with evangelistic ministry in Haight-Ashbury, connected with the conservative Calvary Chapel in Orange County, and helped to grow both a drug rehabilitation centre (The House of Miracles) and a Bible study which drew thousands of people from the counter-culture. Related quasi-denominations developed: Calvary Chapel alone expanded to more than 1,500 churches around the world, influencing mainstream evangelical evangelism, particularly through the ministries of Greg Laurie and John Wimber;[115] the Christian World Liberation Front (CWLF) and Vineyard Christian Fellowship were other examples.[116] Charismatic Christian communities – drawing on Catholic and Anabaptist precedents – were another way of becoming detached from the materialist culture of the West. Although most of these merged, folded or collapsed over the decades, sustained Protestant/Catholic charismatic cooperation could still be found into the new century (e.g. the Servants of Jesus community in Sydney, Australia). At L'Abri in Switzerland, Frances and Edith Schaeffer combined Reformed concerns with the life of the mind and communalist approaches to evangelical spirituality to influence a generation of evangelical university students around the world with their application of reformed theology to all of life. (Schaeffer, a student of van Til, also interpreted the Dutch neo-Calvinism of Kuyper and Dooyeweerd for a

[111] Chris Armstrong, 'Tell Billy Graham: "The Jesus People love him"', *Christian History*, 8 August 2008 (online) http://www.christianitytoday.com/ch/news/2002/nov29.html.

[112] See L. Eskridge, *God's Forever Family*, New York: Oxford University Press, 2011.

[113] Armstrong, 'Tell Billy Graham: "The Jesus People love him"'.

[114] Arthur Blessitt, *The Cross: 38,102 Miles, 38 Years, One Mission*, Colorado Springs: Authentic, 2008, p. 3.

[115] Balmer, *Encyclopedia*, p. 227.

[116] Ray Broadus Browne and Pat Browne, eds, *The Guide to United States Popular Culture*, Bowling Green: State University Popular Press, 2000, p. 439.

broader evangelical audience – influences which later came to him being perceived in the public mind as a theorist for the Religious Right.).[117] New communities, coffee houses, music groups, alternative newspapers (such as *Cornerstone Magazine*), discipleship training centres, outreaches and church forms proliferated out of the Jesus Movement. They became the rootstock for what today is the billion-dollar contemporary Christian music industry,[118] but also less mainline ventures such as Greenbelt Music and Arts Festival in the United Kingdom, or the continuing ministry of 'Cristo è la Risposta' (Christ is the Answer) in Italy, which has fed thousands of converts and leaders into the growing evangelical and pentecostal movements of continental Europe. While the Jesus Movement faltered and institutionalised in 1973–4, becoming sectarian or just plain tired, its longer-term impacts are still evident in contemporary practice. Evangelicalism had morphed once more and embedded its biblicentrist activism in the heart of a new generation.

CAST YOUR BREAD UPON THE WATERS

In March 1995, the 76-year-old Billy Graham preached to a billion people. Using 30 satellites to bounce sermons from his Puerto Rico pulpit to more than 165 countries, his 'Global Mission' campaign was the swansong of a long career of preaching a simple gospel to more people than any evangelist has ever reached in the history of the world. It was an effort made possible by a combination of technology, managerialism, mobilisation of wealth, and a global evangelical community built up over fifty years of ministry. As such, it was symbolic of the course of the post-war evangelicalism which Graham did so much to shape. After the Second World War, evangelicalism went for a ride on post-war expansionism. It intersected with interdenominational, Spirit-driven missions and powerful local movements for indigenisation released by postcolonialism. European and American interdenominationalisms fused with these movements in a 'global-local' axis to create transdenominational, transnational evangelicalism. It co-opted the modernist technological revolution, combined naïve Americanism with U.S. power and finance, absorbed British and Dutch intellectual capital, morphed to meet the needs of majority world peoples and made its way along the pathways described by its evangelical forerunners. By the time (to paraphrase Yves Lambert) the 'axial convergence' of the 1950s was over[119] and the consensus fell apart, evangelical faith was already localised and indigenised in sustainable communities in many parts of the world, from which centres its fragments began to spread in unpredictable ways.

[117] Krapohl and Lippy, *The Evangelicals*, pp. 297–8; Barry Hankins, *Francis Schaeffer and the Shaping of Evangelical America*, Grand Rapids: Eerdmans, 2008.

[118] John J. Thompson, *Raised by Wolves: The Story of Christian Rock & Roll*, Toronto: ECW Press, 2000, p. 36.

[119] Yves Lambert, 'Religion in Modernity as a New Axial Age: Secularization or New Religious Forms?' *Sociology of Religion*, 60 (1999), 303–33.

These centres were not only in the majority world, but also in Tulsa, Oklahoma, along the West Coast of the United States, and in the great melting-pot cities where cultures met and hammered out new ways of communication. The Graham consensus taught the value of pragmatism and provided a vision of what evangelicals could do when they worked together. Increasingly marginal to the secular states in the West, evangelical Christianity had positioned itself to become a mass reality in the majority world.

The intellectual challenge, however, remained. The rapidity of change left a lingering suspicion (especially among European Reformed traditions) that 'evangelical' was not an identity at all, but at best a mode of action towards mission. Rob Warner has described a deep division within evangelicalism,[120] with 'open', engaged evangelicals struggling with those more concerned to defend evangelical distinctives. Both branches had learned lessons from the Second World War. Open evangelicals learned that spirituality should be decoupled from power – leaving them with the task of developing a holistic evangelicalism in the context of global pluralism. Those seeking to protect existing evangelical identities also learned lessons from the war: that the winners are likely to be those with the better organisation and the bigger weapons. Both parties in the fragmented evangelical consensus entered the 1980s seeking to work out the logic of their positions.

[120] Warner, *Reinventing English Evangelicalism.*

8

'The Actual Arithmetic': A Survey of Contemporary Global Evangelicalism

Evangelicals are fascinated by the science of things. From the beginning, they were participants in the gentlemanly sciences. When William Carey sought to demonstrate the extent of Christianity and the world's crying need, it was only to be expected that he would choose to write in the form of the 'gazetteer' (a combined form of geographical and demographical work typical of the age). For evangelicals, numbers have the reassuring attributes of being rational, evidential and semiotic: they are pointers to the action of God in the world, evidences designed to impel Christian obedience. However, as Rodney Stark has pointed out with regard to the commonplace that early Christianity grew at a remarkable rate, such 'evangelical' statistics can lead one astray.[1] 'The "facts" justifying the miraculous assumption were wrong. The only reason people believed that there was an arithmetic need for mass conversion was because no one ever bothered to do the actual arithmetic.'[2] The picture that emerged for Stark when he did the 'actual arithmetic' was in fact far more interesting: early Christianity emerged as a successful, urban, transformative community in and through which marginalised people (particularly women) enjoyed influence and authority far beyond what was possible for them in the broader context. The facts were sufficiently striking without needing to appeal to a miracle. These are observations which can also be applied to the statistics describing global evangelicalism.

Projected onto the global stage, directed scholarship may have political outcomes. In 2006, a former president of Albania, Rexhep Mejdani, sparked a furore by using figures from the *World Christian Encyclopedia* (*WCE*) to demonstrate the decline in the country's Muslim affiliation.[3] The figures, critics said, were 'bogus and biased', 'not serious enough to be cited by a former Albanian president'.[4] The case demonstrates the problems of making definitive statements about the state

[1] Rodney Stark, *The Rise of Christianity: A Sociologist Reconsiders History*, Princeton: Princeton University Press, 1996.

[2] Rodney Stark, 'Reconstructing the Rise of Christianity: the Role of Women', *Sociology of Religion*, 56 (1995), 230.

[3] David B. Barrett, George T. Kurian and Todd M. Johnson, eds, *World Christian Encyclopedia*, New York: Oxford University Press, 2001.

[4] Ines Angeli Murzaku, 'Inter-church and Inter-religious Tensions in Post-Communist Eastern Europe: the case of Albania,' http://www.georgefox.edu/academics/undergrad/departments/soc-swk/ree/Murzaku_Inter-church_Feb%202008.pdf, accessed 29 November 2010.

of large religious communities in globalising contexts. The *WCE* is a systematic conspectus of Christianity around the world (first edition published in 1982, with a second expanded edition in 2001), but it remains the product of developments in evangelical Christian missiology. It did not merely count heads, but provided trend data which would inform evangelical 'missiometrics'[5] – a rational, scientific approach to directing missional energies. Like every statistical tool, its outcomes are shaped by its intentions. It was inevitably 'biased', though not (as its Albanian critics proclaimed) 'bogus'. In a comparative study, Becky Hsu and colleagues have confirmed that the *WCE*'s general percentage data are 'generally reliable.'[6] Unfortunately, the relative lack of interest of the secular academy in evangelicalism has meant that its faults are highlighted by the absence of alternatives. The *WCE*'s relative uniqueness has also made it especially influential among evangelical leaders, particularly through popularisations (such as Patrick Johnstone's *Operation World*, with more than 2 million copies in circulation). By definition it stands in the heritage of the 'Encyclopedie' of Diderot, and as such is based on Western rationalist presumptions,[7] the most sweeping of which is the organisation of statistics by state/geography and by relative 'exposure to Christianity'.[8]

The *WCE*'s critics are numerous. Many find its categorisations difficult to untangle: how do 'independents', for example, come to outnumber 'Protestants' even in the United States?[9] What is the use of a title such as 'Great Commission Christians' when there are no people who identify themselves as such, and there is no methodology which can distinguish between public profession and private motivation? 'These are inadequate and confusing definitions and distinctions', notes Gerald Anderson, 'and therefore the enumeration of them is suspect.'[10] Loose categories can lead to double counting. The estimation of charismatic believers in the United States (at 60 million) is 'not likely,'[11] and estimations of Great Commission believers in France, Italy and other parts of Europe far exceed the number of actual churchgoers. In the end, statistics and the authors' eschatology conflate to sketch hopeful trends in the present work of God. As with the 'myth' of the early church, the 'myth' of 500–600 million pentecostal and charismatic believers

5 David B. Barrett and Todd M. Johnson, *World Christian Trends, AD 30–AD 2200*, Pasadena: William Carey Library, 2001, p. 447.

6 Becky Hsu, Amy Reynolds, Conrad Hackett and James Gibbon, 'Estimating the Religious Composition of All Nations: An Empirical Assessment of the World Christian Database', *Journal for the Scientific Study of Religion*, 47 (2008), 684.

7 J.A.B. Jongeneel, 'Missionary and Missiological Encyclopedias', *Exchange*, 28 (1999), 247.

8 Erica Bornstein, 'Developing Faith: Theologies of Economic Development in Zimbabwe', *Journal of Religion in Africa*, 32 (2002), 7.

9 Gerald H. Anderson, 'World Christianity by the Numbers: A Review of the *World Christian Encyclopedia*, Second Edition,' *International Bulletin of Missionary Research*, 26:3 (July 2002), 129.

10 Ibid., 129.

11 Mark A. Noll, review of Barrett et al., *World Christian Encyclopedia*, in *Church History*, 71 (2002), 451.

located in the global south has become a powerful element in a burgeoning new literature trumpeting the emergence of 'renewalist' Christianity. In the words of Vinson Synan: 'At the end of the twentieth century the explosive growth of these movements forced the religious world to pay increasing attention to understanding the movement and the reasons for its massive expansion in the world.'[12]

And perhaps that was the point: the statistics are themselves 'directed', aimed at motivating Christians towards missionary outreach in the assurance of eventual victory. If they are inflated – as appears likely – then the identification of trends in global evangelicalism needs to be approached carefully. The study by Hsu and colleagues – which generally confirms the reliability of the World Christian Database (WCD) – suggests that this can be done by means of comparing alternative sources and identifying the key biases in the *WCE*/WCD, which trend towards the inflation of Christian numbers and the imposition of arbitrary categories. With these caveats in mind, we may proceed to estimate the extent and location of evangelical Christians.

THE TRANSATLANTIC AXIS

While Christianity was born in the Middle East, evangelicalism was formed in the transatlantic context of the two centuries after the Reformation. Ironically, therefore, the transatlantic world developed both exceptional secularism (in post-Revolutionary France and post-disestablishment northern Europe in particular) and exceptional religiosity (as in the United States), with evangelical Christianity spanning both. Both ends of the transatlantic axis have seen mixed stories with regard to the continuing presence of evangelical Christianity.

On the one hand, American evangelical confidence has been supported by a high, relatively stable average (43 per cent) of the population which self-identifies as 'evangelical' or 'born again'.[13] These categories, however, also apply to 19 per cent of Catholics, 28 per cent of white Protestants and no less than 70 per cent of black people,[14] illustrating the definitional problems inherent in counting evangelicals. It is questionable whether self-identification is a sufficiently objective measure: in an earlier generation, 'Catholic' and 'evangelical' would have been regarded as mutually exclusive categories. A more rigorous survey conducted in 2007 yielded a figure of 26.3 per cent of the population who identified with evangelical churches, and a further 6.9 per cent associated with historically black churches (which are generally

[12] Vinson Synan, 'The Pentecostal Movement in North America and Beyond', *Journal of Beliefs & Values*, 25:2 (August 2004), 153.

[13] Gallup Polls, 2004–2005, see Frank Newport, 'Questions and Answers About Americans' Religion', http://www.gallup.com/poll/103459/questions-answers-about-americans-religion.aspx

[14] Frank Newport and Joseph Carroll, 'Another look at evangelicals in America Today', December 2, 2005, http://www.gallup.com/poll/20242/Another-Look-Evangelicals-America-Today.aspx, accessed 1 December 2010.

evangelical in character). Both figures include pentecostals.[15] Actively committed members of evangelical churches were almost certainly a substantially smaller proportion than this, perhaps as low as 12 per cent. However, even this proportion of the massive population of the United States amounts to around 30 million people, reinforced (the survey evidence suggests) by the 'sympathetic' interest of up to 75 million more. Moreover, in recent decades, 'mainline' liberal churches in the United States have seen significant decline, with the consequence that evangelicals now make up nearly two-thirds of American Protestants. They are, however, very unevenly distributed around the country, being most numerous in the south and thinnest on the ground in the far west and in New England.[16] This geographical distribution impacts on their political and class presence in American debates; their position at the core of the world's political, economic and communications networks will guarantee that their opinions remain important. Proximity to Latin America and the predominance of Catholic and charismatic/pentecostal practice among migrants, furthermore, is effectively making North America not less but 'more Christian'.[17] The danger for the American role in global evangelicalism is not decline, but distraction through the challenges of pluralisation and urbanisation. Concerns about the hollowing-out of evangelicalism in the first world have caused a shift in funding priorities, with church planting emphases often drawing on the resources previously spent on foreign missions. The effect – for example, in relation to Baptist institutions in Zimbabwe – could be challenging.[18]

On the other side of the Atlantic, Europe has become almost a synonym for 'secularisation'. Despite the collapse of the 'hard secularisation theory', as Callum Brown notes, 'secularisation is happening' to the extent that he famously entitled his 2000 book, *The Death of Christian Britain*. Rates of church membership and participation across Western Europe in particular are 'declining precipitously',[19] sparking concerns about the total disappearance of the 'Christendom' heritage and the rising influence of Islam and political violence on both sides of the migration relationship.[20] Church attendance in Britain has certainly substantially declined:

[15] http://religions.pewforum.org/reports, accessed 23 July 2011.

[16] Ibid.; John Wolffe, 'Evangelicals and Pentecostals: Indigenizing a Global Gospel', in John Wolffe, ed., *Global Religious Movements in Regional Context*, Milton Keynes/Aldershot: The Open University/Ashgate, 2002, p. 50.

[17] Philip Jenkins, *God's Continent: Christianity, Islam, and Europe's Religious Crisis*, Oxford: Oxford University Press, 2007, p. 284.

[18] Isaac M.T. Mwase, 'Shall They Till with Their Own Hoes? Baptists in Zimbabwe and New Patterns of Interdependence, 1950–2000', in Lamin Sanneh and Joel Carpenter, eds, *The Changing Face of Christianity: Africa, the West and the World*, Oxford: Oxford University Press, 2005, p. 73.

[19] Frans J. Verstraelen, 'Jenkins' *The Next Christendom*', in Frans J. S. Wijsen and Robert J. Schreiter, eds, *Global Christianity: Contested Claims*, Amsterdam and New York: Rodopi, 2007, p. 96.

[20] Walter Laqueur, *The Last Days of Europe*, New York: Thomas Dunne/St Martin's Griffin, 2007, is only one of a large number of books on this subject. See also Bat Ye'or, *Eurabia: The Euro-Arab Axis*, Madison: Fairleigh Dickinson University Press, 2005.

having been 19 per cent of the population in 1903, by the year 2005, British church attendance was at 6.3 per cent and dropping. One sociologist, Steve Bruce, predicted in 2003 that 'thirty years from now, Christianity in Britain will have largely disappeared.'[21] There is, however, another side to the story. In the face of net overall decline in numbers, there has (especially since 1980) been a growth in evangelical and pentecostal churches sufficiently strong so as to slow or even in some instances to reverse the general trend. Between 1980 and 2005, Anglican weekly church attendance in England declined by a dramatic 37 per cent, from 1.37 million to 870,000. However, the predominantly evangelical Baptists fared much better, dropping only by 11 percent, from 286,900 to 254,800. During the same period, the overwhelmingly evangelical New Churches actually grew by 145 per cent, from 75,000 to 183,600, and the pentecostals by 30 per cent, from 221,100 to 287,600.[22] Moreover, in recent years, there are indications that even the steep Anglican decline is starting to bottom out, and the key diocese of London has actually seen a 70 per cent *increase* in membership between 1990 and 2010. This gain is attributable in part to improved organization and leadership, but also reflects the substantial number of thriving evangelical Anglican churches in the English capital. In 2005, overall church attendance in London was 8.3 per cent, substantially higher than the national average, an indication that in the early twenty-first century, the globalised linkages of a major world city were stimulating resistance to Western secularising trends, particularly among evangelical migrant groups.[23] In 2005, evangelicals were estimated to make up 40 per cent of English churchgoers, up from 30 per cent in 1989.[24]

In continental Europe, too, the picture is more complex than it appears at first sight. In countries where evangelicalism has historically been strong, there has been a marked decline, most notably in the home of Haugean revivalism, Norway. *WCE* figures suggest that the proportion of evangelicals in the Norwegian population fell from 24.5 per cent in 1970 to 10.9 per cent in 2000. However, the same period saw a marked rise in the numbers of charismatic and pentecostal Christians. A similar trend is apparent in the other Scandinavian countries, the Netherlands and Germany, where it is important to distinguish the quite small numbers of *evangelikal* Christians, with beliefs similar to Anglo-American evangelicals, from much larger numbers of *evangelisch* liberal and cultural Lutherans. Apparently using the word in its more restrictive sense, the *WCE* estimates the proportion of evangelicals at 3.8 per cent in 1970 and 1.6 per cent in 2000. Here too, however, evangelical decline is balanced by charismatic and pentecostal growth. A different

21 Steve Bruce, quoted in 'Introduction', in Grace Davie, Paul Heelas and Linda Woodhead, eds, *Predicting Religion: Christian, Secular and Alternative Futures*, Aldershot: Ashgate, 2003, p. 4.

22 Peter Brierley, ed., *UKCH Religious Trends 4*, London: Christian Research, 2003, p. 2.24; idem, *UKCH Religious Trends 7*, Swindon: Christian Research, 2008, p. 2.24.

23 See John Wolffe and Bob Jackson, 'Anglican Resurgence: The Church of England in London' in David Goodhew, ed., *Church Growth in Britain 1980–2010*, Aldershot: Ashgate, 2012.

24 Peter Brierley, ed., *UK Religious Trends 6*, London: Christian Research, 2006, p. 5.15.

pattern applies in countries where Protestants are in a minority, or where Protestant and Catholic numbers are quite evenly balanced. In Belgium, France, Hungary, Italy and Switzerland, numbers of evangelicals appear to have held steady or even to have increased slightly, while there has also been substantial pentecostal and charismatic growth. The strongest evangelical growth has occurred in countries where tiny evangelical minorities had earlier suffered under authoritarian regimes (such as in Poland, Portugal, Spain and Ukraine) and where recent democratisation has also resulted in greater religious freedom.[25]

The *WCE* may well underestimate the extent to which Protestant minorities in predominantly Catholic European countries have become more evangelical in character. Italy, for example, is not only the historic centre of world Catholicism, but is also home to Europe's largest pentecostal movement – more than 300,000. French-speaking scholars have noted the recent substantial growth of a Protestantism that is 'évangélique, conversioniste par essence' at the expense of 'le protestantisme réformé' in both Belgium and France.[26] Since 1950, the number of evangelicals in France has increased from 50,000 to at least 350,000 – a rate of growth which, if it were not compared to the 4–5 million Muslims now in that country, would be considered respectable.[27] Global linkages and migration flows are a significant factor in this evangelicalisation of European Protestantism, especially with the development of African churches, not only in Britain, but also notably in Belgium, the Netherlands, France and Germany. Italian, Spanish and Portuguese connections to Latin America, and Chinese Christian connections to the global market, have created other Christian subcultures throughout Europe.[28] The future for European Christianity, Philip Jenkins concludes, will have a distinctly 'Southern' Christian flavour to it: 'conservative and charismatic',[29] black or Asian, and pentecostal.[30] Comprising (excluding the former USSR) an evangelical population of perhaps 40 million at present, European evangelicals remain important not only as hosts in a location where the world (and hence future Christian mission) is coming to stay, but as subcultural missionaries and thought leaders using their presence at the crossroads of world diplomacy to agitate for the rights of Christians elsewhere in the world.[31]

[25] *WCE*, i. passim. See also Geldbach, '"Evangelikal", "Evangelisch" and Pietism', pp. 156–80.

[26] Luc Nefontaine, 'Les transformations ecclesiologiques et theologiques d'un protestantisme conversioniste en Belgique francophone', in Jean-Pierre Bastien, ed., *La Recomposition des Protestantismes en Europe Latine*, Geneva: Labor, 2004, p. 139.

[27] Agnieszka Tennant, 'The French Reconnection', *Christianity Today*, 49 (March 2005), http://www.christianitytoday.com/ct/2005/march/20.28.html, accessed 12 December 2011.

[28] Gerrie ter Haar, *Halfway to Paradise: African Christians in Europe*, Cardiff: Cardiff Academic Press, 1998, pp. 96–103.

[29] Verstraelen, 'Jenkins' *The Next Christendom*', p. 96.

[30] Maria Mackay, 'Researcher Anticipates Further Church Decline in 2010s', http://www.christiantoday.com/article/researcher.anticipates.further.church.decline.in.2010s/25949.htm, posted 22 May 2010, accessed 5 September 2011.

[31] 'Robert Ekh's speech at the Manifestation', http://www.livetsord.se/default.aspx?idStructure=11388, accessed 1 December 2010.

THE 'OTHER' WEST

Interacting with the traditional transatlantic 'centre' of evangelicalism are those 'other' nations of European settlement: Australia, New Zealand, Canada and, to some degree, South Africa. All these countries experienced rapid population growth through the mass migrations out of Europe between 1840 and 1920 (particularly from the United Kingdom and Ireland, but also Italy, Greece, Spain, Germany and the Slavic countries). They were subject to a second great exodus after the Second World War, creating a situation in which their essential multiculturalism and close proximity to strong alternative cultural forms (to the Asia-Pacific, or to indigenous peoples) saw them experience divergent patterns of religious growth and decline. In this sense, these countries (with other entrepôts such as Singapore and Hong Kong, and transnational networks such as the Chinese diaspora) may be seen as sitting at the intersection of the global north and the global south. On the one hand, mass European migration created in all these countries a 'bedrock' of mainstream Christianity (Anglican, Presbyterian, Methodist, Congregationalist, Roman Catholic and, in South Africa, Dutch Reformed) which had significant impact on the public role of religion. All of these 'cultural Christianities', however, were particularly subject to the effects of pluralisation and secularisation. Their 'European' populations experienced a gradual, and then increasingly precipitate, slide in church attendance, a widening gap between communities of religious practice and an expanding 'no religion' category, and a consequent shift towards sustainable church community formation. The response, as many observers have noticed, was not the decline of religion, as originally projected, but the rise of more energetic, 'sectarian' forms – among which most scholars include 'New Protestant' evangelicalism.[32]

Certainly, evangelicalism has – on the whole – bucked the trends even in the West. There is no particular evidence that evangelical communities are continuing to decline as a whole, although there is some evidence that the emphasis has shifted from the evangelical wings of mainstream denominations to independent evangelical and pentecostal/charismatic forms of the faith. As Peter Lineham notes with regard to New Zealand, 'evangelical churches have a clear focus which often means a committed core'.[33] The cultural role of religion is also different from that in the United States, where polls and subjects have traditionally over-reported the number of people actually attending church.[34] In Australia, Canada and New

[32] Arie L. Molendijk, 'An Alternative View of Christianity: A Troeltschean Perspective', in Hent de Vries, ed., *Religion: Beyond a Concept*, New York: Fordham University Press, 2008, p. 442.

[33] Peter Lineham, quoted in 'Growth in God's Hands', *Marlborough Express*, 5 (November 2008), accessed 6 December 2010.

[34] B. Kirk Hadaway, Penny Marler and Mark Chaves. 'Over-reporting Church Attendance in America: Evidence That Demands the Same Verdict', *American Sociological Review* 63 (1998), 122–30. Roger Finke and Rodney Stark (*The Churching of America, 1776–2005: Winners and Losers in our Religious Economy*, New Brunswick: Rutgers University Press, 2006, pp. 12ff.) detect methodological bias among such critical accounts.

Zealand, the state plays a much larger role in the daily lives of people, the third sector being largely excluded from the political (albeit not the representative) process. The likelihood in these three countries, therefore, is that (as George Rawlyk found in 1996), there is significant *under*-reporting of evangelical association because of perceived social opprobrium,[35] and a much larger 'no religion' category in most censuses. All three societies are advanced secular welfare states, with evangelical constituencies hovering between 3 per cent and 10 per cent of the total population.

In Australia between 1996 and 2001, there was strong growth in pentecostal and some evangelical constituencies (particularly evangelical Baptist churches – although overall, the Baptist Union of NSW experienced zero growth between 1997 and 2006),[36] slow growth in Anglican and Protestant denominations (1 per cent compared to 6.4 per cent across the total population), whereas more generally, Catholic mass attendance declined by 13 per cent (and another 13 per cent between 2001 and 2006)[37] and overall weekly church attendance across all traditions in Australia declined by 7 per cent.[38] By 2007, monthly church attendance in Australia was down to about 17 per cent of the total population, and falling.[39] In large part, these losses came from the mainline churches – particularly the Uniting Church (an ecumenical union that united most Presbyterian, Methodist and Congregationalist churches in 1977), which fell by 11 percent between 1996 and 2001. This church – which in 1911 made up 26 per cent of the Australian population and a very significant segment of the evangelical community – now has less than half of the regular attendees of Australia's largest pentecostal denomination (the Assemblies of God, at approximately 200,000 members), and perhaps as many active evangelicals as the country's next largest pentecostal church (the Christian City Churches, or 'C3', movement: approximately 25,000).[40] There are nearly as many evangelicals in church on any given Sunday as there are Catholics. As a result, evangelical constituencies have become even more disproportionately important among church attendees, although having the numbers and the money does not

[35] G.A. Rawlyk, *Is Jesus Your Personal Saviour?In Search of Canadian Evangelicalism*, Montreal: McGill-Queen's University Press, 1996, p. 119.

[36] Jonathan Pratt, "Awaken O Sleeper": Disturbing a Denomination at the Crossroads", Working Paper No. 1, Baptist Churches of NSW and ACT Directions 2012 Research Project, 29 April, 2009, p. 6, http://baptistnsw.asn.au/working_paper_1.pdf, accessed 9 December 2010.

[37] Michael Gilchrist, '2006 National Church Life Survey: Important Questions Overlooked', http://www.ad2000.com.au/articles/2006/decjan2006p12_2420.html, accessed 6 December 2010.

[38] John Bellamy, Peter Kaldor, et. al., *National Church Life Survey: Initial Impressions 2001*, Adelaide: Openbook, 2002; 'NCLS releases latest estimates of church attendance', Media Release – 28 February 2004.

[39] Ruth Powell et al., 'Why Innovation Is Needed in Church Life', http://www.ncls.org.au/default.aspx?sitemapid=6516, accessed 6 December 2010; and 'Church attenders attitudes to innovation in church life – A comparison across countries and across time', Occasional Paper 14, Sydney: National Church Life Survey, 2010.

[40] Information from Peter Bentley, Christian Research Association, and Secretary, Assembly of Confessing Congregations; Michael Gilchrist, 'What the Census Statistics on Religious Affiliations Reveal', *AD2000*, 12:3 (April 1999), 12.

necessarily translate into 'voice' either in the church or the public square. Growth has been irregular across the various traditions: there is general growth across the pentecostal/charismatic sector, but Vineyard and Christian Revival Crusade churches have declined. The most significant growth across the period (by 20 per cent) was in the mega-church-led Assemblies of God, pointing to the importance of strong organisation and adaptability in the development of counter-secularising community forms. With regard to the market models promoted by Finke and Stark,[41] it is probably not coincidental that the Assemblies of God and the Christian City Churches are amongst the most competitive, globally engaged and culturally adaptive of pentecostal movements in Australia.

Despite complaints that 'church attendance has never been particularly high,'[42] New Zealand-*Aotearoa* has a regular church attendance rate and an evangelical population proportionately larger than that of Australia. As 'the combined Pentecostal churches [now] have bigger attendances than the Anglicans and Methodists combined,' the 'typical New Zealand evangelical' is now more likely to be a pentecostal.[43] Indeed, at the time of writing, a pentecostal was chairman of the National Council of Churches in New Zealand. With such a small overall population, however, relatively small fluctuations in world conditions can have disproportionate results. The effect of global recession and climate change on the Pacific, for example, has meant rapid growth in New Zealand's Pacific Islander (*pasifika*) population. In some cities, such as Auckland, the evangelical church is thus disproportionately Polynesian or Melanesian in its culture, a factor which affects denominational politics and church attendance patterns among the *pakeha* (European) population. Jamieson has suggested that the reliance of pentecostal churches on transfer from traditional denominations may signal a problem for their continued growth over time.[44] Such calculations do not, however, take into account the 'reserve function' of the 'believing but not belonging' constituency reported in many polls (for instance, the Australian census, the Angas Reid World Poll, etc). This group, which shares evangelical values but avoids church engagements, may be as large again as the church-attending evangelical constituency.[45] Nor does it take into account the participation of pentecostal churches in global flows of migration. Increased migration from the majority world has, it is true, increased the Muslim (from the Middle East and Southeast Asia) and Buddhist

[41] Finke and Stark, *Churching of America*, pp. 2–3.

[42] Alan Jamieson, 'The Future of the Church in New Zealand', http://www.evangeliskalliance.dk/icms/filer/future_of_-nz-church.doc, accessed 6 December 2010.

[43] Ibid.

[44] Ibid., and idem., 'Turangawaewae: The Search for A Churchless Faith in New Zealand', *Australasian Pentecostal Studies*, 6 (2004), http://webjournals.alphacrucis.edu.au/journals/aps/issue-56/turangawaewae-the-search-for-a-churchless-faith-in/ – accessed 14 December 2011.

[45] Aileen VanGinkel, *Evangelical Beliefs and Practices: A Summary of the 2003 Ipsos Held Survey Results*, Markham: Evangelical Fellowship of Canada, 2003, p. 7.

(from South and Southeast Asia) elements of Australian and New Zealand populations. It has also, however, supported Catholic numbers (from Africa and South America) and expanded pentecostal congregations (from Africa, Asia and South America).

By way of contrast, Canada carries a double burden: that of operating in a secularised welfare state *and* of dealing with negative reactions to the loud, proactive evangelical community in its larger southern neighbour. Evangelicals in Canada often seek alternative (specifically non-American) public identities as mechanisms for engaging public culture. Calculating the number of evangelicals in Canada is thus a difficult task, made all the more complex by the wrangling within the Anglican Church of Canada which has seen the defection of a significant number of parishes. Roger O'Toole suggests that evangelicals form 7 per cent of the population,[46] Bibby 8 per cent,[47] Hiemstra prefers a number closer to 10 per cent[48] and Rawlyk suggests (using Andrew Grenville's 'Christian Evangelicalism Scale') a number closer to 15 per cent. The Ipsos-Reid survey more recently has claimed 19 per cent.[49] This would suggest that Canada has an evangelical population of between 2.4 million and 3 million people, spread across some 11,000 congregations. Comparison with Australia and New Zealand draws out some salutary issues. In part, pentecostals are so relatively strong in the south because they are more distant (albeit not disconnected) from American comparisons in the secular public mind, and also because these countries did not receive the Mennonite and other European migration which form such a large part of Canadian evangelicalism. Holiness movements (such as the Christian and Missionary Alliance, C&MA) also remain far more potent in Canada. The C&MA in Australia, for example, only had 4,100 regular attendees in 2001,[50] and their growth across the next decade has been largely by migration (particularly by Chinese and Vietnamese). A church like the 6,000-member 'The Meeting House', a multi-locational Anabaptist new-generation church in Oakville, Ontario, would be inconceivable in Australia or New Zealand. Yet there are also parallels – in all three countries, churches that succeed are those which can form sustainable communities with an active response to secularising pressures.

As has already been noted, South Africa was a major portal for the entry of Protestant Christianity into Africa. The presence of a Dutch Reformed 'White Tribe of

[46] Roger O'Toole, 'Religion in Canada: Its Development and Contemporary Situation', in Lori Beaman, ed., *Religion and Canadian Society*, Toronto: Canadian Scholars' Press, 2006, p. 17.

[47] R.W. Bibby, *The Boomer Factor: What Canada's Most Famous Generation is Leaving Behind.* Toronto: Bastian, 2006.

[48] Rick Hiemstra, 'Counting Canadian Evangelicals', *Church & Faith Trends*, 1:1 (2007), p. 1ff; see also Sam Reimer and Michael Wilkinson, 'A Demographic Look at Evangelical Congregations', http://files.efc-canada.net/min/rc/cft/V03I02/Demographic_Look_Evangelical_Congregations-CECS.pdf, p. 5.

[49] 'Survey Shows 19 Percent of Canadians are Evangelical', http://www.evangelicalfellowship.ca/page.aspx?pid=1027, accessed 1 September 2011.

[50] 'NCLS releases latest estimates of church attendance', Media Release – 28 February 2004.

Africa',[51] its articulation of Calvinist and Pietist streams out of Europe, and its contentions with Anglo-German and American forms of evangelicalism have meant that Reformed Christianity has never been disconnected from the key events that eventually gave rise to a nation. As the new century dawned, the Reformed faith was still the largest Christian denomination (42.8 per cent) among whites. In the Church of England in South Africa (CESA), Reformed evangelicalism adopted an apolitical, anti-pentecostal stance that would make it the destination of choice for white Anglicans troubled by the reformist politics of Archbishop Desmond Tutu and the larger Church of the Province of South Africa. Its connection to Sydney evangelical Anglicanism linked it to global Anglican counter-liberal movements.[52] Despite the fact that most South African theology has largely overlooked the 'social turn' in post-war evangelicalism,[53] evangelicals have also been highly active in South African society. Balcomb identifies four evangelical approaches to 'the liberation struggle': radical 'Concerned Evangelicals' involved in open struggle and critical of traditional evangelical dualism; conservatives (such as the Evangelical Fellowship of South Africa and CESA) more interested in fighting against theological 'liberalism' than in upsetting the status quo; 'Third Way' activists (such as Michael Cassidy) involved in reconciliation and change; and protagonists of 'alternative community', such as revivalist Nicholas Bhengu, who countered apartheid through his massive 'Back to God' campaigns in the 1950s.[54] Among the last two groups in particular, the core 'healing' metaphors of charismatic evangelicalism were powerful contributors to passive ('implicit' or 'symbolic') resistance. Evangelicals as a consequence operated right across the range of political positions.[55]

Thus, both through the apartheid period (when a minority governed for their own interests), and the post-apartheid period (when the elites changed, and many South Africans doubted that there was any effective government to speak of), religion remained an important mode of communal organisation and service delivery. Energetic forms of the faith therefore dominate – some 15 per cent of white South African Christians (compared to 33 per cent among non-black and non-European Christians) are pentecostal or Apostolic, as are more than 23 per cent of the 17 million black Christians who associate with the South African Zionist churches, and who make up 80 per cent of all South African 'independent' or 'indigenous

[51] For use of the term, see David Harrison, *The White Tribe of Africa: South Africa in Perspective*, Berkeley: University of California Press, 1981.

[52] Anthony Balcomb, 'Evangelicals and Democracy in South Africa' *Journal of Theology for Southern Africa*, 109 (March 2001), 7.

[53] Clint Le Bruyns, 'Can Any Public Good Come from Evangelicals? Theological Paradigms and Possibilities toward a Transforming South Africa', *Religion & Theology*, 13:3/4 (2006), 350.

[54] Anthony Balcomb, 'Left, Right and Centre: Evangelicals and the Struggle for Liberation in South Africa,' *Journal of Theology for Southern Africa*, 118 (March 2004), 6ff.

[55] Barbara Bompani, 'African Independent Churches in Post-Apartheid South Africa: New Political Interpretations', *Journal of Southern African Studies*, 34:3 (September 2008), 667.

churches'.[56] While many of these were founded in the period between 1890 and 1930, their 'take-off' period was between 1940 and 1960, reaching more than 4.5 million members across South Africa by 1970 and nearly 17 million by 1995.[57] By comparison, *classical* pentecostal and charismatic churches are less numerically significant (particularly when compared to the huge equivalent populations in Nigeria and Ghana), but they remain important as mediators for South African churches with the rest of the world.[58] The visits of Nigerian, Ghanaian and Kenyan preachers in the 1990s rapidly indigenised South African pentecostalism and stimulated rapid growth among the black population. Combined with the Zionist figures, Anderson suggests that up to 40 per cent of the South African population may thus be considered to be broadly 'pentecostal',[59] a contentious claim but one which demonstrates the breadth and depth of evangelicalism's influence on Africa's most advanced economy. After the "Rustenburg Declaration" in 1990, charismatic and pentecostal churches became more active in the social and political life of the country, including in the Truth and Reconciliation Commissions. From Frank Chikane (Director General of the Office of the President), to Ray McCauley (pastor of South Africa's largest 'mixed' charismatic church), and Reinhard Bonnke (whose Christ for All Nations ministry was long based in the country), South Africa has been a critical crucible for evangelical extension in Africa.[60] In the contemporary world, its 'anticipatory refugees' in the South African diaspora have taken their particular emphases around the globe, influencing evangelical/pentecostal church constituencies.[61]

THE DRIFT SOUTH

The significance of the growth of evangelicalism in these Western 'intersection' countries has been not only their mediation of evangelicalism out of the transatlantic axis, but their interpretation of surging indigenous evangelicalism

56 Christoffer Grundmann, 'Heaven Below Here and Now! The Zionist Churches in Southern Africa', *International Journal for the Study of the Christian Church*, 6:3 (September 2006), 257. Grundmann's figures would suggest 9 million Zionists; Anderson's (quoted later in the chapter) would suggest approximately 14.7 million.

57 Grundmann, 'Heaven Below Here and Now!', 257.

58 Allan Anderson, 'New African Initiated Pentecostalism and Charismatics in South Africa', *Journal of Religion in Africa*, 35:1 (2005), 66.

59 Ibid., 67ff.

60 See Kemp Pendleton Burpeau, *God's Showman*, Oslo: Refleks, 2004, and Peter M. Gunnar, *Here am I, Lord, Send Me: The Life of Missionary Leader Rev. William Binnington Boyce*, Annandale: Desert Pea, 2003.

61 On the white South African diaspora, see Nigar G. Khawaja and Lesleyanne Mason, 'Predictors of Psychological Distress in South African Immigrants to Australia', *South African Journal of Psychology*, 38:1 (April 2008), 227; http://www.workpermit.com/news/2008-05-23/australia/immigrating-australia-from-south-africa.htm; Charles Crothers, 'New Zealand Religious Affiliations in the New Millennium,' *Stimulus*, 13:4 (November 2005), 31–49, and *TeAra, The Encyclopedia of New Zealand*, http://www.teara.govt.nz.

back into the West. This 'drift to the [global] south' – often despite rather than because of the activities of formal, denominational missions agencies – involved rapid indigenisation, often in the context of religious revival.[62] As Noll notes, in 1900, 'over 80% of the world Christian population was Caucasian and over 70% resided in Europe.' A century later,

> active Christian adherence has become stronger in Africa than in Europe . . . the number of practicing Christians in China may be approaching the number in the United States . . . live bodies in church are far more numerous in Kenya than in Canada, [and] more believers worship together in church Sunday by Sunday in Nagaland than in Norway.[63]

In the words of Philip Jenkins: 'Over the past century, however, the center of gravity in the Christian world has shifted inexorably southward, to Africa, Asia, and Latin America. . . . If we want to visualize a "typical" contemporary Christian, we should think of a woman living in a village in Nigeria or in a Brazilian favela.'[64] This, as Andrew Walls notes, is another of Christianity's 'great escapes' – not, this time, from one threatened centre to another (for example, Jerusalem to Rome, or Rome to Constantinople),[65] but from somewhere to everywhere, from one or two or a dozen centres to mobile multicentricity.

Much of this expansion of Christianity has been either Catholic or evangelical/pentecostal in nature, and the gap between the West and the South may be seen in by comparing relative growth rates (as in Table 8.1, and Figure 8.1). Reliable comparative source data is available for about 150 countries around the world for the period between 1970 and 2010. Trend data expands this to about 180 countries, although attempts to make larger claims debase the quality of the interpretations. There are, moreover, significant concerns over estimations of evangelical populations, particularly in those countries that figure largely in the missionary mental 'world map'. China is a classic example of this, with estimates ranging wildly from the most recent census figures (which estimate there to be 10 million Protestants in the country, most of whom would fit Bebbington's definition of an evangelical) to the wildly hopeful (which estimate 200 million converts). These 179 case studies, however, might well be taken to be *suggestive* of the whole.

In a world where the global population has been increasing at an average annual rate of 1.6 per cent for the last forty years, we may first note that most evangelical growth is to be found in those countries that exceed the average population growth.

[62] Klaus Fiedler, 'Edinburgh 2010 and the Evangelicals', *Evangelical Review of Theology*, 34:4 (October 2010), 319–34; Andrew F. Walls, *The Missionary Movement in Christian History*, Edinburgh: T&T Clark, 1996.

[63] Mark A. Noll, *The New Shape of World Christianity: How American Experience Reflects Global Faith*, Downers Grove: InterVarsity, 2009, pp. 9–10.

[64] Philip Jenkins, *The Next Christendom*, New York: Oxford University Press, 2003, p. 2.

[65] Tim Stafford, 'Historian Ahead of His Time: Andrew Walls May Be the Most Important Person You Don't Know', *Christian History*, August 2008, p. 3.

TABLE 8.1. *Continent vs. Growth Rate Cross-Tabulation for Evangelical Christian Populations in 179 Countries*

	Annualised Growth Rate, 1970–2010*								
	0	0.01	0.02	0.03	0.04	0.05	0.1	0.11	Total
Africa	1	4	11	18	13	1	0	1	49
Asia	6	5	6	18	6	0	0	0	41
Caribbean	11	5	2	0	0	1	0	0	19
Europe	17	8	3	2	0	0	1	0	31
Latin America	1	1	4	7	6	1	0	0	20
North America	1	1	0	0	0	0	0	0	2
Oceania/Pacific	4	0	11	2	0	0	0	0	17
TOTAL	41	24	37	47	25	3	1	1	179

* Some European growth rates are negative. Overall, these balance out to around zero, which is the baseline used in this table.

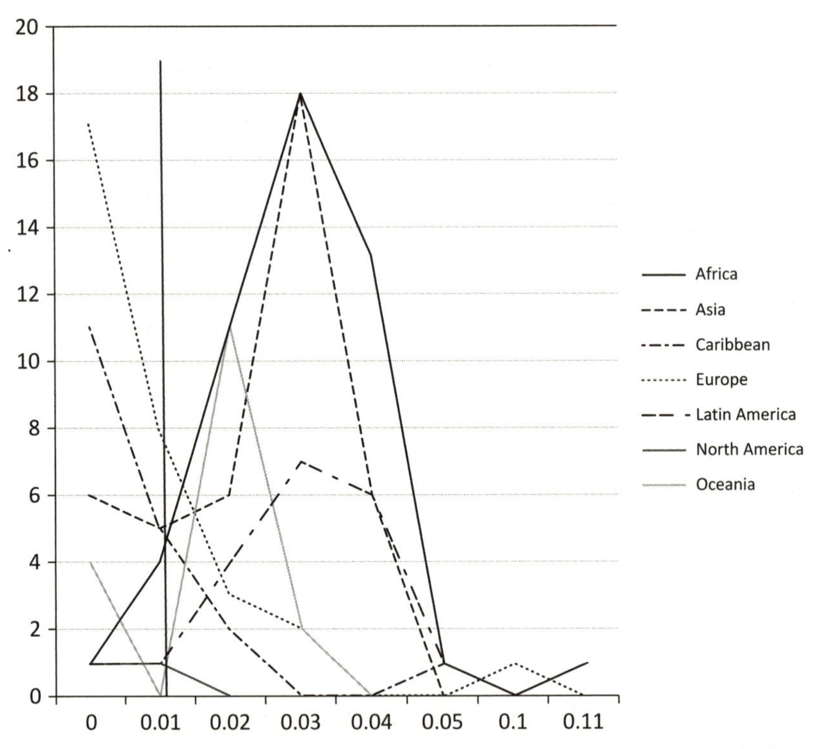

Figure 8.1. Line Graph of Scatter of Annualized Growth Rates Among Evangelical Populations in 179 Countries, 1970–2010. *Note:* Vertical line indicates the annualised global population growth rate, 1970–2010 (1.6%).

Most of those countries which do not exceed that average (of which there are 65), are to be found in Europe (through birth decline) and the Caribbean (largely through emigration), whereas the larger number of countries in the sample (114) have annualised growth rates between 8 per cent and 53 per cent greater than average global population growth rates. Most of these are to be found in Africa, Asia and Latin America.

Africa

The dominance of Islam in the north of Africa is the main reason the evangelical population of the continent is concentrated in the sub-Saharan region. In most countries, non-Islamic religions are highly controlled, leading to prison terms, fines or expulsion of expatriates for (as the law notes in Algeria) 'inciting, forcing or using stratagems of seduction to oblige Muslims to convert to another religion'.[66] Nowhere is this more apparent than in Sudan and Nigeria, where the north/south division was mapped against tribal differences entrenched by imperial fiat, continuing intercommunal tensions and bloodshed, and most recently the separation of a previously unitary country into two. Five out of the ten largest (per capita) evangelical communities are to be found in sub-Saharan Africa. Of the three largest populations of evangelicals, Nigeria and South Africa are the driving economies in their regions, and are highly internationalised. Like the third country, the Democratic Republic of the Congo, these states both have significant social challenges from HIV/AIDS and social disintegration. A bivariate correlation of evangelical growth rates around the world with Transparency International's 2009 Perceived Corruption Index ratings for African countries demonstrates a positive relationship ($r = .471$).[67] Materialist commentators have developed a strong literature exploring the relationships between evangelical religion and capitalism, and tend to read all evangelical political action in the light of the Guatemalan co-option of nationalist 'enthusiasm'. This, however, simply replicates the tunnel vision which Jenkins identifies as typical of Western writing about the rest of the world.[68] This ideological reading is undermined by the fact that, while there is a correlation between state coherency and evangelical communities in Africa, there is no such correlation in Asia (see discussion later in the chapter). It would be more accurate to say, then, that evangelical growth is co-located with rapidly expanding populations in front-line, weak-state globalising situations precisely because it 'makes life better'.[69] Despite its reliance on indigenisation within communities – evident

[66] 'Evangelical Christians Meeting Banned in Tizi Ouzou', http://www.algeria.com/forums/religion-religion/19100.htm, accessed 17 December 2010.

[67] http://www.transparency.org/policy_research/surveys_indices/cpi, accessed 10 December 2010.

[68] Jenkins, *The Next Christendom*, p. 6; see also his 'Christianity's New Centre', *Atlantic Unbound*, Sept. 12, 2002, http://www.theatlantic.com/past/docs/unbound/interviews/int2002-09-12.htm, accessed 10 December 2010.

[69] Wacker, *Early Pentecostals and American Culture.*

in its spread through tribal, ethnic and regional identities in Africa[70] – it is evangelicalism's genius for creating *trans*-communal identities which makes it effective in high-change, socially fractured settings. In 2010, for example, leaked U.S. diplomatic cables confirmed the subversion of the Nigerian state by oil interests and reflected long-standing calls by Christian commentators – such as Felix Oriakhi at the pentecostal Benson Idahosa University – for movement towards a transparent, corruption-free state based on principled social development.[71] In Liberia, 'the proliferation of evangelical Christian churches in Ganta and elsewhere' helps to 'interject more autonomy and change patterns of solidarity (and commerce) in these networks. Local commanders, some of whom are preachers, have played important roles in mediating between [warring] groups.'[72] NGOs such as African Enterprise and Opportunity International have integrated anti-corruption measures into their grassroots training and official-level advocacy measures, cooperating with organisations such as Business Action Against Corruption (BAAC) and the African Institute of Corporate Citizenship (AICC).

For a number of reasons, such as the scandalous human rights record of African Marxist-Leninist regimes prior to 2000, such responses are late and weak. Despite its historical success in creating communities of the individually redeemed, evangelicalism has in itself no well-articulated social theory. Consequently, early African evangelical political and social action tended to be symbolic and corporate – its politicians preached like pastors and its intellectuals (when they could avoid the brain drain which carried away many of the best and brightest, such as Nigerian Ogbu Kalu and Sierra Leonean Jehu Hanciles) were caught up in international biblical and other forms of scholarship which better served the church than the society. Foreign evangelical NGOs and mission agencies tended to be pietistic and non-interventionist. For their part, the evangelical communities on the ground approached politics with a corporatist mindset, which often simply imported the broader culture of corruption into their own circles.[73] But in those countries where evangelicalism managed to grow above five per cent of the population, and thus institutionalise itself in universities, hospitals and social action groups, second

[70] Afe Adogame, 'The Politicisation of Religion and the Religionization of Politics in Nigeria' in Ogbu Kalu, Chima J. Korieh, G. Ugo Nwokeji and Obioma Nnaemeka, eds, *Religion, History, and Politics in Nigeria: Essays in Honor of Ogbu U. Kalu*, Lanham: University Press of America, 2005, pp. 125–6.

[71] 'Checking Godfatherism in Nigerian Politics', *The Tide*, 22 October 2010, online, http://www.thetidenewsonline.com/?p=17641, accessed 10 December 2010; '"We Must Make a Better World Possible" Social Action tasks Nigeria Social Forum', 19 November 2010, http://saction.org/home/index.php?option=com_content&view=article&id=160:we-must-make-a-better-world-possible-social-action-tasks-nigeria-social-forum&catid=51:other-news&Itemid=115, accessed 10 December 2010.

[72] William Reno, 'Anti-Corruption Efforts in Liberia: Are They Aimed at the Right Targets?' *International Peacekeeping*, 15:3 (August 2008), 396.

[73] Paul Freston, *Evangelicals and Politics in Africa, Asia and Latin America*, Cambridge: Cambridge University Press, 2001, pp. 35–6, 66–8.

and third generations of evangelicals who have entered social life have been better educated and better connected to social theory, particularly that generated by the rising evangelical 'third way' and 'left' elements which engage with European and socially progressive thought.

Where the community issues are less overwhelming, one sees slower growth among all Christian constituencies and a higher retention of traditional practices.[74] Naturally, those countries which have had the shortest period of exposure to evangelicalism also rank – because of low starting points – highest in terms of growth rates. So the large evangelical populations in Nigeria and Ghana support church planting into Niger and parts of Mali, which make those countries appear 'active' in terms of evangelical presence, even though the actual evangelical communities of those countries are tiny. Once such irregularities are averaged out, the *least* evangelical countries in Africa (such as Tunisia, Somalia, Niger and Morocco) are all heavily Muslim in character. Others, like Guinea (where evangelicals are caught between a land-poor population which is 85 per cent Muslim and cross-border tribal violence and lawlessness), have powerful and often violent controls over public religious expression or conversion. By way of contrast, the most energetic Christian populations are to be found in east Africa – Kenya (rank one), Uganda (rank two) and Tanzania (rank six) – and southern Africa.

Asia

Whereas in Africa, evangelical growth is related to a country's level of development and such 'perception' indices as the ruling rate of corruption,[75] this is not the case in Asia, where there is no significant correlation between evangelical growth (which surged – on the back of pentecostal and charismatic growth – from 1 per cent in 1975 to 4.4 per cent of the Asian population in 1995)[76] and corruption or development indices. It is not that Asia has no corruption – indeed, some countries (for example, developing India, the Philippines, regional Chinese governments) seem to have organised their economies around it.[77] This suggests that in Asia, one needs to look for intrinsic rather than extrinsic factors which relate to how evangelicalism

[74] Charles Harvey, 'Botswana: Is the Economic Miracle Over?' *Journal of African Economics*, 1:3 (September 1992), 335.

[75] Correlations were against the Transparency International Perceived Corruption Index for 2009, and the UN Human Development indices, found in the United Nations Development Programme's (UNDP) Human Development Report 2010.

[76] Christl Kessler and Jürgen Rüland, 'Responses to Rapid Social Change: Populist Religion in the Philippines', *Pacific Affairs*, 79:1 (Spring 2006), 73.

[77] Sandy Gordon, 'Disillusioned by Rampant Graft Scandals', *The Australian*, 15 December 2010, http://www.theaustralian.com.au/higher-education/letters/disillusioned-by-rampant-graft-scandals/story-e6frgcox-1225971137286, accessed 15 December 2010; John Garnaut, '"Stability" the Buzzword for Establishment Rapine', *Sydney Morning Herald*, December 14, 2010, http://www.smh.com.au/opinion/stability-the-buzzword-for-establishment-rapine-20101214–18vvq.html, accessed 15 December 2010.

associates with a *particular* ethnic, regional or national story. In part, this relates to the 'pull factors' in local needs and contexts, and in part to the disincentives – how, for instance, the local experience of Christianity has interacted with colonialism, or national identity formation. Such stories are not difficult to find. In Myanmar, for example, while most Karen people are Buddhists, the Karen national identity concretely emerged under the influence of Baptist missionaries.[78] The various ethnically structured Baptist Conventions remain important communal organising points. On the other hand, because of the association between the Karen and the British administration (and their mutual cooperation in resisting Japanese aggression in the Second World War), the Karen came to be seen as colonial collaborators, and so enemies of postcolonial Burma, resulting in a long-running quasi-genocidal war with the Burmese state, including conversion to Buddhism either by force or enticement.[79] It is an association only strengthened by U.S. actions against Myanmar elites in international fora on the basis of human rights violations.[80] Evangelical faith plays an important role in maintaining the identities of 2–3 million Karen (approximately 40 per cent of the whole) and 1.2 million Chin (80 per cent of the whole), and provides Burma with (per capita) the seventh-largest evangelical Christian population, and the fourteenth-fastest growing evangelical population out of the forty-two Asian countries surveyed.

Much better known is the story of evangelical growth in South Korea, elements of which have been told elsewhere in this book. Unlike the Burmese experience, Korean Buddhism became associated with Japanese colonialism at precisely the moment of the national encounter with modernity. Christianity, however, became associated with the struggle for national identity, as a result of which 'evangelicalism has often been identified with anti-colonialism and anti-communism. After the Korean War (1950–1953), such identification helped evangelicalism become securely legitimated in South Korea, whose own political identity was constructed largely in opposition to these two "isms."'[81] The result has been the growth of South Korea into one of global evangelicalism's most prominent players – of South Korea's 9 million Protestant Christians, 95 per cent (or 8.55 million) are evangelicals, which helps to power a remarkable global church and missionary presence (in 2004 supporting 12,874 missionaries from 165 agencies in 160 countries).[82]

[78] Yoko Kuroiwa and Maykel Verkuyten, 'Narratives and the Constitution of a Common Identity: The Karen in Burma', *Identities: Global Studies in Culture and Power*, 15 (2008).

[79] U.S. Bureau of Democracy, Human Rights and Labor, 'International Religious Freedom Report 2010: Burma', http://www.state.gov/g/drl/rls/irf/2010/148859.htm, accessed 11 December 2010.

[80] Tom Malinowski, 'The Danger in Lifting Economic Sanctions Against Burma', *The Washington Post*, 8 December 2010, at http://www.hrw.org/en/news/2010/12/08/danger-lifting-economic-sanctions-against-burma, accessed 11 December 2010.

[81] Timothy S. Lee, 'What Should Christians Do about a Shaman-Progenitor? Evangelicals and Ethnic Nationalism in South Korea,' *Church History*, 78 (2009), 69.

[82] Sangkeun Kim, 'Sheer Numbers Do Not Tell the Entire Story: The Challenges of the Korean Missionary Movement from an Ecumenical Perspective', *Ecumenical Review*, 57:4 (October 2005), 463–72.

The lesson of these two case studies seems to be that evangelicalism grows best as a minority religion providing identity to particular groups of people under pressure from majoritarian agendas. In Burma among the Karen, among the Dalits in India, and in Japanese-occupied Korea, minority status provided a defensive identity against oppression. In India, the Dalit use of conversion as a political weapon applies not only to evangelical conversion, but also to conversion to Buddhism and Islam,[83] individual conversion acting to alter the individual's economic and social context, mass conversions acting as a means of protest over political controls and caste-system economic oppression.[84] In the Philippines, it was the pentecostal ability to release spirit-empowered women's ministry that made it effective among matrilineal Kankana-ey tribesmen.[85] In wealthy but oligarchical Singapore, charismatic Christianity has expanded rapidly among youth cultures squeezed out of meaningful public discourse by the expansion of the state and the postcolonial repression of mainline Christianity.[86] Evangelicalism also provides such groups with access to international pressure groups which can speak on their behalf through the United Nations and the U.S. State Department.

Events such as those surrounding the rise of South Korean evangelicalism are rare and by definition unpredictable – something which has not stopped enthusiastic boosters from attempting to predict them. As noted earlier, estimates of the number of evangelical Christians in China vary wildly, from 20 million to 200 million. More sober estimates place the figure between 39 and 65 million. The variance represents a modicum of wishful thinking, as well as of differences between categories. If one accepts a 'middling' number of between 45 million and 65 million, this still only represents between 3 per cent and 4.8 per cent of the Chinese population. To claim (as some have) that therefore there are nearly as many Christians in China as there are members of the Communist Party is to make an invidious comparison; the two are incommensurate categories.[87] There are more evangelicals in the United States than there are members of the Democratic Party – but Obama still won the 2008 elections. It is also a dangerous comparison, as a recent return to 'deterrence' by

[83] 'Dalits convert to Islam, Buddhism and Christianity', http://www.milligazette.com/dailyupdate/20021028.htm; George Oommen, 'Strength of Tradition and Weakness of Communication – Central Kerala Dalit Conversion' in Geoffrey A. Oddie, ed., *Religious Conversion Movements in South Asia: Continuities and Change, 1800–1900*, Richmond: Curzon, 1996, p. 91.

[84] Sathianathan Clarke, 'Dalits Overcoming Violation and Violence: A Contest between Overpowering and Empowering Identities in Changing India', *The Ecumenical Review*, 54 (2002), 278–95.

[85] Julie C. Ma, 'A Pentecostal Woman Missionary in a Tribal Mission: A Case Study', reprinted in *Cyberjournal for Pentecostal-Charismatic Research*, 3 (January 1998) http://www.pctii.org/cyberj/cyber3.html, accessed 13 December 2010.

[86] Daniel P. S. Goh, 'State and Social Christianity in Post-Colonial Singapore', *Sojourn*, 25:1 (2010), 54.

[87] Elinor Wong and Francis Wong, 'Just How Many Christians and Communists Are There in China?' *Ecumenical News International*, 14 September 2005, http://www.eni.ch/articles/display.shtml?05-0691, accessed 13 December 2010.

Chinese authorities indicates.[88] Misplaced evangelical triumphalism can spark the very oppression that it seeks to oppose. The publication of David Aikman's *Jesus in Beijing* (2003), for instance, was greeted in the West as evidence of unstoppable evangelical growth. For many Chinese, it merely confirmed Chinese impressions of American scholars as 'naïve, self-righteous and arrogant'[89] and provoked precisely the sort of crackdown on evangelical churches that the West was so actively protesting against.

No matter how staggering the numbers appear, the annualised growth rate of Christianity in China is no greater than it is in Malaysia, Lebanon or Bangladesh – all considerably more resistant settings than China. It might be better to take a ranked average of 'evangelical proportion of the population' and 'annualised growth rate', which would provide an assessment of how *effective* a particular Asian evangelical population might be. On this measure, the 'hot points' for evangelical growth at a national level (i.e. those 'top ten' ranked countries which have both rapid growth and which represent more than 1 per cent of their national populations) include (in order): Malaysia, the Philippines, India, East Timor (Timor-Leste), Hong Kong, Burma (Myanmar), Indonesia, Mongolia, South Korea and Taiwan.

Whereas the South Korean and Burmese experiences have been described earlier, Malaysia's prominence as a location of evangelical activity may surprise some. Despite the fact that a majority Islamic, oligarchical[90] state is flirting with reversion to sharia law,[91] Malaysia's broadly Christian population makes up nearly 10 per cent of the total. The Christian population quadrupled in the period between 1970 and 2000, growing from 2.5 per cent to 9.1 percent of the total population.[92] The country's political Islamicisation by Mahathir Mohamad[93] and its long-running policy of ethnic bias mobilised these Christian identities, particularly among the threatened Chinese (and, to a lesser extent, Indian) Malay populations. Dahles notes a 'massive conversion to Christianity' among its ethnic minorities with real consequences: 'the ethnic Chinese [26% of the population] ... [alone] hold

[88] 'Police Interrogate Dr. Fan Yafeng; "Operation Deterrence" Looming', *ChinaAid*, 30 November 2010, http://www.chinaaid.org/2010/11/police-interrogate-dr-fan-yafeng.html accessed 13 December 2010.

[89] Philip C. Holtrop, 'On Simplicity, Balance, and Wearing Spectacles: A Discussion of David Aikman's Jesus in Beijing', *Calvin Theological Journal*, 40:1 (April 2005), 111; David Aikman, *Jesus in Beijing: How Christianity is Transforming China and Changing the Global Balance of Power*, Washington: Regnery Publishing, 2003.

[90] See Maznah Mohamad, 'The Ascendance of Bureaucratic Islam and the Secularization of the Sharia in Malaysia', *Pacific Affairs*, 83:3 (September 2010), 505–24.

[91] Thomas Fuller, 'Malaysia's secular vision vs. "writing on the wall"', *New York Times*, 28 August 2006, http://www.nytimes.com/2006/08/28/world/asia/28iht-letter.2619095.html, accessed 14 December 2010.

[92] Heidi Dahles, 'In Pursuit of Capital: The Charismatic Turn among the Chinese Managerial and Professional Class in Malaysia', *Asian Ethnicity*, 8:2 (June 2007), 94.

[93] Albert Sundaraj Walters, 'Issues in Christian-Muslim Relations: A Malaysian Christian Perspective', *Islam and Christian-Muslim Relations*, 18:1 (January 2007), 69.

60 per cent of total GDP and 40–50 per cent of the national corporate assets'.[94] This Chinese ethnic diaspora[95] has found in charismatic Christianity a source of 'spiritual capital' which takes the place of the social benefits 'normatively' provided by citizenship.[96] This charismatic faith of at least 50 per cent of all evangelicals in Malaysia spiritualises the home, business and family network and makes every business leader an evangelist. Legally disadvantaged in their homeland, Malaysian Christian businessmen have a significant presence around the Pacific Rim – particularly in Australia, where real estate prices have made them an unusual Christian presence in the secularising wealthier areas of the society. In Indonesia, similar pressures within a much larger, less economically developed Muslim country produce more muted versions of the same trends.[97] In 2002, Paul Lewis suggested that the pentecostal/charismatic element of Indonesian Christianity alone numbered more than 9 million (approximately 5 per cent of the population).[98] The establishment of Universitas Pelita Harapan in 1994 by James Riady of Lippo Group is an embodiment of the resources and transformational vision current in this evangelical community.

In the Philippines, an annualised evangelical growth of 3.78 per cent has had both a global impact and 'penumbra' effects on other traditions. In the period between 1980 and 2001, the Discipling a Whole Nation (DAWN) Project claimed that 50,000 evangelical churches had been planted across the Philippines, while the charismatic renewal of the 1980s 'attracted many in the developing or aspiring lower classes to form or join "Full Gospel" fellowships that eventually became churches'.[99] The charismatic movement also sparked the laicisation and protestantisation of Filipino Catholicism, as may be seen in Mike Velarde's huge Catholic Charismatic 'El Shaddai' ministry.[100] Pentecostal churches have thus grown at the expense of mainstream Protestantism rather than (compared to Latin America) at the expense of Catholic adherence. Filipino missions were rapidly globalised in 'Evangelical, Charismatic/Full Gospel, Transformational, and Diasporal' modes: by 2003, more than 1,900 Protestant Filipino missionaries (organised by 360 mission agencies,

[94] Dahles, 'In Pursuit of Capital', 90.

[95] On Khoo Kay Peng and Quek Leng Chan, see Michael Backman, *The Asian Insider: Unconventional Wisdom for Asian Business*, Basingstoke: Palgrave Macmillan, 2004, p. 112.

[96] Dahles, 'In Pursuit of Capital', 92.

[97] See Juliette Koning, 'Chineseness and Chinese Indonesian Business Practices: A Generational and Discursive Enquiry', *East Asia: An International Quarterly*, 24:2 (Summer 2007), 129–52.

[98] Paul Lewis, 'Indonesia', in Stanley M. Burgess and E. van der Maas, eds, *New International Dictionary of Pentecostal and Charismatic Movements*, Grand Rapids: Zondervan, 2002 , p. 126.

[99] David S. Lim, 'Leading the Shift Towards Tentmaker Missions: Investigating the Filipino Evangelical Diaspora' in Freston, *The History and Sociology of the Protestant Missions Movement* (forthcoming).

[100] See Mark Hutchinson, 'Wheeler, Rob (1931–), *Australasian Dictionary of Pentecostal and Charismatic Movements*, http://webjournals.alphacrucis.edu.au/journals/ADPCM/q-to-z/wheeler-rob-1931-/, accessed 14 December 2010. Interview, M. Hutchinson with Michael Baré, Pentecostal Heritage Archives, Alphacrucis College, Kessler and Rüland, 'Responses to Rapid Social Change', p. 73.

72 missionary-sending churches and 188 global Filipino churches) were spread around the world, following the pathways established by Filipino expatriate labour migration.[101]

Another surprising entrant into ranks of rising evangelical populations is Mongolia. Within a few years in the early 1990s, the initially struggling Christian church in Mongolia reached 150 churches and 10,000 members which, at a 3.9 per cent annualised growth, would indicate a 2010 membership of around 14,000. The urban/steppe division of the country has played a significant role in evangelical development, with earliest success among young, urban mobile people and most resistance from the communalist nomadic peoples.[102] The timing of the country's opening, and its aspirations to join the Asian tiger economies, has meant that there has been a strong contribution to Mongolian evangelicalism from other Asian countries, particularly Korea (which supplies a third of the total number of missionaries in Mongolia), the Philippines and migrant Chinese workers.[103]

By way of contrast, those locations where evangelicalism is having *least* impact are also instructive as to the religious dynamics of Asia. Five out of the bottom ten are in the Middle East, and in several of these there is the prospect that evangelical communities will actually shrink. In Oman – where 'Non-Muslim religious communities, made up primarily of foreign workers, constitute less than 5 percent of the population', publication of non-Muslim religious material is prohibited, and meeting spaces are often denied – there is little push for change.[104] Kuwait, by way of contrast, has a foreign-worker population larger than its citizenship. Two Gulf wars and dependence on American aid and trade have seen a quite significant evangelical presence (some 40,000) develop among non-citizens. In Turkey, militant Islam struggles with a military-secularist state, a contest in which all sides have been guilty of anti-Christian violence, from Ottoman times onwards. Turkey's desire to join the European Union has caused some change in the status of religious minorities. On the other hand, the ruling Justice and Development Party (AKP) has run a consistent policy of increasing the overtly Islamic nature of the Turkish state.[105] Nationalist/Islamist reactions to the American presence in Iraq have led to churches being firebombed and proselytes and foreign workers being murdered.[106] In Iraq, a decade of war, anti-Western militias and Islamic extremism

[101] Lim, 'Leading the Shift Towards Tentmaker Missions'.

[102] Rustam Sabirov, 'Missionaries of the Steppes', *Transitions Online*, 9.15 (September 2003), online version, accessed 14 December 2010.

[103] Kyo Seong Ahn, 'Christian Mission and Mongolian Identity: The Religious, Cultural, and Political Context', *Studies in World Christianity*, 9:1 (2003), 114–15.

[104] U.S. State Department, 'Oman', International Religious Freedom Report 2010, http://www.state.gov/g/drl/rls/irf/2010/148839.htm, accessed 14 December 2010.

[105] 'Turkey: Ban on AKP for "Anti-Secular Activities" Considered', 31 March 2008, http://becketinternational.wordpress.com/2008/03/31/turkey-ban-on-akp-for-anti-secular-activities-considered/, accessed 14 December 2010.

[106] Yigal Schleifer, 'Turkey's Christians Face Backlash', *Christian Science Monitor*, 99:104 (25 April 2007), 7.

have scattered previously strong Christian communities and curtailed evangelical activities. Wholesale exile or genocide for the traditional Christian communities in the country is the outcome commonly discussed in the press.[107]

While not all countries in the region can be covered, Israel (rank thirty-seven out of forty-two for evangelical impact) is of particular importance, both as a great object of evangelical aspiration and a critical factor in Middle Eastern politics. Hundreds of thousands of evangelicals travel to Israel each year as tourists: the resident population, however, is very small, with the 'Christian' space largely taken up by Arab Christians, Greek Orthodox, Greek Catholic, Armenian and Maronite traditions. These often contend with each other but can act in unity when evangelical Christian organisations begin to emerge in the locality.[108] Messianic Judaism, though widely considered by evangelicals to be an important intermediary form with Judaism, is small, divided and subject to attacks both from orthodox and extremist Jews[109] and from Palestinian Arabs.[110] In 1984, there were as many as 3,000 Messianic Jews in Israel, up from 600 in 1966. By 2010, there were estimates ranging from 6,000 to 15,000 living in Israel.[111] As in other Middle Eastern countries, the success story for evangelicals in Israel may be among migrant-foreign-worker populations rather than the 'Chosen People'.[112] In general, evangelical Christianity does relatively poorly in the Middle East because of the tight association between nationalisms and existing brands of religious identity. In Malaysia,[113] it has been noted, Islam was bureaucratised in order to provide it with the sort of internal control which would support modernisation; in Turkey, that control comes from a secular military, in Israel from Jewish secular nationalism, in other states the previous oligarchical or even despotic controls (e.g. in Yemen) have been challenged by the 'Arab Spring'. Each state has chosen an alternative route to that traced in Europe by Weber from the Protestant Reformation to the 'Spirit of Capitalism'.

The same might be said with regard to the remaining five low-growth Asian countries: Japan, Sri Lanka, North Korea, Bhutan and Vietnam. In four of these, there are very tight controls on proselytism, and usually a powerful alternative

[107] Jim, Muir, 'After Jihad Attacks, Iraq's Christians Live in Fear', BBC News, 10 December 2010, http://doesitallmatter2.wordpress.com/2010/12/13/iraqs-christians-live-in-fear/, accessed 14 December 2010.

[108] Muhammad Shamsaddin Megalommatis, 'Are Evangelicals Triggering Islamic Radicalization in Jordan?' *American Chronicle*, 23 March 2008, http://www.americanchronicle.com/articles/view/56198, accessed 14 December 2010.

[109] Tim McGirk, 'Israel's Messianic Jews Under Attack', *Time Magazine*, 6 June 2008, online edition, http://www.time.com/time/world/article/0,8599,1812430,00.html, accessed 14 December 2010.

[110] Benjamin Beit-Hallahmi, *Despair and Deliverance: Private Salvation in Contemporary Israel*, Albany: State University of New York Press, 1992, p. 34.

[111] McGirk, 'Israel's Messianic Jews Under Attack'.

[112] Barak Kalir, 'Finding Jesus in the Holy Land and Taking Him to China: Chinese Temporary Migrant Workers in Israel Converting to Evangelical Christianity', *Sociology of Religion*, 70:2 (Summer 2009), 130–56.

[113] Mohamad, 'The Ascendance of Bureaucratic Islam'.

ideology encamped in the public space. In the exception, Japan, 'protestantisation' occurred in an economic Weberian sense before it could occur in a religious sense, leaving traditional religious beliefs in place, nuanced by religious innovation in Buddhism which absorbed much of the space taken up by evangelicalism in other settings.[114] In Sri Lanka (where evangelicals account for less than 2 per cent of the population), extremist Buddhism in the 2000s combined anti-Tamil with anti-Christian activities, supporting (through such political organs as the clerical Jathika Hela Urumaya Party, or JHU) the military destruction of the one and the harassment and marginalisation of the other.[115] North Korea is despotic in its control of 'foreign religions', and Bhutan proscribes activities inciting 'religious hatred', a law which at the local level is used to restrain religious pluralism.[116] By way of contrast, Vietnam, with around a million Protestants and another six million Catholics in its population of eighty-five million, may be a 'sleeper' in terms of evangelical development. It has many of the cultural factors which apply to China, and is close to several centres of evangelical activity (particularly the Philippines). With the emergence of a post–Vietnam War global diaspora among which there has been significant numbers experiencing Christian conversion, the interest and cultural resources for successful mission in Vietnam are also already located outside the country.[117] Although the comparison with China is open to debate, it remains conceivable that Vietnam will see significant evangelical growth.

Latin America

One of the great unexpected turns of history has been the protestantisation of Latin America. David Martin's 1990 interpretative study, *Tongues of Fire*, uses the story as a case study to demonstrate the simplifications and ideological content of much 'hard secularisation theory'. In partnership with Peter Berger, Martin identified the counter-trends to global secularisation: counter- as well as anti- and co-modernities which demonstrate the adaptability of faith in modern(ising) settings. Latin America, with its easily accessible links to North America, was a case study demonstrating protestantisation and its theoretical link to modernisation. Guatemala and Brazil in particular drew attention as countries which were

[114] See 'Lotus Politics', *Economist*, 373:8403 (27 November 2004); Pui Yan Lam, 'Religion and Civic Culture: A Cross-National Study of Voluntary Association Membership', *Journal for the Scientific Study of Religion*, 45:2 (June 2006), 177ff.

[115] Neil DeVotta, *Sinhalese Buddhist nationalist ideology*, Washington: East-West Center, 2007, p. 41; Denis D. Gray, 'Tibet's Monk Protests Reflect Rising Activism of Asia's Buddhists', *Manila Bulletin*, 30 March 2008, online, http://www.questia.com/PM.qst?a=o&d=5026299284, accessed 14 December 2010.

[116] U.S. Bureau of Democracy, Human Rights and Labor, 'International Religious Freedom Report 2010: Bhutan', http://www.state.gov/g/drl/rls/irf/2010/148791.htm, accessed 14 December 2010.

[117] Mandy Thomas, *Dreams in the Shadows: Vietnamese-Australian Lives in Transition*, St. Leonards: Allen & Unwin, 1999, p. 10. See also Jenkins, *Next Christendom*, p. 71.

projected to grow pentecostal/charismatic constituencies of between 50 per cent and 60 per cent of the total population.[118] More modest pentecostal/charismatic populations were estimated for Mexico (13 per cent, or 13 million), Chile (30 per cent, or 5 million), Puerto Rico (35 per cent or approximately 1.39 million) and for Costa Rica (18 per cent, or 824,000). At the lower end are the more secularised countries of Uruguay and Venezuela (with upper-end estimations of 10 per cent and 16 per cent, respectively, and lower-end estimations – including pentecostal members only – of 3 per cent and 2 per cent, respectively). The variation – as Martin shows – relates to each country's historical experience with the two great politico-cultural currents affecting nation formation – the 'long war' between Anglo and Hispanic civilisations and the shorter war between political liberal elites and colonial Catholicism.[119]

Overall numbers are difficult to estimate, but given Jenkins's estimation that in 2002 there were fifty million Protestants in Latin America (i.e. not including the larger charismatic leaven in the Catholic host populations of most countries in the region), and a historical annual Protestant growth rate of 6 per cent, there is likely to be a core Latin American evangelical population of around eighty million in 2012. The problem with the numbers is that they are more politically important in Latin America than in many other parts of the world. The cultural exchange which exists between, for instance, the Assemblies of God in Brazil (which has the numbers) and its fraternal organisation in the United States (which has the resources) has been widely noted. For both parties, 'boosting' the numbers has been important to consolidating their positions in the global religious economy and in motivating international opinion towards the protection of evangelical human rights in Brazil itself. For their part, the positions of Catholic authorities and of defenders of the liberal democratic state are best protected by focusing attention only on 'fully committed and practising Pentecosals'.[120] Brian Smith has calculated that between 8,000 and 10,000 people a day are leaving Latin American Catholicism to join pentecostal churches.[121] Edward Cleary,[122] however, properly distinguishes the various functions that conversion plays (including transition towards 'no religion'), rising rates of non-practice, of liberalisation and middle classism, and 'the inability of [Latin American pentecostalism] to retain many of its members'.[123]

[118] Pew Religion Forum, *Spirit and Power: A 10-Country Survey of Pentecostals*, Washington: Pew Research Centre, 2006; Jenkins, *Next Christendom*, p. 61.

[119] Martin, *Tongues of Fire*, pp. 9ff.

[120] Calvin L. Smith, 'Pentecostal Presence, Power and Politics in Latin America', *Journal of Beliefs & Values*, 30:3 (December 2009), 222.

[121] Thomas P. Rausch, 'Catholics and Pentecostals: Troubled History, New Initiatives', *Theological Studies*, 71:4 (December 2010), 933.

[122] Edward L. Cleary, 'Shopping Around: Questions about Latin American Conversions', *International Bulletin of Missionary Research*, 28:2 (April 2004), 50ff; also Edward L. Cleary and Hannah W. Stewart-Gambino, eds, *Power, Politics and Pentecostals in Latin America*, Boulder: Westview, 1998.

[123] Cleary, 'Shopping Around', 54.

This sort of information has become the basis for strategic responses to the rising 'pentecostal threat', such as 'the new evangelization' and localised ecumenism which has seen interdenominational cooperation.[124] Yet despite the arguments of many intellectuals for a preference *for* the poor, the preference *of* many of the poor has been evangelical conversion. Even recognising the difficulties in capturing a true statistical profile, the linkage between Protestantism and modernisation in these countries points to a profound change.[125]

The change has had ramifications well beyond the continent itself. The Latin American diaspora is worldwide, providing linguistic and cultural networks along which evangelism and church planting flow.[126] During the FIFA World Cup in South Africa, for example, Pastor Marcos Grava Vasconcelos ('a handball player turned evangelist') led a group of 200 Baptists to South Africa to carry out missionary work which was particularly oriented towards fans and squad members from North Korea, using the 'world game' to get around regional restrictions.[127] The Comunidad Cristiana de Londres, planted by Peruvian Edmundo Ravelo, has grown to more than 2,000 members and planted other churches in Ecuador, Spain, the United States and elsewhere in Britain.[128] Significantly, it originated in a vision to plant churches in Spain.[129] The largest Protestant church in northern Italy was planted and is run by a Brazilian former youth evangelist for the Catholic Church, Roselen Boerner Faccio – a unique profile for single female expatriates in that country. She is one of several hundred Latin American evangelists active in Italy, some of whom have grown significant ministries.

As Dario Lopez indicates, this is a pattern replicated throughout the Latin world and beyond. The 2006 COMIBAM (Cooperacion Missionaria Ibero-Americano) estimate was that there are more than 10,000 Latin American missionaries working transculturally, many in areas (such as the Middle East) where missionaries of Anglo appearance fall under disabling suspicion.[130] Likewise, there are

[124] Rausch, 'Catholics and Pentecostals', 935ff.

[125] Timothy Wadkins, 'Getting Saved in El Salvador: The Preferential Option for the Poor,' *International Review of Mission*, 97:384/385 (January–April 2008), 32.

[126] Marshall notes the rapid expansion of Latino migration back to Spain in the period between 1996 and 2005 (Steve Marshall, 'New Latino Diaspora and New Zones of Language Contact: A Social Constructionist Analysis of Spanish Speaking Latin Americans in Catalonia', Cascadilla Proceedings Project, http://www.lingref.com/cpp/wss/3/paper1536.pdf, accessed 21 December 2010).

[127] Tom Phillips, 'Evangelists target fans', *Mail and Guardian* online, 4 June 2010, http://www.mg.co.za/printformat/single/2010–06–04-evangelists-target-fans, accessed 20 December 2010.

[128] http://www.comunidadcristianadealicante.es/index.php?option=com_content&view=article&id=20&Itemid=31, accessed 19 December 2010.

[129] Clive Price, 'Hundreds of Latin Londoners Flock to Nightclub to Dance for Jesus', *Charisma Magazine*, June 2005, online, http://www.charismamag.com/index.php/component/content/article/268-people-and-events/11302-hundreds-of-latin-londoners-flock-to-nightclub-to-dance-for-jesus, accessed 19 December 2010.

[130] Dario Lopez, 'Dibujando un Nuevo Rostro Misionero: Un Análisis Inicial del Movimiento Misionero Latinoamericano' in Freston, *The History and Sociology of the Protestant Missions Movement*, (forthcoming).

thousands of churches around the world planted in the Latin economic and political diasporas. Latin American evangelicals – many of whom, like the Peruvian-born former director of the IVCF in Canada, Samuel Escobar Aguirre, are well connected to North American institutions – play a significant role in global evangelical scholarship and leadership. With its particular affinities to Hispanic peoples, the network of evangelical institutions in California has become an important mediating and training location for Hispanic leaders. Most Christian higher-education institutions (Fuller, Azusa Pacific, Biola, etc.) offer programs in Spanish. Hispanic evangelical communities have well-organised social and political networks (such as the National Hispanic Christian Leadership Conference), with people such as Wilfredo de Jesus (pastor of New Life Covenant Church, Humboldt Park, Illinois) running for political office in order to 'extend . . . our commitment to righteousness and justice beyond the pulpit'.[131] The sizeable Spanish market has spawned its own range of global Christian Contemporary Music artists (such as Marcos Witt in Mexico, the Brazilian-born Julim Barbosa performing in Italy and Argentinean-born Freddie Colloca in Miami, Florida), television networks and recording companies. Just as Argentina exported the discipleship movement in the 1970s and a variety of spiritual warfare techniques in the 1980s and 1990s, in the 2000s, Bolivia exported the "G12" approach to cell-based churches, which rapidly grew into a global charismatic network.[132] Luis Palau is only one of the better-known evangelists both to base his work on Latino populations and also to 'cross over' into other settings.[133] If there has indeed been a 'long war' between Anglo and Hispanic cultures for supremacy, in the religious sphere at least, the Hispanic army is something less than defeated.

Oceania

With a relatively small, scattered population, the Pacific has drawn less attention from scholars of evangelicalism than the huge mission-centric populations of Asia. It is a very complex area: with thousands of tribes and linguistic groups, it has produced comparatively little autochthonous literature and demands high levels of cultural and interdisciplinary awareness from authors. As a consequence, it tends to be left out of standard narratives, including the literature on evangelicalism. When the 'Oceanic-Asian' countries and countries of European settlement are taken out, Oceania has a population of only 30 million (34.4 million if New Zealand is included). That population is scattered among Melanesian, Polynesian

[131] Stephanie Samuel, 'A Hispanic Evangelical Goes from Pulpit to Politics', *Christian Post*, 8 December 2010, online, http://www.christianpost.com/news/a-hispanic-evangelical-goes-from-pulpit-to-politics-47983, accessed 20 December 2010.

[132] Dale T. Irvin, 'The Church, the Urban, and the Global: Mission in an Age of Global Cities', *International Bulletin of Missionary Research*, 33:4 (October 2009), 179.

[133] Andres Tapia, 'Evangelist Sets Sights on U.S. Latinos', *Christianity Today*, 40:8 (1997), 68.

and Micronesian ethnic spheres, thirteen countries and twenty-five dependencies which chart the history of imperial (British, French, Dutch, Spanish, Portuguese), hegemonic (the United States) and regional powers who have mediated mandates for others (Australia and New Zealand). More recently, the economic powers of Asia (Indonesia in West Irian; Malaysia in Papua New Guinea; Japan, India and China) have seen the Pacific as a sphere for the extension of influence[134] in search of resource security.

From colonial times, evangelical Christianity has had a powerful impact on the Pacific, to the point where it is the dominant religion of several countries (particularly Fiji and Tonga). In both places, its denominational form has fused with local nationalisms, sometimes with violent results. Fijian nationalism, for instance, has seen sabbatarian acts passed by the nation's military oligarchy, and background support for a 'Christian state' refers back to the Deed of Cession between the Paramount Chiefs and Queen Victoria in 1874.[135] Christian identity provides ultimate authority to those who wish to entrench Fijian ethnic superiority over the economic and educational power of Fijian Indians, and who are responding to regional threats (such as the rise of Islamic states).[136] Classical pentecostals have been critical of this fusion of tradition and faith.[137] Later charismatic and Christian reconstructionist traditions, however, have often fused with this sense of national 'divine destiny', creating conflict with traditional churches and within the renewal movement itself. In Tonga, Methodism is an intrinsic part of the kingdom's identity,[138] albeit subject to high levels of nominalism. Pentecostalism – smaller in Tonga than even Catholicism and the Latter Day Saints – is thus more common among the very large Tongan and Samoan diaspora in the 'New Polynesian Triangle' than it was in the old.[139] (Unlike Tahiti, which earns most of its income from tourism, 80 per cent of private domestic expenditure in Tonga is sourced in remittances from Tongan expatriates in the United States, Australia, New Zealand etc.)[140] Ironically, therefore, first-wave evangelicalism (particularly Methodism) is often at odds with the later waves (pentecostal and charismatic).

[134] For example, 'China to Go on Aiding Vanuatu Without Political Strings Attached: Wen', *China Daily*, 22 December 2010, http://www.chinadaily.com.cn/china/2010–04/13/content_9718941.htm, accessed 22 December 2010.

[135] Jacqueline Ryle, 'Roots of Land and Church: The Christian State Debate in Fiji', *International Journal for the Study of the Christian Church*, 5:1 (March 2005), 59.

[136] Ibid., 60.

[137] Karen J. Brison, 'The Empire Strikes Back: Pentecostalism in Fiji', *Ethnology*, 46:1 (Winter 2007), 21ff.

[138] Ernest Olson, 'Signs of Conversion, Spirit of Commitment: the Pentecostal Church in the Kingdom of Tonga', *Journal of Ritual Studies*, 15:2 (2001), 13.

[139] Brison, 'The Empire Strikes Back', 21–22; Manuhuia Barcham, Regina Scheyvensi and John Overton, 'New Polynesian Triangle: Rethinking Polynesian Migration and Development in the Pacific', *Asia Pacific Viewpoint*, 50:3 (December 2009), 323.

[140] Kathleen Flanagan, 'Refractions on the Pacific Rim: Tongan Writers' Responses to Transnationalism', *World Literature Today*, 72:1 (Winter 1998), http://www.questia.com/PM.qst?a=o&d=95705611, accessed 22 December 2010.

Pentecostal and evangelical churches in the dominant regional players – Australia and New Zealand – are thus often reinforced by more energetic elements of Pacific evangelicalism. A good example is the Harvest Ministry which, founded in Fiji in 1988, by 2006 had 50,000 members in 'Fiji, Vanuatu, Nauru, Pohnpei, Marshall Islands, and Tonga' and missions in Papua New Guinea (PNG), Tanzania, Kenya, the United Kingdom and the United States, running services in English, Fijian and Hindi to congregations around the world through digital technologies.[141]

Those countries in the region with the slowest evangelical growth rates (Australia and New Zealand) are the most secularised and have larger populations. Secular identity fragmentation and the pressure for remittances creates significant identity issues among members of the younger generation in diaspora, and the church can act both as 'village green' and cause for conflict.[142] On the other hand, Australian and New Zealand evangelical and pentecostal churches (particularly the new charismatic churches such as the Christian Revival Crusade and Christian Outreach Centres) have some of their largest constituencies in Pacific nations.[143] Nauru, where the population has been in decline since the end of the country's only viable industry (superphosphate mining), and Fiji, where evangelicalism has reached saturation, and so grows through transfer between older and later versions of Christianity rather than by conversion as such, also have relatively flat evangelical growth rates. Kiribati – one of the Pacific island nations most threatened by climate change – is likewise 96 per cent 'Christian', though 55 per cent of the population is Catholic and 36 per cent are members of the liberalised Kiribati Protestant Church. There are relatively high rates of evangelical growth in those areas where (such as in Papua New Guinea) there remain significant populations of traditional religion practice, or (such as in Vanuatu and the Solomon Islands) the charismatic renewal of traditional churches has been effective. By its fiftieth anniversary, the Assemblies of God in PNG was larger than the Australian AOG which had originally supported missionaries there.[144] Although not on the scale found in Africa, successive charismatic waves have found reflections in Pacific traditional cultures. Silas Eto ('the Holy Mama') of New Georgia draws parallels with Simon Kimbangu of the Congo.[145] In Fiji, independent ministries have emerged among which the Congregation of the Poor (established by healer-prophet Sekaia Loaniceva) has received most attention.[146] Increasingly, the Pacific has become self-propagating as

[141] Brison, 'The Empire Strikes Back', 25.

[142] Stephen R. Koletty, 'The Samoan Archipelago in Urban America', in Kate A. Berry and Martha L. Henderson, eds, *Geographical Identities of Ethnic America: Race, Space, and Place*, Reno: University of Nevada Press, 2002, p. 141.

[143] Allan Anderson, *An Introduction to Pentecostalism*, p. 143.

[144] W. George Forbes, *A Church on Fire: The Story of the Assemblies of God in Papua New Guinea*, Mitcham: Mission Mobilisers, 2001.

[145] Brij Vilash Lal and Kate Fortune, eds, *The Pacific Islands: An Encyclopedia*, Honolulu: University of Hawai'i Press, 2000, p. 256.

[146] Carl Loeliger and Garry Trompf, *New Religious Movements in Melanesia*, Suva: Institute of Pacific Studies, University of the South Pacific and the University of Papua New Guinea, 1985.

a location for evangelical expansion. Frankel notes, for instance, the charismatic 'chain revival' among the Huli in PNG sparked by a Maori evangelist from New Zealand in 1970 and carried by South Seas Evangelical Church (SSEC) evangelists from the Solomon Islands in 1973.[147] In 1984, a similar vision-driven evangelistic outbreak emerged from the SSEC church in Honiara, leading to the establishment of the Deep Sea Canoe Mission. Its indigenisation of evangelical truths is strongly reminiscent of Chinese 'back to Jerusalem' movements, and ultimately led to the excommunication of its most prominent leader, Michael Maeliau, in 2009.[148]

Of all the Pacific communities, PNG is the location for the largest number of evangelical believers, whereas the Solomons and Vanuatu are among the more dynamic in terms of renewal emphases. This overwhelmingly Christian expanse of water, volcanoes and coral atolls has a relatively small but highly mobile population. Compared to the numbers of Koreans, Chinese and Filipinos now missionising their diasporas, they may seem insignificant. Their impact on other countries around the Pacific Rim – particularly Australia and New Zealand, out of which energetic renewal movements have emerged in recent years – indicates that this region probably deserves more attention from scholars telling the evangelical story.

CONCLUSIONS

So, how many evangelicals are there? The common response is a hedging statement like: 'Well, it depends on how you define evangelicals.' The preceding discussion has demonstrated that the very act of definition is subjective and often 'political'. Any suggestions offered here, therefore, are indicative rather than conclusive. Evangelicalism, after all, is counted differently by different people depending on the case being made. Some will define it so that it looks like American religion, ignoring indigenisation in order to make a point about the nature of globalisation. Others define it so that it submerges any taint of Americanism, so as to defend some nationalist or evangelistic agenda. Most definitions struggle with the movement's 'great diversity'.[149] Evangelicalism is not a primary category into which people are converted, but a description of the effects (however gradual) of that conversion on individuals and groups. For many, its major use is as a mediating 'currency' which renders their lives more survivable. It is not the case that people convert for 'merely' economic, personal, cultural or political ends. Rather, one might say (as Rodney Stark has suggested)[150] that people do not in fact convert for any *other*

[147] Stephen Frankel, *The Huli Response to Illness*, Cambridge: Cambridge University Press, 1986, p. 34.

[148] Sinclair Dinnen and Stewart Firth, *Politics and State Building in Solomon Islands*, Canberra: ANU E-Press; Asia Pacific Press, 2008, pp. 205–7.

[149] Rosemary Dowsett and Samuel Escobar, 'Evangelicals 1910–2010', in Todd M. Johnson and Kenneth R. Ross, eds, *Atlas of Global Christianity*, Edinburgh: Edinburgh University Press, 2009, p. 97.

[150] Rodney Stark and W. Sims Bainbridge, *The Future of Religion*, Berkeley: University of California Press, 1985, p. 524.

reason apart from the change that the new religion makes in their lives. People in the majority world, as Andrew Walls has noted, have a view of the world which is much more akin to that in the New Testament – and consequently, they have a right to expect that the application of the biblical text will have real world outcomes.[151]

Statisticians cannot directly count by the categories which (as noted in Chapter 1) evangelicals use to define themselves. They have, rather, developed three general uses of the term, which may be compared so as to obtain a general idea as to the size of the evangelical community at the core and in its shifting 'borderlands'. As a community of spiritual practice, evangelicalism is primarily an activist impulse of personal spirituality centred on communities of people responding to the biblical 'message of the Cross'. This community is best identified by counting spiritual *practitioners* (i.e. 'members' rather than adherents). Secondly, there is the self-identifying evangelical community of mission resulting from a common interest in the outcomes of the 'message of the Cross.' This would suggest that one needs to count card-carrying members, and members of the *affiliates* of evangelical organisations, such as the World Evangelical Fellowship, evangelical missions organisations and NGOs. Thirdly, there is the 'penumbra' *affected* by evangelical activism, the large number of people affected by the conscientisation which engagement with evangelical communities brings. This group includes many Catholic charismatics, African Independent church members moving towards more normatively evangelical positions, those strange categories (found in many religious encyclopaedias) with titles such as 'Indian radio/TV believers', crypto-evangelicals in anti-evangelical cultural settings, the 'evangelically inclined' in churches (such as the Uniting Church in Australia) which have evangelical traditions but which might be run by those Christians of a more liberal theological persuasion, and non-churched people with evangelical beliefs who work out their fundamental beliefs in settings not normally considered to be evangelical (such as secular NGOs, politics, etc).

With these three 'types' of evangelicalism in mind, a review of the available sources was undertaken to remove double counting, idiosyncratic categorisations, and the inconsistent inclusion and exclusion of pentecostals/charismatics. A summary of the results (see Table 8.2) provides some idea of the core community (the 'Community of Practice' described by the *WCE* in its conflation of evangelical and pentecostal numbers of *members*), those in the extended evangelical community (such as pentecostals and neo-charismatics not otherwise included in the core 'Protestant' groupings by, for example, Stanley Burgess,[152] and their affiliates and those outside evangelical churches and organisations (e.g. Catholic charismatics, indigenous pentecostal groupings, etc.). The result gives some idea as to the location of evangelicalism in at the time of writing this book (2010–2011), although the conflicting categories between, and inconsistency within, sources suggests that the

[151] Andrew Walls, *The Cross Cultural Process in Christian History*, Maryknoll: Orbis Books, 2002, p. 19.

[152] Burgess and van der Maas, *International Dictionary of Pentecostal and Charismatic Movements* p. 284 ff.

TABLE 8.2. *Distribution of Evangelical Communities by Continent* (millions) (approximate figures only), Comparing Sources*

	Evangelical Members 2010 (Barrett 2000, projections)	Pentecostals & Neo-Pentecostals (Burgess 2002 projections)	Charismatics 2010 (Burgess 2002 projections)	Pew Foundation Estimates 2005, Pentecostals/ NeoPentecostals***
Africa	132.20	104.64	40.84	107
Asia	114.08	80.30	28.27	138
Caribbean	3.21	2.22	3.34	
Europe	39.70	7.98	20.40	
Latin America	48.64	71.17	53.77	75
North America	86.40	59.58	22.99	17
Oceania	6.28	1.86	2.51	
	430.51	327.76	172.13	

* overlap in counting by different sources removed, census data extended to 2010 by projecting per country annualised growth rates 1970–2002/2005/2007 (as relevant on latest available data).

** CCR, indigenous church, and other figures estimated using available population % projections from available sources.

*** http://pewforum.org/Christian/Evangelical-Protestant-Churches/Spirit-and-Power.aspx, accessed 24 December 2010.

North American figures are probably too high and the African and Latin American figures too low.

Taking a different tack, and working backwards from projected country religious affiliation percentages (derived from census figures – usually in 2005–2007, and latest known scholarship, without increase, and dividing 'pentecostal' from evangelical returns), we arrive at the following figures:

TABLE 8.3. *Distribution of Evangelical Communities by Continent* (millions) (approximate figures only)*

	2010 Population	Evangelicals	Pentecostals/ Neo-Pentecostals*
Asia	3,879.00	65.94	135.77
Caribbean	40.81	3.26	4.08
Latin America	580.09	29.00	58.01
North America	340.75	4.79	17.04
Europe	831.00	8.31	8.31
Africa	1,000.01	150.00**	250.00
Oceania***	35.67	3.57	3.57
	6,707.32	344.88	476.77

* not including denominational charismatics. Gross population figures extracted from OECD reports, 2007–2010; evangelical and charismatic figures from projections (2000–2010) based on reconciliation of figures provided by *WCE* and Burgess (2002).

** notional division of evangelicals (15%) and pentecostals (30%).

*** including New Zealand.

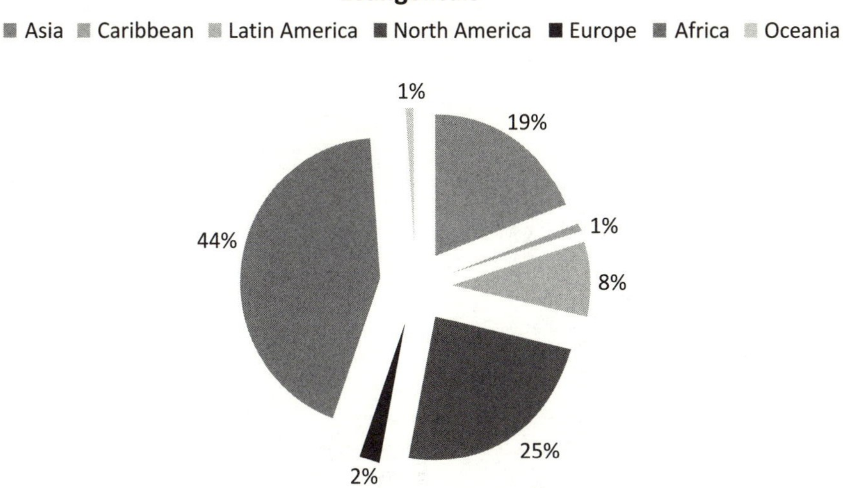

Figure 8.2. Evangelical Distribution by Region.

Although statistical estimates vary, such a comparison confirms the general conclusions of the contemporary literature. The 'leading edge' of evangelicalism in two-thirds of the world is largely pentecostal and charismatic in nature, and evangelicalism as a whole is a majority world religion.

A large number of attempts have been made to explain evangelical growth, and there is no space in which to canvass them here. Rosson and Fields, for example,

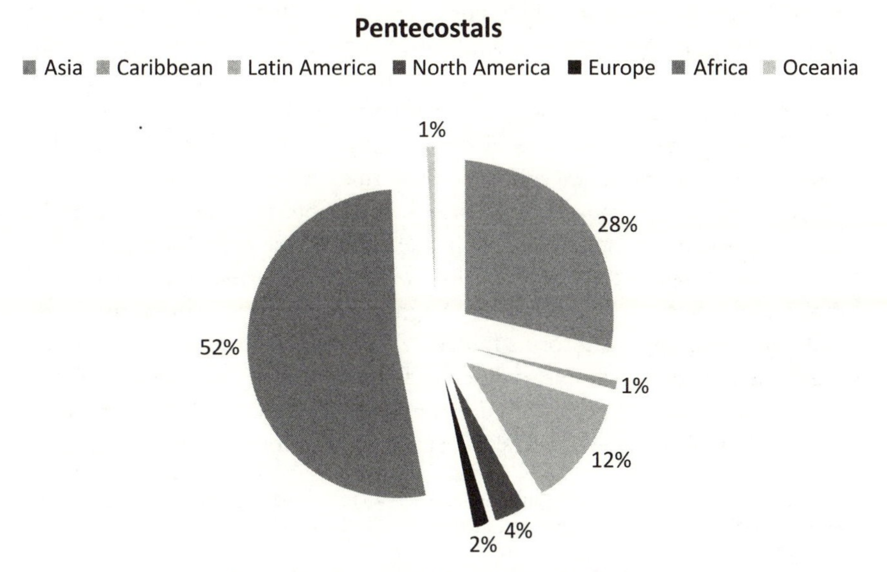

Figure 8.3. Pentecostal Distribution by Region.

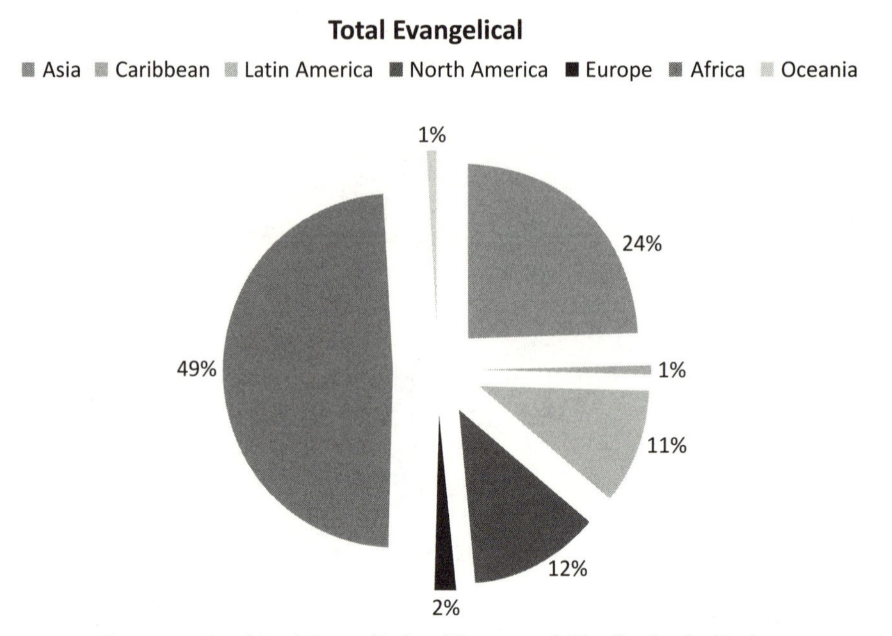

Figure 8.4. Combined Evangelical and Pentecostal Distribution by Region.

use Geert Hofstede's dimensions of national culture to suggest that 'higher levels of power distance and lower levels of individualism' are 'both positively related with growth in evangelical Christianity in a country'.[153] The foregoing survey, however, suggests that there are both general *and* particular conditions for such growth or decline. It may be true that in high power distance settings (in which people are happy to accept power to be distributed unequally), as Rosson and Fields (2008) note, the personal, evangelical Jesus is 'an ultimate ideal boss . . . who affords grace to the less powerful and provides a substitute for dependence on the powerful established religions', while collectivism provides ready networks for the spread of values.[154] There are always exceptions to these rules, however: evangelicalism, for instance, is relatively strong in the United States, a country which is high on the individualism scale, and relatively weak in France, which has an orientation towards higher power distance relationships. This is where the *particular* events of national history are important. The Hofstede categories point to the general attributes which make evangelicalism (or its functional equivalent) attractive. They do not explain the differential success of different *forms* of evangelicalism (for instance, reformed as against pentecostal) in different settings. For this, Martin's theory of 'downward mobilisation' is preferable, explaining as it does how evangelical faith

[153] Thomas Rosson and Dail Fields, 'Cultural Influences on the Growth in Evangelical Christianity: A Longitudinal Study of 49 Countries', *Review of Religious Research*, 49:3 (2008), 269.
[154] Ibid., 274–5.

acts as a form of empowerment for the poor, while fitting into the broad historic-cultural movements of a region.[155] Each of these theories, however, is best applied within the particular historical events impacting on subcultures and countries. Nicholas Taleb's concept of 'black swan' events warns theorists that the 'exception' to theories which apply everywhere will eventually become the rule somewhere.[156] Very few contemporaries picked the rise of evangelicalism in Korea, or Argentina, or in the mobile, high-technology global cultures which inform much of modern life. Over extended historical periods, therefore, those seeking to apply general theories to evangelicalism should be prepared to be surprised.

[155] Martin, *Pentecostals*, 29–33.
[156] Nicholas Nassim Taleb, *The Black Swan: The Impact of the Highly Improbable*, New York: Random House, 2007.

9

Localism and Transnationality: 1970s to 2010

'It had worked for me for a long time. Then it stopped working.'

Kristen Bell

In 1973, the Organization of Arab Petroleum Exporting Countries (OAPEC) protested at the U.S. decision to resupply the Israeli military during the Yom Kippur War. The emergence of a powerful oil lobby realised U.S. fears about its strategic weakness, especially in the light of its extended and failing defence of South Vietnam. The consequences for evangelicals everywhere were significant. Dispensationalist millenarians predictably saw the crisis as foreshadowing the end of all things – and certainly, it would be the end of some things. Broad-based American evangelical support fell in behind the Israel lobby. In Latin America, the exposure of weak economic structures to the roller-coaster ride of global capitalism directly impacted the effectiveness of emerging democracies and the civic role of the rapidly growing evangelical communities that supported them. In Africa, the front lines between Christians and Muslims became increasingly tense. On the Day of Atonement 1973, there were only 17 million Africans who described themselves as 'born-again Christians'. Over the next three decades, that number would grow to more than 400 million.[1] Mainline denominations, even some in Keswick circles (such as the SIM-related Kale Heywet Word of Life Church in Ethiopia), which had earlier resisted pentecostal spirituality, were energised by an indigenous, charismatic spirituality. By the turn of the century, such charismaticised evangelical communities were facing resurgent fundamentalisms in the Middle East and Asia, and struggling with 'secular' states from France to China. These tensions fed back into the internal conversations framing civic evangelical thought and action around the world. They produced a fractured evangelical community searching for positive agendas which could be worked in the light of the new transnational realities.[2] Over this period, evangelicalism would face the collapse of Christendom and the crises of a divided world by developing new symbolic rhetorics, new forms, and new relationships.

[1] 'Slain by the spirit', *Economist*, 396:8689 (1 July 2010), http://www.economist.com/node/16488830, accessed 7 November 2010.

[2] Jeffrey Haynes, 'Transnational Religious Actors and International Order', *Perspectives: Central European Review of International Affairs*, 17:2 (Winter 2009/10), 43–4.

The 1970s presented a new and complex world, a world of conflicting narratives. On many fronts, evangelicals seemed to be advancing, even as the old structures of Christendom were slowly collapsing. As Callum Brown notes with regard to Britain, in the 1950s 'religion mattered', Christianity 'intruded in very personal ways into the manner of people's comportment through their lives.... But it started to stop mattering in the 1960s.'[3] The decline of traditional denominational Christianity was not merely the disappearance of a collection of musty deans; it was the fragmentation of a national culture under the pressures of consumerism, materialism and individualism. Church attendance statistics were merely indicators of a substantial refiguring of the Western mind, and what made for the good (or bad) society. There was, for instance, a rapid shift in Western legislation governing public morality – the decriminalisation of homosexuality (for example, in Canada in 1969) and abortion, "probably the fastest social revolution in American history" (United States, *Roe vs. Wade*, 1973),[4] and the facilitation of divorce (Australia, 1975).[5] Another outcome was the collapse of voluntarism. This was not only a major blow to traditional denominational forms, but a challenge to the way evangelicals preferred to exert social influence.[6] The existence of a generalised 'improving' impulse had been the foundation for evangelical campaigns for anti-slavery and women's rights. Evangelicals would now have to find another means to be 'salt and light'. The slow-motion train wreck of the traditional denominations carried with it many of the best available theological resources in the Protestant world (not to mention a still-substantial influence on political and social elites). The Evangelical Lutheran Church in America anticipated the need to close a full 50 per cent of its congregations in the period between 2007 and 2017;[7] average Sunday attendance in the Anglican Church in Melbourne, Australia, more than halved (from 50,000 to 21,000) between 1981 and 2006;[8] and others projected similar figures, even to the point of complete disappearance. The plan (common enough among those evangelicals who had remained in traditional denominations) of 'outwaiting' the liberals and then 'overplanting' traditional congregations could only succeed if there was something left to overplant. As Donald Bloesch warned: 'The striking resurgence of evangelicalism in America may be an Indian summer before the total

[3] Callum Brown, *The Death of Christian Britain: Understanding Secularisation, 1800–2000*, London: Routledge, 2001, p. 8.

[4] James Risen and Judy L. Thomas, *Wrath of Angels: The American Abortion War*, New York: Basic, 1998, p. 36.

[5] Sheila B. Kamerman, *Family Change and Family Policies in Great Britain, Canada, New Zealand, and the United States*, Oxford: Clarendon, 1997, p. 186.

[6] Brown, *Death of Christian Britain*, p. 13.

[7] Stephen Ellingson, *The Megachurch and the Mainline: Remaking Religious Tradition in the Twenty-First Century*, Chicago: University of Chicago Press, 2007, p. 58.

[8] Peter Corney, 'The decline in the Australian Protestant Church – How we got to where we are', Foundations: Perspectives on the Christian Faith and Culture, http://petercorney.com/, accessed 5 November 2010.

collapse of organised religion in this country.'[9] Evangelicals clearly needed to do more than just wait.

EVANGELICAL PRESENCE AND INFLUENCE

The decline of the mainline denominations created a public plausibility problem for evangelicals as religionists. In many Western countries, the story of irreversible secularisation was applied indiscriminately by those who greeted it as the triumph of modernism. Secularism was winning, religion was losing. The result, when evangelicals *did* emerge into the limelight, was a rolling 'moral panic' among enclosed Western intellectual elites. As activists and biblicists, evangelicals sought mechanisms by which they could overcome marginalisation and express biblical witness in the public square. A number of overlapping strategies may be identified. In many countries, particularly those like the United States where electoral success was tied up in established networks, or where 'lobby politics' had become a dominant form, there were attempts to exert pressure on existing parties or through policy directions. In some countries (such as Australia, Brazil and the Philippines), particularly when evangelical voices have been excluded, there have been attempts to organise specific Christian political parties. As part of the indigenisation process, evangelicalism had already (as in the United States) interpolated itself into patriotic or nationalist identities or, in turn (as in Northern Ireland or Guatemala), been co-opted by these. The movement's core christocentrism, however (as we have seen with the Scottish Disruption) tended to resist such co-option, and so many evangelicals have preferred to work in transnational settings. Here the vast emerging world of nongovernmental organisations has been a field of operation, with some evangelical NGOs growing to have significant roles on the global stage. Where squeezed out of the public space, evangelicals have learned from models of subcultural protest in the 1960s to develop a range of non-political public action. Finally, as citizens and consumers in the global economy, evangelicals in all these settings have learned to exploit media and consumerism in order to build sustainable communities and maintain public witness.

Lobby Politics and Evangelical Political Parties

In the United States, the election of an openly evangelical and Democratic president (Jimmy Carter) in 1976 ushered in 'The Year of the Evangelical': 'Suddenly people . . . thought, *My God, there are millions of these people out there, this must be a right-wing explosion.* No, they've always been there, you've just never noticed

[9] Donald G. Bloesch, *Crumbling Foundations: Death and Rebirth in an Age of Upheaval*, Grand Rapids: Academie Books, 1984, quoted in Rob Warner, *Reinventing English Evangelicalism 1966–2001: A Theological and Sociological Study*, Milton Keynes: Paternoster, 2007, p. 4.

them.'[10] The hardening of public secular pluralism, it is true, had made traditional evangelical approaches to public influence decreasingly effective. By the 1970s, for instance, the 'chaplain to society' role of Billy Graham was fading, in the midst of the failure of governments to satisfy either civil or religious visions. The 'competent and compassionate' Carter presidency – afflicted by energy crises, economic recession and the consequences of Islamic revolution in Iran – satisfied neither reformist nor conservative evangelicals. The Carter administration's accommodations to progressive social reform (feminism and homosexual rights among them) tapped into more widely held social fears about the seeming dissolution of standard gender, social, race and religious identities, and the consequences of this for 'the righteous nation'. Carter was defeated at the next election, in part through skilful manipulation of evangelical divisions by Ronald Reagan, who became the 'conviction candidate'.[11] While the Reagan presidency captured a large proportion of the white evangelical vote, policy outcomes for many evangelicals were disappointing. Although their methods had not changed – as in the 1880s, evangelicals in the 1980s continued to be involved in social reform – many struggled with seeing themselves written off as conservatives, as the 'new Christian right'.

One of the more high-profile examples of this ethical anachronism was the Moral Majority, founded in 1979 by Baptist pastor and radio preacher Jerry Falwell.[12] It became symbolic of a global rise in institutional 'evangelical assertiveness', an assertiveness also seen in the high profile of Paisleyite Protestantism in Northern Ireland, the founding of the Logos Foundation in Australia and (for different reasons) the rearguard actions of the Dutch Reformed Church in South Africa. The same period saw the rise of evangelical influence in Latin America, Nigeria and South Korea. Guatemala (with a rapidly growing pentecostal or charismatic Christian population, which would eventually total 60 per cent of the entire population) would return a significant number of Christian politicians to high office. Again, this 'new assertiveness' was in part illusionary: it was 'new' only in the sense that it was 'unexpected', quite counter to secular presumptions as to the decline of evangelicalism in general.

Such influence was won at a cost. Falwell's evangelicalism was 'Word' focussed, and proclamatory, and tapped into the now-rudderless radical activism of the 1960s.[13] To liberals, however, its positions smacked of the theocratic fundamentalism which had recently expelled America from Iran. The rhetoric of the U.S. Secretary of Health and Human Services in labelling Falwell an 'Ayatollah Khomeini'

[10] Katie Bacon, 'Christianity's New Centre: Interview with Phillip Jenkins', *Atlantic* Unbound, 12 September 2002, http://www.theatlantic.com/past/docs/unbound/interviews/int2002-09-12.htm, accessed 5 November 2010.

[11] John Dumbrell, *The Carter Presidency: A Re-Evaluation*, Manchester: Manchester University Press, 1995, p. 80.

[12] David Snowball, *Continuity and Change in the Rhetoric of the Moral Majority*, New York: Praeger, 1991, p. 3.

[13] Preston Shires, *Hippies of the Religious Right*, Waco: Baylor University Press, 2007, pp. 200–1.

was picked up and reused by both politicians and anti-religious opinion makers around the world.[14] Such typifications divided the Majority's base: 'Its candidates all lost. Its legislative initiatives uniformly failed'. Eventually, however, it failed not because it lost at the ballot box, but 'because it could not find the words that would be acceptable to both its most devoted followers and to a broader spectrum of the American public'.[15] By 1986, the Moral Majority was in the process of collapse.[16] Despite later moderation,[17] its co-option of the evangelical identity had already driven a generational wedge into the evangelical conversation. Robert Wenz of the National Association of Evangelicals later called it 'an aberration and a regrettable one at that'.[18] Journalist David Brooks witnessed firsthand the profound 'sense of embarrassment' among younger evangelicals with 'proclamation' people – 'like Jimmy Swaggart, Tammy Faye Baker, Jerry Falwell' – who blundered out into the public square with the norms of fundamentalist subcultures firmly on display.[19] This 'sense of revulsion' among younger evangelicals 'was . . . natural and profound',[20] and fused with a growing generational reaction against the dominance of a post-war 'proclamatory' evangelicalism built on 'gathered church' assumptions. Even though they often admired their older fellows for their commitment to the battle, younger evangelicals increasingly thought the fight for 'the Christian nation' to be the wrong war.

The shift reflected a deeper ambivalence in evangelical activism. Evangelicals (*qua* evangelicals) are not interested so much in politics or even in theology, but in 'perceived spiritual action'. The evangelical self-identification with God's action in the world causes them to 'read' political positions and candidates in terms of their projected 'spiritual communion' with God: whether a candidate prays, goes to church, or 'performs' the Christian life.[21] Having gathered (often merely impressionistic) information, the individual conscientised evangelical chooses to support candidates, sometimes almost regardless of their actual politics. This 'repertoire' approach makes evangelicals important 'swing' actors in many political settings. In the absence of explicit, spiritual leadership, their vote may be steered in a variety of ways by those prepared to 'perform' the Christian life. The development of a

[14] See Jeffrey Hadden and Charles Swann, *Prime-Time Preachers*, Reading: Addison-Wesley, 1981, p. 149.

[15] Snowball, *Continuity and Change*, p. 3.

[16] Ibid., p. 151.

[17] Ibid., p. 154.

[18] 'Moral Majority Was "Regrettable Aberration," Says Evangelical Leader', *Church & State*, 58:3 (March 2005), 17.

[19] Transcript, telecast of the 700 Club, September 13, 2001, http://www.democraticunderground.com/discuss/duboard.php?az=view_all&address=389x909250, accessed 5 September 2011.

[20] Rick Warren and David Brooks, 'Myths of the Modern Megachurch', Pew Religion Forum, online, 23 May 2005, http://pewforum.org/Christian/Evangelical-Protestant-Churches/Myths-of-the-Modern-Megachurch.aspx, accessed 5 September 2011.

[21] David Smilde, 'Contradiction without Paradox: Evangelical Political Culture in the 1998 Venezuelan Elections', *Latin American Politics and Society*, 46:1 (2004), 75–102.

'Third Way' in politics by the British prime minister Tony Blair (whose memoir, one critic declared, 'reads like a management school textbook written by an evangelical preacher'),[22] for instance, reinvented the Labour Party in order to expand its attractiveness to evangelical voters while not alienating secular supporters.[23] Similar social mobilisation approaches were followed by the churchgoing Kevin Rudd in his short-lived 'post-ideological age' as Australian prime minister, and by Barack Obama in his desire to connect 'red and blue America'.[24] In Canada, the conservative prime minister Stephen Harper demonstrated that this balance could only be maintained while keeping one's religious convictions quiet. Whereas 'liberal' leaders promoted faith to broaden their constituency,[25] conservative leaders have had to overcome community assumptions that evangelicalism would render their conservatism extreme.[26]

In the period between 1980 and 2000, evangelicals entered political discourse on the back of widespread re-democratisation and pluralisation away from historic Catholic nationalism (in Latin America), in the context of widespread public corruption (in Africa), and in the context of pluralisation and a dominant liberal agenda (in Australia).[27] Evangelicals around the world had to position themselves – often without a consistent political philosophy – within a confusing range of options ranging from reactionary Catholicism to various types of revolutionary Marxism. The range of appropriations of the traditional European Catholic title 'Christian Democrat' indicate the problems the movement was having converting its support base into votes: parties emerged under that title, for instance, as an anti-Catholic party in Guatemala and as a conservative minority evangelical party in Australia. Where evangelical liberty of conscience was not at issue, Paul Freston notes that 'the disadvantages of such parties tend to prevail.'[28] Conditions of threat have been significant motivators for generating evangelical political involvement

[22] James Kirkup, 'Tony Blair's "A Journey" Reads Like an Evangelical Self-help Manual', *Daily Telegraph*, 1 September 2010, http://blogs.telegraph.co.uk/news/jameskirkup/100051993/tony-blairs-a-journey-reads-like-an-evangelical-self-help-manual/, accessed 11 November 2010.

[23] 'Introduction', in Gerry Hassan, ed., *After Blair: Politics after the New Labour Decade*, London: Lawrence & Wishart, 2007, p. 8.

[24] Hon Kevin Rudd MP, Member for Griffith, First Speech to Parliament, 11 November 1998, Parliament of Australia, Hansard, http://www.aph.gov.au/house/members/firstspeech.asp?id=83T, accessed 11 November 2010.

[25] Rodney Smith, "How Would Jesus Vote? The Churches and the Election of the Rudd Government", *Australian Journal of Political Science*, 44:4 (December 2009), 613–37; and idem., 'Questioning the Influence of the Christian Right in Australian Politics', ABC Religion and Ethics, 3 August 2010, http://www.abc.net.au/religion/articles/2010/08/03/2971958.htm, accessed 11 November 2010.

[26] Douglas Todd, 'Why Stephen Harper Keeps his Evangelical Faith Very Private', *Vancouver Sun*, 10 September 2008, http://blogs.vancouversun.com/2008/09/10/why-stephen-harper-keeps-his-evangelical-faith-very-private/, accessed 2010.

[27] Paul Freston, 'Evangelicals and Politics in Latin America', *Transformation*, 19, 4 October 2002, p. 271.

[28] Ibid., p. 273.

or action.[29] In most other settings, evangelicals were just as likely to vote in ways not distinguishable from the rest of the populace, and even *against* 'branded' 'Christian' parties. This was as much the case in Venezuela in 1998, where the alternative was the socialist/nationalist ex-coup leader Hugo Chavez, as it was in Australia in 2010, where the alternative was the Labor Party or the environmentalist Greens.[30] Despite this, the high profile of fundamentalist groups and their targeting by secularist ideologues tended to portray evangelical politics as universally conservative.

Evangelicalism and Contemporary Nationalisms

As a process of personal and communal transformation, evangelicalism intersects *with* politics as opposed to being driven by or towards politics. Evangelicals may intersect with politics out of interest in single issues, or more generally out of a developing regional 'theology' of witness. Lamin Sanneh makes a useful distinction between 'global Christianity' and 'world Christianity', the former referring to colonising extensions of transatlantic evangelicalism, the latter to indigenous appropriations.[31] In the latter (particularly strong in Africa), a coherent biblical worldview can often make a community disproportionately influential. In poorly formed states, it can even help to construct an otherwise missing sense of the civic in 'unconsolidated democracies'[32]. This has been a driving impetus behind the formation of Christian universities in Africa, and even of the abortive proclamation in 1991 of Zambia as a "Christian nation" under the MMD government of Frederick Chiluba.[33]

The collapse of the Moral Majority in the United States was a lesson which had to be learned locally in every locality around the world. The bloody counterinsurgency tactics of Efraín Ríos Montt in Guatamala is only one example of the use of evangelical identities to mobilise popular opinion in profoundly nationalist, ambivalent ways.[34] Are such actions a form of nationalism, a form of religion, or a syncretic amalgam of both? The growth of pentecostal/charismatic churches in East Africa saw a swing towards socially conservative and politically liberal outcomes: in Uganda, for instance, legislation against homosexuality resulted from

[29] Ibid., p. 273.

[30] David Smilde, 'Contradiction without Paradox: Evangelical Political Culture in the 1998 Venezuelan Elections', *Latin American Politics and Society*, 46:1 (April 2004), 75–102. 'Australian Christian Voter', 1 September 2010, http://austchristianvoter.blogspot.com/, accessed 8 November 2010.

[31] Quoted in Terence O. Ranger, 'Evangelical Christianity and Democracy in Africa: A Continental Comparison', *Journal of Religion in Africa*, 33:1 (February 2003), 113.

[32] David J. Simon, 'Democracy Unrealized: Zambia's Third Republic under Frederick Chiluba' in Leonardo A. Villalo'n and Peter von Doepp, eds, *The Fate of Africa's Democratic Experiments: Elites and Institutions*, Bloomington: Indiana University Press, 2005, p. 202.

[33] Ibid., p. 199.

[34] Edolphus Towns, 'Extension of Remarks', U.S. Congressional Record, 28 November 2001, p. 23300.

anti-AIDS campaigns by leaders such as Makerere Community Church's Martin Ssempa,[35] whereas in Kenya, the growth of charismatic churches stiffened resistance to organised Muslim demands for bans on proselytism and so advanced the cause of individual rights.[36] In Nicaragua, the rapid growth of evangelical churches after the collapse of the Sandinista regime meant that evangelicals could be found in every section of the political spectrum. In each place, the public discourse was different, and evangelicals had to learn new ways of speaking in public. The cultural nationalism factor also varies from country to country: in Canada, for example, 'Politicians with strong religious convictions who do not abandon their beliefs at the door of the legislature risk being labeled 'too American' or 'un-Canadian'.'[37] The Australian prime minister John Howard's appearances on stage at Sydney's Hillsong Conference drew a howl of protest and cultural interpretation from the Australian press.[38] In both countries, being 'too evangelical' was equated with being 'un-Canadian' or 'un-Australian'. In Northern Ireland, the survival of nationalised evangelical identity was as much a problem for its protagonists as an advantage, and over the years has propelled many minority evangelicals to seek alternatives.[39]

Evangelicals and Internationalism

Three major international events dominated or influenced evangelical action on the international scene during the period under review, even as the various communities continued with their now long-running campaigns against poverty and human rights abuses. The first of these was the outbreak of the AIDS scourge, which rapidly globalised and presented a challenge to evangelical communities which mere preaching could not meet. The shift from values community to scientific meritocracy annihilated the public function of preaching: 'the good' had been definitively detached from religious values and reattached to clinical success and harm minimisation. In Africa, where AIDS became a pandemic, it exposed evangelical naïveté with regard to human sexuality and fuelled criticisms of intolerance and insensitivity to 'the human plight'.[40] Secondly, the emergence of *perestroika* in the Soviet Union (in 1987, leading to its collapse in 1991), undermined those premillennial assumptions which drew support from the threat of nuclear annihilation. It also released a surge of foreign missionaries into the previously

[35] Lisa Miller, 'Pastor Rick Warren Responds to Proposed Antigay Ugandan Legislation', *Newsweek*, 29 November 2009.

[36] Arye Oded, *Islam and Politics in Kenya*, Boulder: Rienner, 2000, p. 85.

[37] David M. Haskell, *Through a Lens Darkly: How the News Media Perceive and Portray Evangelicals*, Toronto: Clements, 2009, p. 55.

[38] See for instance, Marion Maddox, *God under Howard: The Rise of the Religious Right in Australia*, Sydney: Allen & Unwin, 2005.

[39] For example, see the discussion of Zero28 later in the chapter.

[40] James Nkansah-Obrempong, 'Evangelical Theology in Africa: Ways, Perspectives, and Dilemmas', *Evangelical Review of Theology*, 34:4 (2010), 296.

closed eastern bloc.[41] Early practices abroad often seemed to point out that many missionaries had not learned much from two centuries of previous experience, and highlighted the need for greater social awareness. As Grigori Komendant, president of the Evangelical Christians-Baptists of Ukraine, stated, 'Russia is not a Third World country. The church has been here a long time, and we are not interested in the Americanization of our church.'[42] A resurgence in the influence of the national churches, such as the Russian Orthodox Church (ROC),[43] inevitably meant conflict with the new evangelicals, sometimes with international ramifications. For the ROC, evangelical expansion was 'not Christian mission, it is spiritual colonialism.'[44] Even evangelical social work was seen as 'material inducement' in breach of the UN's International Covenant on Civil and Political Rights (1966).[45] Apart from attacks on individuals and restrictions on normal civil rights for evangelical groups, local legislation was often used to blackmail or browbeat the 'foreigners'. For their part, evangelical human rights advocates campaigned against Orthodox anti-Semitism and use of state mechanisms against evangelical churches. The triumphant entry of the evangelical gospel into the former eastern bloc was thus not without consequences.

The destruction of the World Trade Centre on 11 September 2001, and the responses to the attack of a self-professedly evangelical U.S. president, also deepened the problems associated with Christian identity in the Middle East and Africa. It raised community tensions in Turkey and Syria, where secular states struggled with a significant Islamist presence, and saw the use of Pakistani 'blasphemy' laws and Iraqi 'premeditated ethnic cleansing'[46] against often long-established communities. These frictions raised the stakes for evangelical missionaries and social welfare agents, particularly in the kleptocracies (for example, Somalia, the borderlands of Afghanistan, etc.) which survived on traditional drug, extortion and assassination practices. Ten members of the International Assistance Mission Nuristan Eye Camp in Badakhshan in 2010 were accused of proselytism

41 Peter Deyneka and Anita Deyneka, 'Evangelical Foreign Missionaries in Russia', *International Bulletin of Missionary Research*, 22:2 (April 1998), pp. 56–60.

42 Quoted in ibid.

43 Zoe Knox, 'Russian Orthodoxy, Russian Nationalism, and Patriarch Aleksii II', *Nationalities Papers*, 33:4 (December 2005), 533. See also Robert C. Blitt, 'How to Entrench a De Facto State Church in Russia: A Guide in Progress,' *Brigham Young University Law Review*, 3 (1 April 2008), 707–78, accessed 11 November 2010.

44 Metropolitan Kyrill of Smolensk and Kaliningrad, 'Gospel and Culture', in John Witte, Jr. and Michael Bourdeaux, eds, *Proselytism and Orthodoxy in Russia: The New War for Souls*, Maryknoll: Orbis, 1999, pp. 73, 75.

45 Mark Elliott, 'Evangelism and Proselytism in Russia: Synonyms or Antonyms?' *International Bulletin of Missionary Research*, 25:2 (April 2001), pp. 72–5; 'Open Letter of Protest from Kyrgyz Churches, March 15, 2009', *Religion in Eastern Europe*, 1 May 2009, pp. 40–5.

46 'Iraq archbishop: "Christian People... should Escape the Ethnic Cleansing"', http://blog.beliefnet.com/deaconsbench/2010/11/iraq-archbishop-christian-peopleshould-escape-the-ethnic-cleansing.html#ixzz14wKdb9Wv, accessed 11 November 2010.

and murdered, simply because of their association with a Christian organisation.[47] Such events deepened the growing division between those evangelicals who ignored (and so absorbed) culture in the proclamation of an absolutist Word and those who sought to swim in their particular culture while critiquing it. The question in suburban America was 'what is the gospel?', whereas in democratising Russia and expanding China, it was 'what is the gospel *here*?'.[48]

One example of evangelical symbolic influence in the public square is Charles Colson. While he was mired in the public scandal of the Watergate fiasco which destroyed the Nixon presidency, and with his political career in tatters,[49] a reading of C.S. Lewis' *Mere Christianity* gave Colson a spiritual methodology through which to face the political problems, death threats, and public pillorying elicited by Watergate. While in prison, Colson founded a group he called Prison Fellowship (PF). On his release, it grew rapidly, especially after the Bush administration established the Faith-Based and Community Initiatives in 2001. By 2005, PF had become 'the largest prison outreach program in world history', serving 8 million prisoners worldwide, as well as in every U.S. state.[50] Attempting to create a program based on action, influence and perceived authenticity[51] in the public square, however, exposed Colson's evangelicalism to assessment as a methodology for effectiveness in social reform.[52] On its own data, PF's approaches have resulted in an 11 per cent drop in recidivism, improved prison operations, and mobilised huge voluntary forces against a major social evil, but do not eliminate criminality.[53] Its critics were less sanguine.[54] Colson's increasingly close association with other conservative Catholic and evangelical causes – from religious approaches to AIDS prevention, gay marriage, school prayer and abortion to support for the State of Israel – have made PF (in the words of one critic) a 'primary enemy' to secular organisations and lobby groups around the world doing the same sort of work.[55] The difference in public reception of this program compared to those of nineteenth-century evangelical reformers suggests much about the relationship which evangelical social

[47] 'Foreign Medical Workers among 10 Killed in Afghanistan', BBC News, 7 August 2010, http://www.bbc.co.uk/news/world-south-asia-10900338, accessed 11 November 2010.

[48] Holtrop, 'On Simplicity, Balance, and Wearing Spectacles', 116.

[49] Jonathan Aitken, *Charles W. Colson: A Life Redeemed*, New York: Doubleday, 2005, pp. 202–3.

[50] Davis Bunn, 'Evangelical and Post-Evangelical Christianity', *European Judaism*, 38:1 (Spring 2005), 10.

[51] Jonathan Aitken, 'A Man for All Seasons', *American Spectator*, 35:6 (November/December 2002), 47.

[52] Ken Newton and Jan W. van Deth, *Foundations of Comparative Politics: Democracies of the Modern World*, Cambridge: Cambridge University Press, 2006, p. 294.

[53] Tucker Carlson, 'Deliver Us from Evil', *Policy Review*, 62 (Fall 1992), pp. 72–7.

[54] Mark A.R. Kleiman, 'Faith-Based Fudging: How a Bush-Promoted Christian Prison Program Fakes Success by Massaging Data', *Slate*, 5 August 2003, http://www.slate.com/articles/news_and_politics/hey_wait_a_minute/2003/08/faithbased_fudging.html, accessed 11 November 2010.

[55] Rob Boston, 'Charles Colson's Transition from Prison Reformer to Religious Right Reactionary', *Church & State*, 56:3 (March 2003), 7.

action has with its moral environment. Colson, who had built his social service empire on the back of his ability to capture the *national* conversation of American evangelicals, inevitably became entangled in the transnational concerns of oppositional conversations. Having achieved the national microphone, like many logos-driven evangelicals, Colson failed to appreciate that symbolic effectiveness relies on leaving some things unsaid.[56]

Non-political Public Action

Part of the generational division emerging among evangelicals during the 1990s related to a tiredness over being co-opted for what were often battles of apparently minor interest to society at large. Younger evangelicals in particular objected to being represented by organisations such as Concerned Christians Canada or the Australian Christian Lobby. Traditional methods of political representation drew evangelicals into supporting protests over such causes as opening prayer in Parliament (Australia), or specific mention of God in the Constitution (Europe) and into conflicts with other minority proponents which (like Green/environmentalist parties in Europe, Australia and the United States, or the organised gay-rights lobby)[57] inhabit the same 'minority' space. Given the range of evangelical attitudes to the state, divisions were inevitable. Squeezed out of public debate and unable to agree on political platforms, evangelicals have searched for 'non-political' methods of public witness. The London City March for Jesus, for instance, originated in the public witness events of neo-charismatic groups Pioneer, Ichthus and Youth with a Mission. Fifteen thousand people who marched in 1987 became, by the year 2000, some 7 million people from thousands of centres around the world in the 'Global March for Jesus'.[58] The objective was not specific change (although by definition it was a challenge to the secular/private split which dominates modern societies); rather, it was the expression of pure symbolic witness.

In many Latin countries – including Italy and Spain – the mobilising fear, and therefore the basis for unity and political effectiveness, has been the defence of religious rights in the secular constitution against a projected resurgence of oppressive Catholicism.[59] In Africa – particularly in the northern states of Nigeria – the threat of the imposition of sharia law has likewise mobilised common action,

[56] On the cultural value of silence, see Silvia Montiglio, *Silence in the Land of Logos*, Princeton: Princeton University Press, 2000, p. 4.

[57] See 'Greens MP's Gay Hate Claims an Outrageous Slur Against ACL', http://australianchristianlobby.org.au/2010/11/greens-mp%E2%80%99s-gay-hate-claims-an-outrageous-slur-against-acl, accessed 5 September 2011.

[58] Gerald C. Ediger, 'The Proto-Genesis of the March for Jesus Movement, 1970–87', *Journal of Pentecostal Theology*, 12:2 (2004), 249.

[59] Paul Freston, *Evangelicals and Politics in Asia, Africa and Latin America*, Cambridge: Cambridge University Press, 2001, p. 22.

even in the face of violent responses.[60] In Europe, even ostensibly secular states (France, Italy, Greece) continued to reinforce a form of religious monopoly through laws regarding religious sects and proselytisation.[61] As a result, evangelicals in one country may find themselves aligned with an oppressive regime against which other evangelicals were working in the cause of human rights, whereas in another country they may be found marching in the streets alongside political liberals and reformists.[62] In all these countries, in addition, there are sectarian churches such as the Christian Congregation (in Brazil), the Christian Churches in North America (unorganised) and the Assemblies of God in Italy, which either refuse combined action or (on quietist principles) disregard the state as a valid sphere of action.

'Culture is Politics'

The compromise inevitable in modern states meant that religious influence at the ballot box was cyclical. When evangelicals could exert power, they found their own candidates as corruptible as anybody else. Demographics also play a large part. In Latin America, the 'private religion of salvation' grew into a mass movement because of the failure of capitalism to advance according to its own ideological program.[63] Rather than entering political discourse through the front door – through elite membership, or the passport of education – Latino pentecostal evangelicals gained political representation through populist pressure and by leveraging the pathways of social mobility (the pastorate itself is often a first step towards professionalisation in majority world contexts). They did so in ways which were not directly tied – in any simplistic Weberian way – to capitalist self-interest, but often (through microcredit, or patterns of voting on altruistic principle) in ways which were equally adapted to the new economies of developing countries.[64] The purchase of the Brazilian national network 'TV Record' by the Universal Kingdom of God Church in 1989 was a spectacular example of how an indigenous pentecostal movement leveraged its mass base into political representation by buying into the oxygen of politics – the media.[65] The failure of Pat Robertson's 1988 presidential campaign in the United States, on the other hand, demonstrates that media assets did not automatically translate into political influence.

60 Ranger, 'Evangelical Christianity and Democracy in Africa', p. 113.

61 Kyriakos N. Kyriazopoulos, 'Proselytization in Greece: Criminal Offense vs. Religious Persuasion and Equality', *Journal of Law and Religion*, 20:1 (2004–5), 149–245.

62 http://www.chiesavaldese.org/pages/archivi/index_commenti.php?id=916, accessed 8 November 2010.

63 Freston, 'Evangelicals and Politics in Latin America', p. 272.

64 Smilde, 'Contradiction without Paradox', p. 75; Ranger, 'Evangelical Christianity and Democracy in Africa', p. 117.

65 Freston, *Evangelicals and Politics*, pp. 17–18.

A more effective role for evangelicals has been to act as interpreters of meaning for rising cultures in need of a greater sense of meaning than that provided by the programmatic political rationality traditionally offered as the pathway to modernisation. Evangelicalism in the developing world provides political actors with 'symbolic effectiveness'.[66] American evangelical support for Israel, with all its consequences, has, after all, really been a form of civil religion. It was about protecting a reified American civic covenant – a national biblicist symbolism which ties America's prosperity 'under God' to its continued performance of the faith. The American sense of being 'God's people' has enormous populist appeal, as may be seen in sales of the books of John Hagee, an independent mega-church pastor and Christian Zionist. Simply tying an evangelical presence to patriotism (as Robertson did in 1988), however, threatened to alienate other evangelicals either suspicious of civil religion or disturbed by the effect that American foreign policy had on the world's poor.[67] Opposed to people like Hagee were those like Lauren F. Winner, whose memoir of conversion to Christianity from Judaism (entitled *Girl Meets God*) brought her widespread if abashed notice from evangelicals and non-evangelicals alike. Winner's was a faith emblematic of the wider search for an authentic, humane, intellectually satisfying journey self-assembled from the pieces of spirituality available in the postmodern marketplace.[68] Her self-critique deliberately undercut the missionary triumphalism associated with 'conversion of the Jews', in part to avoid becoming one more symbol caught up in the culture wars of plural societies. It was a deliberate acknowledgement of the importance of cultural forms in communicating authority.

EMBRACING PLURALITY

By end of the twentieth century, evangelicalism had been proclaiming its ascendancy for fifty years. There had been plenty of disappointments on the way: they were no longer 'the Moral Majority'; evangelical appropriations of the media had been tarnished so as to make the word 'televangelist' a postmodern swear word; 'evangelical' preachers and their associations with conservative politics around the world were entangled in all the usual corruption that one had come to expect from the political process. Playing the numbers to compete against other lobbies for political traction (that form of post-Graham evangelical entrepreneurialism which in the English context Warner calls 'Calverism' after the leader of the Evangelical Alliance)[69] had, in most countries, achieved little that was not later eroded.

[66] Uribe and Lander, quoted in Smilde, 'Contradiction without Paradox', p. 77.

[67] David John Marley, *Pat Robertson: An American Life*, Lanham: Rowman & Littlefield, 2007, p. 130.

[68] Sarah Hinlicky Wilson, 'Christ via Judaism', *Christianity Today*, 47:7 (July 2003). http://www.christianitytoday.com/ct/2003/july/39.65.html, accessed 14 November 2010.

[69] Warner, *Reinventing English Evangelicalism*, chapter 1.

The very nature of post-1989 politics required more than negative opposition: it required a positive platform for the world as it was. The worldwide collapse in voluntarism – both secular and religious – presented evangelicals with both a challenge (the voluntary society had been their traditional form) and an opportunity to move from interdenominational *re*action (particularly reaction to the 1960s moral revolution) to trans-denominational *pro*action through cooperative action regardless of traditional race, class, gender or religious barriers.

This evangelical *aggiornamento* took different shapes in different places, depending on the cultural issues at stake. A minority of American evangelicals – many of them children of the 1960s – for instance, had long recognised that biblical ideals could not be easily squared with U.S. foreign policy or the 'virus' of American nationalism.[70] But what would evangelicalism look like detached from the national frameworks within which they had worked since 1776? The process required re-thinking, a re-centring on the human. This was not an abstract pursuit but part of a broader recognition of the state of the world. One result was the re-emergence of evangelical philosophy, under the leadership of the Reformed philosophers Nicholas Wolterstorff and Alvin Plantinga. Others drew on counter-Enlightenment influences such as Nikolai Berdyaev and Søren Kierkegaard (or, in Wolterstorff's case, Thomas Reid) to construct a 'radically biblical' evangelical philosophy. Wolterstorff in particular notes the influence of Africa's anguish after a visit there, mediated by his friendship with black reformed theologian Allan Boesak: 'I was confronted with the faces and voices of people suffering injustice.'[71] Such people understood the need for Christian involvement in politics, but not as a set of moral demands or as church agitation for ecclesiastical privilege. Rather, politics was a human field of activity in democratic societies and, like all human fields of endeavour, should be the field for Christian action.[72] There were, moreover, ways of influencing the culture which did not involve forming a party or standing for office.

In Britain, Warner describes the fracturing of evangelicalism into what he calls pre-charismatic (normally Reformed biblicist) evangelicals and entrepreneurial evangelicals. With the withdrawal of the former under the leadership of Martyn Lloyd Jones in 1966, the latter were left to reconstruct a pan-evangelicalism largely made up of Anglicans and Baptists, drawing on a combination of Graham-like 'big event' evangelism and approaches developed by the British neo-charismatic New Church Movement.[73] The failure of this bureaucratised pan-evangelical alliance to

[70] Jon Trott, 'A Christian Thinker Critiques Obama and McCain on Foreign Policy vs. "American Exceptionalism"', Blue Christian on a Red Background, http://bluechristian.blogspot.com/2008_09_01_archive.html, 23 July 2011.

[71] Nicholas Wolterstorff, 'The Grace That Shaped My Life'; Nicholas Wolterstorff and Terence Cuneo, *Inquiring about God*, vol. 1, New York: Cambridge University Press, 2010, p. 2; http://www.calvin.edu/125th/wolterst/w_bio.pdf, accessed 7 November 2010.

[72] Alan Storkey, 'Inadequate Christian Politics', *Third Way*, 4 May 1978, p. 3.

[73] Warner, *Reinventing English Evangelicalism*, pp. 48–9.

fulfill its promise reaffirmed the reaction against organised religion which motivated its more left-wing members. The potential members of evangelical organisations were not so much *anti*-evangelical (they conceived of themselves as reacting against the classical evangelical tendency to be anti-everything which did not agree with established doctrine and authority) as *pro*-human – and that in broader categories than the national categories of traditional evangelicalism allowed. Sales of middle-brow monthly evangelical magazines steadily declined during the 1980s, whereas those of TEAR Fund's magazine 'grew rapidly' – from 20,000 in 1979 to 170,000 in 2001.[74] Socially based evangelical activities countered the decline in comparable formally organised institutions. The rewriting of Holy Trinity Brompton's 'Alpha Course' so that it connected to non-believers, for instance, went 'viral' from 1990 to 2000 through evangelical and later even Catholic circles. By 2005, it was running in more than 150 countries, had national offices in 29 countries, and had seen 8.5 million people pass through its doors.[75] Centred on accessible technology and a holistic 'mere Christianity' which did not seek to advance from 'universal truths',[76] it successfully managed to bridge the public and private by relocating the spiritual conversation from the office, the church, the street and other public places to the dining rooms of the laity. A local church-based phenomenon, linked to a global community, its success in the midst of widespread criticism pointed to a re-centring of evangelicalism on real communities.

As one form of evangelicalism was opening its doors to the world, between 1990 and 2010, Reformed evangelicals increasingly defined their borders and took the advice of Martyn Lloyd Jones: they left, divided or conquered those in their denominations who were not like themselves. This too had global impacts, becoming, for instance, an important catalyst in the formation of the evangelical Global Anglican Futures Conference (GAFCON) in Jerusalem in 2008. While sparked by the consecration of a gay bishop in the Episcopal Church in the United States, the issues were deeper than mere theology or even church discipline. The divisions – led by 'confessing' bishops from Africa, Canada, Australia and many other places – mapped the global divisions in the Anglican communion. Evangelicals were dominant in the churches of the global south, liberals in the global north. The concerns of the churches were necessarily different. The resistance in 1998 of Lambeth and New Hampshire (and, before that, Perth and Vancouver) to the claims of Lagos and Sydney bore fruit in GAFCON's 2008 declaration of intent to 're-form' the Anglican communion worldwide, by political and disciplinary means where possible, or by schism and separation where necessary. The geographical restraints on church relationships were redefined and alternative organisations were created. In North

[74] Ibid., pp. 90–91.

[75] Charles Foster, 'From Knightsbridge to the Nations: The Alpha Movement and the Future of Christendom,' *Contemporary Review*, 288:1682 (Autumn 2006), 322.

[76] Graham Tomlin and Sandy Millar, 'Assessing Aspects of the Theology of Alpha Courses', *International Review of Mission*, 96:382/383 (July/October 2007), 258.

America, evangelical, charismatic and Anglo-Catholic congregations dissociated themselves from the Protestant Episcopal Church of the United States and placed themselves under bishops in Argentina, Bolivia or Uganda.[77] The appointment in 2010 of Mary Glasspool as the first lesbian bishop in the Anglican communion led the Fellowship of Confessing Anglicans to call for the de-recognition of the Episcopal Church in the United States and its replacement by the Anglican Church in North America.[78] The consequences for local congregations in terms of property and resources were profound. In the Anglican Church in Canada (already financially challenged by 'cultural genocide' settlements with indigenous peoples), legal cases threatened to bankrupt formerly strong evangelical parishes. Those with a sense of history would have recognised the patterns from 1662 (the Great Ejection) and 1843 (the Great Disruption). These too were not 'evangelical' events as such, but by their nature evangelicals in these important communions were inevitably and deeply affected.

CHASING GLOBAL REVIVAL

Charismatic evangelicals faced a similar problem. With the fading of the charismatic renewal of the 1970s, the early rhetoric of the unstoppable wave of the Spirit was replaced with reflection on the reasons for Spirit baptism. Many – like Andrew Walker – concluded that the renewal had been personal and temporary. Walker converted to Greek Orthodoxy in search of a more profound theology.[79] Others migrated out of their startlingly unrenewed mainline denominations into independent congregations or mega-churches. The convention form of organised charismatic renewal (such as Spring Harvest in the United Kingdom) was swept into the orbit of the emerging mega-churches or became part of the floating population chasing global revival. As a significant re-formation of evangelical community, the former will be dealt with at more length below. The latter, however, formed something of a progressive convention which attempted to avoid institutionalisation by attaching an evangelical gospel to ecstatic experiences. Revival moved from Argentina (1983), to Toronto, Canada (1993–4),[80] to London (1994), to Brownsville, Florida (1995) and to many other places. Its public manifestations were not in organisational structures, but in the media and material culture.

[77] 'About us', Diocese of Western Anglicans, http://www.westernanglicans.org/index.html, accessed 15 November 2010.

[78] Communiqué from the Primates Council of GAFCON/FCA, 10 April 2010, http://www.gafcon.org/news/communique_from_the_primates_council_of_gafcon_fca, accessed 15 November 2010.

[79] Thomas Smail, Andrew Walker and Nigel Wright, *Charismatic Renewal: The Search for a Theology*, London: SPCK, 1994.

[80] Martyn Percy, 'Adventure and Atrophy in a Charismatic Movement: Returning to the "Toronto Blessing"', *Journal of Contemporary Religion*, 20:1 (January 2005), 71.

Essential to this was the proliferation of a baptised consumerism – Christian music, films, books, and the 'holy hardware' (from bumper stickers to key rings) which populated the symbolic worlds of evangelicals and linked home to church. The 'bust to boom' story of Mel Gibson's *Passion of the Christ*, apart from demonstrating the increasing closeness of evangelical Catholics and catholic evangelicals, also illustrated to the moneymen of Western popular media that the evangelical dollar was a significant player. The search for 'the crossover' – a media form which could appeal to both Christian and non-Christian audiences – was a prominent theme from the 1990s onwards. In a globalised world, rhetoric matters; culture is politics. The success of bands such as Switchfoot (a Christian band which has found a broader following through 'mere Christian' lyrics and secular film scores) and on the other hand U2 (a non-Christian band with a religious edge) were examples of this sort of fusion and the broader leverage it could generate.[81] The success of the 'Narnia' films demonstrated the continuing appeal of C.S. Lewis's mere Christianity, while that of a film about William Wilberforce (*Amazing Grace*, 2007) capitalised on an interest in period pieces as a means of moral reflection.[82] Whereas Christian bookstores remained sparse on the ground in Britain (many collapsing financially after 2007), they proliferated elsewhere, with the Koorong network in Australia becoming the third-largest bookseller of any type in that country, and the publishing houses based in Grand Rapids and Colorado in the United States achieving such success that one, Zondervan, became a target for purchase by the Murdoch News Corporation empire. Massive sales (such as that of Rick Warren's *Purpose Driven Life*) could be parlayed into cultural influence.[83] Christian Contemporary Music (CCM), the offspring of the marriage of the Californian Jesus Movement and New Zealand Latter Rain worship,[84] expanded into a billion-dollar industry, largely on the back of the rapid spread of contemporary worship styles.[85] Participant scholars of evangelicalism (such as Warner or Dawn)[86] have tended to be dismissive, referring to such music as 'the inconsequential enthusiasms of evangelical juvenilia', or as a mode of theological compromise.[87] Forgetting the gospel origins many of their own forms, secular observers also tend to dismiss it as an adulteration of popular music. Such studies tend to miss what the genre means for its consumers, however, namely the potency of the medium in creating community, as a mechanism for cultural bargaining and adaptation in the secular context.[88]

[81] Quentin J. Schultze and Robert Woods, *Understanding Evangelical Media: The Changing Face of Christian Communication*, Downers Grove: InterVarsity, 2008, p. 26.
[82] Ginia Bellafante, 'Sick of Jane Austen Yet?' *Time*, 147:3 (15 January 1996).
[83] Warren and Brooks, 'Myths of the Modern Megachurch'.
[84] Knowles, 'Music as an Indicator of New Zealand Pentecostal Spirituality and Theology'.
[85] Paul Y. Chang and Dale J. Lim, 'Renegotiating the Sacred-Secular Binary: IX Saves and Contemporary Christian Music,' *Review of Religious Research*, 50:4 (June 2009), 396.
[86] Larry Eskridge, 'Slain by the Music', *Christian Century*, 123:5 (3 July 2006), 20.
[87] Warner, *Reinventing English Evangelicalism*, p. 86.
[88] Chang and Lim, 'Renegotiating the Sacred-Secular Binary', 397.

Whatever one's opinion, any global assessment of contemporary Christian worship music – from its chart-bending success in Australia, to its impact on missions in Africa, to the growth of mega-churches in Singapore – needs to conclude that it is anything but inconsequential. At their worst, evangelical media productions generated kitsch;[89] at their best, they redefined authenticity and became a means of cultural subversion and recreation.[90]

SEEKING NEW FORMS: CHURCH 2.0.

Changes in culture and relationships with their denominations necessarily implied changes in evangelical ecclesiology. By the 1980s, as Robert Bellah noted, American individualism and materialism had slowly gutted the institutional forms imported along with waves of migrants over three centuries.[91] Americans had not forgotten how to be Christians, but their hold on how to 'do church' seemed to be slipping. Neither traditional churches nor the convention form nor the pan-evangelical institution (such as the Evangelical Alliance) could provide the sort of local framework for community required for continuing faith. Evangelicals responded to the issue of 'sustainable size' by growing both larger and smaller, depending on their context. The mass urbanisation which gave rise to cities such as Sao Paolo, Brazil and Lagos, Nigeria, involved highly mobile populations and a radical redefinition of the 'local'. Localities became less geographical places and more 'glocal' places interconnected by new communication and transportation technologies. The extension of this – as Robert Putnam famously explored in his *Bowling Alone* – was the undermining and redirection of traditional forms of civic voluntarism.[92] Not coincidentally, these centres also became seedplots for some of the world's fastest-growing mega-churches.

In the United States, evangelical mega-church growth has been shown to follow high-fertility 'exurban' white family formation and aspirational urban black and Hispanic family settlement. For the masses of people made mobile by global urbanisation, churches were often the means for imposing communal form on new urban and 'exurban' areas of development, incorporating many of the aspects of everyday life. In Brazil in 2009, for instance, the 8 million member 'Universal Church of the Kingdom of God' gained planning permission for a new 10,000-seat church in Sao Paolo, which would include 'a car park for 1,000 vehicles, TV and radio

[89] Heather Hendershot, *Shaking the World for Jesus: Media and Conservative Evangelical Culture*, Chicago: University of Chicago Press, 2004, pp. 2, 52.

[90] Steve Stockman, *Walk On: The Spiritual Journey of U2*, Orlando: Relevant Books, 2005, p. 153; Hans Weisethaunet and Ulf Lindberg, 'Authenticity Revisited: The Rock Critic and the Changing Real', *Popular Music & Society*, 33:4 (October 2010), 471.

[91] Robert N. Bellah et al., *Habits of the Heart: Individualism and Commitment in American Life*, New York: Harper and Row, 1985, pp. 220–1.

[92] Robert Putnam, *Bowling Alone: The Collapse and Revival of American Community*, New York: Simon & Schuster, 2001, pp. 49–50.

studios, classrooms for 1,300 children' in a building designed around the measurements of the biblical Temple of Solomon.[93] The development of the networked mega-church – of which Hillsong in Australia (and now in the Ukraine, Britain, France, Sweden, South Africa and the United States) is an example – is another realisation of this 'redefinition of the local' in a globalised world.[94] This has a direct impact on spirituality: mega-churches offer a sort of de-iconised space within which God is made 'palpable' through 'an alternative semiotics and performance which reconciles the individual's private spiritual encounter with "the mega"'. The church's very size and 'success' is a materialisation of the word preached, a concrete ideology.[95] Mega-churches are thus not driven by organisation so much as organised *spirituality*, the force of which has caused a fundamental shift from the historic situation where evangelical churches acted locally (entrusting their more extended interests to denominations or para-church ministries), to the situation where local churches, regardless of their size, are increasingly able to internalise direct action towards the global.[96] John Vaughan reports that 'known non-Catholic churches having a weekend attendance of 2,000+ people each weekend' rose from about 150 in 1986 to 'about 1,700 churches that size' in 2009. In 2010, some 1,400 of these were in the United States.[97] While the overall growth rate in numbers of mega-churches in the United States was approximately 10 per cent per annum between 1970 and 2005, their annualised growth in numbers doubled between 2000 and 2005, and their average size increased by 47 per cent.[98]

A participant in both trends (towards the formation of both larger and smaller communities), Seattle pastor Mark Driscoll describes three types of church response to changing urban contexts: Church 1.0 (traditional, institutional, assumes central place in culture), Church 2.0 (contemporary, business orientation, fights marginal place in culture, pastors are CEOs marketing spiritual goods and services to customers), and Church 3.0 (postmodern, pluralistic, accepts marginal place in culture, pastors are local missionaries).[99] Mega-churches are, in his terminology, 'Church 2.0' responses. For evangelicals looking for good news in the

93 Stephen Kennett, 'Giant Brazilian mega-church gains planning approval', http://www.building.co.uk, accessed 4 November 2010.

94 John Dar 'Flexible Megachurches Rival Denominations', *Christian Century*, 125:20 (October 2008), 14.

95 Robbie B.H. Goh, 'Hillsong and "Megachurch" Practice: Semiotics, Spatial Logic, and the Embodiment of Contemporary Evangelical Protestantism', *Material Religion*, 4:3 (2008), 291.

96 Robert J. Priest, Douglas Wilson and Adelle Johnson, 'U.S. Megachurches and New Patterns of Global Mission', *International Bulletin of Missionary Research*, 34:2 (April 2010), 101.

97 John Vaughan, 'The Term "Megachurch"', *Church Growth Today*, reprinted 2010, http://hubpages.com/hub/Megachurches-Today, accessed 4 November 2010; 'Hartford Seminary Database of Megachurches in the U.S.', accessed 5 November 2010.

98 Barney Warf and Morton Winsberg, 'Geographies of Megachurches in the United States', *Journal of Cultural Geography*, 27:1 (2010), 35.

99 Mark Driscoll, 'A Pastoral Perspective on the Emergent Church', *Criswell Theological Review*, new series. 3:2 (Spring 2006), 87–93.

face of denominational collapse, the growth of large churches is a metrics-based form of self-affirmation. Mega-churches seek relevance on a community level, locating themselves as the means for combining 'high, deeply personalized religiosity with cultural relevance by appropriating the aesthetics and media technologies of popular culture' within corporatised structures.[100] Just as social voluntarism was a major organising principle in the nineteenth century, organisational theorists such as Peter Drucker have identified the rise of the corporation as the most significant sociological phenomenon of the twentieth century. As the value-driven form of the corporation, the mega-church, according to Drucker, is 'the only organization that is actually working in our society'.[101]

The mega-church, however, has many critics, many of whom have professed concern (often from within denominational traditions threatened by their development) about the theological and pastoral aspects of mega-church growth, whereas others see the form as a form of clever managerialism.[102] These approaches ignore two facts: first, many clever managers in the mainline denominations have attempted to grow their churches, without lasting success; and secondly, the founders of many contemporary mega-churches are themselves among the most surprised that they saw remarkable growth in often merely doing what others did. Their confusion is only increased when, pressed to turn their approach into a transportable technology, churches like Yoido Full Gospel (Seoul) and *Misión Carismática Internacional* (Bogotà) have found that their approaches do not result in the same sort of growth in different cultural settings. Mega-church growth does have theological and managerial aspects, but these vary enormously: 'Although megachurches are disproportionately evangelical,' Bird notes, 'theology only modestly influences the number of participation opportunities.'[103] Within the United States, the largest number of mega-churches are independent evangelical churches, followed by Baptist, then pentecostal and charismatic identifications. In Australia, by contrast, 14 out of the 16 Protestant churches with membership exceeding 2,000 are pentecostal/charismatic ones. Theologically, they are enormously varied, from the neo-Reformed theology underlying Willow Creek and Stephen Tong's evangelical Reformed evangelism in Indonesia, to the 'Youngsan' theology at Yoido Full Gospel Church. The rise of the new form, therefore, must be seen mostly as a response to the needs of *mission* in mobile social contexts. London's largest mega-church, for instance, is Matthew

[100] Miller, quoted in Omri Elisha, 'Sins of Our Soccer Moms: Servant Evangelism and the Spiritual Injuries of Class,' in Melissa Checker and Margaret Fishman, eds, *Local Actions: Cultural Activism, Power, and Public Life in America*, New York: Columbia University Press, 2004, p. 141.

[101] 'Managing to Minister: An Interview with Peter Drucker,' *Leadership Journal* (April 1989), quoted in Warren Bird, 'Megachurches as Spectator Religion', PhD thesis, Fordham University, 2007, p. 26.

[102] This is the tone of both Warf and Winsberg and Patrick Malloy, 'Rick Warren Meets Gregory Dix: The Liturgical Movement Comes Knocking at the Megachurch Door', *Anglican Theological Review*, 92:3 (Summer 2010), 439–53, among many others.

[103] Bird, 'Megachurches as Spectator Religion', p. 196.

Ashimolowo's Kingsway International Christian Centre (KICC), the membership of which is largely West African in origin, whereas the largest English-originated church is Kensington Temple, recently restructured on the G-12 model imported by Colin Dye from the Columbian church model of Cesar Castellanos' *Misión Carismática Internacional*.[104] Hillsong's London church and Holy Trinity Brompton both draw heavily on the 'invisible' diaspora of Anglo expatriates from New Zealand, Australia and South Africa. Yoido's church planting has likewise followed Korean expatriates into Japan, Australia and the Pacific Rim.[105]

Indications of why this may be happening can be drawn from the study of that other great religious revolution – the Reformation. Steven Ozment notes that in pre-Reformation towns such as Rostock, traditional forms of church life in the 1510s suffered many of the same issues as traditional churches in the 1980s: high investment in fixed assets supporting comparatively large numbers of highly trained and relatively inflexible staff for low attendance returns from the surrounding culture.[106] As, periodically, many Western economies went into periods of economic stagnation, the ideological pressure for more efficient ways of conducting the mission of the church was reinforced by economic pressure.[107] In the majority world, mega-church growth is a response to urbanisation and its impact on land prices, particularly in land-poor locations such as Singapore and South Korea.[108] The adoption of corporatised management approaches applied to relatively large, laicized 'commuter' congregations decreases the relative cost of ministry and makes such organisations more directive and missional in their orientation. If they were 'taking energy away from older and smaller churches', often it was because the missional challenges facing churches in urbanising societies had outgrown the ability of traditional churches to service the objects of their own discourse.[109] In rapid-change contexts (such as industrialising South Korea, war- and poverty-wracked Colombia or Nigeria, the troubled 'powerhouse of West Africa'), some of the largest mega-churches became 'de facto replacements for denominations', acting as centres for fundraising and the establishment of training institutions, missions and even universities (such as Hansei University in Seoul and Covenant University in Nigeria).[110] While some mega-churches – such as Saddleback Church in California, New Life Assembly of God in Chennai, India, and Hillsong Church in Australia – remain within denominations in their own countries, most act as

[104] 'Cell Vision at KT', http://www.kt.org/cellvision/, accessed 23 June 2011.

[105] Mark R. Mullins, *Christianity Made in Japan: A Study of Indigenous Movements*, Honolulu: University of Hawai'i Press, 1998, p. 181.

[106] Steven Ozment, *Protestants: The Birth of a Revolution*, New York: Doubleday, 1993, pp. 17–18.

[107] Robert Wuthnow, *The Crisis in the Churches: Spiritual Malaise, Fiscal Woe*, New York: Oxford University Press, 1997, p. 19.

[108] Harvie M. Conn and Manuel Ortiz, *Urban Ministry: The Kingdom, the City and the People of God*, Downers Grove: InterVarsity, 2001, p. 243.

[109] Wuthnow, *The Crisis in the Churches*, p. 236.

[110] The Hartford Group reports that 69% of mega-churches did their training in-house. 'Flexible Megachurches Rival Denominations', *Christian Century*, 7 October 2008, p. 14.

pseudo-denominations through their international mentoring, 'resourcing' and church planting activities elsewhere.[111]

With increased resources come increased challenges. Sustainable mega-churches need to proliferate the channels through which individuals can be meaningfully engaged in the larger community. The upsurge in 'prosperity' preaching often co-located with these churches is a temporary, if effective, anodyne for many, as the association between mega-church growth and aspirational poverty around the world demonstrates. A leading symbol for this association has been the 20,000-member World Changers International Ministries Church[112] in College Park, Georgia, pastored by Creflo Dollar. Largely African American in membership, the church 'crystallizes the spirit of the Word of Faith movement' which developed out of the teachings of E.W. Kenyon, and grew around the edges of the healing revival of the 1950s.[113] The development of T.D. Jakes' 30,000-member Potter's House Church in the Dallas-Fort Worth metroplex reflects the same combination of gifted individual, empowering message, urban growth and aspirational marginality.[114] In other settings, particularly in Korean mega-churches, alternative 'technologies' (such as cell-based discipling programs, or prayer mountains) are used to transform ethnic association into religious association and conviction.[115] Although many such churches hold theological positions which place them beyond evangelical orthodoxy (and not a few beyond financial transparency standards),[116] their innovations are examples of the enculturation of evangelical spirituality at the level of personal need in marginalised communities.

SEEKING TO CONNECT: CHURCH 3.0

As the 'huge shift' of archetypical mega-churches, such as Willow Creek, away from seeker-oriented services and towards 'greater depth to mature believers'[117] shows, mere size was only an organisational solution. It did not necessarily deal with *individual* perceptions of utility. As broader social fascination with mere corporate success faded externally in the 1990s, so did the utility of merely organisational responses. Catholic critics such as Metz had long been pointing to the emergence of a 'postbourgeois age'.[118] The separatist educational foundations of the 1930s and

[111] Warren and Brooks, 'Myths of the Modern Megachurch'.

[112] Various attendance numbers are given in the literature, ranging from 15,000 (Hartford Institute) to 30,000 (Warf and Winsberg).

[113] Milmon F. Harrison, *Righteous Riches: The Word of Faith Movement in Contemporary African American Religion*, New York: Oxford University Press, 2005, p. 132.

[114] Robert V. Kemper, 'Dallas-Fort Worth: Toward New Models of Urbanization, Community Transformation and Immigration', *Urban Anthropology*, 34:2–3 (March–June 2005), 132.

[115] Michael W. Foley and Dean R. Hoge, *Religion and the New Immigrants: How Faith Communities Form Our Newest Citizens*, New York: Oxford University Press, 2007, p. 135.

[116] Adelle M. Banks, 'Change of Address', *Christianity Today*, June 2008, p. 13.

[117] Matt Branaugh, 'Willow Creek's "Huge Shift"', *Christianity Today*, June 2008, p. 13.

[118] See Johann Baptist Metz, *The Emergent Church*, New York: Crossroad, 1986.

1940s had, ironically, produced better-educated younger evangelicals less satisfied with simplistic answers and badly trained clergy. As a media generation, they were alert to the manipulation of systems and aware of their value to 'the organisation'. Mass evangelism and results for this generation were less important than being permitted to pursue meaningful lives. The traditional evangelical 'growth towards grace' was, through the early 2000s, reformulated to the pursuit of spiritual quests 'not so much for group identity and social location as for an authentic inner life and personhood'.[119]

Mega-churches responded through 'growing smaller' internally (through, for example, careful management of small groups), whereas others decided to restart with the small in mind and to take culture seriously. What Driscoll refers to as 'Church 3.0' – variously referred to elsewhere as 'emerging' or 'emergent' church paradigms – was a convergence of the strategic reaction (among younger leaders in the 'Leadership Network') to changes in the evangelical place in U.S. culture, as well as British and Australasian responses to denominational decay.[120] Indeed, it was an *acceptance* of those changes, based on a value assessment about the nature of modern communication. To this cohort of younger evangelicals, the continued defence of a privileged position in a culture which devalued privilege essentially voided the power of the gospel as a communicative act. Starting, instead, with the assumption of evangelicalism as marginalised within its culture, Church 3.0 thinkers drew on missiologists such as Lesslie Newbigin (England) and David Bosch (South Africa) to reconstruct themselves as 'Christians seeking to be effective missionaries wherever they live'. Leaders such as Brian McLaren in the United States, Andrew Jones in the United Kingdom, and Michael Frost in Australia built on the emergence of evangelicalism as an object of scholarly interest attended by a proliferation of books and articles.[121] So objectified, they could more readily choose the elements they found useful, and reorient evangelical ecclesiology as a postmodern practice.[122]

Divisions within the evangelical theological fraternity helped. 'Christian theology,' Wolfgang Vondey noted, 'has simply become too large, too divided, too abstract, and too worldly to connect God and a pluralistic reality.'[123] An attempt by the U.S.-based Evangelical Theological Society to reject open theism (2001) and expel protagonists such as Clark Pinnock and John Sanders (2003) exposed the

[119] Wade Clark Roof, *Spiritual Marketplace: Baby Boomers and the Remaking of American Religion*, Princeton: Princeton University Press, 1999, p. 7.

[120] Mathew Guest and Steve Taylor 'The Post-Evangelical Emerging Church: Innovations in New Zealand and the UK', *International Journal for the Study of the Christian Church*, 6:1 (March 2006), 49–64.

[121] Driscoll, 'A Pastoral Perspective on the Emergent Church', 89.

[122] See Mark Hutchinson, 'The Hamburger Index: Determining Evangelical Interests 1960–2010', online, http://alphacrucis.academia.edu, accessed 17 November 2010.

[123] Wolfgang Vondey, *Beyond Pentecostalism: The Crisis of Global Christianity and the Renewal of the Theological Agenda*, Grand Rapids: Eerdmans, 2010, p. 2.

fragility of the evangelical theological consensus. It also exposed the ecclesiological problems of a movement united by nothing but its pragmatism and its theological institutions.[124] The widely reported suggestion from the conservative core that progressive thinkers should (in the words of Wayne Grudem) 'consider leaving'[125] was confirmation to Church 3.0 thinkers that they should do just that. McLaren's *A New Kind of Christian* (2001) spoke into this broader sense of ecclesiological crisis, sparking interest in postmodern approaches to the standards of evangelical spirituality, sidestepping the charismatic option and providing a means of renewal which seemed to be philosophically based. It promised an integration of the life of the mind within Christian community which many people coming out of evangelical backgrounds had not encountered since the 1970s.

The emergent movement gained in structure as interest swelled and discussion groups became churches and networks.[126] Here was a movement which took culture and human individuality seriously and contained a response to 1950s evangelicalism's totalising emphasis on method, on external compliance over internal change or social justice.[127] Critical of the Enlightenment presuppositions of their forebears, the new generation sought new symbols and new collocutors. Often, they created bridges through the ironic use of traditional symbols – as might be seen, for instance in the title of a book by Gareth Higgins, co-founder of Zero28 in Northern Ireland: *How Movies Helped Save My Soul*.[128] Up for critique were gender distinctions in ministry, implicit racism or anything else (including the mere experientialism of the charismatic movement) more about power than about the gospel. At the same time, they were in search of a new holism which responded to the charismatic communitarian critiques of evangelicalism's individualism and orientation towards personal salvation. 'It's not about the church meeting your needs,' emergent founder Brian McLaren noted, 'it's about you joining the mission of God's people to meet the world's needs.'[129] Having held out the invitation to converse, he found hundreds of thousands happy to oblige. The world's needs were not hard to find. Defining 'God's people' would prove more elusive.

This synthesis fed on the increasing fragmentation of older evangelical subcultures. Some of the children of the fundamentalists crossed over to pentecostalism or Catholicism, but as a whole, their minds were too full of the counterarguments

[124] See David Hillborn, 'Principled Unity or Pragmatic Compromise? The Challenge of Pan-Evangelical Theology', *Evangel*, 22:3 (Autumn 2004), 81; Eric Gorsky, 'Evangelical Theologians Reject "Open Theism"', *Christian Century*, 118:34 (12 December 2001), 10.

[125] E.g. Chris Tilling, 'ETS adopt Chicago Statement on Biblical Inerrancy', Chrisendom blog, http://www.bpnews.net/bpnews.asp?ID=24424, as Douglas Wilson argued in relation to the Reformed rejection of charismatic gifts (*Mother Kirk: Essays and Forays in Practical Ecclesiology*, Moscow, ID: Canon Press, 2001, p. 63).

[126] 'Loose Emergent Churches to Have More Structure', *Christian Century*, July 2005, p. 14.

[127] Bunn, 'Evangelical and Post-Evangelical Christianity', p. 9.

[128] Brett McCracken, 'Hipster Faith', *Christianity Today*, 54:9 (September 2010), http://www.christianitytoday.com/ct/2010/september/9.24.html, accessed 17 November 2010.

[129] Quoted in Andy Crouch, 'Emergent Mystique', *Christianity Today*, November 2004, p. 39.

of their parents: 'We grew up in churches where people knew the nine verses why we don't speak in tongues, [but] had never experienced the overwhelming presence of God. . . . Life in the church had become so small. It had worked for me for a long time. Then it stopped working.'[130] Many dropped out of church altogether, and some out of faith. As Elaine Bolitho has shown for Baptist churches in New Zealand, and Rob Warner has demonstrated for evangelical churches in England, myths of evangelical growth long hid a significant 'back door'.[131] 'For every one hundred new members to the Baptist churches of New Zealand' in the early 2000s, reported Alan Jamieson, 'one hundred and eight left.'[132] Nick Mercer refers to 'the large numbers of nomadic ex-evangelicals' which typify British religious life,[133] and similar 'back doors' have been discovered in Australia, Canada and the United States. The evidence points to a significant number of people of evangelical conviction, but also to increasing resistance to standard evangelical ecclesiology. Some prominent figures – including former Presbyterian minister Charles Bell, Franky Schaeffer (son of leading reformed apologist, Francis Schaeffer), Campus Crusader Peter Gilquist and charismatic founder and John Stott's former curate, Michael Harper – reacted to the 'crisis' by transferring allegiance to Orthodox traditions.[134] For these evangelical refugees, Orthodoxy had the advantage of being a real community (bound together by the invisible bonds of global diaspora), with the reassuring depth of Eastern tradition, subtle philosophical resources, spiritual disciplines, and a (Holy) Spiritual praxis which had been largely eliminated from the evangelical traditions by the rationalisers of the nineteenth century.[135] For those who did not want to leave evangelicalism, emergent church forms absorbed many elements from these alternative Christian approaches. Rob Bell, for instance, consciously sets up a counterpoint to the Cartesian Western tradition in phrases like: 'We're rediscovering Christianity as an Eastern religion, as a way of life.'[136] In short, the emergent movement provided a mechanism for cultural osmosis.

Appropriately for a movement which has taken symbolic action seriously, emergent churches operate through a semiotics of culture. They meet in deinstitutionalised settings – bars, warehouses, nightclubs – places where the script written over the location deliberately repositions the message. In her study of the ikon and

[130] Kristen Bell, quoted in Crouch, 'Emergent Mystique', p. 37.

[131] E. E. Bolitho, 'In This World – Baptist and Methodist Churches in New Zealand 1948–1988' unpub. PhD Thesis, Victoria University of Wellington, Wellington (1992), p. 114; Warner, *Reinventing English Evangelicalism*, passim.

[132] Quoted in Alan Jamison, 'Turangawaewae: The Search for a Churchless Faith in New Zealand', *Australasian Pentecostal Studies*, 5–6 (2004), http://webjournals.alphacrucis.edu.au/journals/aps/issue-56/turangawaewae-the-search-for-a-churchless-faith-in/, accessed 17 November 2010.

[133] Nick Mercer, review, '*The Post-Evangelical*', *Third Way*, September 1995, p. 30.

[134] Vigen Guroian, 'Dancing Alone – Out of Step with Orthodoxy', *Jacob's Well* (Fall 1995).

[135] Stuart Piggin, 'Historical Streams of Influence on Evangelical Piety', *Lucas: An Evangelical History Review*, 18 (December 1994), 5–19.

[136] Crouch, 'Emergent Mystique', p. 38.

Zero28 networks in Northern Ireland, Gladys Ganiel notes the operation of this semiotics among thirty Protestants meeting in a Catholic bar, or at an art show on secular premises.[137] Mars Hill Bible Church in Michigan meets in a former shopping mall; Cityside congregation of Shirelive church, Sydney, Australia, meets in an urban music school. Alternative ways of communicating draw from mystical spirituality and secular discourse. For instance, as a singer from divided Ireland, Bono deliberately does not call himself a Christian, but infuses his concerts with 'a lot of Christian imagery'.[138] Likewise, many emergent church members do not call themselves Christians, preferring terms like 'Christ follower'. It is the church of studied ambivalence, where organizing metaphors range from 'the ark' (the church as the body of Christ's saved) to 'the journey' (where the body is discovered processionally). But is it a new form of evangelicalism, or a prophetic voice within evangelicalism, or schismatic fragments becoming something else altogether? As Scott McKnight suggests, it is all of the above, the missional orientation of the churches defining themselves in terms of their object rather than their tradition.[139] In part, the ambivalence is also because of their recent origins – Zero28 (named after 'the only thing which Catholics and Protestants have in common' – the Northern Ireland phone dialing code) began in 1999 over social justice issues; *ikon* commenced in December 2001 over a desire to engage arts expression and contemporary culture. Inevitably, for a movement defined by its theological schools and a core confessional reformed element, the movement sparks conflict. Driscoll describes the postmodern approach to authority as 'conversation becoming a conflict',[140] as there is 'no source of authority to determine what constitutes orthodox or heretical doctrine'.[141] At the end of the first decade of its existence, the emergent phenomenon was already old enough to be critiqued by conservative evangelicals[142] and even by some of its founders, who had grown disillusioned and moved on to 'post-emergent' approaches.[143] Still largely 'white, well-off and Western',[144] emergent energy is increasingly directed towards development of forms

[137] Gladys Ganiel, 'Emerging from the Evangelical Subculture in Northern Ireland: An Analysis of the Zero28 and ikon Community', *International Journal for the Study of the Christian Church*, 6:1 (March 2006), 38–48.

[138] Warren and Brooks, 'Myths of the Modern Megachurch'.

[139] Scot McKnight, 'Five Streams of the Emerging Church', *Christianity Today*, 19 January 2007 (edition of February 2007) http://www.christianitytoday.com/ct/2007/february/11.35.html, accessed 17 November 2010.

[140] Driscoll, 'A Pastoral Perspective', p. 91.

[141] Ibid., p. 91.

[142] E.g. David Wells, *The Courage to be Protestant*, Grand Rapids: Eerdmans, 2008; and D.A. Carson, *Becoming Conversant with the Emerging Church: Understanding a Movement and Its Implications*, Grand Rapids: Zondervan, 2005.

[143] See Trevor P. Craigen, 'Emergent Soteriology: The Dark Side', *The Masters Seminary Journal*, 17:1 (Fall 2006), 177–90.

[144] Soong-Chan Rah and Jason Mach, 'Is the Emerging Church for Whites Only?' *Sojourners*, May 2010, http://www.sojo.net/magazine/2010/05/emerging-church-whites-only, accessed 17 November 2010.

and content which can move into the majority world. In the words of Rob Bell, 'People don't get it. They think it's about style. But the real question is: What is the gospel?'[145]

THE END(S) OF EVANGELICALISM?

Driving criticism of emergent innovation is the conservative fear that, rather than being a solution to the 'serious decline' of the Western church, it may trigger the collapse of evangelical identities. The disproportionate attacks on Rob Bell's slight book *Love Wins* in 2011 were indicative of the defensiveness which emergent theology elicits. In an age when all identities are relativised – at least in the West – the fear is not unjustified. It is entirely possible that 'evangelicalism' as it was constructed after the Second World War may disappear as a category. Countering this, however, is the strength of evangelical organisation and conviction in the majority world. Evangelical Christianity, after all, is not a particular ecclesiology or ethnicity; rather, as Bebbington noted, it is a historical convergence of convictions (biblicism, crucicentrism, activism, conversionism) which link personal and local experience with a universal mission.[146] Much of the debate is thus not about what evangelicalism *is*, but rather how evangelicals are to *recognise* one another outside their local tribes. What are their common ends? Evangelicalism is not – for most of its adherents – a primary identity. Very few people are converted to 'evangelicalism' as such. Most are converted to Jesus, and then sustain their faith through evangelical catechism, community and spiritual practice. It is the uniqueness of Christ – 'as the Father sent me' – which informs the work of evangelical theologians in the majority world such as Rene Padilla (Argentina) and Vinoth Ramachandra (Sri Lanka), rather than evangelical identity as such.[147] Evangelicalism is a connectional category, a mechanism for missional unity or community formation. The rise of internal reform movements is a constant, as method and form outlive their missional usefulness, and the synthesis creates pressures for redefinition.

The post-evangelical/emergent church debate is in part a debate about the nature of mission and the role of the human. It can be seen, for instance, in the 'humanitarian front line' created by the increasing conflict between Western secular powers and Islamic resistance during the early 2000s.[148] Dispersed networks (such as churches and religious organisations) often proved to be more effective in

[145] Crouch, 'Emergent Mystique', p. 41.

[146] D. W. Bebbington, *Evangelicalism in Modern Britain: A history from the 1730s to the 1980s*, London: Unwin Hyman, 1989, pp. 2–4.

[147] Samuel Escobar, 'A Theology of Evangelism in the Global South', *Lausanne World Pulse*, April 2008, http://www.lausanneworldpulse.com/themedarticles.php/923/04-2008?pg=all, accessed 19 November 2010.

[148] Bruno de Cordier, 'The "Humanitarian Frontline", Development and Relief, and Religion: What Context, Which Threats and Which Opportunities?' *Third World Quarterly*, 30:4 (October 2009), 663ff.

aid delivery than government services. This not only provided an alternate mode of Christian presence in the world, but energised evangelical church networks which had previously rejected the idea of a 'social gospel'. Pentecostal churches in particular (which, as leading missiologist Melvin Hodges noted in 1977, had historically seen charitable ministries as mere 'by-products of evangelism, not primary means to that end') have demonstrated an 'explosion' of interest in social work as incarnational presence.[149] Adaptive evangelical pragmatism demanded a response to global poverty, inequality and injustice and found it largely among its socially oriented, transnational NGOs. There are now thousands of these scattered throughout the world: Christians Against Poverty (CAP) is an example of a local response to debt counseling which has been replicated in other countries by imitation since its foundation in 1996. Two leading transnational examples – Opportunity International and World Vision – illustrate the global dimensions of such activity on a larger scale.

Founded in 1971 by Bristol Myers International Corporation executive Al Whittaker and Australian entrepreneur David Bussau, Opportunity International developed 'trust group' approaches to microfinance delivered through partners, before moving on to the establishment of 'formal financial institutions' and 'microinsurance' designed to bridge the gaps in developing countries. By 2010, they had more than 1.3 million clients (85 per cent of whom were women) in 42 countries, 11,000 staff and more than US$500 million in assets.[150] Their models have been widely emulated beyond Christian circles and have reignited a nineteenth-century interest in business as a vocation. While some of the 'Kingdom business' discussions are shallow and temporary, the work on social entrepreneurship and the role of churches in building social capital has drawn attention from state and trans-state actors.[151] In 2008, David Bussau was nominated 'Senior Australian of the Year' in recognition of his work elevating people from poverty.

An even larger organisation (and perhaps, among Christian NGOs, uniquely influential) is World Vision. Founded to care for Korean orphans in the 1950s, by 2005 its budget was US$1.5 billion, it employed 22,000 people and was nearly ubiquitous in development and disaster relief. 'A U.S. ambassador once exclaimed, "You've got more people in Mozambique than the U.S. government has in all of

[149] Kent Duncan, 'Emerging Engagement: The Growing Social Conscience of Pentecostalism', *Encounter: Journal for Pentecostal Ministry*, 7 (Summer 2010), 1; Murray W. Dempster, 'The Structure of a Christian Ethic Informed by Pentecostal Experience: Soundings in the Moral Significance of Glossolalia' in Wonsuk Ma and Robert P. Menzies, eds, *The Spirit and Spirituality: Essays in Honour of Russell P. Spittler*, New York: T & T Clark, 2004, p. 109.

[150] Tamsin Morrison, 'What £32 Can Do in Ghana,' *New African*, 447 (January 2006), 17.

[151] Evan Carmichael, 'Five Talents Joins a Consortium of Fellow Christian NGOs to Support Microfinance Program in Sudan', http://www.evancarmichael.com/, accessed 17 November 2010. Donald E. Miller and Tetsunao Yamamori (*Global Pentecostalism: The New Face of Christian Social Engagement*, Berkeley: University of California Press, 2007) have traced this development in detail.

Africa!"'[152] After a period of 'drifting apart' from churches ('We got impatient with the church.... It was easier to do it ourselves.'),[153] the 'social turn' of evangelical churches from the 1990s has brought the NGO into much closer contact with both donor churches and network/distribution churches in the majority world. A landmark 2010 case in the United States defending the organisation's 'profound sense of religious mission' was a marker both of its determination to remain evangelical and its ability to mount the appropriate defence.[154] In many cases, national faith-based NGOs are finding co-option by the secular state difficult to resist.[155] Significantly, then, it was a transnational, rather than a state-based, evangelical actor which demonstrated the irreducibility of religious rights, both in the national context and within transnational frameworks such as the UN Universal Declaration of Human Rights.[156]

Despite being socially conservative, transnational evangelicals have demonstrated marked ability for political flexibility, and so remain useful to national leaders. This political range is illustrated by the fact that all nine U.S. presidents from Carter to Obama – regardless of politics – were self-proclaimed (if faulty) people of faith. Even when not personally evangelical, such leaders have in part been successful by energising evangelicals to consider their social agenda above their political biases. Newer evangelicals and post-evangelicals – activist and pragmatic – are even more politically diverse. They are to be found everywhere in social justice circles – cooperating with Palestinian Christians, seeking peace from Israel, on both sides of a Gaza blockade. Even conservative evangelicals now make common cause on issues of concern with Catholic, Orthodox and even Muslim groups. Mega-church leaders (such as Rick Warren) cooperate with media figures in the cause of AIDS relief and majority world development issues. There is also growing intellectual cooperation with Catholic institutions, particularly following the publication of Mark Noll's influential book, *The Scandal of the Evangelical Mind* (1995), and his transfer from Wheaton College to Notre Dame University (2006).[157] The Carter Center has led the way in cooperating with non-Christian NGOs and

[152] Quoted in Tim Stafford, 'The Colossus of Care', *Christianity Today*, 49:3 (March 2005), http://www.christianitytoday.com/ct/2005/march/18.50.html, accessed 17 November 2010.

[153] Stafford, 'The Colossus of Care'.

[154] 'World Vision Wins Right to Hire and Fire on Faith Basis', *Christian Century*, 21 September 2010, p. 18.

[155] 'Anglicare Flags Withdrawal over Gay Adoption Bill', ABC News, 7 August 2010, online http://www.abc.net.au/news/2010-08-07/anglicare-flags-withdrawal-over-gay-adoption-bill/935728, accessed 18 November 2010; Stephen Judd and Ann Robinson, 'Christianity and Australia's Social Services' in S. Piggin, ed., *Shaping the Good Society in Australia*, North Ryde: Macquarie University, 2006.

[156] 'Flexible Megachurches', p. 14; seminar by Anne Robinson, Chair, World Vision Australia, 20 May 2011.

[157] See in particular Mark A. Noll and Carolyn Nystrom, *Is the Reformation Over? An Evangelical Assessment of Contemporary Roman Catholicism*, Grand Rapids: Baker, 2005.

state actors in conflict reduction and service delivery programs. Some, such as the 'Imam and the Pastor' program of the Muslim-Christian Interfaith Mediation Centre in Kaduna, Northern Nigeria, began as local events, only to become global because of their engagement with common issues. Contemporary evangelicals are also sociologically aware. Intellectual activists such as Tony Campolo's Evangelical Association for the Promotion of Education have helped to fund progressive evangelical activities (such as Zero28 in its startup phase, and the 'Beyond Borders' social justice organisation). The cooperative campaign – typified in the Jubilee 2000 and Make Poverty History campaigns; in the pressure for Millennium Development Goals; and the role of evangelical reformers in the ending of apartheid in South Africa – are all examples of how evangelicals stepped beyond the confessional barrier in order to put the end before the means.[158] It was more than a new expression of social awareness – indeed, given the 'social leaven' activities of nineteenth-century evangelicals, it was hardly even new. It was (as Thomas notes) a recognition that the evangelicalism which in the 1950s had become global was now truly a transnational citizen, an essential participant and supporter of global civil society.[159]

CONCLUSION

By the end of the first decade of the twenty-first century, evangelical Christianity was irretrievably widespread and diverse, and yet more active than ever before. A fundamental shift had occurred in its organising principles, which called for continuous re-clarification of its identity. On the one hand, a tradition born in the division of Christendom into many little christendoms in the sixteenth century had finally developed forms detached from dependence on particular national myths and traditions. It was now truly global in its presence, but still learning how to be transnational in terms of organisation. Whereas most of its members were in the global south, and its workforce was coming from everywhere to anywhere, most of its resources still lay in the north. Impatiently pragmatic, some evangelicals found the sort of civil politeness required in plural societies difficult to come by. With no central policy organisation determining what battles to fight – or whether the metaphor of battle was indeed at all useful – action could only be determined location by location. And despite having become increasingly transnational, evangelicals (particularly when organised) continued to be considered by some majority-world actors (particularly Muslim organisations and left-wing activists) in the light of anti-colonialism. The irony of slogans such as 'World Vision go

[158] Josef Boehle, 'The UN System and religious actors in the context of global change,' *Cross Currents*, 1 September 2010, p. 383.

[159] Thomas (2005), quoted in Boehle, 'The UN System and Religious Actors', p. 385.

home'[160] was that evangelicals no longer had a 'home' to go to. Living with the reality of having many houses but increasingly no 'home' is reflected everywhere in evangelical conversations, from the language of 'the house' widely found in mega-church circles to missional 'journey' language among emergent churches. The detachment of evangelical distinctives from their traditional stories, and reattachment to local identities engaged in global realities, is a change of the first order.[161] This was not the Evangelical Alliance club of 1846, struggling to transcend national and demominational divisions, but a porous and ever-changing space of mutual recognition dealing with the fundamental issues of the human condition. For good and for bad, whether they were willing or not, evangelicals were now global pilgrims.

[160] Michael Lee, 'World Vision, Go Home!', *Christian Century*, 16 May 1979, pp. 542–4; see also the Internet coverage of Muslim protests in Hebron over World Vision engagement with Gaza: http://www.youtube.com/watch?v=EXUUexaI9vo, accessed 19 November 2010. See also Soong-Chan Rah, *The Next Evangelicalism: Freeing the Church from Western Cultural Captivity*, Downers Grove: InterVarsity, 2009.

[161] Claudia Währisch-Oblau, *The Missionary Self-Perception of Pentecostal/Charismatic Church Leaders from the Global South in Europe*, Leiden: Brill, 2009, p. 142.

10

Conclusion

Evangelicalism has always been a 'surprising work' which evangelicals themselves have ascribed to God. It seemed to emerge from nowhere and quickly spread to everywhere. It was a movement of diverse origins – a confluence of transatlantic diasporas (English, Irish, Scottish, German and Dutch, to name a few of the nationalities involved in its beginnings) with sources in Europe, but meeting and blending into new forms in America. Taking a longer view, just as the original founders of the Massachusetts Bay community considered themselves to be pilgrims on the way to the *city* of God, it might be said that from the beginning, evangelicals saw themselves as citizens of an emerging global *kingdom*. Evangelicalism was part of a long-term process of dissociation from national frameworks. In the days before sophisticated telecommunications and modern health care, evangelical spirituality warmed the heart and provided a bedrock for the soul in the midst of the social turbulence of the Old World, the tossing waves of the wild Atlantic and the trackless forests of the New World. Western historians have tended to tell the story of evangelicalism, where it has been remembered at all, as if it were a minority interest in the midst of great state churches. Such a view, organised around national frameworks, misses the dynamism of the movement, its emergence as a people 'in-between': in between classes, in between countries, in between continents, languages and cultures. There has also been a great deal of work tracing the course of evangelicalism as if it were primarily a theological construct, or an economic influence or a form of political or social capital. This work has been valuable. Most, however, is concentrated on the West, and thus isolated from the movement's largest present-day communities, or focused by disciplinary perspectives in ways which detach it from what evangelicalism functionally *is*.

Typifying evangelicalism as a diasporic movement, a perspective gained on the shoulders of this previous literature, clarifies aspects of the movement which have been overlooked. Evangelicalism emerged from the conversation (and occasionally conflict) between scholastic Calvinists and holiness Arminians who took for themselves 'the harmless name' given to them by others – that of 'Methodist'.[1] Wesley originally understood the word to indicate the 'method' by which the members of

[1] Richard Watson and John Emory, *The life of the Rev. John Wesley . . . founder of the Methodist Societies*, New York: Mason and Lane, for the Methodist Episcopal Church, 1840, p. 16.

his Holy Club remained mutually accountable, under the statutes of Oxford University. There is a sense in which evangelicalism thereafter remained not so much a 'chiliasm of despair'[2] as a readily adaptable 'spiritual technology', a way of doing things that made their small number of not very unique theological doctrines effective in building integrated persons, communities, institutions and eventually a form of stability which, when adopted by elites, could become a means of effective social organisation. Before his death some years ago, the doyen of the study of continental evangelicalism, W.R. Ward, used to enjoy shocking church-related conferences by defining evangelicalism as 'a penchant for building orphanages'.[3] Ward pushed the ends of the eighteenth-century evangelical axis from Northampton, Massachusetts, to Estonia, Russia, and eastern Germany. His quip captures something about the sense of mobile order, of concretising activism which evangelicalism carried from its beginning and which David Bebbington captured in that element ('activism') of his quadrilateral definition.[4]

Another aspect more implicit than explicit in Bebbington's quadrilateral is the powerful sense of ambivalence which evangelicals held towards the powers that be. Part of the evangelical insistence on the perspicuity of the Bible was the understanding that any person could read it and come to a saving faith and a vision of what God desired for his people to do in the world. The visions actually resulting were extremely various, interacting with local contexts and issues of the moment. It was part of the evangelical genius, however, that with the Bible in hand and the Holy Spirit in mind, a reflected biblical vision of the future could be worked up out of the ground almost anywhere. This was the function of envisioning in early evangelical hymns, in the immediacy of evangelical preaching, in the notion of heart-warming experiences. In all effective evangelical preaching, there is a strong emphasis on transformation in the present, an experience of the condescension of God to the sinner. Evangelicals were thus at their best as leavening, transformative minorities, in small groups and coherent communities. On the rare occasion when they became truly powerful, as in early Victorian Britain or the later-twentieth-century United States, their methodical, if disparate, visions often meant that their influence did not last for long. Their moments of transformation, however, were of lasting influence. In human rights, politics, the arts, social welfare, international relations, science, indeed most of the cornerstones of the modern world, evangelicals have made a contribution and continue to do so. From public rhetoric expressing concern for the poor to the banners and bunting of political conventions so reminiscent of revival crusades, evangelicalism has left its cultural mark. More important to international discourse, however, has

[2] E.P. Thompson, *The Making of the English Working Class*, Harmondsworth: Penguin, 1968, pp. 411–40.

[3] W.R. Ward, in M. Hutchinson and O. Kalu, eds, *A Global Faith*, Sydney: CSAC, 1998, p. 20.

[4] D.W. Bebbington, *Evangelicalism in Modern Britain: A history from the 1730s to the 1980s*, London: Unwin Hyman, 1989, pp. 2–3

been the tendency to name a problem as an opportunity for solution and wider transformation.

In many cases, that contribution has been contentious. During the Enlightenment, it was contentious because of the evangelical insistence not simply on the supernatural, but on the rationality and reality of the spiritual. In the nineteenth century, before organised labour took up the refrain, evangelicals helped to civilise capitalism, and were often the anvil against which the ideas supporting the liberal state were hammered out. In the twentieth century, evangelicals have acted as a scapegoat for overly confident secularism within the public square, and as societal glue outside it. The emergence of the intergovernmental sector in the West and the vast network of voluntary associations and NGOs which now support the fragile nations of the majority world, and thus the 'international system', was a field of disproportionate influence for evangelicals. Entering the twenty-first century, this movement has never been so successful in the majority world, and never more hated in the West. It may well turn out that this is more to do with the contentions inside the secular public square than with evangelicals themselves. Still, the venom with which the so-called tolerant society of the West treats one of its older minority cousins says much about their relationship and the nature of high modernity. It also says something about evangelicalism, however. An aspect of Bebbington's biblicism is that it assumes a plastic world on which the biblical template can be applied. Evangelicalism has therefore always been political, even when quietist. Motivated, disciplined communities with an understanding of the possibility of change inevitably impact on their contexts.

This review of evangelical history reminds us that evangelicals have also been relentlessly integrative. Paradoxically, that could lead to schism, leaving them with a reputation for divisiveness. Even schism, however, was often a means by which evangelicals sought to retain or to regain integrity, either in their individual consciences, within their communities or within some important cause. Some scholars have thought it odd that evangelicals on the one hand seem to be anti-modern and on the other, early adopters of technology and facilitating advances, particularly when it comes to education, medicine or missions and communications. Understanding the (re)integrative nature of evangelical imagination, which seeks to bring all the created order under the lordship of Christ, helps to overcome this seeming conundrum. Through revival journals, missionary biographies and the other productions of their vast writing and publishing endeavours, most evangelicals carried a good sense of their origins. Their movement was born in the same context as modernity itself, and so while never entirely co-opted by it, they were prepared to recognise its shared heritage and benefit from its advances. If modernity was rationalist, evangelicals were rational; if society was advancing, evangelicals too were moving ahead; if restless capitalism made the whole house of creation one room, evangelicals were determined to carry the light into every one of its corners.

This co-emergence with modernity has, on the emergence of postmodernity, however, created the same sort of issues for evangelicals as it has for others (such as sporting clubs, newspapers, national governments and the like) whose primary social functions have been defined by trends in social capital generation and maintenance. As a 'speaking religion', evangelicalism's major internal issues relate, on the one hand, to tensions over *what* should be communicated and, on the other, *how* it should be communicated. Symbolic self-representation – through writing, media, non-political public demonstrations, 'good works' and the like – has been an essential element of evangelical action. In an age when culture is politics, however, the evangelical urge to be *definite* is often misunderstood. This metaphorical evangelical understanding has always made them good local, regional and national citizens. Evangelicals are active in service and self-maintaining in lifestyle precisely because of their emphases on the cross and the Bible as transformed through the personal synthetic act of conversion. They were salt to the eighteenth century, light to the nineteenth, a mustard seed in the twentieth, and in the twenty-first century a very great tree in which 'the birds come and perch in its branches' (Matthew 13: 32). There are some indicators that they are now less than sure what the appropriate metaphor is for their life together in the future: are they to be yeast or pilgrims, soldiers, servants or seed? Certainly, as a whole, they have little understood either the process by which they have been repositioned as the 'repugnant cultural other' in modernising settings[5] or the way in which they have themselves contributed to that negative stereotyping. Adaptation to becoming 'global citizens' is still ongoing, and the future shape of their role undetermined. Part of the repositioning of mega-churches, post-evangelicals and emergent churches in the period after the 1990s may be seen as a response to this growing plausibility gap between function and communication, between national assumptions and missional impetus and between ecclesiological legacies and the imperatives affecting community formation. This repositioning has been a necessary concomitant of evangelicals recognising not just that they *are* a minority (voiding the plausibility of triumphalism), but that being a creative force actually relies on that minority status.

Taking such a contextualist, cultural approach to defining and explaining the course of evangelicalism over its first three centuries also explains why many of the great divisions within the movement have occurred. The recurring conflicts between doctrinalists and 'method-ists' is rooted deeply in the movement's history, and is, in fact, a necessary element of its ability to change and adapt. The movement swings between its missional, experiential and doctrinal self-definitional touchpoints as it encounters new situations, negotiating between effectiveness and self-definition. Occasionally these break into the public press, often over

[5] Brian Howell, 'The Repugnant Cultural Other Speaks Back: Christian Identity as Ethnographic "Standpoint"', *Anthropological Theory*, 7 (2007), 372.

particular doctrinal emphases (from predestination to evolution to emerging church reformulations), leading to the expectation that what is being witnessed is the dissolution of the movement. In each case where this has occurred (for instance, in the division between Wesley and Whitefield, or over higher criticism, or in the aftermath of the Scopes trial), evangelicalism has re-emerged with one or another of its quadrilateral elements acting as a new basis for continued cooperation. Often, however, the greatest challenges for evangelicalism do not occupy the headlines of the *Times* (either in New York or in London), but are on the 'frontiers' of its growth. The greatest contemporary challenge for evangelicalism is probably not whether a pastor from Grand Rapids, Michigan, is right about the doctrine of hell,[6] but the issues surrounding global pluralism, and the sustainability of the experiential 'détente' which knits together evangelicalism and pentecostalism.

The growth of experiential elements within evangelicalism is a reflection of globalisation; disconnection from continuity renders theology abstract. Evangelical spirituality, however, is concrete and so reverts to present experience when this happens. Much of evangelicalism's 'credibility' – from Moravian missionaries to Argentinean apostles – has been derived from its ability to tie doctrinal definition together with spiritual 'effectiveness'. Whereas liberal theologians had the seminaries, as a whole, evangelicals could comfort themselves with the understanding that they had the numbers. As Andrew Walls has noted, however, in general the 'numbers' in the majority world were not the result of direct evangelical missionary action, but of cultural indigenisation and appropriation by majority-world actors (through, for example, Bible translation).[7] In other words, the 'cultural edge' of evangelical influence is as important as its core self-understandings. Disconnection from its growing, charismatic edge in the majority world would do more than remove a method of legitimisation; it would nullify the revivalistic impulse which has been essential to this movement's growth from the beginning. There is little likelihood of this happening; having expanded on the back of indigenising experientialism, one may expect majority-world communities to move towards greater intellectual and social definition. Conversely, the minority status of evangelical communities in the West may cause them to move towards new forms of experientialism. The rise of short-term 'missions as tourism', of technologically connected global churches acting as networks (as opposed to denominations) for mobile, professional young evangelicals, and the ready integration of the charismatic into most contemporary evangelicalisms are perhaps indicators that these shifts are already underway. Their timing and extent will depend on the cycle of crises in nation states which, driven by international competitiveness need increasingly to

[6] Erik Eckholm, 'Pastor Stirs Wrath With His Views on Old Questions', *New York Times*, 4 March 2011, http://www.nytimes.com/2011/03/05/us/05bell.html, accessed 23 August 2011.

[7] Andrew F. Walls, *The Missionary Movement in Christian History: Studies in the Transmission of Faith*, New York: Orbis, 1996, p. 40.

rely on voluntarist social capital formers such as evangelicalism, but are also caught on the petard of their core secularism and inevitable pluralism.

In 2006, the Evangelical Alliance in Britain complained publicly to Channel 4 for its airing of Richard Dawkins's 'documentary', titled 'Root of All Evil', a 'film . . . so viciously biased against faith-communities, and against evangelicals in particular, that in the interests of balance and freedom of speech the station ought to offer a substantial right of reply.'[8] It did not get it, for the same reason that in 2011 the Australian Broadcasting Corporation did not change its description of the Norwegian mass murderer Anders Behring Breivik as a 'Right-wing Christian' even after it became clear that he was not associated with any tradition to which that term is usually applied.[9] The outburst of what Terry Eagleton has called the 'lunging, flailing [and] mispunching'[10] about religion in contemporary media reflects deeper shifts in the nation-state, besieged on the one side by globalisation and on the other by the seemingly insoluble problems created by two centuries of bureaucratic rationalisation. It is understandable that in the midst of these crises, evangelicals (less politically coherent than the Catholic Church, and less problematic for public figures than extremist Islam) have become a target for secularists seeking to assert their hegemony in the public square and liberals wanting a 'whipping boy' against whom to expand their conception of individual rights. Evangelicalism, for many who shape public opinion in the modern age, is the religion which refused to die in the late Enlightenment, when the light of reason was shone upon it; or which blunted the revolution that England needed to have.[11] While evangelicals do not present the visible icons of Catholic medievalism, their experientialism and the perception that they are obscurantist and reactionary, combined with general public ignorance as to its history and variety, have made them an ideal blank canvas for counter-ideological statements by spokesmen such as the prominent scientific atheist Richard Dawkins and the late controversial journalist Christopher Hitchens.[12] Evangelicals, it may be argued, are not 'the problem', but standing as they do at the crossroads of change, they are readily identified as a symptom of a syndrome which their critics little understand.

[8] '"Dawkins' programme viciously biased against faith communities", says Evangelical Alliance', http://www.eauk.org/media/dawkins-programme-bias-against-faith-communities.cfm, accessed 29 August 2011.

[9] Noted in live coverage on ABC News, but see also 'Norway did not see far-right as "serious threat"', http://www.abc.net.au/news/2011-07-23/norway-did-not-see-far-right-as-27serious-threat27/2807566, accessed July 23, 2011.

[10] Terry Eagleton, 'Lunging, Flailing, Mispunching [review of Richard Dawkins, *The God Delusion*', http://www.lrb.co.uk/v28/n20/terry-eagleton/lunging-flailing-mispunching, accessed 29 August 2011.

[11] On this, see J.A. Jaffe, 'The "Chiliasm of Despair" Reconsidered: Revivalism and Working-Class Agitation in County Durham', *Journal of British Studies*, 28:1 (January 1989), 23–42.

[12] See Richard Dawkins, *The God Delusion*, London: Bantam Press, 2006; Christopher Hitchens, *God Is Not Great: How Religion Has Poisoned Everything*, New York: Twelve, 2007, p. 34.

Among historians, however, the reductionist ideological categories used to describe evangelicals in the literature of the 1960s (by Manning Clark, for whom they were 'men in black', philistines and moralisers;[13] or by E.P. Thompson, for whom evangelicals were agents of capitalist domination) are now much less common. It is hoped that this book, along with other recent attempts at a more global understanding,[14] will help to inform more nuanced discussions of evangelicalism in its huge variety around the world. It has not embraced 'the whole world and all that is in it': no book can. The increasing subtlety of scholarship by evangelicals themselves and the growth of interest in religion among non-evangelicals have, however, provided the basis for a more accurate understanding of who evangelicals have been and who they are becoming. An analysis of Library of Congress and British Library holdings indicates that this is probably more advanced in the integrative space of historical studies than in other disciplines, but that real interest is emerging in the applied social sciences.[15] What this book *has* attempted to do is to reference, summarise and relocate the now received arguments about evangelicalism and to extract a critical narrative which takes evangelicalism seriously in ways that are recognisable both to itself and also to others. Whatever one's personal experience or opinion, that is the least that a reader should be able to expect from treatments of such a significant contributor to the rise of the modern world.

[13] Among many other examples, see C.M.H. Clark, *A History of Australia* (ed. M. Cathcart), Carlton: Melbourne University Press, 1997, p. 222 and Thompson, *Making of the English Working Class*.

[14] Such as Mark Noll, *The New Shape of World Christianity*, Downers Grove: InterVarsity, 2009; and Jay Riley Case's *An Unpredictable Gospel: American Evangelicals and World Christianity 1812–1920*, New York: Oxford University Press, 2012.

[15] Mark Hutchinson, 'The Hamburger Index: Determining Evangelical Interests 1960–2010', online, http://alphacrucis.academia.edu, accessed 17 November 2010, pp. 8–10.

Further Reading

This short note complements the detailed references in the footnotes by highlighting works that are likely to offer the most fruitful initial further reading. Despite an extensive popular literature, the scholarly study of evangelicalism as a global movement remains undeveloped, with most material focused on particular cases or countries. Moreover, much which is useful is not yet in English. The following list, therefore, concentrates on those English-language studies which particularly contribute to understanding of global interconnections.

WORLD CHRISTIANITY

Carey, Hilary, *God's Empire: Religion and Colonialism in the British World, c. 1801–1908*, New York: Cambridge University Press, 2011.

Gilley, Sheridan and Brian Stanley, eds, *World Christianities, c. 1815–c. 1914*, Cambridge: Cambridge University Press, 2006.

Kim, Sebastian C.H., *Christianity as a World Religion*, London: Continuum, 2008.

McLeod, Hugh, ed., *World Christianities c. 1914–c. 2000*, Cambridge: Cambridge University Press, 2006.

Sanneh, Lamin and Joel A. Carpenter, eds, *The Changing Face of Christianity: Africa, the West, and the World*, New York: Oxford University Press, 2005.

GLOBAL EVANGELICALISM

Case, Jay Riley, *An Unpredictable Gospel: American Evangelicals and World Christianity, 1812–1920*, New York: Oxford University Press, 2012.

Hempton, David, *Methodism: Empire of the Spirit*, New Haven: Yale University Press, 2006.

Lewis, Donald M., ed., *Christianity Reborn: Evangelicalism's Global Expansion in the Twentieth Century*, Grand Rapids: Eerdmans, 2004. This contains two useful survey chapters on earlier periods.

Martin, David, *Pentecostalism: The World Their Parish*, Oxford: Wiley-Blackwell, 2008.

May, Cedrick, *Evangelism and Resistance in the Black Atlantic, 1760–1835*, Athens: University of Georgia Press, 2008.

Noll, Mark A., *The New Shape of World Christianity: How American Experience Reflects Global Faith*, Downers Grove: InterVarsity, 2009.

Noll, Mark A., David W. Bebbington and George A. Rawlyk, eds, *Evangelicalism: Comparative Studies of Popular Protestantism in North America, the British Isles, and Beyond, 1700–1990*, New York: Oxford University Press, 1994.

Shaw, Mark, *Global Awakening: How 20th-Century Revivals Triggered A Christian Revolution*, Downers Grove: InterVarsity, 2010.

Ward, W.R., *The Protestant Evangelical Awakening*, Cambridge: Cambridge University Press, 1992.

Ward, W.R., *Early Evangelicalism: A Global Intellectual History, 1670–1789*, Cambridge: Cambridge University Press, 2010.

A five-volume *History of Evangelicalism: People, Movements and Ideas in the English-Speaking World* is currently in course of publication by Inter-Varsity Press (UK). The first three volumes covering the eighteenth and nineteenth centuries have already appeared: Mark A. Noll, *The Rise of Evangelicalism*, 2004; John Wolffe, *The Expansion of Evangelicalism*, 2006 and David W. Bebbington, *The Dominance of Evangelicalism*, 2005. The volumes covering the twentieth century are due to appear in the next few years: Geoff Treloar, *The Disruption of Evangelicalism* and Brian Stanley, *The Global Diffusion of Evangelicalism.*

NORTH AMERICA

Brint, Steven and Jean Reith Schroedel, eds, *Evangelicals and Democracy in America*, vol. 1, *Religion and Society*, New York: Russell Sage Foundation, 2009.

Christie, Nancy and Michael Gauvreau, *The Christian Churches and Their Peoples, 1840–1965: A Social History of Religion in Canada*, Toronto: University of Toronto Press, 2010.

Noll, Mark A., *American Evangelical Christianity: An Introduction*, Oxford: Blackwell, 2001.

Noll, Mark A. and Luke E. Harlow, *Religion and American Politics: From the Colonial Period to the Present*, New York: Oxford University Press, 2007.

Stackhouse, John G., *Canadian Evangelicalism in the Twentieth Century*, Toronto: University of Toronto Press, 1993.

EUROPE

Bebbington, D.W., *Evangelicalism in Modern Britain: a History from the 1730s to the 1980s*, London: Unwin Hyman, 1989.

Ganiel, Gladys, *Evangelicalism and Conflict in Northern Ireland*, New York: Palgrave Macmillan, 2008.

Hempton, David and Myrtle Hill, *Evangelical Protestantism in Ulster Society 1740–1890*, London: Routledge, 1992.

Railton, Nicholas, *No North Sea: The Anglo-German Evangelical Network in the Middle of the Nineteenth Century*, Leiden: Brill, 1996.

Warner, Rob, *Reinventing English Evangelicalism, 1966–2001: A Theological and Sociological Study*, Milton Keynes: Paternoster, 2007.

W.R. Ward's two books listed previously are crucial for continental European evangelicalism in the eighteenth century; publications in English on later periods remain fragmentary. There is a very extensive literature in German and a number of Slavic languages, and in Italian, where trans-cultural figures such as Giorgio Spini have developed important pan-European studies.

ASIA

Austin, Alvyn, *China's Millions: The China Inland Mission and late Qing Society, 1832–1905*, Grand Rapids: Eerdmans, 2007.

Frykenberg, Robert, *Christianity in India: from Beginnings to the Present*, Oxford University Press, 2010. In the absence of a specific study of evangelicalism in India, this book is the best starting point.

Lumsdaine, David H., ed., *Evangelical Christianity and Democracy in Asia*, Oxford: Oxford University Press, 2009.

Phan, Peter C., ed., *Christianities in Asia*, Oxford: Wiley-Blackwell, 2011.

Xi, Lian, *Redeemed by Fire: The Rise of Popular Christianity in Modern China*, New Haven: Yale University Press, 2010.

AFRICA

Adogame, Afe, ed., *Christianity in Africa and the African Diaspora: The Appropriation of a Scattered Heritage*, New York: Continuum, 2011.

Eshete, Tibebe, *The Evangelical Movement in Ethiopia: Resistance and Resilience*, Waco: Baylor University Press, 2009.

Hanciles, Jehu, *Beyond Christendom: Globalization, African Migration, and the Transformation of the West*, Maryknoll: Orbis, 2008.

Korieh, Chima J., et al., eds, *Religion, History, and Politics in Nigeria: Essays in Honor of Ogbu U. Kalu*, Washington: University Press of America, 2005.

LATIN AMERICA

Freston, Paul, ed., *Evangelical Christianity and Democracy in Latin America*, New York: Oxford University Press, 2008.

Martin, David, *Tongues of Fire: The Explosion of Protestantism in Latin America*, Oxford: Blackwell, 1990.

Sanchez Walsh, Arlene M., *Latino Pentecostal Identity: Evangelical Faith, Self, and Society*, New York: Columbia University Press, 2003.

OCEANIA

Breward, Ian, *A History of the Churches in Australasia*, New York: Oxford University Press, 2004.

Chant, Barry, *The Spirit of Pentecost*, Lexington: Emeth Press, 2009.

Lange, Raeburn, *Island Ministers: Indigenous Leadership in Nineteenth Century Pacific Islands Christianity*, Christchurch and Canberra: University of Canterbury and Australian National University, 2006.

Piggin, Stuart, *Evangelicalism in Australia: Spirit, Word and World*, Melbourne: Oxford University Press, 1996.

Newman, Keith, *Bible & Treaty: Missionaries Among the Maori – A New Perspective*, Auckland: Penguin, 2010.

Sivasundaram, Sujit, *Nature and the Godly Empire: Science and Evangelical Mission in the Pacific, 1795–1850*, Cambridge: Cambridge University Press, 2005.

Stenhouse, John and Jane Thomson, eds, *Building God's own Country: Historical Essays on Religions in New Zealand*, Dunedin: University of Otago Press, 2004.

Index